D0151188

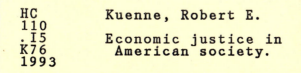

DATE			

BAKER & TAYLOR

Economic Justice in American Society

———————————————

Economic Justice
in American Society

Robert E. Kuenne

PRINCETON UNIVERSITY PRESS

PRINCETON, NEW JERSEY

Copyright © 1993 by Princeton University Press
Published by Princeton University Press, 41 William Street,
Princeton, New Jersey 08540
In the United Kingdom: Princeton University Press,
Chichester, West Sussex

All Rights Reserved

Library of Congress Cataloging-in-Publication Data

Kuenne, Robert E.
Economic justice in American society / Robert E. Kuenne.
p.   cm.
Includes bibliographical references and index.
1. Income distribution—United States.   2. United States—
Economic conditions.   3. Social justice.   I. Title.
HC110.I5K76   1993   330.1—dc20   93-16273

ISBN 0-691-03219-x

This book has been composed in Postscript Baskerville

Princeton University Press books are printed
on acid-free paper and meet the guidelines for
permanence and durability of the Committee on
Production Guidelines for Book Longevity
of the Council on Library Resources

Printed in the United States of America

1   3   5   7   9   10   8   6   4   2

To the Memory of My Sisters

Margaret Ruth Kuenne Harlow

and

Dorothy Jane Kuenne Stearns

CONTENTS

FIGURES

TABLES

PREFACE

AMERICA is entering, unprepared, an age of acute economic discord with no strategic principles to provide guidelines for the resolution of the ensuing debate. The next thirty years of domestic economic concerns will be dominated by the struggle to channel income distribution to an unprecedented extent away from market-dictated patterns to a socially determined configuration.

The conflict has already begun and has forewarned of the intensity of the struggle ahead. Few indeed are the economic decisions by federal, state, and local policymakers that do not have an important and contested distributive content. And the frequency of the "tax revolts," as well as the near-impossibility of raising federal taxes by even 1 percent of gross national product during the last decade to alleviate a fiscal deficit almost universally recognized as unacceptable, are portents of the social strains that will confront the nation.

Each of the contenders for income entitlements will frame demands in terms of "economic justice" with no felt need to define that concept. It becomes an incantation designed to mask self-interest and instill guilt in opponents, and it is frequently effective because no present consensus exists in the nation defining the overarching principles of economic justice that give perspective to competing claims.

John Stuart Mill perceived the social dangers that the failure to define an explicit and formal body of such principles entails and the social weakness that is exploited by interest groups in their absence:

> The powerful sentiment, and apparently clear perception, which that word [justice] recalls with a rapidity and certainty resembling an instinct, have seemed to the majority of thinkers to point to an inherent quality in things; to show that the Just must have an existence in Nature as something absolute, generically distinct from every variety of the Expedient, and, in idea, opposed to it, though (as is commonly acknowledged) never, in the long run, disjoined from it in fact.[1]

This book proposes a theory of economic justice appropriate to the moral basis of American society: *the theory of dualistic individualism.* Mill, in the quotation above, notes the inevitable relationship between notions of justice and the "expedient." My definition of "appropriateness" echoes this perception in requiring that the theory conform to the nation's "ethos," or that central core of values, beliefs, and institutions that ultimately defines the nation's unifying social consciousness. The "should be" is not the "is," nor can the "should be" be derived from the "is": but any theory of the "should be" that has pretensions of becoming a future "is" must be constrained by the present "is," when that "is" accurately reflects the nation's moral first principles. The desire to conjoin the abstract principles of economic justice to the American ethos is an important theme of my effort.

My hope is to inspire debate concerning principles of economic justice that will give as much definition to proper governmental conduct in the economic terrain as the American Constitution does in the political. With that in mind I have framed a notional "bill of economic rights and obligations" embodying the theory of dualistic individualism to emphasize the need for formalism. The alternative is to accept the present method of resolution of distributive conflict: ad hoc decisions reflecting in largest part the politically disproportionate power of well-organized and well-funded interest groups.

A mea culpa: by training an economist, I have encroached on the academic terrain of the social philosopher and the sociologist. In designing the theory I have sought to understand and extract the economic relevance of important thinkers in the area of social ethics, and I have studied present thinking of sociologists concerned with the nature and content of the national ethos. The sin is one of trespass, not hegemony, but I am well aware of the dangers of such trespass: a failure to fully grasp the subtleties of thought that are discerned only after career-long dedication to these foreign fields. The result may well be what Edward S. Mason termed the "cross sterilization of the social sciences." My excuse must be that the nature of my perceived task required the excursion, and I hasten to deny any ambitions of aggrandizement.

I am also sure that critics will correct my misperceptions quite readily, and that is the purpose of the debate I hope to inspire. I recall that once, after Bertrand Russell delivered a particularly convoluted public lecture on "The Future of the Cosmos," Alfred North Whitehead rose to congratulate him on the skill with which he "left the dense fog that enshrouds the subject unobscured." My hope is that the reader will not feel like sentiments are appropriate to this effort.

I have been fortunate in the referees who devoted intensive critical efforts to the manuscript. Professor Elizabeth Kiss of Princeton University and Professor Michael Mcpherson of Williams College have deepened my understanding of moral and political philosophy and corrected misconceptions in a number of areas or suggested further reading in others. I have not, at my peril, taken all of their advice, so they must be excused my missteps. But the book has benefited immensely from their devotion of time.

My thanks are due once more to my wife, whose patient forbearance of neglect over a long period of time of dedication to the work was of an order beyond the bounds of commutative justice, not to mention uxorial duty.

PART I

American Conceptions of Economic Justice

Chapter 1

THE IMPLICIT ECONOMIC ETHIC IN
THE MARKET ECONOMY

THE IMPORTANCE OF A WELL-DEFINED ECONOMIC ETHOS

In the definition of the principles that shape and constrain their governing institutions, societies are notorious muddlers. But even in those instances in which political rules of governance are given explicit formulation, as in the case of the American Constitution, the deeper philosophical notions of the individual's rights and obligations in the social context are left to be discerned and debated. Somewhat paradoxically, perhaps, in the social area at least, submerged foundations are not uniquely determined by the visible architecture nor does their structure have much direct visible influence on the additions to and modifications of the superstructure as practical usage dictates.

This reluctance to give form to a comprehensive ethos for governmental guidance is nowhere as evident in American society as in the economic sector. Indeed, a marked ambivalence toward the free market mechanism that determines the allocation of goods and resources in the individualistic sector of the economy exists in the rhetoric that surrounds its functioning.

On the one hand great attraction attaches to the ideal notions of individual responsibility, the opportunity to advance to the limits of one's abilities, competition among individuals and firms on the basis of relevant characteristics only, and rapid progress in the material basis of society that the market economy purportedly fosters. But on the other hand earning profits is considered somewhat suspect, protection against competitive market forces is viewed as necessary for some groups, and the social changes introduced by market-driven innovation and rapid growth are deplored or deflected. That the contradictory nature of these sets of attitudes, frequently held by the same individual, is not intellectually disturbing serves to buttress the assertion that a clear and self-consistent economic philosophy does not inform the public consciousness.

That the greater portion of the reservations concerning the free market economy finds its source in that system's distributive mechanisms— that is, in the manner in which the economic system divides the year's social product among the owners of the resources which cooperate to produce it—is not fortuitous. The imperfect allegiance rendered capitalism in the hazy ethos of its adoptive society is grounded in the system's efficiency. The economist, the businessperson, and other advocates of the system, assisted by the poor or nonperformance of alternative economies, have been successful in arguing that competitive markets allocate resources during the year and across the years in a manner that "maximizes social output" in definable senses poorly understood by the public. If one argues that in doing so they distribute claims on that output "equitably" or "justly" or "morally," however, one must expound a well-defined theory of economic equity that rests of necessity on value judgments with far less universal appeal than "more is better than less." Theories of economic equity are much more difficult to formulate and defend convincingly than are theories of economic efficiency.

A holistic economic "constitution" for a society, therefore, contains an integrated body of accepted beliefs concerning the efficiency and equity with which the economic mechanism, assisted by or supplemented with the governmental economic apparatus, performs its allocative and distributive functions. That constitution must cohere as a social ethos guiding government action and inaction, and, as a practical political matter, it must be widely accepted by the citizenry. In a sense that is even more true than it is for its political analogue, that body of philosophic economic principles has not been formulated in a convincing and understandable form in the United States, especially as it deals with the equity aspects of income distribution. Congressional, executive, and judicial actions, therefore, follow no deeply embedded, universally accepted body of guiding precepts. Rather, and notably with respect to distributive equity questions, they consist of incremental movements about the status quo, largely motivated by the political strengths, election leverage, or publicity success of parties whose distributive welfare rests on prospective policy.

Perhaps this formlessness is not prima facie undesirable and indeed it may help to achieve social stability. Democratic government must be flexible enough to reflect the changing social attitudes and power structures of an evolving society. The sclerotic tendencies of rigid philosophies that are not readily translatable into current specifics may impede adaptations necessary to political functioning. Democracy is "policy incremental" by its nature; where successful it is continuously subject to the pulls of its competing interests and strives for constrained accommodating movements from the status quo. It is not ideally constituted for periodic upheavals in its institutional basis to permit substantial adaptations in the social ethos—an inability it shares with most other governmental forms.

But on the other hand, where the everyday functioning of government as social agent is sensitive to the shifting pressures of vested interests, and where almost without exception every economic measure has direct or indirect distributive implications, a danger to system stability inheres in the governmental process absent a clearly defined economic ethic. The unattainably ideal democratic political process prescribes a form of "political pure competition"—that is, a condition in which no group of participants wields a degree of power disproportionate to the relative size of the group. The telecommunications revolution has made the organization of vested interests and their concerted exertion of pressure on elective officials routine. Where distributive decisions are at issue, such groups have strong financial incentives and consequently resources to pursue their own advantages. More or less subtle forms of "influence peddling" in the guise of protecting constituents' interests flourish in an elective process in which it becomes increasingly expensive to participate.

Nor does the argument carry conviction that citizens who organize in groups thereby reveal a greater intensity of concern about certain issues and are entitled to more than proportionate weight in decisions involving such issues. Indeed, in logic such individuals are likely to be those who benefit most by favorable action in these instances and, as interested parties, should be excluded from influence to ensure that impartial decisions will be made by disinterested parties judging the issues in the light of a prevailing economic ethic.[1] Without an explicit economic ethic, governmental intervention in economic process, and particularly redistributive process, will result frequently in subsidization of politically successful groups by a broader citizenry whose countervailing interests have simply been ignored.

With a view to filling this national ethic vacuum, this work will consider questions of economic equity in five steps:

1. A first question addressed is the manner in which an idealized market economy performs its distributive functions, and the implicit economic equity principles that are consistent with the economy's operations and are implemented and supported by it. In chapter 4 I will distinguish social ethics from social justice, both of which constitute social equity. The work is concerned almost wholly with social, and more narrowly, economic justice.
2. From an understanding of the cultural leanings of the U.S. society, guided by the isolation of the market economy's implicit equity principles, an attempt is made to formulate the fuzzy set of principles constituting the nation's creed of economic equity.
3. To help in formalizing this credo into a consistent body of economic equity principles, a review of prominent theories of social equity is conducted to extract their explicit or implicit economic content. With a schema of six structural questions, the strengths and weaknesses of each of the existing

theories are examined as a means of judging their acceptability and usefulness within the American ethos.

4. The difficult task of formulating an economic ethic that codifies principles
   consistent with the American social ethos is then performed.

5. To judge the degree of conformance of the income distribution pattern of
   the present U.S. economy to the proposed economic ethic, a study of its
   structure is presented in some detail with judgments concerning the feasibility of policies to move it into greater conformance. The prospective demographic, sociological, and economic trends of relevance to income distribution patterns thirty years hence are then discussed to assess longer-term
   feasibility of redistributive programs in the light of the potential desirable
   adaptability of the nation's ethos.

The Cultural Reinforcements of Capitalism

The economic equity ethos that we seek as a preliminary to presenting a
formal theory of economic equity has evolved within the framing cultural outlines of a capitalistic economy. With respect to that theory and
the discussion in the previous section, even were it considered desirable
by a substantial portion of the citizenry—and the evidence is that it is
not—a wrenching movement to a radically different economic system in
the foreseeable future would not be feasible. Any theory of economic
equity meant to be operational must be consistent with a vigorous capitalist economy. One of the virtues of a free market economy is that it
permits a substantial amount of flexibility in the political and cultural
institutions with which it coexists: indeed, one of the liberal embarrass-
ments of this century is the catalog of repressive political and social
regimes within which capitalism flourished. Nonetheless, in a deeper
sense, the institutions of a free market mechanism reinforce or implant a set of values, beliefs, and attitudes—an *ethos*—that have a direct
relevance to judgments of equity and justice beyond the economic
arena.

A capitalistic or free market economy is most simply seen as a very
large complex of markets in which buyers and sellers of goods and services (agents) meet to exchange such goods and services for money. In
each market decisions are taken by the agents wholly in accord with their
individual self-interest and these are converted by the market's functioning into prices and quantities exchanged of each good and service. The
complex of markets is integrated into a single social decision-making
mechanism by the flow of prices among markets. Agents focus on the
subset of prices relevant to their decisions and act accordingly in the
subset of markets in which they participate. Given each agent's portfolio

of factor services to sell and the market prices of those services, the agent's income is determined.

Prices, incomes, and goods preferences lead consumers to choose a basket of consumer goods and savings that maximizes their satisfactions. Prices of factor services, technology, and demands for goods guide each firm in the production of those goods in those qualities and quantities that maximize its profits, which is to say the difference between its total revenues and total costs. With the same goal in mind firms determine their optimal amounts of advertising, product differentiation, product innovation, and investment on the basis of conditions in the relevant markets.

The net result of the functioning of this vast network of interdependent markets is a determination of the fundamental economic decisions a society must make for the majority of its materialistic needs. In the ideal market economy, which is never achieved realistically, each good is produced in the quantities that are required to satisfy buyers' desires plus desired additions to stocks, so that no wastage of resources or queue-induced shortfall occurs. Goods are produced efficiently, with the society's scarce factor services distributed over their competing uses most effectively. When economic power is atomized in all markets, as it is in the ideal under discussion, so that no agent has a discernible power over price exercised through his or her decisions to buy or sell, the prices of all products are exactly equal to the economic costs necessary to produce the goods and services. Product flows among sectors of the economy are coordinated so that, for example, just enough steel is produced to meet the demands of automotive, construction, defense industries, and so forth. This phenomenal task of coordination of economic activities—consumption, production, investment, advertising, product differentiation and innovation—is accomplished without any costly central direction by the flow of price information. That information is inexpensive to transmit, is readily understandable by all agents who must process only a small subset of it, and hence constitutes the most efficient manner yet devised by societies to determine and effect vital interdependent allocation and distributive decisions.

Of course, this is an idealized picture of a market economy that assumes, in addition to atomization of power in all markets, that information is known with certainty by all interested agents, that adjustment processes are instantaneous, and that individuals' decisions do not affect others adversely or advantageously in perceptible degree. Many reservations and modifications would have to be added to bring the tableau closer to its real world counterpart. But such corrections and alterations affect mainly the *efficiency* characteristics of the description without much affecting my primary concern at this point: the implicit criteria that are behind a market economy's choices and the value system that is sustained by or supports those criteria. I identify and discuss four of the most important elements in this cultural complex.

Individualism

Markets are energized by individuals or firms accustomed to act on their own initiatives in furtherance of their egoistic self-interest. Therefore, the market economy can function only in a legal structure that holds individuals responsible for their contractual obligations and protects their ability to dispose freely of property whose acquisition, ownership, and transfer are guaranteed rights. The pure market economy places the obligation of material support of the citizen and his or her family squarely on the individual acting to acquire income through the sale of resources via markets to other individuals and firms in voluntary transactions. The market economy is a *voluntaristic* mechanism firmly grounded on individual rights and obligations and on a recognition of the propriety of agents to act solely to further their own material welfares. The market economy simply has no capability to incorporate in its decision making motivations that are social in character in the sense that they consistently include consideration of the welfare of persons other than the individual and his or her dependents.

A market economy, therefore, is *individualistic* in these senses, at once a beneficiary and reinforcer of these traits in the culture. Its inability to provide social goods (the economist terms them public goods) and its inherent incapacity to perform charitable distributive actions require that a dual economy—the governmental—function alongside the individualistic market economy. To produce those public goods and redistribute income away from its market-dictated recipients (and to perform corrective or preemptive regulatory functions which I ignore in this discussion), the state must divert resources from the market economy largely via taxes. In the strongly individualistic ethos fostered by capitalism, such diversions are always deeply resented and are difficult to effect regardless of the absolute levels of affluence achieved by a society. In general, the individualistic market society tends to devalue social ends that interfere with devotion of social resources to the achievement of individual goals, the latter being implicitly perceived as the proper end for the usage of available resources.

This strong individualistic trait which is reinforced by the market mechanism and is required for its successful functioning defines the individual as the proper social unit; accepts his or her welfare as constrained by resource ownership and the voluntary actions of other individuals via markets as the primary economic end; recognizes the individual's right to maximize the radius of his or her free choice within such constraints; and obligates the individual to provide the materialistic basis for his or her existence without the charitable assistance of other individuals. These rights and obligations in turn reinforce such institutions as private property, civil and political freedom, freedom of contract, and freedom of expression. Unfortunately, however, from the point of view of the proponent of the liberal society, such reinforcement may fall far short of requiring the establishment of such freedoms in a market society, and the market economy can function with the narrower concept of individualism embodied in the making of decisions within the economic domain proper.

Economic individualism in the form in which it underlies the capitalistic economy has been deemed by many critics as excessively egoistic in its implications for social welfare, especially as they concern the distributive economic functions and the neglect of public goods. The term socialism was intended to contrast with the individualism of the market economy and to imply a variety of economic mechanisms that stressed resource allocations driven less by individualistic and more by cooperative motivation. Less dramatic departures from the market's regime have been urged continually by many types of reformers who wish to retain the capitalistic framework but to temper its dictates with greater emphasis on social goods and subsidization of various groups in the interest of charity or their interpretations of broader social welfare.

Materialism

The market economy functions both as a decision *maker* and as a decision *effectuator*. Not only must the capitalistic economy decide where resources are best employed according to its implicit choice criteria, but it must induce the owners of those resources to voluntarily place them there. The major rewards and sanctions that it has to effect these desired placements are the promise of greater remuneration or denial of such returns. For such enticements to work effectively, the owners of the resources must be sufficiently attracted to material rewards and sensitive to relatively small increments and decrements in material returns. This implies that a successful market economy must implant or exploit an already existent value system that places great stress on material well-being. Since money is the homogeneous unit of the material in a market economy, this is equivalent to saying that the culture of the society must be monetized; that is, it must be deeply conditioned to the importance of progressing in the acquisition of money income and wealth, frequently at the expense of values to which other societies might give greater allegiance.

In the market society money assumes cultural functions that transcend its economic functions. Its acquisition becomes a major means of attaining status in a market society as income and wealth serve as social distancing factors. Power and position are highly correlated with its receipt in the market economy proper, and even in extra-market domains where other criteria for success may dominate—the arts, academia, government, the ministry—it serves as a token of relative success. Income plays a strong role in choice of occupation, determination of position within those occupations, the adoption of a circle of friends and acquaintances, and the choice of life-style. In an individualistic society, of course, it is a major source of material security and provision of material benefits, but the attraction of money goes beyond those important needs as a consequence of its success symbolism.

The successful market society is to a large degree materialistic and monetized in its culture, therefore, and of necessity must be. This is not to say—as is too lightly done by critics—that such values cannot coexist with other artistic and cultural interests, nor indeed that such interests do not benefit from the affluence the successful market society enjoys. Such cultural traits are not excluded by the monetized value system, and may be enhanced by it. Rather, my point is that generally the materialistic vein in the culture is dominant, with the important consequences that follow from that position. Much of the intelligence, imagination, and talent that might enter the priesthood, government, artistic endeavor, or the university in other types of societies flow into market occupations. Artistic and religious concerns, although they may retain a position in the individual's life, are relegated to the periphery of his or her active interests. Subtly or otherwise the striving for material gain and its symbolic representations are uppermost in the value systems of most of the market society's inhabitants.

Rationalism

Max Weber, one of the most astute scholars in the field of economic sociology (and many others), believed that the most important distinguishing characteristic of modern cultures from those of previous ages was *rationalism*. By this term he meant the tendency to systematize and routinize social functions in whose performance previous societies permitted much more spontaneity and randomness. It is not the pursuit of profit under capitalism, for example, that distinguishes it from commercial enterprise in earlier periods, he argues, but rather the development of procedures and techniques that permitted its continuous, regulated, planned achievement.[2] Such tools as double-entry bookkeeping, the limited liability corporation, management science, and business bureaucracy permit the institutionalization of profit making as a routine procedure. Government in the market society is also rationalized through bureaucratization and the creation of the civil service.

But by the term rationalism I mean to identify a gestalt that includes but extends beyond this conception. Thorstein Veblen among other analysts commented on the necessity of a modern market economy to foster a cause-and-effect world view among the working population in order to make the new technology workable.[3] This penetration of a scientific approach to everyday life, he felt, would inevitably make the acceptance of the mystic approaches of religion or the nationalistic credo of patriotism more difficult to instill, so that the market society would foster an ideology in which the intensity of mystical and symbolic belief would decline.[4] Joseph A. Schumpeter also felt that the dollars-and-sense, profit-and-loss, bottom-line mind-set fostered by the market culture would lead to a decline in the emotional or nonrational elements of the social ethos. Attachment to historical or traditional institutions would yield to the demand for functional or utilitarian usages; the "passion and glamour" attached to previous ruling classes—feudal warrior lords or vestment-clad clergy—which provided an emotional social cement to hold society together would dissipate in the prosaic aura surrounding the business elite. And artists and intellectuals, who would lose status in a predominantly technologically and scientifically oriented milieu, would feel threatened and would actively attack the culture.[5]

Many other social analysts and, notably, literati have diagnosed these rationalizing forces in capitalism. Charles Dickens, echoing the criticism of Thomas Carlyle, decried in his "social novels"—*Hard Times, Dombey and Son, Bleak House, Little Dorrit,* and *Our Mutual Friend*—the encroachment of a rationalizing culture. In *Hard Times* explicitly and more subtly in *Dombey and Son* he depicts what he perceived as the crushing of imagination in the new society in favor of "fact, fact, fact" and the alienation of individuals from their fully dimensioned potential by the technological need to shape "hands" for the burgeoning factories. Matthew Arnold interpreted the rationalizing strains as the ascendancy of the "Hebraic" values at the expense of the "sweetness and light" of the "Hellenic" virtues in his *Culture and Anarchy*, and his poem *Dover Beach* echoes these feelings of loss on the "darkling plain." The novels of Sir Walter Scott, AlfredTennyson's *Idylls of the King*, and James Russell Lowell's *Vision of Sir Launfall* are oblique attacks on the emerging rationalized and unglamorous social ethos, and were perceived as such by Mark Twain, who attempted unsuccessfully in his *Connecticut Yankee in King Arthur's Court* to defend the new American ethos.[6]

More recently such authors as Sinclair Lewis (*Babbitt*) and Kurt Vonnegut (*Player Piano*) have deplored the perceived trivialization of values and denial of meaningful labor such rationalizing forces encouraged. In the 1950s and 1960s such social critics as those of the Frankfurt Institute of Social Research—Horkheimer, Adorno, Marcuse, and Fromm—employed a Marxist-Hegelian-Freudian analysis as mentors of the New Left to attack the same rationalist syndrome.[7] The catalog of criticism in this vein can be extended indefinitely—few have been the literary critics who have not decried the rationalizing influences of the market economy to which their artistic leanings have sensitized them.

It is this group of traits of consciousness that I wish to denote by the term *rationalism*. Of course, the market economy is merely one of the contributors toward its implantation: the advances of science and the secularization of society begun in the Renaissance have been important—and perhaps not totally independent—sources. But the market mechanism is a powerful and continuous prime mover in the creation of the gestalt, and any acceptable theory of economic equity must conform to it.

Nondiscriminatory Egalitarianism

There are three varieties of economic egalitarianism that are relevant to an analysis of economic equity:

1. equality of reward
2. equality of opportunity for reward
3. equality of competition for reward.

The market economy's implicit judgments concerning the propriety of each are extremely important in eliciting its implicit economic equity precepts.

1. *Equality of Reward.* The market society is thoroughly inegalitarian in its distribution of income, as I will show in some detail in chapter 9. The allocation of social product in the idealized market economy is performed through the markets for factor services by pricing them at the levels that equate the amounts demanded and supplied and paying the owners of those resources at those prices for each unit of the factor offered. Therefore, the individual's income depends on (1) the amounts and types of factor services owned and sold, and (2) the market-determined values of those factor services.

Those values in turn relate to the relative scarcity of the factor service in the economy, that is, the amount of the factor service supplied relative to the demand for its use. The supply of brain surgeon labor is quite limited, and the demand for it is insensitive to its price because for those requiring it there are no acceptable substitutes. Therefore, brain surgeons command a high price for each hour of their labor. On the other hand a ditch digger's skills are in much more ample supply, the demand for them is conditioned by the availability of machinery, and as a consequence his or her wage rate is much smaller than the brain surgeon's.

Thus, the individual's reward for a period of the market economy's functioning depends on the quantities of factors owned and the relative scarcity of those factors. This income distribution is dictated by the implicit *efficiency* drives that inhere in the allocation mechanism and that must, as I have noted, exercise a great attraction to any society. Judgments concerning the *equity* of this distributive result might be based on an independent theory of social justice quite unrelated to efficiency considerations, but its practical implementation must recognize that a trade-off with efficiency will occur. John Stuart Mill believed in the mid-nineteenth century that in the capitalistic economy production was subject to the laws of nature but that distribution of income was independently determinable by human law.[8] But now, as Arthur Okun notably has argued, the interdependence of production and distribution cannot be ignored, and society must accept some decline in social output if it opts for greater equality of income distribution.[9]

2. *Equality of Opportunity for Reward.* Similarly, the market economy does not provide for equality of opportunity to pursue occupation, income, or position, either when that equality is defined to accept natural abilities as constraining on the individual or as compensated in some manner.[10] Individuals begin each period with different endowments of factors, some of which are acquired by inheritance or gift or natural endowment, and the market economy is indifferent to method of acquisition. Family income and educational levels differ among individuals, benefitting some in the race for achievement and penalizing others. The market, with its motive forces designed to achieve efficient allocations, rewards and punishes correlatively with resource and natural endowments and makes no corrective compensations with respect to any notion of equity.

3. *Equality of Competition for Reward.* There is, however, one facet of egalitarianism that is actively reinforced by the motive drives of the market mechanism: that which I have termed "equality of competition for reward." This is the motivation of the market to ignore all features of the individual that are irrelevant to the economic choice at hand. The

market moves to choose the lowest bidder to perform a task, assuming that bidder possesses the necessary skills, regardless of race, sex, religion, political bent, or other inessential characteristic. Similarly, the market's strong propensity is to hire the best qualified individual for a job, to reward the firm whose product and price best fill the needs of buyers, and to serve all customers with the requisite effective demand. In all of these senses the market is nondiscriminatory except in those efficiency dimensions that have a direct bearing on economic choices. This constitutes an extremely important form of egalitarianism in a liberal society.

Milton Friedman has pointed out these antidiscriminatory features of the market economy's operation.[11] He stresses their strong reinforcement of the freedoms of the liberal society, since they permit the political nonconformist to find employment and they reinforce civil liberties in their blindness to color, sex, and religion. Also important, however, are their impacts on the horizontal equity of the market economy. One universally accepted tenet in any theory of social equity based on the moral equality of individuals is that all who possess the same relevant characteristics in any particular situation must be treated equally, absent some unusual overriding social constraint or goal. Were the market economy's forces dominant in all economic relations, the profit motive would bring about horizontal equity in the labor and other factor service markets and the consumer's desire to maximize satisfaction would yield the same result in the patronage of suppliers. Should a black or female worker with the same skills as a male white be discriminated against in wage or salary terms, competition among employers would bid those compensations up to parity with the favored employee. Should one storekeeper be forced to offer lower prices than others because of consumer discrimination on religious or other grounds, competition among buyers would speedily correct the discrepancy. The market economy's drives toward nondiscriminatory treatment of agents are deep-seated and persistent, even in the presence of other social barriers to its implementation.[12] Once social barriers of a noneconomic origin begin to fall, the market economy offers a strong reinforcement of these corrections of inequities.

A DISTILLATION OF THE INFORMALLY ACCEPTED ECONOMIC ETHIC

The first section of this chapter indicated that no formally codified bill of economic equity particulars exists in the United States, and that it would be difficult to identify a cogent, consistent and near-universally accepted philosophy of economic justice in its social ethos. Nonetheless, there exists a body of precepts that derive from court interpretations of the political constitution of the country, from legislative enactments, and from the broader social outlook distilled from the folkways, mores, and traditions developed in the nation's cultural history. The discussion in that section indicates the difficulty inherent in attempting to distill this ill-defined corpus of moral principles that serves to shape economic policy, debate, and opinion. Fortunately, however, much of it is firmly grounded in the cultural proclivities of the market economy discussed in the second section, and that insight can be used to isolate the quietly influential precepts.

The first tenet of that informal ethic is that *the individual is entitled to the returns from his or her ownership of economic resources determined by a market in which no agent possesses a power over price, but with important constraints and reservations.* Underlying this basic acceptance of the market's dictates is a hazy perception of such recompense as the contribution of the factors to the social product and therefore, on the basis of physical ascription, the factors' just returns. This view is reinforced by a feeling that what others give voluntarily through the complex of markets to the owners of factors when those owners do not extract such payments through fraud or price manipulation are equitable receipts. This precept therefore receives support from contributory and voluntaristic interpretations of the market's factor pricing.

The voluntaristic nature of American society is deeply embedded in the economic ethos, as is its individualistic leanings, but the nonsocial character of their interpretation by the economy is importantly tempered in the operational ethos. *Labor is most importantly perceived to be a factor that has supereconomic claims for consideration, with a right to organize into groups with market power over its price and to be protected in its working conditions.* These attitudes lead to important qualifications concerning the market's distributive results and to the preeminent consideration wages are given as just economic returns. They rest in large part on a belief that in some vaguely formulated manner labor is the prime contributor to the economic product and is entitled to such special consideration. Also, labor service is thought to require a greater psychological cost in its rendering than other factor services, and on this ground as well is set apart.

As a complement to these attitudes toward labor, *profits and their interest and dividend derivatives are viewed as necessary and therefore just payments for a free market economy, but are always somewhat suspect in terms of their size and the degree to which market power has contributed to their receipt.* "Unearned income" is grudgingly accorded the status as a factor return though the contributions of capital and entrepreneurial inputs to the productive process and to risk-bearing; but they are seen as somewhat uncertain of origin and as psychologically painless. There exists as well a feeling that their magnitude (which itself is not well known) in large part arises from monopolistic power within product markets and, to a lesser extent, to "exploitation" of labor in some ill-defined sense that implies that labor is getting less than it "deserves," perhaps in the sense of contribution.

Market power exercised in product markets by suppliers is always unjust, but in cases where government uses such pricing power to protect agents whose welfare is deemed socially worthy of preservation, such usage is deemed equitable. Usually the primary concern in protecting such groups is is that of job preservation for laborers or conservation of a desirable life-style, such as farming. In both instances the ethos reveals the labor bias noted above. Industries deemed to be vital to the social welfare or to be suffering from "unfair" pricing policies of foreign competitors also may qualify for such protection. In general, however, the exercise of pricing power in product markets is perceived as an inequitable practice and subject to condemnation.

Each individual may be justly asked to benefit from the market economy only to the extent that his or her ownership of resources and possession of market-valued talent permits, but society must accept some responsibility to develop the individual's capabilities and to assure that he or she does not fall below an income floor deemed to be necessary for support. Individualism and voluntarism tempered with social responsibility for individual welfare dictate that differences in resource or natural endowment should result justly in differential incomes, even where resources are obtained without the individual's effort (e.g., through inheritance). But these entitlements are subject to some minimum income necessary to sustain life and dignity without interfering with the incentive to accept responsibility for earning a living. I have termed this "dualistic individualism" in recognition of its rather antagonistic components. Moreover, although inequality of starting positions is seen as just, or at least noncorrectible by just means, social responsibility for providing the opportunity to lessen this inequality through education or other skill development is accepted. But underlying this restrained commitment is a belief that for the motivated and qualified individual, the market society provides sufficient opportunity to prosper without great social intervention. Social responsibility, therefore, is quite secondary, and individual responsibility overriding.

In the competition for rewards and position in the society only those aspects of character, capability, or terms of offer that are relevant to the situation at hand should be taken into account in the decision making concerning it. Fairness requires that only in the most unusual of circumstances should this equality of competition for reward be violated. One of the most deeply rooted concepts of fairness in economic dealings is this interpretation of equality of competition for reward. The intensity of the social debate surrounding its contravention in recent reverse discrimination policy in the United

States, whose social purpose was purportedly to correct intergenerational inequity suffered by minorities, is a witness to the depth of commitment of the society to this precept. The dedication to the notion of the "level playing field" in areas other than economics—in the competition for political office or academic tenure or athletic events, for example—is a further indication of the prominence of this concept of equity in the American social ethos.

The most appropriate function of economic resources is their dedication to the satisfaction of individualistic desires as registered in the marketplace, and any diversion of such resources to social purposes must be strongly justified on the grounds of necessity, efficiency, or justice. To accord with the equity-based desire for equal sacrifice, such diversions effected through taxation must rise progressively with income. Legitimate social demands for resources exist and must be met through state provision, but their certification must be carefully granted. The individualistic basis of the economy must be treated as dominant in importance and sustenance of state projects granted grudgingly. Although nonprogressive types of taxes are permitted, ability to pay is accepted as the dominant guideline shaping the tax structure. This precept, as well as the suspect nature of profits, implies that heavy taxation of firms is just.

An Analysis of the Informally Accepted Economic Ethic

There is a consistent structure in the precepts I have identified as components of the informal American economic ethic. The first is the delineation of a core belief and the second a delineation of potential relaxations of its dictates. There is, therefore, an inherent tension between the two components that form the basis for much of the social debate and dissension surrounding distributive decisions in the American democracy.

The core components are the reflections in the informal code of social justice of the value system fostered by the market economy, as presented earlier. They have been absorbed from or reinforced by the individualism, materialism, rationalism, and constrained egalitarianism that spring from the energizing motivations of self-interest and the operational methods of the market economy. *The most notable feature of these motivations and methods is the implicit interpretation it gives of the rights and obligations of the individual agent in the social setting.* In the idealized perfectly competitive market's implicit view, society is a *passive* actor in the individual's search for an extremum outcome. The individual agent's impacts on the welfares of others are either insignificant because of the negligible amount of pricing power possessed in a competitive environment or, when others' welfares are impacted noticeably, such effects are incapable of capture and therefore ignored. The individualism of the market economy is the individualism of the particle that perceives itself myopically as an isolate, capable and with the inherent right of acting without conscious and active consideration of social consequences.

This first and dominant strain in the conception of economic justice is the egoistic ethic, which confirms the rights of individuals to act wholly with self-interest as motivation, to pursue that self-interest in such manner as to maximize their material welfare within the constraints of their resource and natural limitations, and to be rewarded by an impersonal market mechanism that takes into account only those characteristics of relevance to the allocation at hand. The correlative obligations of the individual are to accept the responsibility for his or her welfare and that of immediate dependents, to be obligated by contracts freely entered into, and to act in ways that do not seek or exploit market power.

Society is viewed as existing, to be sure, and functioning as an environmental milieu within which the individual is active and isolated. Economic contact with other individuals is incidental to the necessary transactions, and these individuals are treated in their economic dimension wholly as means to the satisfaction of wants. The individualism of the market is an impersonal force, asocial in its structure and in the conditioning of those who participate, linking agents in a "cash nexus" stark in its rationalism and devoid of interpersonal meaning.

The egoistic ethic contributes much, nonetheless, to social existence. As noted above, it is supportive of allocative efficiency, which increases the material basis of the society and must be an important goal of any society. Moreover, it inculcates the values of individual responsibility and initiative—attributes that are generally considered desirable as character traits. *But it cannot form the whole of an operational, effective economic ethic because of its failure to include an active consideration of the social fabric.* The second and dual component of the economic ethic isolated in the previous section is a *social* ethic containing two strains of values that take into account the impacts of individual decision making extending beyond the agent's own welfare.

The first strand in the social ethic is a *corrective* component, which establishes the propriety of the society, acting through its governmental agency, to reduce, eliminate, or compensate for the effects of individual actions that are perceived to affect the welfare of others in ethically unacceptable ways. A first instance of such actions is the possession and exercise of pricing power in markets. Monopolistic power to raise prices or exclude competitors is perceived to be an unacceptable departure from the market structure for which the egoistic ethic is valid, and, at least in theory, should be eliminated. A second instance is that of externalities, in which individual actions have nonnegligible spillover effects on the well-being of others the costs of which the market does not have the capability of levying against the causal agent. Social equity demands that such costs be borne by the offender via taxes, or that the action be terminated, or that those who suffer be compensated. Environmental pollution is the prime example of such violations of equity, but less dramatic instances are those of traffic congestion and peak-hour usage of utility services.

The second and most important body of values in the social ethic for a theory of distributive justice consists of the assumption by society of the obligation to provide for the material welfare of those members who are judged to be unable to assume the responsibility of providing for themselves and their dependents or who are believed to be worthy of such support for transcendent social reasons. I will term this strain in the social ethic the "compassionate" strain. It consists of a body of extramarket values that recognizes the obligations of individuals in a society to assume an active concern for others' economic welfares via state action in cases where the market economy is incapable of sufficient provision. As such it is in rather radical conflict with the egoistic equity beliefs fostered by capitalism, and may be viewed as imposing constraints on the implementation of the distributive patterns dictated dominantly by that system.

In the American society, where the egoistic equity values are dominant, economic debate most frequently revolves about the role that is to be assigned the social value system. Such issues as welfare mothers with dependent children, payments to mothers with dependent children, food stamps, price supports to subsidize farmers, voluntary restrictions on imports, punitive tariffs, affirmative action, day care for children, Social Security payments that are insensitive to need, and so forth, are policy issues whose ethical basis is immediately challenged by the individualistic values instilled by the market economy. The intensity of opposition to such proposals is frequently out of all proportion to the demands they make on social resources and must be understood as the result of conflict between two acknowledged ethical standards that find coexistence difficult. A practical complication of this inherent tension is the opportunity the compassionate value system affords many vested interests to seek moral justification for what are realistically egoistically motivated attempts to further their material advantages. The suspicion of such demands fostered by egoistic equity pleas is deepened by the experience with such ploys.

Any theory of social equity that rests on a basis of dignity, therefore, of the individual and the inviolability of the sense of self-worth that rests on that dignity must confront two implications of the term "individualism." The first is the necessity of giving the individual the freedom and responsibility to assess his or her own needs and desires, of assuming that the individual is capable of reasonable judgment and intelligent action in fulfilling those goals, and of believing that the individual is capable of achieving a sufficient number and variety of goals to permit him or her to live in a manner that is meaningful to the individual. The second implication is that this manner of material provision must not be allowed to become such as to undermine the feeling of self-worth that underlies the individual's dignity. Where the individual does not conform to the presumptions of the first implication, for reasons that the society judges to be excusable, society must assume the responsibility of providing through compassion the wherewithal to permit the basis for its social equity to exist.

Hence, the primary distributive conflict in the market society is the inherent contradiction between the egoistic strand in the informal economic ethic and the compassionate strand.[13] Historically, in the United States, that conflict centered about the tension between the egoistic component and the corrective strand of the social component. In the last quarter of the nineteenth century through the 1920s it was the proper role of regulation versus the individualistic ethic that generated most debate. Since the New Deal era of the 1930s, however, the social ethical component has been dominated by the compassionate strand, and economic policy with its implicit economic ethical implications has focused on the tension between it and the egoistic component. As will be shown, that debate is likely to intensify in the future.

THE MORAL BASIS OF DUALISTIC INDIVIDUALISM

It is important for the understanding of the philosophical and political economic argument to follow that I make explicit the relationship of the *prescriptive, predictive,* and *pragmatic* aspects of my analysis.

First, explicitly and unapologetically, I accept the American ethos as I have defined it as morally desirable in its content and necessitous of preservation as the ethical soul of American polity. In my view it is based on a vision of the good and the right in social living that strives to free the individual from the historic restraints or outright evils of a wide variety of organic alternatives. It grants the individual protection from the arbitrary actions of others by imposing a set of obligations on his or her behavior that reflect and reinforce self-respect. It permits the expression of individuality and a social mobility that are unsurpassed if equaled in other societies, and that urge the suppression of stereotypical, irrelevant judgments and barriers to that mobility on the basis of their violation of that individuality. It has oriented the goals of individual and social life to the desirable and innocent pursuits of improving human material existence, and it has done so by fostering a mind-set that encourages the discovery and rapid empirical implementation of rational means of so doing.

That in its role of *Zeitgeist* it is the ethical status quo is neither an argument for nor against its moral legitimacy. That in its practical application in guiding everyday individual and social action it fails—sometimes seriously—to approach its ideals I readily admit, but I know of no other operational ethos that does not nor whose inevitable failures are consistently more benign nor that affords corrections through internal mechanisms more readily. That in its very consistency it implies conflicting strands of desirable behavior that must be reconciled in compromise I accept: indeed, it is the very beginning of my prescriptive argument.

As noted in earlier sections, there inheres in the American interpretation of individualism two antagonistic implications that I have termed the egoistic and the compassionate. Both in my view are morally justifiable and must be preserved in any prescriptive theory of economic justice that could be or should be accepted pragmatically or "operationally" by American society. As I interpret the core problem of any theory of economic justice within the context of a liberal society, it is the determination and justification of the domains granted these two implications of individualism.

My argument that the present balance of emphasis on them is not just is based on an observation of the level of economic attainment of the American economy and the distress of individuals within it. I believe that any attempt to define the just balance must take both aspects of reality into account. It is this distinguishing characteristic of economic justice that makes it so challenging to the theorist: its principles are of necessity a function of the poverty or affluence of the economic context. The principles of economic justice for the subsistence economy will be quite different from those of an economy whose per capita income is $100,000 per year—a consideration that theorists like Rawls have neglected, at least in their static analysis.

Exercise of the compassionate strand interferes with and restricts directly the economic welfare of individuals who are forced in a liberal market economy to yield up income the fundamental institutions of that society lead him or her to believe are justly earned. I know of no theory of morality that requires the individual to sacrifice his or her life, health, or basic necessities for the benefit of another: heroism is a supramoral quality. What may justly be demanded of the individual for support of others in these terms inescapably depends on his or her resources.

Hence my theory of dualistic individualism is at once a prescriptive one, arguing the degree that the role given the compassionate strand should be altered in the interest of justice and, at the same time, is a pragmatic one, seeking to judge the limits of feasibility imposed by the community's perception of its ability in justice to demand sacrifices of its individuals who also have claims in justice on their earnings. Of necessity, such judgments must consider the degree of distress suffered by groups in the society, and, for good or for evil, their ability to impact the social consciousness concerning that distress.

Being to some extent a consequentialist in my approach to economic justice, I will examine these practical matters in the discussion to follow, but I do not wish to be interpeted as believing matters of justice can be settled by considerations of the ability of the disaffected groups to exert social blackmail through exercise of political power or worse. Indeed, it is the prevalence of this manner of deciding the balance issue currently and the need to counter it with formalized frameworks of just action that motivate my own theory.

The claims that the individual has on that which he or she has earned through the market without force or fraud, and the claims of the individual who is incapable of reaching a level of economic existence through voluntarist mechanisms that permits health and self-respect, are just claims based on the moral implications of individualism. That level of sacrifice and support which satisfies the demand of justice must be determined at any period by a social consensus that depends in large part on the economy's level of affluence. That consensus will also be affected by the objectively observable levels of distress of claimant groups. Justice demands that the consensus be conformant with the constitutive values, beliefs, and institutions that comprise and implement the ideals of the society, and this is best done by formalizing their most fundamental content in expressions of rights and obligations. By definition, justice is distinguished from morality in the recognition of the social importance of a universal adherence to its principles through supporting them with legal sanction. These are the bases of the theory of economic justice I have called *dualistic individualism*—a theory that is at once prescriptive and pragmatic, supportive and importantly critical of the status quo of income distribution in American society.

Last, I argue in a predictive vein that presently forseeable trends in the growth of those groups that constitute the loci of poverty or need in the American society—the aged, single mothers, especially minority single mothers, and the undereducated underclass—will make the importance of these growing pressures increasingly clear and should force the content of social consensus to be different from what it would or should be in their absence. The political power of these groups over the next thirty years probably will grow, and that will be a factor in the urgency. But far more important is the rise in social consciousness that these trends will inspire, especially as the American economy grows more affluent. As in the past, in my view, the growth in the compassionate strand of individualism has not occurred because of a felt threat concerning social stability but rather from need for reform felt by the more affluent electorate within the American ethos.

These are the primitives in my theory of economic justice, and I believe they are subscribed to implicitly if vaguely by the large majority of American citizens. The American ethos—or that portion of it I have defined as relevant to my quest—is a constraint on the rapidity and degree to which any theory of economic justice can be implemented. But it is a desirable constraint whose content limns out the good and the right to which the American polity should subscribe. I will quarrel with emphases within it, with shortcomings from the ideal, and with outright violations of it in historic practice: the status quo in any period can violate the dictates of the ethos as expressed above (slavery, treatment of native Americans, and so forth). These were violations of individualism, were discerned as such by perceptive members of the society, and (admittedly after long lags) were recognized as unjust by the majority by virtue of the tensions generated within the ethos.

In summary, in a nation in which distributive economic measures constitute a major and increasing portion of governmental policy, it becomes important therefore to obtain a consensus on an economic ethic. The informal ethos inherent in the market system must be examined for its consistency and conformance to the nation's deeper values. This need to obtain a formal basis for an accepted, consistent set of principles for economic justice will become even more important in the future as the demands for redistribution become more intense. And simply as a matter of intellectual cogency, the development of an ethic whose constitution permits the discernment of the fundamental factors involved in distributive policy highlights the conflicts among such factors that require resolution and suggests philosophical guidelines along which those resolutions could occur is desirable. The remainder of this book is dedicated to suggesting a framework for the discussion of these issues.

A Summary

Several goals have been accomplished in this chapter that have laid the groundwork for performance of that task. Because of the importance of the economic factor in the life of the nation and the intensity of the motivating forces in the market economy, the implicit economic ethic that characterizes much of the policy discussion in American society has been treated as shaped in large part by the values that the economy imposes and reinforces. In an important sense, the market economy is an active factor in shaping the value and belief system of a society in which it is embedded, because in order to function as a smooth decision maker and effectuator, it must instill a certain vision of life that cannot be confined to the economic sector alone. Four important components of that value system have been isolated as instrumental in forming the dominant portion of the unwritten economic ethic:

1. An individualism that stresses the rightness of egoistic motivation of agents, the responsibility of individuals for their material well-being, the acceptance by individuals of their resource and natural capacities in the economic process, and the subordination of concern for the external impacts of individual decisions.

2. A materialistic view of existence, in the sense that the earning of income and enjoyment of the goods it provides are worthy goals of life constituting an important element in the definition of the good in any operational theory of social ethics and should provide important motivation in the selection of location, career, associates, and so forth.

3. A rationalistic world view that emphasizes cause-and-effect explanations, the useful, the bottom line, profit and loss, costs and benefits, the technical and scientific, the efficient, the formal organization. In this "vision" the mystical, the traditional, the artistic, the intellectual, the spontaneous, the informal tend to be subordinate.

4. The acceptability of inequality of income and opportunity, but an insistence on selection processes among agents that ignore all qualities but those relevant to the purpose of the exercise: a rejection of all selection modes that depend on characteristics other than "merit" in the sense defined above.

Each of these values in its own way, and most particularly the first and the last, conjoin to establish the first and dominant strain in the informal American economic ethic. I have termed it the *egoistic* strain, which justifies the individual's rights, obligations, and constraints in seeking to maximize his or her satisfactions without consideration of the social matrix within which the economy is embedded.

But this lack of extrapersonal dimensionality is corrected by a *social* strain in the informal ethic that is formed by two components: the corrective strand and the compassionate strand. The first recognizes that individual actions within the market economy may occur within contexts that violate the implicit requirement of atomization of power or that have harmful spillover effects on others that cannot be ignored. The second—and in recent decades more important—component is the recognition that economic justice requires that society provide to some degree for the individual who is incapable of obtaining a minimum standard of living. It is this second component of the social strain in the economic ethic that conflicts with the egoistic strain and produces most of the tension in the policy reflections of the ethic.

Is it possible to draw from this set of vaguely defined value and belief allegiances and include desirable modifications that constitute a formally precise economic ethic providing a better understanding and management of the conflict between the egoistic and social strands? To what extent do existing theories of social ethics cast light on the problems we face in formulating an economic ethic for the American society? Can the individual citizen be aided in reaching an economic ethic that conforms to his or her own value system? Finally, after deciding on an economic ethic that in my opinion is most appropriate for a society grounded firmly on the notion of the inviolability of the individual's free will within a social context, I ask how its implications compare with the present and prospective distribution of income in the United States? Further, I seek to judge the feasibility of programs in furtherance of the principles in view of the adjustments in the nation's prevailing ethos that will be necessary in the future.

PART II

Theoretical Bases for Economic Justice

Chapter 2

THEORIES OF SOCIAL EQUITY:
EGOISTICALLY ORIENTED THEORIES

THE INDIVIDUALIST CONSTRAINT

At the core of traditional liberal thought is the notion of the individual as the fundamental unit of moral concern. Whether the precept is grounded in religious or secular principles, the sanctity of the individual's life, the respect for his or her dignity on the basis of recognized moral equality, the protection of the freedom of will and action of the individual in the face of all but the most exigent social circumstances, and the basic rectitude of his or her search for personal gratification are corollaries of this fundamental notion of the integrity of the personality, the individuality of moral being.

As noted, support for this view has been drawn from the sacred origin of the human soul in Christian belief and from the doctrine of natural rights, but I shall accept it as a "primitive" of the analysis to follow, or an axiomatic statement from which other propositions are derivative.[1] Any acceptable and potentially useful theory of economic equity designed for western democratic societies must conform to this bedrock ideological tenet of the liberal society. I propose that it is and should remain the moral keystone of the American ethos. Consideration therefore will be given only to theories of social equity that are individualistic in this sense.[2]

As noted in chapter 1, the individualism that is relevant is embedded in a social context and is conditioned by that circumstance. The social rights that originate from the recognition of the uniqueness of the individual carry with them the obligations not to transgress the same rights of other individuals. But those obligations extend to a concern for the welfare of others that was termed dualistic individualism in chapter 1. That concern may well seem to contravene or limit the claims to autonomy based upon a passive social interpretation of individualism, both for those who sacrifice for the sake of the social concern and for those who benefit from it. With the acceptance of this active social concern for the welfare of the individual, for example, it may be right for the society to restrict access to drugs, to require the wearing of seat belts, and to prevent suicide, as well as to tax away resources earned through the market to implement programs for those designated by society as deserving.

Theories of social equity vary significantly in the relative weights they give to the egoistic or asocial interpretation of individual rights and to the active social compassion interpretation. It is convenient to group such theories into categories depending on the dominant orientation they display in this dimension. A good deal of judgment, no doubt arbitrary at times, enters such a dichotomization, but the framework is a valuable analytical construct. As indicated in chapter 1, the central difficulty in constructing a theory of economic equity that possesses a potential for consensus is the attaining of a balance between the egoistic and the social compassionate strands of equity. The classification, by focusing upon this balance in the theories, will aid in the judgment of the acceptability of their insights.

This chapter is devoted to the presentation of social equity theories in which the egoistic strand stressing individual entitlements is dominant. Such theories treat society as a rather neutral medium within which the individual pursues selfish goals; a necessary entity to be sure, but like the atmosphere, to be taken for granted and making few demands upon the agent. Social action, where appropriate, generally is viewed as protective of the individual's rights, with perhaps some corrective and compassionate functions more or less grudgingly conceded.

CONTRIBUTORY THEORIES OF CAPITALIST DISTRIBUTIVE EQUITY

In chapter 1 it was stated that under the idealized conditions of pure competition, each factor service receives as a reward for its use in production a return consisting of its market-clearing price. Contributory theories assert implicitly or explicitly that it is morally wrong to deprive an agent of that which he or she created without equivalent compensation. What can be said in general about the nature of the price received by the factor service in capitalism as an index of contribution and what justification in terms of equity can it be given?

The Marginal Productivity Theory

Assuming that *diminishing returns to variable factor services* rules—by which is meant that as any factor is added to a body of all other factors whose quantities are held constant the additional product will be positive but will diminish in its size as the variable factor becomes more plentiful—every profit maximizing firm will be led to hire each factor service to the point where the last unit hired adds just as much to revenue as it does to cost. These incremental revenues that occur at the edge or margin of the amounts of variable resources hired are called *marginal revenue products* by the economist. In the equilibrium solution of the ideal competitive system, therefore, each factor service "earns" its marginal revenue product, in the sense that its payment is that amount of income that would be lost if that unit of factor service were withdrawn, all other units of factor services remaining employed in their current positions.

The distribution of the social product therefore is derived by multiplying the price of the factor service (= marginal revenue product) by the number of units of that service controlled by each person and summing these products over the set of factor types possessed. Each individual therefore presents claims against the total social product based upon the amount of factor service and a price that hinges on the presence of the last (and least productive) unit of each resource in the market for that resource. The larger the amount of the resource available, all other factor quantities being constant, the smaller will be the marginal revenue product because of diminishing marginal physical returns and the need to reduce the price of the product slightly to sell the additional physical product. Importantly, the smaller will be the return to every unit of that resource in the economy. This is because every unit receives the incremental revenue that would be lost if any one unit of it were withdrawn. Of course, the amount of the resource available depends upon the quantity in existence at the start of the time period as well as the willingness of its owners to sell its services in the market.

In the thought of some economists explicitly, and to many laissez-faire ideologues implicitly, the fact that the market rewards factors with the revenue product that they (i.e., their marginal units) have "earned" is a testimony not only to the capitalist economy's efficiency but to its equity as well. The marginal revenue product is viewed by these advocates as the "contribution" of the factor to the social product, and with the additional but generally unstated assumption that justice requires the factor service to obtain what it provides society in the way of productivity, the equitable return to that factor. The just distribution of income reflects, via ownership of such resources, these just factor service rewards.

John Bates Clark, who developed the notion of marginal productivity at the turn of the twentieth century, wrote, for example:

> It is the purpose of this work to show that the distribution of the income is controlled by a natural law, and that law, if it worked without friction, would give to every agent of production the amount of wealth that agent creates. . . . They [marginal products] are the theoretically "natural" rates which science has been seeking.[3]

Given the prominence of natural rights theories of economic equity in the seventeenth, eighteenth, and nineteenth centuries, it was a small step for Clark from "natural law" to "just"; indeed the identity was self-evident as it is less explicitly (or unconsciously) with many free market supporters.[4]

The Marxist Contributory Theory: An Average Productivity Theory

It is somewhat paradoxical that Karl Marx—the most influential critic of the capitalist economy—joined its staunchest defenders in embracing a contributory theory of economic equity. Whether or not his total system of analysis permitted him to endorse such a theory is a matter of debate among Marxist scholars.[5] But a straightforward reading of *Capital* and his later works certainly lends credence to this interpretation of his exploitation theory, and it was the dominant theme in his followers' critiques of the market economy until the intellectual popularity of the alienation thesis dominated it in western thought after World War II.[6]

Marx distinguished capitalism as a distinct mode of production on the basis of the presence in it of two unique institutions: a market on which labor power is sold at its true exchange value "voluntarily" by laborers and a capitalist class that owns the means of production without which the labor power of the worker is unusable. Marx *assumed* that although capital goods are physically productive, they could convey to their products only the value of the depreciated labor their wastage delivered. Hence, capital goods, which are simply congealed labor as opposed to living labor, contribute to the value of the social product only their depreciation. No net return to the capitalist is due as a result of contribution. One of the more important "contradictions" in capitalism in Marx's view was the fact that the production of commodities was of necessity a social endeavor, yet the essential means of employing labor productively are held as private property.

All net value is the product of living labor, which alone has the capacity of vitalizing capital goods and creating exchange value. Hence, on a contributory basis, the entire value of the social product (after depreciation) is justly that of the laborers, which is to say that in terms of equity, labor should receive its average net product. Interest (or, equivalently, profit) in capitalism therefore is the result of labor exploitation made possible by the private ownership of the means of production. Because all other shares in the distribution of income are derivatives from the surplus value—rents, retail and wholesale profits, advertising salaries, and so forth—Marx was not interested in the manner in which other income shares were determined and spent little time with the means by which this process of "expropriation of the expropriators" was carried on.

It seems to me that this interpretation of Marxist exploitation theory is explicit in Marx's model of capitalism and his discussion of it in *Capital*. Yet its meaning and rationale have caused all manner of difficulties for Marxists. Peffer, for example, writes that "Marx never gives a clear-cut definition or explication of his concept (or concepts) of exploitation."[7] He goes on to assert, however, that one need not adopt a labor theory of value to explain its existence: one need only assume that there is something important about how much time one labors—or compare what percentage of society's labor time one contributes and what percentage of society's wealth one receives in return![8] In a similar vein, Buchanan argues that one need not assert that labor is the sole source of value: one merely distinguishes between necessary labor time [presumably the laborer's wages] and surplus labor time, as if the distinction could be meaningful in the absence of Marx's assumption of labor's exclusive role in creating value.[9]

Marx wrote relatively little about his perceptions about the distribution of income in the socialist and communist modes of production which he saw ahead, and what he did write was rather sketchy and ill thought out.[10] In *The Critique of the Gotha Program*, where the greater part of his thinking along these lines was outlined, he saw a role for contributory determination of income distribution in the socialist transitional mode between capitalism and communism. In both the socialist society and the communist society which would succeed it, Marx foresaw that the total social product would have to be reduced before distribution to the laborers by depreciation, net investment, and insurance or reserve funds, and that charity deductions for such purposes as support of those unable to work would also be deducted. Further, the expenditures on public goods would be greatly increased. After such deductions, the remaining product would be available for distribution to the laborers.

In the socialist mode, however, still contaminated with the residues of its capitalist predecessor, the distribution of this net product would be based on contribution. Each worker would receive a certificate stating the amount and "intensity" or quality of labor rendered. Unequal incomes would result from unequal endowments of ability and capacity for work, but Marx insisted that this is a form of equality since such inequalities would not arise from class differences but from the equal application of a standard common to all. This contributory basis for the division of social product is just in the Marxist sense for this transitional mode of production because of the need to incentivize workers still infected by the capitalist virus: justice can never rise higher than the economic structure of the society and its implied cultural development.

In the communist mode of production, however, the contributory theory can be rejected. Division of labor will have been eliminated and the distinction between physical and intellectual labor will have vanished. Work will have become a rewarding means of self-fulfillment, and no incentivization of the worker will be necessary. Such attitudinal changes will have raised the social product to levels that permit egalitarian justice to be established. In such conditions, the guideline for distribution will be that enunciated by Louis Blanc: "From each according to his ability, to each according to his need."

Marx's attitudes toward the contributory theory of equity are difficult in their complexity, but an attempt to summarize them is made in the following manner. Capitalism as an economic system implies the unjust exploitation of the laboring class which fails to receive its contribution to the net value of the social product. In the transitional socialist period a contributory basis of distribution will have to persist, which will be just in the sense that class exploitation will have vanished, and such inequalities as do arise from the distinctions among laborers reflect the application of a standard that is uniform for all. Moreover, such inequalities must be justified on the basis of the need to incentivize and to attain the larger social product that can only emerge in a completely cooperative society. Hence, Marx's basic quarrel with capitalism in terms of its contributive aspects is as a class phenomenon, not as to its inegalitarian implications for individuals within the class. Finally, the culminating stage of social evolution—communism—with its classless society will feature workers' contributing to production in step with their abilities, but drawing from the product according to their "needs" in some undefined sense.

NATURAL RIGHTS OR ENTITLEMENT THEORIES

Theories of social equity that are based on natural rights assert that the individual is given by natural law a protection against arbitrary exactions, actions, or interference with desired conduct by other individuals or the state. Such intrusions on the individual's property or action space are acceptable (nonarbitrary) only if the individual has agreed to them and the intruding agent has conformed to all contractual obligations that may be specified in that agreement. In the case of the state, successful assertion of a right that obligates the individual hinges upon demonstration of the individual's voluntary and explicit agreement that serves as the basis of that state's legitimacy.[11]

The Hobbesian Challenge

With the passing of the medieval period and the dissolution of the spiritual unity of Christendom entailed by the Reformation, moral philosophers began to search for explanations of good and evil, right and wrong, just and unjust, that did not rest wholly on the arbitrary will of God. Was there not some other facet of the Divine Essence from which emanated the principles of the moral and the just—a facet whose manifestations were more readily perceived by the imperfect mind of man? Indeed, might not God have bound Himself, out of His infinite goodness, to principles that were neither arbitrary nor capricious?

Philosophers in the sixteenth century reached back through Scholastic thought to the Stoics, Cicero, Augustine, and Thomas Aquinas to focus on the "law of nature" as divine principles of right reason which were independent of revelation and directly perceivable by rational men. Because they were so readily perceptible they were binding upon all men with intact faculties and reflected the Divine Reason that had shaped the universe. Grotius (1583–1645) was an influential thinker in the seventeenth century who viewed man as led by his nature to seek peaceful coexistence with his neighbors through his understanding of natural law. Man's conformance to that law, therefore, and his ability to form societies were based upon the faculty of right reason implanted within him by his Maker. Man understood the laws of nature, sought to obey them, and could be forced to conform to them by virtue of a faculty of reason that was independent of revelation.

Hobbes accepts the doctrine of natural law and the ability of man's reason to discern it. But in *Leviathan* he believes man's egoistic drives toward the attainment of pleasure by means of power over his fellow men lead him to act contrary to his natural inclination to desire a peaceful life.[12] Man, therefore, obsessed by pleasure and power, and essentially equal in ability with his fellows in the Hobbesian natural state, is unsocial, brutal in his treatment of others, utterly selfish in his goals, and frightened of the consequences of the like motivations of others for his life and freedom.[13] Life in such conditions is a "war of all against all," "solitary, poor, nasty, brutish, and short." But each person in this state has the natural right to employ his or her power for self-protection, and indeed is required to defend his or her life by natural law. The first strand of natural law—a general rule discerned by reason—is that the individual seek peace, but the second is that he or she defend his or her life by all means. More generally, "the Lawes of Nature therefore need not any publishing, nor Proclamation; as being contained in this one Sentence, approved by all the world, *Do not that to another, which thou thinkest unreasonable to be done by another to thy selfe.*"[14] It incorporates both strands of the first law.

In the state of Nature, however, the war of every man against every other is not unjust or wrong because such terms do not exist in such a state. Moral law is man-made and men must agree upon the individual or individuals who should make it. The fear of death, which is a strong passion in everyone, suggests the establishment of an agency that can define moral law and enforce it. The solution is at hand in the mutual transfer of power by contract to a party (legislature or monarch) who is given sole authority to write the natural law into statutory law and to inflict penalties on those who transgress it. Hobbes believes the keeping of contracts is another law of nature and, indeed, injustice is simply failure to abide by a contract.[15]

Hobbes asks one of the fundamental questions of ethics: why should the individual follow moral dictates when they contradict his or her self-interest? His answer is uncompromising: in the absence of compulsion individuals will ignore the urgings of the natural law under such conditions. Therefore, the power that defines and enforces the laws protecting each against all must be absolute in its power to punish and to command obedience.

With the passing of the divine right of kings, social analysts were seeking the source of sovereignty and limitations of power of the state, and Hobbes found both in his acceptance of the unrelieved egoism of human nature. Individuals in the Hobbesian natural state will form a society for one reason only: protection against their fellows. The natural law will rule only if the political system imposes sanctions on those who disobey it. The state therefore arises from a social contract in which sovereignty is given by individuals to a government for the purpose of protecting each from the depredations of his or her fellow citizens. Moreover, to ensure the comprehensive observance of the laws, the granting of sovereignty must be absolute: only when the dictates of religion, other social mechanisms, and the individual conscience are subordinated to the absolute dictates of the state, limited only by the natural law it is seeking to enforce, can the individual be assured of protection.[16]

The desideratum is the establishment of natural law, which Hobbes associates with the negative form of the Golden Rule quoted above. But natural law morality *is wholly dependent on the existence of the absolute sovereignty of the state and the juridical institutions it establishes.*[17] Hobbes seems contradictory at this point: man is capable of understanding the natural law through reason, but the sovereign is empowered to interpret and establish that law in statutory form. As a subject of God, the sovereign is bound by natural law, yet he or it is incapable of breach of contract since he or it is not a party to the social compact. The individual is bound to obey that law even though he or she may believe it is contrary to the natural law. The only condition under which the sovereign can no longer be obeyed is if he or it loses the power to protect the individual. However, it is not clear how the individual is to decide at what point this incapacity arises.

Hobbes had little to say about economic distributive equity, since in the civil society it is wholly the province of the sovereign. The first law is distribution of the land of the commonwealth as the legislature or monarch deems fit. Beyond that:

> It belongeth to the Commonwealth, (that is to say, the Sovereign,) to appoint in what manner, all kinds of contract between Subjects, (as buying, selling, exchanging, borrowing, lending, letting, and taking to hire,) are to bee made; and by what words, and signes they shall be understood for valid. And for the Matter, and Distribution of the Nourishment, to the severall Members of the Commonwealth, thus much (considering the modell of the whole worke) is sufficient.[18]

In the state of Nature, however, Hobbes is an egalitarian. Because all persons are equal in this state, resources that cannot be divided equally should be held in common where possible, and where sufficient exists no limit should be set on consumption and usage. Failing this, if necessary to ration scarcities, equal distribution as the law of Nature dictates distribution among individuals by lottery.[19] Provision for the creation of private property in the state of Nature is not stated in Hobbes's theory, and its existence in civil society is at the whim of the sovereign.

Hobbes's thought was seminal in leaving the seventeenth and eighteenth centuries three central questions to ponder:

1. Was man in the natural state so completely egoistically driven, his motivation so dominated by the drives for pleasure and power, and his psychological state of mind so dominated by the fear of death? And was human nature in a type of Prisoners' Dilemma game led rationally to violate the natural law it rationally understood as desirable for individual survival?
2. Was the necessary grant of sovereignty to the state by the social contract absolute and constrained only by its own interpretation of a natural law it imposed as principles of morality?
3. Was society to be doomed to be nonharmonistic in the sense that an absolute state continuously struggled to restrain war among the citizens for power and possessions? Might one not expect periodic challenges to and disruptions of such government? Must mankind look forward to such a society of constrained discord?

Lockian Natural Law

The responses to the Hobbesian challenges were immediate and multiform in their approaches. The Cambridge Platonist moral philosophers (especially Cudworth and Henry More) argued that moral truth was as objective as mathematical laws and independent of both divine and human will, although rooted in divine reason, and was apprehended by man's intellect. More asserted that a "boniform" faculty or sense of virtue gave rise to a feeling of true pleasure. But while they challenged the

Hobbesian notion of morals as established by the will of the state and in the case of More anticipated the arguments of the Sentimental School, they did not provide reasons why individuals would suppress egoistic drives for pleasure and power.[20]

Shaftesbury (1671–1713) confronted Hobbes's conception of human nature directly in asserting that man's emotions coexisted with his reason and led him to feel affections for his fellows which tempered his egoistic drives and suppressed those that were malevolent. The psychological basis for morality was independent of the need for religious implantation and provided the countervailing "moral sense" that permitted egoism and altruism to coexist. Francis Hutcheson (1694–1747) viewed the psychological enabling force for the harmonistic society to be a sense of virtue that coexisted with the five physical senses and led directly to benevolent action. His student Adam Smith (1723–1790) denied the existence of any separate moral faculty and instead urged that it was the human ability to empathize with others that was based in the imagination and provided the foundation for a harmonistic society. It also underlay the notion of retributive justice as a proper demand of the victim of crime. The derivative conscience of the individual leads him or her to choose a moral life rather than one of Hobbesian egoism.

Joseph Butler (1692–1752) is another influential thinker in this "sentimental" vein whose challenge was to Hobbes's narrow delineation of human nature. Like Shaftesbury, he argues that social conscience, though weaker than egoism, exists in the human psyche and leads men to choose benevolent as well as selfish actions. Unlike Shaftesbury, however, he believes that conscience is a form of reason acquired by contemplation of the results of actions. The state and its institutions are unnecessary to lead the rational individual to choose the moral. Conscience defines a "reasonable self-love" that leads us to the higher satisfaction acquired from benevolent actions.

All of these theorists sought to find faculties in the human psyche other than "reason" in the narrow sense of logical capacity that led human participants in a society to extend consideration beyond their narrow self-interest to the welfare of their fellows. In one sense or another, they argued, man possessed innate ability not incorporated in ratiocination to accept the obligations discussed in chapter 1 under the heading of the compassionate strand of equity.

But the most influential moral architect of his age—John Locke (1632–1704)—in responding to Hobbes and erecting a new foundation for social contract theory did not choose this route. Rather, he elected to found his theory of natural law and the social justice that was based on it on the narrow faculty of man's reason. The mind of man had no innate ideas implanted by God, but it did possess intuition, with which the individual was aware of his or her own existence, and the faculty of reason with which man deduced truth from the evidence of the senses and the faculty of inward perception.[21] In the Lockian natural state that preceded the establishment of a civil society by social contract men are capable of understanding and acknowledging through reason and intuition (not innate ideas) a natural law whose tenets included the following:

1. All men are born free and equal, by which Locke meant that in the state of Nature the individual had "a liberty to follow [his] own will in all things where that rule [i.e., natural law] prescribes not, not to be subject to the inconstant, uncertain, unknown, arbitrary will of another man, as freedom of nature is to be under no other restraint but the law of Nature."[22]

2. Each individual has the obligation not to harm any other individual and indeed *to take steps to preserve other individuals* to the extent his or her own preservation is not endangered. The individual possessed the right to punish violations of the natural law with a degree of force proportionate to the severity of the infraction and the need to deter infractions.

3. Freely entered contracts among individuals must be honored. However, because no person has the power to end his or her own life, and because slavery can exist only if the slave holder has the power of life and death over the slave, no contract is valid in which an individual puts himself or herself under the absolute power of another.[23]

4. In the natural state nature's gifts are held in common by all until any member of society mixes his or her labor with such gifts, at which time the resultant product becomes the property of that member. But this right to establish the claim of private property is subject to certain important restrictions to be discussed below.

5. Parents have power over children until attainment of adulthood, but are obligated to nurture them until that maturity.

The Lockian natural state therefore is one in which society is organized in families, in which contracting exists, and citizens assume certain obligations with respect to less fortunate neighbors. It is a far cry from the continuously life-threatening aggressive anarchy conceived by Hobbes. However, disputes among individuals, in whose actions self-service is a dominant motivation, as in Hobbes, do arise and are not arbitrated in a satisfactory way. Violations of natural rights go unpunished, and disputes therefore have the potential for violent resolution. Under such threats to individual and social peace, a social contract is instituted in which individuals as a body assign a portion of their sovereignty to a government sufficient to permit the latter to safeguard their physical safety and their property.[24]

The limits to that delegated authority are set by the powers that are just necessary to impose the natural law on all inhabitants of the society.

If the government fails in its obligations to enforce the natural law, it forfeits its legitimacy. On the other hand those who accept the benefits of its legitimate protections may not opt out of the social contract because by accepting its protections individuals tacitly consent to the contract.

Despite the rational comprehension of the natural law by the society's citizens, civil and religious sanctions are necessary, since Locke viewed the body of natural law to be dictates of God. Their establishment and legitimization therefore were not dependent on civil institutions (as Hobbes asserted), but ultimately were grounded in divine dictates in whose effectuation the state functioned as agent.

In Locke's theory, therefore, no faculty other than reason, sharpened by experience and deepened by contemplation, is necessary to lead individuals to accept the rule of natural law in the definition of social equity. In his *Essay on Human Understanding* Locke asserts that moral ideas are absorbed through the senses, but that the logical monitor within each individual integrates them into moral law—a law which (adopting the Cambridge Platonist view) is demonstrable with mathematical precision. Everyone accepts its rule as an individual seeking to maximize his or her own self-interest, maximizing individual good conceived of as pleasure and avoidance of pain, not in trying to maximize some overriding social welfare concept. However, that self-interest incorporates an ability to accept some responsibility for the welfares of others in the society without the need for state exactions for that purpose. Moral good, or conformance to the moral law, consists of a higher pleasure derived from that conformity.

Locke's thought involving economic equity is almost entirely concerned with the natural right to private property, and the structure of his theory is not clear in these respects. One has the distinct feeling that Locke was not satisfied with it, and in this sense that it was incomplete. In the natural state, initially all of Nature's gifts are held in common. Each person, however, can alter the status of such resources to one of private property by mixing his or her labor with them, with one major reservation:

> Whatsoever, then, he removes out of the state that Nature hath provided and left it in, he hath mixed his labor with it, and joined to it something that is his own, and thereby makes it his property. It being by him removed from the common state Nature placed it in it hath by this labour something annexed to it that excludes the common right of other men. For this "labour" being the unquestionable property of the labourer, no man but he can have a right to what that is once joined to, *at least where there is enough, and as good left in common for others.*[25]

Every person has property in himself or herself, and labor, as a projection of that natural quality, provides the basis of private property in the state of Nature. However, because of his concern for the origin of private property, Locke remains for the most part with the conditions of an agricultural community in which land is a free good or at least in abundance. Thus the normal case is that where "there is enough and as good" left for others. Even when this is true, however, man's natural right to private property in land is limited by needs; no person is entitled to land whose product, even when derived from his or her labor, spoils or decays because it exceeds the person's ability to consume it.[26]

Hence, Locke's discussion of the natural law basis of property is limited to the tilling of land or keeping of livestock in a subsistence economy and is constrained by the individual's or family's ability to consume. Under these conditions Locke estimates that labor contributes about 90 percent of the raw value of the products of the earth, and perhaps 99 percent of the final consumed agricultural product. It is difficult to understand why ownership of land in any amount would not be consistent with natural rights when land is a free good, but it is clear that even in such conditions Locke is uncomfortable with the notion of a natural right to unlimited acquisition.

Locke's proviso provides a clearer limit to private property when land becomes scarce in the state of Nature and it must be rationed for all men to survive. Natural law then presumably would dictate that the legislative body established by the social compact limit land ownership to a sufficiency for survival. But a complication arises, Locke says, when the community invents money as a means of exchange and a store of value, for then such production as cannot be consumed in the period of its production can be "stored" for future consumption in the form of deferred claims. In the state of Nature the limit to property possession was not defined by size but in the spoiling of produce; however, that limit can be avoided when money is adopted as an instrument of exchange.

What, then, in the money economy sets limits to the acquisition of private property? Locke becomes uncomfortable with the question and fails to answer it. Because money is useful only by the convention of its general acceptance and it does not exist in the state of Nature (although why it does not is unclear), its usage is not a provision of the social compact and hence does not have a clear foundation in natural law. Thus, the bounds to property ownership in this more advanced society are set by the legislative authority, which is bound by the laws of Nature, and this authority has accepted a "disproportionate and unequal possession of the earth."[27]

The fact that the ability to store value permits more land to be used for the production of more product to heighten the welfare of the society is

not considered by Locke in his concern for the equity of property ownership. He is uncomfortable with the notion of the unlimited acquisition of
property, primarily of land, but develops his ideas no further as they
concern the postcompact society. This fact, plus the limitation of his
analysis almost wholly to land and the products of land, means that he
left the natural law basis for the existence of private property in a modern society tenuous. To add to the confusion, Locke does establish the
right of inheritance as a natural right.[28]

Finally, in the First Treatise, which was probably written after the Second, Locke gives explicit support to the social compassionate facet of
economic equity as overriding egoistic rights in cases of distress. The
quotation is also interesting in asserting the justice of the product of
"honest industry" and of the legacies of "fair acquisitions" from forbears:

> But we know God hath not left one man so to the mercy of another that he
> may starve him if he please. God, the Lord and Father of all, has given no
> one of His children such a property in his peculiar portion of the things of
> this world but that he has given his needy brother a right in the surplusage
> of his goods, so that it cannot justly be denied him when his pressing wants
> call for it; and, therefore, no man could ever have a just power over the life
> of another by right of property in land or possessions, since it would always
> be a sin in any man of estate to let his brother perish for want of affording
> him relief out of his plenty; for as justice gives every man a title to the
> product of his honest industry and the fair acquisitions of his ancestors
> descended to him, so "charity" gives every man a title to so much out of
> another's plenty as will keep him from extreme want, where he has no
> means to subsist otherwise.[29]

Nozick's Entitlement Theory

Among the more strenuously egoistic theories of distributive equity is
that endorsed by the libertarians, which grounds the existence of the
state and its rightful powers in the natural right of the individual to organize for self-protection. The most recent influential theory of this type
is that of Robert Nozick,[30] which starts from the acceptance of Locke's
natural state and natural rights. The libertarian theory will be presented
within his framework.

Nozick's work is one in political philosophy, and in it he seeks to deduce three sets of theorems from the natural rights that exist in a Lockian natural state:

1. The state as an institution would arise in such a state of nature as the result
   of contractual relations among individuals entered into voluntarily to seek
   protection of their individual rights. The state therefore possesses legiti-

macy in that it violates no one's natural rights, but it possesses no independent power that is not granted voluntarily by the individuals who have formed it.

2. However, the only state that is consistent with the naturals rights of individuals is the *minimalist* state, which confines itself essentially to protecting those individuals from the attempts of their fellows to trespass on those rights without permission or compensation.

3. If one analyzes the goals of utopian theorists one discovers that the only framework that accomplishes their ends is also the minimalist state.

It is the first and second of these theorems that are relevant to the theory of economic equity. From them Nozick derives the three principles of economic justice:

1. The principle of *justice in acquisition*, which states that if the holdings (income-earning assets, wealth of a nonearning type, objects, etc.) of an individual have been acquired by means that are just, the holdings are justly his or hers.

2. The principle of *justice in transfer*, asserting that if one individual transfers holdings to another voluntarily, by way of payment for goods or services or through gift or legacy, those holdings are the just property of the recipient.

3. The principle of *rectification* of justice in holdings. If present holdings of an individual have been obtained by unjust methods—fraud, force, theft, or other violation of the voluntarism precept—then justice requires that the resulting holdings be returned to their just owners, or the heirs of such owners, or that compensation be paid.

A notable feature of Nozick's theory of justice in economic holdings is that it is a process theory rather than an end-state theory that holds up a structural template framing the desired distribution of holdings (either at a slice of time or intertemporally) to judge conformance of the actual distribution to the just. The principle of entitlements in holdings is therefore a historical principle of justice, depending wholly on the justice of the processes by which a structure of distribution has emerged rather than the shape of the emergent structure itself. Nozick also distinguishes his entitlements theory as an historical process from what he terms "pattern theories," which assert that a just distribution conforms to distribution that correlates with some variable or attribute—moral worth, contribution, intelligence, and so on—or some weighted sum of such qualities. Puzzlingly, he refers to such theories as a subset of historical theories, but they fit quite neatly into the end-state or template theories identified above.

Nozick's notion that economic justice must be defined and gauged wholly by process rather than by end result—making his theory a "non-

consequentialist" doctrine—is an important contribution and one that
must be confronted by anyone seriously interested in deriving an economic ethic for a liberal society. Through it, distribution of material
goods is wholly divorced from any concept of desert other than voluntarism. It is a logical correlate of his starting point in the Lockian state of
nature[31] and of his interpretation of natural rights as narrowly focused
on the individual's benefit (what is termed the egoistic strand of economic equity in this work). Those institutions that would arise through
the voluntary actions of individuals acting wholly out of self-interest and
constrained only by restraints designed to protect the same natural
rights of others are alone just. Explicitly, those side constraints upon the
individual's right to maximize self-interest in his or her actions do not
require sacrifices for the benefit of others:

> "Why not . . . hold that some persons have to bear some costs that benefit
> other persons more, for the sake of the overall social good? But there is no
> *social entity* with a good that undergoes some sacrifice for its own good.
> There are only individual people, different individual people, with their
> own individual lives. Using one of these people for the benefit of others,
> uses him and benefits the others. Nothing more. What happens is that
> something is done to him for the sake of others. Talk of an overall social
> good covers this up. (Intentionally?) To use a person in this way does not
> sufficiently respect and take account of the fact that he is a separate person,
> that his is the only life he has. *He* does not get some overbalancing good
> from his sacrifice, and no one is entitled to force this upon him—least of all
> a state or government that claims his allegiance (as other individuals do
> not) and that therefore must be *neutral* between its citizens.[32]

Thus, Nozick embraces the narrower version of individualism that treats
society passively, in the terminology of chapter 1, and is led to the conclusion that forcing upon the individual the acceptance of some degree
of responsibility for others' economic welfares, or the social compassionate aspect of economic equity, is an unjust exaction by a nonneutral state.

The rights to property possessed by the individual are constrained
only by the restraints appropriate to the minimal state. If an individual
has acquired holdings in conformance with the first, second, and third
principles, that property is justly his or hers. Since property rights are
ultimately rights to restrict usage, the individual's use of the property is
constrained only by restrictions on its imposition of negative externalities upon others. Such invasions of the boundaries of others' natural
rights must be forbidden or compensation must be paid, and the watch-
man state has the duty to enforce these restrictions. Hence, the equity of
state actions in enforcing the corrective strand of social equity is recognized, at least in minimal degree.

But Nozick in defining the limits of this corrective obligation must wrestle with the thorny social implications of private property ownership that bothered Locke as discussed above. The first of these concerned the origin of property ownership in the natural state. Nozick's first principle, which establishes the justice of the origin of holdings, does not confront in any great detail what determines the justice of original holdings. Locke asserted that an individual has a natural right to the result of mixing his or her labor with unowned resources. However, I have indicated that Locke conditioned this prerequisite with the stated proviso that "there be enough and as good left in common for others."

The Lockian basis for legitimizing private property is an outmoded explanation for modern economies. Nozick essentially grounds his legitimation in voluntaristic transfer processes and begs the question of original holdings by limiting his interest in application of the principle of rectification of justice in holdings to a small number of prior generations. But he devotes more time to interpreting the Lockian proviso within the confines of his entitlement theory of economic equity. In what sense is it incorporated into the constraints on individual pursuit of self-interest and thereby into the obligations of the minimal state to exercise its corrective functions?

Importantly, Nozick asserts that no "adequate" theory of justice in acquisition can exist without a weak version of the Lockian proviso. He interprets its function as insurance that others' situations are not worsened by the acquisition of property by an individual. This is an ambiguous proposition, and Nozick sharpens it in applying it to his theory of entitlements: "A process normally giving rise to a permanent bequeathable property right in a previously unowned thing will not do so if the position of others no longer at liberty to use the thing is thereby worsened."[33] Once its applicability has been determined, the individual must compensate those adversely affected or the acquisition must be forbidden. But when are others' positions worsened?

In advanced societies, Nozick believes the proviso is applicable most often to conditions under catastrophe, as when an individual monopolizes a vital life material. For example, if an individual discovers the sole source of a new material whose existence was previously unknown, others have not suffered because they did not use the material before its monopolization. Or if a medical researcher discovers a cure for a dread disease and refuses to use it to cure sufferers from that disease, the proviso is not violated, on the same grounds. However, in cases like the latter, some easing of the interpretation must be instituted, since when property rights are based on new discoveries, their acquisition limits the rights of future generations to make those same discoveries, which we may assume would occur. Therefore, it is acceptable to put a time restric-

tion on such rights, as is done in the case of patents, or to limit them to
the discoverer's lifetime by prohibiting their bequest.

However, in summary, Nozick expresses the belief that the conditions
under which the proviso will be appropriate in a market economy are
quite rare: "I believe that the free operation of a market system will not
actually run afoul of the Lockean proviso."[34]

The essential principles of Nozick's theory of entitlements therefore
are not altered by the proviso. If the individual's acquisitions are just in
the light of the three principles of acquisition, they are just in the context of a minimal-state society, and state interference with them for redistributive purposes is unjust. Pattern or end-state theories of social justice
assume that goods come into existence as manna falls from heaven, and
that redistributive actions can be justly applied. But in Nozick's theory
such goods arrive attached to individuals who are entitled to them, and
their redistribution is a violation of those natural rights based entitlements. To give others rights to such goods or services of admittedly great
importance to life as medical care or shelter or to attempt to equalize
opportunity for the disadvantaged by taxing the just entitlements of involuntary benefactors are unjust impositions of the state. In effect such
exactions give others property rights in the taxed individual, rendering
him or her effectively a slave. Such benefits must be granted voluntarily
or not at all if justice is to rule. In Nozick's summarization:

> From each according to what he chooses to do, to each according to what
> he makes for himself (perhaps with the contracted aid of others) and what
> others choose to do for him and choose to give him of what they've been
> given previously (under this maxim) and haven't yet expended or trans-
> ferred."

And even more succinctly: "From each as they choose, to each as they are
chosen."[35]

Nozick's strict application of his passive social interpretation of individualism results in a theory of property rights that Locke would not
accept. The latter, as we have seen, accepted the obligations of social
charity for those in dire need.

But are not certain acceptable actions of the minimal state redistributive? For example, the provision of fire protection or police protection to
those too poor to pay taxes has the effect of taxing some to provide
benefit to others. Nozick's reply is that the definition of "redistributive"
hinges upon the intent of the program, not its effects.[36] Since the intent
of providing such protective services to those too poor to pay for them is
not to redistribute goods but rather results from the nature of public
goods, these are acceptable state actions.

JUSTICE-AS-FREEDOM THEORIES

A group of theories of economic justice which are less ambitious in their architecture and consequently less rigorously constructed revolve about the notion of the economic mechanism of a society as an instrument whose major equity goal is the preservation or maximization of the individual's radius of egoistic free choice. Because such an objective tends to inhibit the social corrective and compassionate strands of economic equity, these theories tend toward the libertarian or constrained-libertarian positions in social theory.

Their supporters therefore are almost invariably supporters of free market capitalism and a circumscribed, if not minimalist, state. Freedom of choice for individuals in any aspect of behavior—social, political, religious, economic, and so forth—involves the resolution of conflicting convictions, preferences, and tastes. This school of thought favors social mechanisms that resolve such conflicts and encourage cooperation in manners that minimize coercion, most particularly the coercion of the state. Just treatment of the individual therefore implies a minimization of the roles of coercive institutions. Historically, such institutions have been religious, political, and economic in nature, and justice therefore requires that these potential tyrannies be blocked by institutional means. Because in the modern period the threat of religious abuses of individual freedom of choice has essentially vanished in western societies, the focus of these philosophies is upon the limitations of the political and economic power of the state.

A rather large number of thinkers—in largest part, economists—may be grouped in this rather broad category, although their emphases may differ within it. The so-called Austrian school, whose leaders are Ludwig von Mises and Friederich von Hayek, is prominent, and the Chicago school of economists featuring F. H. Knight, Henry C. Simon, Milton Friedman, and George Stigler among others, are members with prominent economic credentials. Because my concern is primarily with an economic ethic, the presentation of the analysis will be limited to these writers, with a heavy emphasis on the writings of Milton Friedman, who has been most influential in the American intellectual milieu and has developed the notions of economic equity most explicitly.

Friedman's Economic Ethic

Friedman is explicit in defining his assumption of the *summum bonum* of human life: it is the provision of the individual with the opportunity to live his or her life with the maximum radius of freedom of action that is

consistent with the similar rights of others.[37] Therefore, society must be
structured in such manner as to permit the individual's preferences to
be satisfied with as little interference as is necessary to enforce peaceful
coexistence; correct, where appropriate, negative externalities; provide
public goods when it is not feasible for individuals to do so; and, to some
extent, enforce the compassionate strand of equity.[38]

To Friedman, the power of government to limit the choice field of the
individual and potentially to threaten basic liberties is the single power
source in society to be feared, as long as the free market economy is in
place to decentralize economic power. Friedman asserts, on the basis of
his experience, that the American economy functions effectively as a
perfectly competitive economy, with such monopoly power as exists either created by government preferential treatment of vested interests or
effectively subdued by active rivals.[39] Such decentralization, while not a
sufficient condition for political liberty, is a necessary condition, he believes, because it assures that the political rebel or dissident cannot be
deprived of a livelihood by a political power which also has centralized
control over the economy. One of the fundamental attractions of a market economy to a liberal of this persuasion is that it is the only effective
manner of splitting off political power from economic power, thereby
aborting *the major potential source of social injustice.*

The anonymity of the market—the impersonal individualism of the
institution, as described in chapter 1—permits the political or social
nonconformist to obtain employment. It protects the worker, Friedman
says, against an unfair employer by permitting the employee to find a job
elsewhere. It permits the individual consumer to obtain goods that are
close to his or her ideal configurations because the market can cope with
conflicting tastes by differentiating products, once again, therefore permitting maximum individual choice. And, most important, the profit
motive that energizes the market economy protects civil liberties, in the
sense that it strives to effect what was termed *equality of competition for
reward* in chapter 1. Irrelevant personal characteristics are disregarded
in the search for the most efficient factor mix, or cheapest price, or
highest bid in exchange situations. Friedman also views the market economy as the only means to attain efficient resource allocation and management, of course, but this part of his argument is disregarded in order
to focus on the social equity content. It should be said, however, that
because any adequate theory of economic justice must be conformant
with other social goals, and because one of those goals must be efficiency, this assertion concerning the functioning of capitalism cannot be
dismissed out of hand. *However, because of the emphasis that Friedman places
on the capitalistic system as the maximizer of individual freedom, one must as-*

sume that even were it shown to be importantly inefficient the case for its institution in society would still be quite strong.

On the other hand, government almost invariably restricts the freedom of the individual. When decisions are made by it the outcomes are frequently binary: either an action is to be taken or it is not to be taken. No spectrum of alternatives is possible as is true in the market's decision making. Under majority rule, therefore, 49.9 percent of a citizenry may have to accept what only 50.1 percent decide to effect. Hence, not only to improve efficiency, but to meet the overriding need for maximizing individual choice, as many functions as possible must be ruled over by the market. In the United States, for example, the postal service and national parks should be turned over to free enterprise and run for profit, permitting efficient service to be performed and costs apportioned proportionately to those electing the benefits of such services. Nor need universal education be public education. It was Friedman who devised the notion of education vouchers being issued to parents by the state in lieu of providing the education by entrenched educational bureaucracies, so that students could attend private educational institutions that were forced to compete in quality and price of services provided.

Even worse, when government decides to intrude on the individual's rightful exercise of job choice by imposing licensing restrictions or zoning regulations, it deprives the individual of liberties and restricts consumers' right to choose. Hence, the state's licensing of plumbers or physicians, or its institution of building codes, are usually instituted at the behest of the vested interests of incumbents in those callings who wish to restrict supply.[40] Corrective actions such as antitrust prosecutions or price supports or the vetting of medicines ignore the more efficient operation of competition, create more costs than benefits, are designed to protect vested interests, and limit individual choice.

So dreaded is government intervention in restriction of individual preferences that Friedman hesitates to give the state the power to enforce nondiscrimination statutes or even to control such natural monopolies as public utilities. In the former case he believes that the state has no just right to enforce upon the discriminating individual its preferences, no matter how morally despicable the prejudices of that individual. It is morally preferred to permit sex, religious, or racial prejudice to exist than to use the state's power to prevent it.[41] As far as public regulation of monopolies is concerned, Friedman believes that government interference with their functioning or setting of the rate structure results in greater inefficiency than permitting them to function in unregulated fashion.

In that restricted field of government regulation that is necessary, bureaucratic discretion must be minimized. A rule of law, not of men, is required in the name of justice. Regulations must be spelled out in detail so that no government functionary can effect personal interpretations of statutes.[42] Individuals functioning under the mantle of government power are dangerous threats to individual liberty when that power is not reined in by strict limitations.

What role remains for government in economic justice, then, beyond its minimalist corrective functions? Does it extend into the social compassionate protection of the individual's self-respect? Friedman's inclinations are rather more liberal in this regard than Nozick's. He believes, for example, that the early New Deal relief measures were necessary.[43] It was Friedman who suggested that welfare support be in the form of a negative income tax, in order to maximize consumer choice and increase efficiency in rendering support to those deserving such aid. Its attraction is that it assures minimum necessary subsistence without harming the character or independence of the individual and retaining personal incentives. With its introduction and the gradual conversion of the Social Security program to a voluntary plan, he believes that remaining social services can be provided by private charity.[44]

Equality of opportunity in the usual sense of the phrase—active social programs to correct or ameliorate disadvantages that are capable of such treatment—is not an obligation of society, in Friedman's view. Individuals must benefit from a market economy within the constraints of their natural abilities and differentially advantaged opportunities to develop them. In later work Friedman defines away the problem by identifying equality of opportunity with what was called *equality of competition for reward* in chapter 1:

> No arbitrary obstacles should prevent people from achieving those positions for which their talents fit them and which their values lead them to seek. Not birth, nationality, color, religion, sex, nor any other irrelevant characteristic should determine the opportunities that are open to a person—only his abilities.[45]

Finally, Friedman's attitude toward the distributive equity implied by capitalistic income distribution—rather surprisingly—is qualified and guarded. The ethical principle implicit is the marginal productivity contributory principle:

> The ethical principle that would directly justify the distribution of income in a free market society is "to each according to what he and the instruments he owns produces." The operation of even this principle implicitly depends on state action. Property rights are matters of law and social con-

vention. . . . their definition and enforcement is (*sic*) one of the primary functions of the state. The final distribution of income and wealth under the full operation of this principle may well depend markedly on the rules of property adopted.[46]

There is no appeal to natural law principles as one might expect from a liberal, but a seeming Hobbesian recognition of the right of the state to adopt property institutions that deny entitlements to the market receipts from owned resources. This is a marked departure from Nozick's libertarianism, even taking into account his updated Lockean proviso.

After discussing some of the expressed objections of others to capitalistic distribution principles, such as the right of inheritance, Friedman continues:

> The fact that these arguments against the so-called capitalist ethic are invalid does not of course demonstrate that the capitalist ethic is an acceptable one. I find it difficult to justify either accepting or rejecting it, or to justify any alternative principles. I am led to the view that it cannot in and of itself be regarded as an ethical principle, that it must be regarded as instrumental or a corollary of some other principle such as freedom.[47]

He then goes on to assert that the implied contributory basis for distribution is a feature of the basic core of values in society and is accepted as an "absolute" principle, not simply as an instrumental institution (presumably necessary for efficient allocation).[48]

This statement is a reaffirmation of the preeminent position Friedman gives individual freedom in judging social institutions. But it is also an uncharacteristically nebulous ethical nondefense of the distributive patterns that are so vigorously supported on grounds of maximizing freedom and efficiency in Friedman's writings. Abstracting from these desiderata, he finds no basis in natural rights or individualism or entitlements that would justify such patterns. His realization that their defense as simply instrumental in achieving other social goals severely weakens their ethical basis finally leads him to assert that the marginal productivity contributory basis for distribution is accepted by the American society as a kind of intuitionist principle with no other philosophical buttressing. The argument seems a bit confused:

1. A capitalistic market economy must be accepted as a necessary condition for the attainment of the ultimate good which is the maximum of freedom for the individual (or family);
2. The distribution of income in such an economy—surely one of its most socially important dictates—cannot be defended independently in terms of equity but must be justified by its instrumental contributions to achieving the ultimate good;

3. But the social acceptance of the income distribution goes beyond its instrumentality to be "explained" by its presence in a core of values whose origin is obscure.

Justice has not been done to the other writers mentioned in this category of thinkers, whose theories of economic equity parallel in large measure Friedman's ethic but do reveal important variations. Hayek, for example, in his *Road to Serfdom*, which appeared at the end of World War II, anticipated some of Friedman's argument in urging that any movement toward the welfare state was a start down the road to the loss of individual freedom. In later work, Hayek argued against all attempts to alter the market's distribution pattern on the basis that the market gives to each person the value of the benefits he or she confers upon others.[49] He does not assert a strict contributory theory, in that he does not argue that this is in some teleological sense the actual contribution of the individual to the social product, nor does he assert a Nozickian entitlement theory in that he does not explicitly discuss such receipts as gifts or legacies. Nonetheless, his argument is in the spirit of both Nozick and Friedman.

BARGAINING THEORIES OF ECONOMIC EQUITY

A last category of egoistically oriented theories of economic equity has a somewhat schizoid orientation and has only a doubtful claim to inclusion in considerations of justice-directed frameworks. It is the rather large set of bargaining theories concerning the attainment of a distributive solution when all persons with a stake in the outcome must consent to that outcome, and where the distributive portions received by one or more of the participants directly affect those obtained by others.

Bargaining theories are driven by egoistic self-seeking that is made effective by the power of participants to impose solutions on other participants—hardly the environment from which one expects a theory of economic equity to emerge. Moreover, such situations arise primarily in micro-analyses, with significance for a relatively small number of individuals, whereas I am primarily interested in the derivation of equity frameworks for society as a whole.

Nonetheless, in order for determinate solutions to such bargaining problems to emerge it is necessary to impose certain patterns of behavior or expectations on participants that can be viewed as concerns for others' welfares, albeit a concern that is shaped by rational self-interest in the light of knowledge concerning others' self-interest. These patterns therefore have some claim to being axioms in frameworks involving definitions of economic equity, and some space will be devoted to considerations of their relevance to the search for an adequate theory for American capitalism.

One of the best-known of such theories is Nash's cooperative solution to an *n*-person non-zero-sum game.[50] Suppose there exists a compact and convex set of outcomes, Ω ,which consist of potential distributions of income among *n* individuals. Each individual has a von Neumann-Morgenstern utility index over incomes, so that for every potential outcome in Ω there exists a vector, $X = [x_1, x_2, \ldots, x_n]$, of utility payoffs over the affected individuals. The whole set of *X* defined over Ω defines the bargaining region, *S*, within which a solution vector X^* must be determined.

Assume further that in the absence of the participants selecting some X^* by bargaining among themselves there is some *default solution* in *S*, $D = [d_1, d_2, \ldots, d_n]$, that is imposed on all parties. Finally, define the subset S^+ of *S* which consists of all *X* such that $X > D$, that is, all utility distributions which yield every participant more utility than the default solution does. How, then, might the participants proceed to select a solution $X^* \in S^+$ that would avoid *D* and make each better off?

If four axioms shape the behavior and expectations of all participants, Nash shows that a unique X^* will be determined:

1. *Pareto optimality.* Every person will be willing to permit others to receive as much utility as possible as long as it costs him or her nothing in utility. That is, X^* must yield every person at least as much utility as any other *X* in S^+ and at least one person more than he or she receives in *X*.

2. *Symmetry.* If all individuals derive the same utility from income (that is, if all consumers have the same von Neumann-Morgenstern utility index except for the definition of an arbitrary origin and size of calibration unit) they should receive the same income in the solution. No individual should receive special consideration other than what is reflected in his or her ability to enjoy income and the power reflected in the default level of utility.

3. *Independence of Equivalent Utility Representations.* It is well known that the von Neumann-Morgenstern utility index is unique up to a positive linear transformation. If every participant's initial utility index is transformed by a change of origin and/or unit of measurement, then X^* must be transformed into $X^{*\prime}$ by the same set of transformations. Hence, no real changes in utility must occur.

4. *Sen's Rationality Property* α. Suppose a solution $X^* \in S$ is determined but that a subset of *S* (which contains *D*), *T*, is obtained by reducing the choice field. Suppose also that $X^* \in T$. Then the new solution must be X^*. The best item in any set must be the best item in any subset of which it is a member.[51] This implies that X^* is a true maximum, and behaviorally this implies that the participants are shaping their actions to achieve such a maximum.

If all participants' behavior conforms to these four axioms, Nash has shown that a unique solution X^* is obtained that is equivalent to maxi-

mizing the geometric means of the differences between individuals' actual utilities, x_j, and their default utilities, d_j. Let Y be any distribution-
of-utility vector in S^+ other than S^*. Then S^* is such that

(1) $$\pi_j(S^*_j - d_j) > \pi_j(Y_j - d_j)$$

The operational problem is that participants are following their own
egoistic self-interest and certainly would not act consciously to maximize
the geometric mean of their joint incremental gains from negotiation.
Such behavior would have to be imposed on them by a governmental
authority that accepted the four axioms as rational criteria for a solution,
that is, criteria that, when explained to all participants, would be accepted by them as equitable. The first three axioms do have an appeal to
intuitive reasonableness, but does the last? Would individuals agree that
a solution S^* accepted in a larger field of choice would, when available
as a solution in a smaller field of choice, still be preferred over all others?

Consider this more realistic scenario. Let X^o be the vector of *ideal* utility outcomes, defined as follows. For participant i, let x^o_i be the highest
utility outcome he could obtain in S^+ when all other participants j are
receiving at least their default payoffs d_j. This is participant i's ideal outcome, and the vector X^o contains all such payoffs as elements. Normally,
it is not in S and hence is unobtainable; of course, if $X^o \in S$, then $X^* = X^o$
trivially. Egoistic behavior would lead the individual to seek to get as
close to his or her ideal payoff as possible. Suppose, now, that a Nash
solution X^* is obtained from set S. Suppose further that S shrinks to T,
where T is contained in S. Assume further that S^* remains a potential
solution in the new situation, but that in the shrinkage X^o has changed,
so that some participants' ideal payoffs have changed. Is it rational that
all parties would still accept X^* as the fair or just solution, as Nash's
Axiom 4 requires? Two hypotheses can be asserted with some justification:

1. Egoistic desires to do as well as possible will change the behaviors of those
   persons whose ideal payoffs have changed; and
2. Those participants whose ideal points have not been affected would not
   believe it was fair that the payoffs to those whose highest potential payoffs
   have been reduced should receive their earlier imputations.

Gauthier proposes as an alternative to Nash's solution in (1) above the
following. Let X^g be the Gauthier solution and $Y \neq X^g$ be any other utility
payoff vector in S^+. Then X^g is determined such that

(2) $$\min_j\{(x^g_j - d_j) / (x^o_j - d_j)\} > \min_j\{(y_j - d_j) / (y^o_j - d_j)\}$$

for all y in S^+. That is, in the Gauthier solution, the participant whose
incremental gain from negotiation is the smallest proportion of the ideal

incremental gain (the least advantaged participant) obtains a larger proportion than the least advantaged participant in any other solution Y.[52] More succinctly, the least advantaged person in terms of this proportion must be as well off as possible. A *maximin* solution is achieved.

This solution is consistent with the first three of Nash's axioms but violates the fourth (Sen's α property). It is not therefore a social maximum position in the usual sense. In lieu of that postulate, the following procedural axioms must be accepted:

1. Each participant proposes his or her ideal payoff solution.
2. In the face of the infeasible X^0 proposed in 1, each person expects that there is a set of concessions that will lead to an outcome in S such that every rational person is willing to make the required concession if every other person is.
3. Suppose participant i considers all other participants' proposals, and computes $(x_i - x_j)/(x_i - d_j)$ for each other participant j. When the minimum of these ratios is less than the minimum he expects some other rational participant has calculated he reduces his proposed reward if he is assured all others are willing to follow the same route.
4. No participant will make a concession unless 2 and 3 are met.

But it is not clear that these rules of procedure are indeed those that would be followed by a rational self-seeking decision maker, nor is it clear on what grounds the outcome X^g can be described as equitable. The participants' concessions are not guided by wholly voluntaristic motives if such rigid rules are followed, and if society forces their use the theory of economic equity is a procedural one in the sense of Nozick, and the basis of its claim to equity is not clear.

Enough has been said to indicate that bargaining theories of social equity have an aura of ambiguity about them. If they are theories about how rational self-seeking individuals *would* behave in the bargaining process, it is not self-evident that the results have a prima facie claim to being economically equitable. If they are frameworks prescribing individual behavior in order to achieve a certain outcome considered equitable by society, so that they become mechanisms for achieving pattern distributions, they are essentially uninteresting in themselves and rely for their plausibility on a rationale for the desired pattern.

A SUMMARY

At the core of Western liberal social thought concerning the principles on which society is justly organized and functions are the concepts of *individualism* and *voluntarism*. Two dual aspects of individualism which are often at odds in shaping social philosophy and policy have been identified. Both strands of interpretation rest upon the inviolable nature of the human personality, the respect due its uniqueness of characteristics, the vulnerability to hurt that springs from its self-consciousness, and the essential correctness of its search to fulfill its desires in accordance with its own preferences. Social institutions, therefore, and the principles that define their structure and functioning, must be shaped in such manner as to conform to the individual's pivotal importance in society's moral priorities. Of course, it is recognized that rights that spring from these axioms are conditioned by the obligations of each individual to honor those rights for others.

The first strand of interpretation, and the dominant one in American culture, emphasizes the rightness of individual self-seeking, the individual's voluntary selection of goals and objects, and the ownership and transfer of property. At the same time, and on the same philosophical basis, it imposes the obligation that individuals provide for the material welfare of themselves and their dependents and abide by freely undertaken contractual obligations.

The second strand of individualism, and one which also springs from the sanctity of the individual personality, implies the obligation to preserve the life and self-respect of those individuals who are incapable of providing for the material welfare of themselves and their dependents for reasons beyond their control. Compassion at the expense of the more narrowly egoistic urgings of the first interpretation is a correlate of this second strand.

Effectively, theories of economic equity search for the axiomatic means to determine the emphases to be given the rights and obligations that are implied by these two facets of individualism, as well as that to be placed on the corrective role of government in monitoring the establishment and functioning of the institutional mechanisms that effectuate those emphases. In other terms, the basic principles of economic equity determine (1) the manners in which the individual is to benefit from the resources he or she applies to his or her self-advantage, (2) the sacrifices in those individual benefits that are justly due the disadvantaged, and (3) the governmentally administered sanctions necessary to prevent practices that subvert the principles. These principles have been termed the (1) egoistic, (2) social compassion, and (3) social corrective principles of economic equity in chapter 1.

In this chapter I have reviewed the prominent theories of economic equity whose derivative principles give dominant protection to the egoistic strand and subordinate the two social strands. Four major approaches to the derivation of such principles have been identified and discussed: (1) contributory theories, (2) natural rights or entitlement theories, (3) maximization-of-freedom theories, and (4) bargaining theories.

The common axiomatic basis of the contributory theories is the intuitive notion that every individual is rightfully entitled to that which can be shown to be his or her contribution to the social product, and that it is unjust to give the individual less than this contribution. Paradoxically, many justifications of both the free market economy and Karl Marx's alternative to it are based on this unstated axiom.

The natural rights theories are grounded in the axiomatic base laid in the seventeenth and eighteenth centuries which emerged from the inquiry into the nature of the state and the locus of its legitimate sovereignty. These debates centered about the nature of man in a world without institutions and the types of such artifacts that would emerge through the voluntary cooperation and contractual agreements among individuals. It was deduced that governments of one kind or another would be established primarily for the purpose of protecting the life and property of the individual, and the duties and limitations enacted with respect to such governments defined, among other systems, the principles of economic equity.

The most recent and ambitious theory of this type is Nozick's entitlements theory, and its principles have been developed in some detail. It asserts that economic justice should be judged by the nature of the processes by which individuals acquired holdings of material possessions rather than by the pattern of such holdings established at any particular time. The touchstone that determines the legitimacy of those processes is the voluntarism of the actions that define those processes, interpreting that term to imply the lack of fraud, force, or incompetence. The corrective functions of government must be minimal, and the charity claims of individuals exercised through governmental exactions on other individuals are unjust. Nozick's principles of economic justice are explicitly the most oriented toward the egoistic strand of any investigated in this chapter.

The maximization-of-freedom theories interpret the implication of individualism as the need to maximize the radius of free will of the individual agent, acting within its natural limitations and the constraints imposed by other agents so acting. Such constrained maximization must be protected by decentralizing power in the society that might seek to interfere with the individual in arbitrary manners. Each agent must be protected in seeking to benefit from the voluntary actions of others in their behalf, primarily from the purchase of the factor services it controls. Government, as the greatest threat of instituting such unjust interferences with the individual's freedom, must be severely restrained in its functions. And the capitalistic market economy, which at once splits the economic power in the society from the political power and decentralizes that economic power, affords the individual the greatest protection of the right to choose freely.

In terms of the principles of distributive equity, contributory theories differ from entitlement theories in confining their notions of entitlement to provable claims of product or value creation and excluding the voluntary gifts or legacies accruing to individuals. Maximization-of-freedom theories place the emphasis in their distributive principles on the voluntarism of individual actions that effect the distribution, as do the entitlement theories, but accept such distributions as ancillary to the primary goal of maximizing freedom of will. But both theories differ only in their placement of emphasis—the one on the process through which voluntarism is effected, the other on the degree to which voluntarism is achieved.

Bargaining theories are of a different breed from those discussed above and somewhat unclear as to positive versus normative content, and therefore as to equity import. If they are intended to define rational self-seeking behavior for a set of participants, they may yield an indeterminate solution. If maximization principles are used to permit a solution to be obtained, it may be questionable as to what equity base the instrumental maximization possesses. If rules of procedure are imposed on the individual by society in order to achieve a desired distribution, the procedure has no independent interest and interest focuses rather on the rationale for the desired pattern.

An adequate theory of economic equity that is conformant with the American ethos must contain some balance between the egoistic and the social strands implied by individualism and voluntarism; some balance must be sought between such strands that is not captured by the theories just reviewed. It is necessary, therefore, to study important systems of distributive equity that emphasize the social strands, and this will be done in chapter 3.

Chapter 3

THEORIES OF SOCIAL EQUITY:
SOCIALLY ORIENTED THEORIES

THE SOCIAL CONTENT OF ECONOMIC EQUITY

In chapter 1 the general model presented for the analysis of a theory of economic equity highlights two antagonistic strands of concern that are sourced in the multifaceted implications of individualism. Prominent theories that feature the first of those themes—the egoistic—were presented in chapter 2. This chapter continues the exposition with the focus on theories with the other orientation—that of the social. Of course, the emphases in both cases are less than total in either direction, but they are sufficiently in evidence to make the distinction meaningful.

The social content of the concept of equity recognizes the obligations individuals assume toward one another by virtue of their very social existence. Those duties are in part the obverse of the rights we exercise in furtherance of our selfish interests, such rights being of necessity constrained by the like rights of others. When individuals act in manners that trespass on others' liberties or property—through fraud, force, imposition of externalities, or exercise of an undue amount of market power—the first type of social equity is violated. Society, acting through its governmental agent, is obligated to exercise its corrective function to prevent, punish, or ensure that compensation is paid for such infractions.

This function is an important one in the economic area, and I do not mean to demean that importance by failing to discuss it in great depth in this work. However, the litigious nature of the function has assured that a great deal of legal and legislative attention has been paid to it, a large body of theoretical and applied work exists dedicated to defining its proper scope and content, and although debate is active and some extreme dissents exist (Friedman's strictures on government action are an example) a rather stable consensus on that scope and content has congealed in American society. I shall therefore expend most analytical effort on the second facet of social equity, for it is not characterized by any of these attainments.

The *compassion* obligation in economic equity is based on the positive or active interpretation of social living discussed in chapter 1. At the least, it registers the obligation of a society to provide the *opportunity* to all citizens, within constraints on individual self-denial, to achieve the preparatory basis for at least a minimum acceptable standard of life. And it accepts the right of all persons who are incapable for reasons outside of their control of attaining the minimum standard that maintains health and self-respect to be provided with the necessary wherewithal for it. At the other extreme, some proponents urge an "equal" distribution of income and/or wealth with or without ownership by the society of nonhuman resources as an instrumentality for such a distribution. Obviously, the perceived role of egoistic motivation correlates negatively in the theories with the position on the compassion spectrum adopted by their authors.

This chapter presents summaries of the major arguments of three theories that are interpreted as located at the right, middle, and left positions of that spectrum. At the minimum position I place what I interpret to be the economic equity implications of Kant's moral theory. The placement of Kant among these theorists is admittedly subject to argument, as many of those implications are fully acceptable to such egoistic strand theorists as Friedman. However, the strong emphasis in Kant on the positive role of social duty in defining moral action warrants his inclusion in this chapter.

At the middle position one finds the act-utilitarianism of Bentham and John Stuart Mill. Narrowly read, each could be interpreted as advocating an extreme egalitarian position, but neither could escape the persistent appeal of the egoistic rights of expression of the individual and the attractions of institutions that permitted the exercise of those rights. Also, Mill in particular found it difficult to accept the assumptions necessary for the theory to advocate income or "utility" equality.

Finally, and unambiguously at the left extreme, John Rawls's recent and influential theory of justice is presented. He is clearly egalitarian in doctrine and intent although grudgingly permissive of some departure from equality if it achieves other goals and is bounded.

As in chapter 2, the purpose of this chapter is to present the economic equity implications of the three theories accurately but uncritically where it is possible to exposit clearly without critical comment. Appraisals of the usefulness of the doctrines in the attainment of an operational economic equity framework for the United States will be presented in chapters 4, 5, and 6.

The Kantian Rational Imperatives

Immanuel Kant's profound and difficult probing into the essence of morality is an attempt to isolate its most fundamental principle.[1] What are the pure forms of morals, or the a priori principles that are derivable by logic alone, independent of the particulars of the real world or of human

nature other than the fact that man is a rational being? Ethical philosophers who sought these principles in perfecting humanity, the search for
pleasure, the intuition of moral senses, or the fear of God delved in the
realm of human motivation or aspects of human nature. The principles
they derived, therefore, were conditioned by the experience of the natural world, since man was an object in it.

But nature is nonmoral, and the fundamental essence of morality—
those principles that must hold independent of the state of the world—
cannot be sought within its confines. The laws that govern understanding and reason—the forms of such faculties—have no empirical content,
and these are the laws that must govern the search for basic moral principles as well. Those principles to be fundamental must establish obligations of unconditional necessity; that is, their acceptance must not be
contingent on any particular state of the world or facet of human nature.
Only logic—the method of reason—applicable because man is rational,
can isolate this moral law, and the possibility of doing so is self-evident
from the ideas of duty and morality revealed in the common man's
moral consciousness.

Kant argues that reason asserts that *the only absolute good—good that is
unconditional—is a good will.* The will is a product of reason which permits
the individual to deduce a set of maxims or self-imposed rules of action
from principles. With it the individual determines ends. A good will is
one that chooses as the supreme end the performance of duty for its own
sake, contrary to the natural inclinations or self-interest of the individual, and regardless of the consequences of the action. Such action is the
basis of all morality. Morality therefore is concerned wholly with the motivation underlying actions, not with their consequences.

How then does the will discern moral duty and the path of the supreme good? It must perceive an objective principle of action that it
recognizes as obligatory, a principle in the nature of a command with the
form of an *imperative.* That imperative must command that a certain action be taken immediately and unconditionally, that is, it must be a categorical imperative. It specifies an action that the individual perceives as
a universal law binding on all rational beings, and duty is the absolute
necessity of conforming to it. Indeed, the First Formulation of the categorical imperative is so defined: "Act only on that maxim whereby thou
canst at the same time will that it should become a universal law." As
noted, a maxim is a self-imposed rule for voluntary action in the real
world. Hence, one should act in that manner that is consistent with reason and, therefore, which one can will that all individuals follow under
the same circumstances.

For example, it is unreasonable to assert the proposition that "all persons should observe their contractual obligations unless it violates their
self-interest" as a universal law. For obviously were all individuals to act in

this manner the concept of "contract" would lose meaning—the maxim is inconsistent with reason. To the extent a functioning society requires a means of binding obligations in order to permit secure expectations, all rational beings will perceive the maxim as nonsupportable. Therefore, if an individual violates a contract, society can force him or her to honor it on the basis that the inconsistency of the action with reason would force that person to admit the culpability of the action—would lead the individual to convict him- or herself of unacceptable behavior. Interestingly, this was the manner in which Kant interpreted the concept of the social contract: it was a hypothetical instrument that existed only in the sense that if the individual were confronted with its body of principles, his or her reason would force that individual to subscribe to it.

By what logical route does Kant arrive at his proposition that the only absolute good is a good will? If Nature's purpose for man was the attainment of happiness, she would have endowed him only with instincts or natural inclinations. This would have been a better mental structure for that purpose, for clearly men with some degree of culture and sensitivity use their reason to devise a life plan that frequently interferes with happiness. Man is a compound of the world of the senses (which endow him with the natural inclinations) and the world of reason (which permits him to choose his actions autonomously). Hence, man's life has a nobler purpose than simply the attainment of happiness—although that is a good in life—and the definition of that nobler end is what reason is intended to give man. Its purpose is to produce as *summum bonum* the will as an end in itself. Hence, a good will is the supreme good among all goods, and there is nothing inconsistent with Nature's wisdom in using reason to attain it even though it interferes with the attainment of the lesser good—happiness.

In possessing will and the ability to perceive categorical imperatives, man understands that he has freedom to choose his ends. Freedom is the property of being independent of foreign causes and is embodied in his being subject to the moral law. He is not driven like nonrational beings to react to external causes, nor is he limited to a mechanical, unthinking search for happiness. He exists as an end in himself, therefore, not simply as a means to be manipulated by other wills. This leads Kant to a Second Formulation of the categorical imperative: "So act as to treat humanity, whether in thine own person or in that of any other, in every case as an end withal, never as means only."

In contrast to the categorical imperative, a hypothetical imperative is conditional upon an individual's desire to produce the result of an action or to achieve happiness. For happiness is a good, and the desire to achieve it springs from man's natural inclinations. Therefore, it may be assumed to be an end for all men, although they realize it to have lesser value than the search for moral ends. Ends either have value or dignity: attainment of skills has market value; developing one's wit or imagination has fancy value; but only morality has dignity.

What is the reward of achieving dignity through good will? After all, one frequently must sacrifice happiness to act on the categorical imperative. Kant answers a bit vaguely: The return is a deeper satisfaction of realizing oneself as an end and of participating in the "legislation" of universal laws. To what extent these compensate for sacrificed pleasure is unclear: certainly the Kantian road to morality can be one of extreme self-denial if the categorical imperative makes demands too frequently or with great abnegation.

But at least reason does not dictate that others should seek to force one into the path of morality. The moral nature of the individual is personal and individual, and the only authority for its dictates is internal to the individual. The search for moral perfection therefore is a product of the individual's will, and reason dictates that one not try to shape his or her neighbor's moral consciousness. For the individual is an end in himself or herself, and one's moral desire to treat him or her as an end implies one's acceptance of his or her own ends. Since one of the universal ends of mankind is happiness, and every person desires the aid of others to attain it, the happiness of others must become one's ethical end in defining actions toward them.

Kant's fundamental principles of morality accommodate a number of operational theories of economic equity. One that recommends itself is a constrained egoistic interpretation. Individuals should be allowed to seek maximum satisfaction subject to their conformance to the categorical imperative in treatment of others. That is, that search for happiness should be limited by the need to treat other human beings to a meaningful degree as ends, not means. That implies an active social concern for the economic welfare of others and the obligation to promote their well-being. This application of Kantian principles to the derivation of an operational ethic lifts the search for "happiness" to an accepted realistic role in the economic affairs of daily life and introduces the more elevated moral precepts as means of bounding selfish motivation. It grounds the economic ethic solidly in an individualistic context, yet without merging the individual's goals into a social goal it intrudes the claims of other individuals on the basis of their just claims to dignity as rational beings.

As noted earlier, it is this insistence by Kant that the fundamental principle of morality inheres in the imperative of each to treat all others as ends with the explicit obligation to aid them in their search for fulfillment that leads to the inclusion of his theory in the category of compassion-oriented. All moral action involves an active consideration of its impacts on others and the desirability of such action as a general mode of behavior. This coexists, therefore, with a recognition of the just self-seeking of the individual as a sustained search for a higher end out of a sense of duty to community.

Utilitarianism

Among the most ancient and influential schools of ethics are doctrines that define the ultimate good of the individual's life experience as that which Kant subordinated: the enjoyment of pleasure and freedom from pain. The definition of the moral for the individual is the selection of actions that maximize these states of sensation. In some theories the extension to social ethics was straightforward: the social good was the sum of pleasure (considering pain as negative pleasure) in the society and the morally right was the maximization of this body of social good.

The roots of such theories can be traced as far back as ancient Greek philosophy. The Cyrenaics—a post-Socratic sect that was active in the third and fourth centuries B.C.—were inspired by the Socratic insistence on the desirability of rationalizing life with an organizing principle. They identified that principle as acting to seek the good, which end they found in the search to attain pleasure and avoid pain.[2] Epicureanism as a post-Aristotelian sect, which was influential between the third century B.C. and the fourth century A.D., argued that happiness in the sense of gratifying the senses and the appetites was the supreme individual good and pain the supreme evil and that only those activities (tempered by consideration of their externalities on others) that contributed to happiness were virtuous.

Modern utilitarian doctrines emerged in the seventeenth and eighteenth centuries' search for the harmonizing principles of social organization and their implications for a just balance between the individual's egoistic urgings and his or her social obligations to others. Cumberland (1632–1718) asserted that the preeminent law of nature was the obligation to establish the "common good," that state including the happiness of individuals and the perfection of human nature. Hutcheson (1694–1747) was the first to state the principle of greatest happiness: "That action is best which procures the greatest happiness for the greatest numbers, and the worst which in like manner occasions misery."[3]

In the *Essay Concerning Human Understanding*, Locke identifies good and evil for the individual in terms of pain and pleasure:

> Things then are good or evil, only in reference to pleasure or pain. That which we call *good*, which is apt to cause or increase pleasure, or diminish pain in us; or else to procure or preserve us the possession of any other good

or absence of any evil. . . . By pleasure and pain, I must be understood to mean of body or mind, as they are commonly distinguished.[4]

Moral good and evil entail pains and pleasures in the form of punishments and rewards at the hands of the lawmaker:

> Moral good and evil, then, is only *the conformity or disagreement of our voluntary actions to some law, whereby good or evil is drawn on us, from the will and power of the law-maker*, which good or evil, pleasure or pain, attending our observance or breach of the law by the decree of the law-maker, is that we call *reward* and *punishment*.[5]

Such pronouncements do not make Locke a utilitarian by any stretch of the imagination: they were more in the nature of precepts in the analysis of human nature and the functioning of the mind and human institutions.

Similarly, Hume (1711–1776) was more interested in discerning the motives for human actions and acceptance of institutions than in designing theories of individual or social ethics. Two fundamental qualities of the human psyche were an ability to empathize with the happiness or pain of others and the strength of expected feelings of pleasure and pain in the determination of human actions. As an antirationalist in the theory of morals, Hume argues that feelings of morality are grounded in the emotional nature of man, not the reason, for the latter was the servant of the former, not vice versa. It was not contrary to reason, Hume argued, to prefer the destruction of other human beings to the scratching of one's own finger, but the moral opposition rather springs from man's sympathy for others' suffering. "Reason is, and ought only to be, the slave of the passions, and can never pretend to any other office than to serve and obey them."[6] "Morality, therefore, is more properly felt than judged of."[7]

Morality, as a theory of the motivation of human actions, therefore is grounded in man's emotions, not his reason, since the reason does not lead to action. Utility and sympathy form our moral judgments. But Hume's view of the role of reason is somewhat cloudy when it comes to the motivation to obey moral rules when they counter self-interest: "In general, it may be affirmed that there is no such passion in human minds as the love of mankind, merely as such, independent of personal qualities, of services, or of relation to oneself."[8] Empathy therefore does not extend to the moral duty to conform to rules that contravene our egoistic welfare. Rather, there seems to be a role for reason leading us to do so out of self-regard: an *artificial* virtue is created where the *natural* ruled out above does not exist by a recognition of the long-run disadvantages to ourselves if others infringe the rules. Given the human tendency to discount the future, it is difficult to accept such a recognition as a type of long-run utility return. Rather, Hume's rejection of reason in the formation of moral rules does not seem to hold in considering the motivation to accept them. But then, how can one formulate moral rules without the implication of accepting them as bounds on one's behavior?

Indeed, in the *Inquiry*, which was published twelve years after the *Treatise*, Hume seems to retreat from his view of the lack of a general regard for mankind in the *Treatise* with the appeal to a form of reason and finds the motivation to conform in such a concern rather than long-run self-interest:

> It appears that a tendency to public good and to the promoting of peace, harmony, and order in society does always, by affecting the benevolent principles of our frame, engage us on the side of the social virtue.[9]

On balance, then, Hume must be marked as an antirationalist theorist of morals who viewed man as motivated by feelings of personal pleasure and pain as well as those of others. Both forms of utility shaped individual actions and decisions, with those with moral content dictated largely by the latter, though perhaps with some influence of an understanding of long-run consequences of a general disregard for moral rules.

But Hume was not a complete moral theorist in that he did not concern himself with the content of moral rules, but rather with their origins. The individual's primitive drives to obtain pleasure and pain in both egoistic and altruistic dimensions simply are viewed as "original existences." Their relation to the good in individual life or to right is not explored. It is therefore a theory more in the lineage of the psychology-of-motivation doctrines of Shaftesbury, Hutcheson, Butler, and Smith.

One of the first who found the criteria for moral behavior as well as the motivation in the search for pleasure was Paley (1743–1805). In his interest in justifying the moral results of the individual's behavioral search for utility, he was a utilitarian in the true sense of the term. But Paley linked the moral basis of this search to the will of God and His desire for the happiness of man. God judged the social value of individual actions on the basis of their tendency to increase or decrease social welfare, and man's motivation to perform the moral was linked to the expected utility of such social acts in the form of rewards and punishments in the afterlife.[10] This strong dependence of morality on divine will in a period in which moral philosophy was struggling to free itself from such a basis militated against Paley's acceptance, and the leadership of the Utilitarian School passed to a writer who was a dedicated secularist.

Benthamite Utilitarianism

The seminal figure in the establishment of utilitarianism as the most influential school of social ethics in the nineteenth and twentieth centuries was Jeremy Bentham. His Damascene conversion to the doctrine occurred during his reading of Hume's *Treatise,* and its use with explicit relevance to distributive justice dates from his prolific writings.

Bentham presented the act-utilitarian theory in its simplest, most comprehensive, and least compromising terms. In a famous quotation, he establishes the fundamental article of faith for the utilitarian:

> Nature has placed mankind under the governance of two sovereign masters: pain and pleasure. It is for them alone to point out what we ought to do as well as to determine what we shall do.[11]

This governance is part of the natural order: it is not susceptible of proof nor is there any need for such proof, and this also implies that it is impossible to disprove the assertion as a proper guide to individual conduct.

Since pleasure (and continuing to treat pain as negative pleasure) is the good, the right is the pursuit of it by the individual *and the society.* The morally right and the socially just therefore are derivative from the definition of the good and are defined formally as the maximization of the good.[12] The morally right for both the individual and society therefore is implemented in the "greatest happiness principle." That principle, applied to society, is "the greatest happiness of the greatest number," which translates into a meaningful statement if the number of individuals in the society is taken as given. Otherwise, when social policy is capable of affecting population size, and the primary objective is the maximization of numbers, the aim becomes a total utility concept which may imply an average level of utility at subsistence.

Individual and state should act to maximize the happiness of all persons whose interests are involved in an individual or social action of whatever kind. Whether the action impacts a single individual or, at the other extreme, affects every person in the society, the greatest happiness principle is the only right and just guide to moral behavior. A person has an interest in an action if it affects in any way his or her sum of "utility," which is a property in a good or action that produces "benefit, advantage, pleasure, or happiness," considered synonymous in Bentham's view.

Bentham makes it clear that his primary interest is in social ethics rather than individual morality:

"But it is never, then, from any other consideration than those of utility, that we derive our notions of right and wrong?" I do not know: I do not care. Whether a moral sentiment can be originally conceived from any other source than a view of utility, is one question: whether upon examination and reflection it can, in point of fact, be actually persisted in and justified on any other ground, by a person reflecting within himself, is another: whether in point of right it can properly be justified on any other ground, by a person addressing himself to the community, is a third. The two first are questions of speculation: it matters not, comparatively speaking, how they are decided. *The last is a question of practice: the decision of it is of as much importance as that of any can be.*[13]

In an independent assumption, society is conceived to be simply an assemblage of individuals with a social utility equal to the sum of equally weighted individual utilities. Individual utilities are taken to be cardinally measurable and interpersonally comparable, so that such a social sum is derivable and meaningful. As will be discussed below, Benthamism has rather contradictory attitudes toward individualism, but certainly in the prescription of its fundamental premises it is assertively individualist. The state's primary welfare obligation to its citizens based on the utilitarian concept of right is the negative one of minimal interference with their egoistically motivated actions. For any action of the individual, the state must total the pleasures received from it over all interested parties and deduct from it the pain inflicted on other interested parties. If the net utility is positive, the state is forbidden to interfere with the action; if the net is negative, the state is obligated to take action to preempt or prevent the individual's action.

Governmental action to counter individual actions that interfere with the maximum happiness principle may take three forms. The first is a reliance on education and indoctrination of the young. Bentham adopted Hartley's associationist psychology, which taught that the individual learns by grouping sensations into categories such as "hot" and "cold," "sweet" and "sour," or "good" and "bad." It followed that with proper instruction in youth to associate socially benevolent actions with "good" and harmful actions with "bad," much of the need for governmental action against individuals would be eliminated.

A second route is the creation of social institutions that bring about an "artificial harmony" of interests in the presence of egoistic motivation that might interfere with the maximization of social utility. The free market economy, which yields "optimizing" social solutions from inputs of egoistic self-seeking, was one such institution in Bentham's view (until James Mill convinced him of the validity of the Malthusian doctrine). Another was representative government, which employed the vote as a means of bringing the self-interest of the governors into harmony with the interests of the governed. Benthamism evinced a great deal of interest in such social engineering, based upon a faith that it was possible to use constitutional methods to move societies toward institutionally designed harmonistic solutions to social problems.

Last, in the event such measures failed to deter the individual from performing antisocial acts, the state must impose sanctions and rewards to induce proper behavior. However, the greatest happiness principle dictated that the degree of punishment or reward be just enough and no more than that needed to deter the action. This had obvious implications for penology, an area in which Bentham took an active interest in reforming.

In the area of distributive justice, the application of the greatest happiness principle in a market society required an active and continuing government interventionist role. Maximizing social utility requires that the marginal utility of income for each citizen be equalized—a result which the contributory distributive mechanism of the market does not accomplish. This implication, together with the role of the state in educating the young in the ways of harmony, implied a program of governmental action whose scope clashed with the inclinations of the classical laissez-faire economists who embraced Benthamite doctrines.

A number of criticisms of the simple form which Bentham gave the theory arose as the first half of the century progressed. Among the more important in terms of the later development of the theory are the following.

1. *The Measurability of Utility.* The ability to use the indicated criterion of justice depended on the means of measurement of utility for each individual with two demanding properties:

   a. The numbers assigned in the measurement procedure must have sufficient uniqueness to permit meaningful first differences to be obtained between them.
   b. These incremental differences (and the utility measurements from which they were derived) must be comparable interpersonally.

Bentham had no doubts that it would be possible to derive such utility measurements in order that income redistribution dictates could be obtained operationally. To date, except in situations of risk and on the assumption of certain plausible but not incontestable attitudes toward risk, economists have been unable to achieve measurements that conform to the first requirement. And in no case have they succeeded in achieving measurements that meet the second.

Utilitarians quickly devised means of circumventing the necessity of such measurement. If all persons' abilities to enjoy income are roughly equal at birth, and if differential capacities for enjoyment are the result of opportunities that are themselves caused by income inequalities, the condition of equal marginal utilities among individuals can be obtained by equal incomes. This was not acceptable to all utilitarians but was welcomed by those who leaned toward egalitarianism as a social ideal; it flavored the utilitarian doctrines, which endorsed democratic representative government, with an additional egalitarian spice.

2. *The Maximization of Total Utility.* Benthamite utilitarianism called for the maximization of the total utility summed over the population. If population growth were more rapid than the rise in the material basis of utility, this might imply the decline in per capita utility. The utilitarians took an active role in instituting methods of limiting a population growth they believed to be following Malthusian income response patterns. Theorists like John Stuart Mill and Knut Wicksell converted the maximization problem to one of per capita utility.

3. *The Submergence of Individual Protection.* A strict use of the maximum happiness principle by the state to define its actions could result in the most outrageous violations of the integrity of the individual and the rights guaranteed the individual in liberal societies. The oft-quoted example of the innocent person sacrificed to the vengeance of the mob in order to prevent a larger number of deaths is one instance. Less dramatically, an individual's private property might be condemned for a public purpose when the balance of social utility was only slightly positive, contrary to the prevailing doctrine that such state uses of eminent domain are just only under compelling circumstances. And the deviant whose public behavior was considered bothersome by a large number of people might be institutionalized for the comfort and convenience of the population, at the expense of his or her right to liberty in the absence of genuine threats to the health or lives of others.

In these respects the simple sum of utilities was a threat to the most basic tenets of natural rights and constitutional protection of the individual. Some type of constraints on the use of the maximum happiness principle—total or per capita—to protect these aspects of individualism from the threat of social expediency seemed necessary.

4. *The Lack of Qualitative Discrimination among Utilities.* One reflection of Bentham's stress on egalitarianism was his assertion that pleasures could not be ranked in terms of quality. Poetry, he asserted, was no more valued in the scale of social welfare than pushpin, a children's game. The state must be equally protective of the individual's right to pursue either, and must not give unequal weights to the utilities derived from either. This lack of discrimination on grounds of quality disturbed critics who harbored a nagging belief that intellectual or artistic pleasures must be graded by a civilized society above mere physical sensations.

Indeed, was sensual experience a true definition of happiness? Might not the experience of a more refined needs fulfillment involve a quantum of dissatisfaction? Should not society recognize such a grading of the inputs to the felicific calculus? How would such qualitative distinctions be determined and enter into the social utility aggregate?

5. *The Basis of Moral Obligation.* To assert that it is moral for individuals to consult the impacts of their actions on others' happiness and to weight those changes equally with their own utility increments is to establish a moral obligation or binding legal requirement to so act. Bentham treated the greatest happiness principle as a self-evident prescription, but based as it was on the notion of happiness as the sole end of individual existence, capable of neither proof nor disproof.

However, a theory of morality must establish a firmer rationale to claim the acceptance of so self-denying a principle. Why should the individual seek happiness—however defined—as the sole end of life? Why does another person have an equal claim to his or her own happiness in calculations of utility? What provides the persuasive force for such a moral code? Is the only basis an appeal to intuition, and if so, does this suffice?

The Refinements of John Stuart Mill

John Stuart Mill's contribution to the utilitarian doctrine was to address most of these objections in an attempt to place the theory on more solid foundations than Bentham left it, necessarily at the expense of some of its simplicity. He was not wholly successful in providing satisfactory solutions to these problems, but he succeeded in making some of its core doctrines more acceptable to intuitive notions of justice. His restatement was the most influential treatise on utilitarian ethics in the nineteenth century.

Why is the utility derived from acts the sole good for persons and their aggregate, society? Mill's answer goes beyond Bentham's. In the narrow sense of proof, Bentham is correct: ultimate ends are not possible of direct proof. "Whatever can be proved to be good, must be so by being shown to be a means to something admitted to be good without proof."[14] But there is a broader meaning of the term "proof," which is to present considerations which the reason (not intuition) can agree to or disagree with. This is equivalent to proof, in Mill's view. His argument is straightforward: the only evidence that happiness is desirable is that persons desire it.[15] Hence, happiness is *a* good. To establish that it is the *only* good, he argues that all other aims in life—virtue, for example—are simply means of achieving happiness.

Mill stressed more than Bentham the social dimension of utilitarianism, even within the narrow scope of individual decision making. The greatest happiness principle was a criterion not for the individual's selfish happiness but for the collective happiness of all whose interests are at stake. In most instances, Mill insisted, this involves a relatively small group of people known to the actor, so that the injunction is a feasible constraint on the individual's decision making. He or she is obligated to act as an impartial judge in weighing own benefits against the possible disutilities inflicted on others by such action. The ideal essence of the utilitarian ethic is captured in the Golden Rule. Indeed, as Mill presents the notion of utility as a guide to action, it is so strongly oriented to the benefit of others as to require a substantial amount of self-sacrifice. It is true that society can justly ask the individual to sacrifice his or her happiness only if that of other individuals is disturbed to a greater extent than he or she benefits: but in that case he or she is morally or legally obligated to desist.

But is this a rational requirement? Others' incremental or decremental pleasures are externalities to the individual. What claim on his or her allegiance to this principle of morality can be made on the egoistic decision maker of *homo economicus* fame? What would motivate the individual, for example, to seek to maximize average social utility by massive income redistribution at his or her own cost? And this *is* an instance when the individual is asked to take into account the welfare of all other individuals in the society rather than a tight circle of peculiar concern. Participation in effecting the principle of economic justice is a process involving the individual in global social concerns.

Mill's provision of motives has several lines of argument. The first is that man's rationality would lead him to accept the Golden Rule or Kant's categorical imperative as an ideal ethic. Reason would lead to a realization of the undesirable social consequences if everyone acted in a manner that disregarded the comfort or safety of fellow citizens.

Second, to the extent reason fails to provide the necessary foundation for such universal good will, the plastic nature of the human mind can be indoctrinated through education, institutions, and the sanctions of religion and public opinion to associate happiness with the socially cognizant and pain with antisocial acts. In these arguments Mill follows Bentham closely, urging the engineering of harmony when it does not emerge from volition.

But most fundamental in Mill's belief that men would find the greatest happiness principle congenial in the definition of their moral claims and obligations is his faith in the deep-seated social aspirations of mankind. Not as an innate idea, but as an early acquired sentiment, the desire to live at harmony with his or her fellows makes the individual's consideration of the social implications of his or her actions quite congenial with perceived self-interest. Cooperation is a natural consequence of this longing for integration into a society.

Sympathy for one's fellows grows with the progress of civilization, as class barriers are reduced, but exists in the earliest phases of social existence as well. It progresses beyond mere consideration of others' happiness to a state of coordinate importance with one's own. The only society consistent with these sentiments of self-interest and altruism is the civil egalitarian:

> Now, society between human beings except in the relation of master and slave, is manifestly impossible on any other footing than that the interests of all are to be consulted. Society between equals can only exist on the understanding that the interests of all are to be regarded equally.[16]

Equality of "treatment," in Mill's phrase, becomes an ambiguous term in his usage. In his quotation above, taken from his extensive analysis of justice, it seems to refer to equality before the law and impartiality in the administration of justice. In general, his primary concern in this discussion of the concept is with its civil rights elements. But this is not an exclusive concern:

> The equal claim of everybody to happiness in the estimation of the moralist and of the legislator, involves an equal claim to all the means of happiness, except in so far as the inevitable conditions of human life, and the general interest, in which that of every individual is included, set limits to the maxim; and those limits ought to be strictly construed. As every other maxim of justice, so this is by no means applied or held applicable universally; on the contrary, as I have already remarked, it bends to every person's ideas of social expediency. But in whatever case it is deemed applicable at all, it is held to be the dictate of justice. All persons are deemed to have a *right* to equality of treatment, except when some recognised social expediency requires the reverse.[17]

The means of happiness would seem to include income for the provision of material goods. Does the right to equal treatment in Mill's view include income equality or, more exactly, equality of satisfaction?

Happiness of such greater worth may in fact imply some dissatisfaction. In this sense Mill distinguishes happiness from pleasure. Satisfactions that appeal to a finer faculty frequently are alloyed with such seeming pain. But capable human beings would not trade such dissatisfaction for the pleasures of animals or dunces because of a sense of human dignity. Better a human being dissatisfied than a pig satisfied, or a Socrates dissatisfied than a fool satisfied. Utilities are qualitatively differentiated with respect to the level of refinement of faculties to which they appeal.

But men differ in their capacity for enjoyment of such happiness:

> A being of higher faculties requires more to make him happy, is capable
> probably of more acute suffering, and is certainly more accessible to it at
> more points than one of inferior type; but in spite of these disabilities he
> can never really wish to sink into what he feels to be a lower grade of exis-
> tence.[18]

Finally, Mill's valuable analysis of the concept of justice and its relation
to morality stresses the individual's right to freedom from the arbitrary
actions of others, including threats to his or her life and property. Man's
sentiment for the institution of rules of justice is grounded in his strong
desire for self-protection and his ability to sympathize with his fellow
beings embracing all persons in the society. Justice is contradistin-
guished from morality by the notion that the former creates a duty on
the part of one agent and a correlative right of another, whereas the duty
exists in the latter case but no agent has a right to demand performance.
The distinction is that in the philosophy of ethics between duties of *perfect* and *imperfect* obligation. Hence:

> Justice is a name for certain classes of moral rules, which concern the essen-
> tials of human well-being more nearly, and are therefore of more absolute
> obligation, than any other rules for the guidance of life; and the notion
> which we have found to be of the essence of the idea of justice, that of a
> right residing in an individual, implies and testifies to this more binding
> obligation.[19]

Rules for specifying which tenets of morality should have the sanction of
justice can only be determined by the total of social utility their adoption
entails. But the utility or disutility that arises from the acceptance or
violation of such rules by individuals is of a qualitatively distinct nature
from ordinary utility:

> Our notion, therefore, of the claim we have on our fellow-creatures to join
> in making safe for us the very groundwork of our existence, gathers feelings
> around it so much more intense than those concerned in any of the more
> common cases of utility, that the difference in degree (as is often the case
> in psychology) becomes a real difference in kind.[20]

But if in fact these feelings related to the rules of justice are qualitatively
different from ordinarily utility, does their justification reside in the
greatest happiness principle? Might they not be treated better as constraints on that principle?

Specifically, if an individual has a right to protection in his or her
pursuit of a living, should this interfere with the equality Mill envisages
for the greatest happiness principle? He seems to support the notion of
such a right:

Thus, a person is said to have a right to what he can earn in fair professional competition; because society ought not to allow any other person to hinder him from endeavouring to earn in that manner as much as he can. But he has not a right to three hundred a-year , though he may happen to be earning it; because society is not called on to provide that he shall earn that sum.[21]

Do such rights form part of the "inevitable conditions of human life and the general interest" that limit equal claims on the means of happiness? If so, they impose substantial departures from the equality that Mill believes utilitarianism demands. Is the nonright of the individual to a specified amount of income a denial of society's obligation to provide minimum or equal entitlements to society's goods?

Despite Mill's lucid clarification of the relation of justice to morality, when he attempts to tie the determination of the rules of justice to the social felicific calculus, the outlines of the just economic system become fuzzy. He seems torn between the belief that utilitarianism would dictate an economic egalitarianism in one of several senses or would require substantial protections of the individual's egoistic rights in a free market system. The struggle to reconcile his vigorous views on personal liberty, including that relevant to economic actions, with his inclinations toward economic egalitarianism are reflected in the changing views of ideal economic organization he held over his lifetime.[22] From the beginning of his argument, his view of the depth of communitarianism in the concept of utility committed him to a degree of social organicism that his commitment to individualism and laissez-faire never permitted him to admit.

Was Mill consistently an act-utilitarian, as I have implicitly interpreted him? There are two points at which Mill reveals an understanding of the meaning of rule-utilitarianism and seems to endorse it. In defending the charge that utilitarianism places too great a responsibility on the shoulders of the individual in deciding the net social benefits of his or her actions, Mill argues that society embodies precepts concerning moral actions in rules which are subordinate to the principle of utility but which are available to the individual for guidance. Also, in his definition of utility he refers to the rightness of actions that *tend* to promote global happiness, which implies that he is classifying such actions in the manner of rules, since individual actions cannot have tendencies.[23]

RAWLSIAN RATIONAL PRUDENCE

Certainly the most influential theory of justice in the last forty years is the rationalist, social contractarian theory of John Rawls.[24] It is especially relevant to the present investigation because its primary contributions and most controversial propositions are concerned with economic

equity. The Rawlsian structure is ambitious in its goals, complex in architecture, polished in the many qualifications of its arguments, rather pro-
lix and repetitious in presentation, and, most challenging to the reader,
continuously altered in its most fundamental notions. The reader is ad-
vised, therefore, to read the work in the original to grasp the magnifi-
cence of Rawls's performance: one cannot hope to do justice to the theory in this brief summary.

Rawls's theory of justice as fairness has evolved through three phases,
at each stage becoming more complex, more heavily qualified, and
more difficult to grasp as a whole or even to understand in its most fundamental arguments. In Phase 1, which predated the publication of the
Theory of Justice, Rawls's goal was to develop a set of principles utilizing
wholly self-interest via a bargaining process in a society among agents
knowledgeable about their positions in society and their consequent
benefits from such principles. Phase II succeeded and was codified in
The Theory of Justice, dropping the notion of the the original position as
one of strict bargaining and converting it essentially into a type of Kantian natural state within which the individual can reason essentially in
isolated fashion.[25] Finally, Phase III involves the reorientation toward
political philosophy discussed below and to be found in the articles ref-
erenced in note 24.

Rawls poses the framing questions of his inquiry in the following
terms. Assume, for simplicity, that a society is self-contained with no in-
tersocietal relations. Then:

1. Assume that a nation of *moral persons* is organized into a *well-ordered*
society and seeks a set of principles of justice with which to organize its
most basic structural institutions. A moral person is one who has a desire
for principles of justice and assumes others will have also, and who will
act according to those principles and expects others to do so when they
are forthcoming. A well-ordered society is one in which such principles
regulate actions within the realm of justice adopted by moral persons
who view each other as *free* and *equal* citizens, where freedom implies that
persons are entitled to participate in the design of the principles of justice and to pursue ends. Equality demands an equal right to participate
in the determination of the principles and to assess them in due reflection.

2. The well-ordered society Rawls envisions is a constitutional democracy viewed as a cooperative endeavor among free and equal moral persons with the principles of justice to be sought providing the guidelines
for distributing the benefits of that enterprise. Those principles of right
are not meant to provide a full-fledged moral philosophy, nor are they
designed as appropriate to all societies regardless of history, traditions,
and state of development.[26] Moreover, the principles of justice derived

must conform to the deeper, latent convictions and common sense principles of moral behavior that override the pluralistic moral convictions of groups with different religious, philosophical, and social convictions of the ultimate goods in human existence. That is, the principles derived must achieve an "overlapping consensus" among such groups and hence a "reflective equilibrium" brought about by an interactive adjustment process between these deeply held convictions and the justice principles derived.

3. The constructivism that Rawls chooses for moral persons, acting individually or as representatives of groups to derive these principles of justice, is the original position. Suppose such persons were *rationally autonomous* in the sense that in their decision making they are freed from notions of antecedent principles of right and are permitted to seek their maximum advantage in fulfilling their rational life plan, being "disinterested" in the welfares of others who are not their charges and feeling no envy toward others who might gain more favorable treatment if fair.

These provisions intrude the rational into the choice process, but it must be supplemented by and indeed be subordinated to the reasonable, which introduces the deeply ingrained notions that fair terms of cooperation must be incorporated into the derived principles, so that all who cooperate in social endeavors benefit or share burdens in an appropriate fashion. Rawls's procedure for doing so is to introduce constraints that create a "thin" veil of ignorance, denying to the participants all knowledge that would bias their choices toward self-advantage and effectively deny the equality of disinterested choice necessary. Since the procedures guiding the decision making are rationally autonomous yet reflect a symmetry of self-knowledge among the participants, the propositions emerging are the result of *pure procedural justice* and are *fair*: hence, justice as fairness.

4. But although these propositions reflect the decision making of moral persons seeking their "highest-order" goods or goals, they must be taken into the real world conflicts among ends and values that exist in a constitutional democracy, to confront the "strains of commitment" such abstract principles create. There ensues, therefore, a dialectic of reflection between the principles and these deeper values and beliefs derived intuitively or osmotically from the traditions and historical evolution of the institutions of the society—which I have characterized as the "ethos" of the society. That ethos is not sacrosanct, but will yield to the compelling rationality and reasonableness of the proposed propositions in important respects, for example, the unacceptability of racial or sexual discrimination for irrelevant reasons. But the propositions will probably be forced to compromise with the ethos in other respects, perhaps, for example, in the degree of economic equality they seek to institute or in

programs of affirmative action they might condone (or might not). The tension between these two bodies of principles is resolved in a synthesis termed *reflective equilibrium* by Rawls and an overlapping consensus among groups committed to a variety of ideological allegiances achieved.[27] In such a context the moral person achieves full autonomy in that he or she acts in the pursuit of goals he or she defines for self-benefit but at the same time treats others as equals entitled to the respect and self-respect necessary in the well-ordered society.

This emphasis in the later Rawls on the reflective equilibrium and its achievement of an overlapping consensus, somewhat demoting the original position propositions from their earlier claim to a slightly tempered allegiance because of their abstract origin in fairness and their moral objectivity because of their unanimous agreement by participants, marks a reorientation of Rawls's theory away from moral theory toward political philosophy. The sociopolitical relativity of principles of justice, the necessity of their bending to the reasonable sanctions of the ethos (again, my term, not Rawls's), and the role of justice as political precepts for the shaping of basic social institutions in a constitutional democracy rather than a discovery or construction of immutable systems validated by epistomology or metaphysics are at the least important changes in the emphasis to be found in *Theory of Justice* arguments.[28]

Despite the increased emphasis on reflective equilibrium and consensus, the core of the Rawlsian contribution to social justice is the body of principles emerging from the original position. Rawls is not specific about the compromises that would have to be made to achieve reflective equilibrium and overlapping consensus in American society, and one does depart his discussions with the notion he believes them to be minimal and that they should be. I shall therefore give greatest attention to the derivation and content of the abstract principles.

Justice as Fairness

As noted, in Rawls's view, the principles of justice are best derived from the theory of rational choice within the context of voluntary contractual agreement of the social compact type, when the individual's essentially egoistic motivation is constrained to incorporate "reasonableness." The framework is Kantian in approach, for to Kant, as pointed out earlier in the chapter, the proper interpretation of the social contract was as an abstract exercise in rational decision making. If an individual violates a categorical imperative (e.g., refusing to pay a legitimate debt) he or she may be forced to honor the obligation on the grounds that his or her reason would lead to an acceptance of the universal law of honoring contracts. Even if the individual had never assented to such a clause of the "social contract," the effect of the intellectual experiment is the same, for he or she can be shown to be a prisoner of his or her reason.[29] Paradoxically, only by virtue of that servitude is man truly free or autonomous, and within the context of the voluntary agreements arrived at in the "social contract" he expresses that freedom.

Rawls proceeds therefore to place individuals in a hypothetical state wherein they mutually agree on the principles of justice that will provide the framework for their rights and obligations—the duties of perfect obligation. That state—a particularization of the initial situation in which individuals decide to arrive at a social contract whose constructivist intent is to create the principles defining basic institutions of justice—is the *original position*.

The Original Position

The original position envelops the participants in the social contracting process in a veil of ignorance designed to deprive them of the opportunity to advance a knowledgeable self-interest. The principles of justice should be derived from a procedure in which (1) no one should be aided or harmed by natural endowments or social circumstances; (2) no one can tailor the principles to fit his or her circumstances; (3) the personal inclinations or conceptions of the good peculiar to individuals cannot affect the results; and (4) all persons are free and equal in the contracting process and rationally autonomous.

Behind the veil of ignorance, the participants are aware of several characteristics of the society whose rules of justice they are designing. They know that it is a society that will follow such rules and the "general organizational facts" (size, institutional structure, natural environment) concerning it, and they know that they already occupy a place in it. They also know the basic outlines of human psychology. In more personal affairs, they know they will live by a rational plan but do not know the content of the plan. However, they are aware that the fulfillment of that plan will require receipt of the "primary goods"—tangible and intangible—whose distribution their agreed principles will determine, and that they will be better off with more of such goods than less. These primary goods, sought by the individuals or those they represent, are (1) basic liberties, (2) freedom of movement and occupational choice, (3) powers and prerogatives of office and positions of responsibility, (4) income and wealth, and (5) the social bases of self-respect.[30] They are concerned for the welfare of themselves, their families, and at least two generations of their descendants. Moreover, they are mutually disinterested in the welfare of all others: explicit altruism is lacking but they display no envy of others' potentials. They know that such welfare is positively correlated with the receipt of primary goods, in that they will be able to exercise their moral powers to pursue their highest-order interests with such goods, and so they evaluate competing sets of principles by their ability to deliver these primary goods weighted in some fashion.

But no person knows:

1. his or her occupational position in society, class position, or social status;
2. his or her natural assets and abilities;
3. his or her conception of the good or final end as embodied in the rational plan he or she will follow;
4. the special features of his or her psychology, *including attitudes toward risk*;[31]
5. the generation to which he or she belongs.

Under such conditions no bargaining can occur, for the participants are ignorant of the import of any principles for their welfare.[32] In the absence of the possibility of bargaining, no coalition formation among parties is rational. The parties will consider a list of alternative theories to determine the principles and rank them in terms of preference, in terms of primary good implications.[33]

Decisions will be arrived at unanimously in the Kantian glow of reason, extended from the determination of personal maxims of behavior to social. For the original position is not an actual gathering at some point in time; rather, it is a hypothetical set of conditions within which to reason. If any rational person is selected at random and placed within such a framework, he or she will arrive at a given ranking. But since all persons are the same in respects reason, they all would arrive at the same decision if placed in the original position. Hence, Rawls argues, unanimity will occur, and a type of moral objectivity will characterize the principles.

Although the individual's motivation is self-regarding in the extended family sense, Rawls denies that the principles derived are egoistic. The veil of ignorance achieves the same results as benevolence without having to assume it because it forces each to take into account the welfare of others since they are in the same position as oneself. But the resulting principles of justice "are those which rational persons concerned to advance their interests would accept in this position of equality to settle the basic terms of their association." [34] Since those interests are their "highest-order" interests in gaining primary goods to pursue the goals of moral persons, their choices are not be be confused with egoism.[35]

The Principles of Justice as Fairness

Under the conditions of the original position, with the equality of all and with all in a state of ignorance, an environment of fairness is established, and hence the principles chosen unanimously will be fair. In Rawls's reasoning, the set of principles that would emerge from the original position are the following:

1. *First Principle.* Each person is to have an equal right to the most extensive total system of equal basic liberties compatible with a similar system of liberty for all.
2. *Second Principle.* Social and economic inequalities are to be arranged so that they are both:
   a. to the greatest benefit of the least advantaged, consistent with the just savings principle; and
   b. attached to offices and positions open to all under conditions of *fair equality of opportunity.*
3. *First Priority Rule.* The principles of justice are to be ranked in lexicographic order[36] and therefore liberty can be restricted only for the sake of liberty:
   a. a less extensive liberty must strengthen the total system of liberty shared by all; or
   b. a less than equal liberty must be acceptable to those with the lesser liberty.
4. *Second Priority Rule.* The Second Principle is lexicographically prior to the principle of efficiency and to that of maximizing the sum of advantages; and fair opportunity is prior to the *difference principle.* There are two cases:
   a. an inequality of opportunity must enhance the opportunities of those with the lesser opportunity;
   b. an excessive rate of saving must on balance mitigate the burden of those bearing the hardship.

As a general summary statement, which abstracts from some of the refinements stated above: *all social primary goods—liberty and opportunity, income and wealth, and the bases of self-respect—are to be distributed equally unless an unequal distribution of any or all of these goods is to the advantage of the least favored.*

The social structure in Rawls is viewed as split into two sectors: that which deals with the provision and protection of the equal civil liberties and that which rules over the distribution of income and wealth and of authority and responsibility. The First Principle and its conjugate First Priority Rule are concerned with the first part of the social structure and assure that basic freedom and civil rights are equally distributed and cannot be traded away as commodities by individuals. In the original position the selfish interests of each participant will lead to the assignment of such rights on an equal basis in order to assure that conditions will not be attached to their award that would work to the disadvantage of the individual. They are either actively endorsed or passively consistent with all of the alternative theories considered in chapter 2 and the present chapter. Further, little more need be said in this work concerning them, since one of the primitives in the investigation is the assumption of individualism made in chapter 2.

The controversial principles are those contained in the Second Principle and Second Priority Rule whose more important content is summarized in the general summary statement. They must be explained and motivated in somewhat greater detail than their summarization above. A systematic approach will prove valuable.

1. *Groups in the Original Position.* In the Rawlsian version of the state of nature—the original position—participants discuss the futures of aggregated segments of the population distinguished by their positions or status in the society on the other side of the veil of ignorance. Rawls discusses their fates in terms of a "representative man" in each, and his expectations are used to judge the expectations of the group as a whole. The groups are ranked from top to bottom in social fortune, with the "least-advantaged" group being singled out for the statement of the principles. It may be identified with the least skilled element of the laboring class, or perhaps the unemployable elements in society, with a representative man (or woman) embodying its attributes and symbolizing its status.

Rawls's discussion of the interrelatedness of the welfare of this hierarchy of groups is not always clear in the progression of the analysis. Assume that a classification of groups has been accepted and that the categories are ranked in descending order from most to least advantaged. The *chain connection* assumes that when the least-advantaged representative person is benefited all groups benefit, but it says nothing about what happens when the least-advantaged group is reduced in welfare. Hence, as the most-advantaged groups receive increases in primary goods, when the least-advantaged group's receipts of such goods decline the intermediate groups may rise or fall in their receipts. On the other hand, in the society that is *close-knit,* whenever any representative person rises or falls in welfare, all groups' representative persons rise or fall as well.

Rawls assumes at one point that close-knittedness always holds in the society so that when the least-advantaged class experiences an increase or decrease in its status all other groups do also, and, similarly, when more advantaged classes raise their expectations, all other classes including the least-advantaged do as well.[37]

But if this is true, and if for simplicity it is assumed that social welfare is the sum of interpersonally comparable utility levels, the Second Principle would place no limits on the departure of the most-advantaged class from an egalitarian position unless it were imposed for reasons other than the behavior of utility functions. Indeed, Rawls does say that some upper bound on inequality must be emplaced in order to prevent undue political influence from accruing to more advantaged classes. Yet at other points in the work Rawls implies that the society is not close-knit: a limit on the inequality of income distribution is set at the point where the utility of the least-advantaged class as a function of the utility of more advantaged classes reaches a maximum.

But Rawls's Second Principle would not be very distinctive if close-knittedness always characterized the society, since it would not provide a meaningful bound on inequality. The general case should be assumed to be one where the utility of the least-advantaged representative man would, as a function of utility received by more advantaged classes, rise to a maximum and then decline, because, for example, as inequality surpasses a certain degree, interpersonal comparisons endanger the self-respect of the least-advantaged.

2. *The Difference Principle.* These terms permit us to discuss the difference principle, which is the core concept behind the Second Principle. It asserts that one of the tenets of justice that would emerge from the negotiation of the original position is the rule that the distribution of primary goods among persons would be equal except that departures from inequality would be allowed more advantaged groups if and only if the least-advantaged group benefited. Figure 3.1 illustrates the concept. The horizontal axis labeled Y depicts *increments of income above an equal income distribution* received by the representative person of the most-advantaged class, and the vertical axis labeled U_2 shows *the total additional utility obtained from the unequal distribution* by the least-advantaged representative person. The function, $U_2 = f(Y)$, reaches a maximum at A; hence, the utility received by the least-advantaged class reaches a maxi-

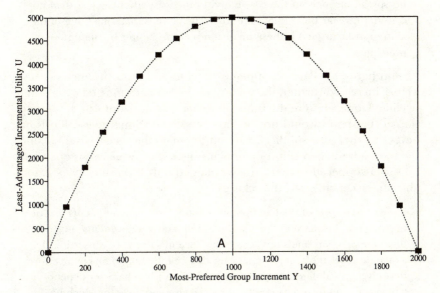

FIGURE 3.1. The Difference Principle

mum at this incremental income level of the most-advantaged. Close-knittedness does not hold in this case because the function declines after A. Were $f(Y)$ to become horizontal beyond A the difference principle dictates that inequality cease at A, since the least-advantaged class does not benefit after that point.

The fairness in Rawls's view of this principle is that it distributes the products of society's cooperative efforts in a manner that diverts the advantages of attributes whose possession is a gift of nature or of advantaged circumstances from personal to social benefit:

> Now those starting out as members of the entrepreneurial class in property-owning democracy, say, have a better prospect than those who begin in the class of unskilled laborers. It seems likely that this will be true even when the social injustices which now exist are removed. What, then, can possibly justify this kind of initial inequality in life prospects? According to the difference principle, it is justifiable only if the difference in expectation is to the advantage of the representative unskilled worker. The inequality in expectation is permissible only if lowering it would make the working class even more worse off. Supposedly, given the rider in the second principle concerning open positions, and the principle of liberty generally, the greater expectations allowed to entrepreneurs encourages them to do things which raise the long-term prospects of the laboring class. Their better prospects act as incentives so that the economic process is more efficient, innovation proceeds at a faster pace, and so on. Eventually the resulting material benefits spread throughout the system and to the least advantaged. I shall not consider how far these things are true. The point is that something of this kind must be argued if these inequalities are to be just by the difference principle.[38]

At A in figure 3.1 Pareto optimality is achieved in this instance because were Y increased further, the welfare of the least-advantaged class would decline. However, were the function to become horizontal at A, the solution at that point would not be Pareto optimal. Nonetheless, Rawls believes that the "just" solution at A would remain the socially optimal one: the most-advantaged cannot complain since their welfare is dependent on social cooperation that can be obtained only if the society is reasonable and acceptable to other classes:

> It seems to be one of the fixed points of our considered judgments that no one deserves his place in the distribution of native endowments, any more than one deserves one's initial starting place in society. The assertion that a man deserves the superior character that enables him to make the effort to cultivate his abilities is equally problematic; for his character depends in large part upon fortunate family and social circumstances for which he can claim no credit. The notion of desert seems not to apply to these cases. Thus

the more advantaged representative man cannot say that he deserves and therefore has a right to a scheme of cooperation in which he is permitted to acquire benefits in ways that do not contribute to the welfare of others. There is no basis for making this claim.[39]

Note Rawls's tendency to slip in and out of the mode of speaking of benefiting the least-advantaged class or benefiting "others": it is frequently unclear whether he is assuming close-knittedness or not. However, if close-knittedness holds, there is little point in singling out the least-advantaged.

Rawls asserts other advantages for the difference principle. It permits the concept of "fraternity" to enter social justice principles and it allows for the existence of a meritocratic society at the same time that it promotes the self-respect of the least-advantaged by limiting the range of hierarchy and inequality. If the difference principle would permit a degree of inequality that was socially undesirable because of such social structural concerns, an upper bound must be placed on it in order to prevent infringement of the rightful political power of the least-advantaged. However, given the operation of the right to "equality of fair opportunity," which will be defined below, the degree of inequality in a liberal society should diminish as individuals develop their talents and reduce differentials in primary goods as a result.

Finally, even though in the purest sense the amount of information necessary to implement the difference principle perfectly will never be available, a practical advantage of the difference principle in a democracy is its relative ease of fulfillment in a policy sense. A legislature is charged with the responsibility of maximizing the "common interest," an impossible charge if interpreted as a multiple objective maximization of all classes' welfare. Effectively, a natural democratic objective would be the maximization of the primary goods of the least-advantaged:

> It seems that the policies in the justice of which we have the greatest confidence do at least tend in this direction in the sense that this sector of society would be worst off should [equal liberties and fair opportunity] be curtailed. These policies are just throughout even if they are not perfectly just. The difference principle can therefore be interpreted as a reasonable extension of the political convention of a democracy once we face up to the necessity of adopting a reasonably complete conception of justice.[40]

Additionally, such a policy has the advantage of ease of application, as compared with, for example, the utilitarian's goal of maximizing total or per capita satisfactions.

3. *Fair Equality of Opportunity.* The second component of the Second Principle was the notion of "fair equality of opportunity," which, like the concept of equal opportunity in Friedman's theory, is given a meaning

that differs from the conventional in Rawls. "Equal citizenship" in the Rawls lexicon includes equal rights and liberties (First Principle) and the principle of fair equality of opportunity. The basic meaning is that offices and positions in the society that lead to wealth and authority must be open to all, not simply in the *legal* sense but in the sense that "all should have a fair chance to attain them."[41]

Not only must liberties be equal among citizens, but the "worth of liberty" must be equalized. In extension:

> Offhand it is not clear what is meant, but we might say that those with similar abilities and skills should have similar life chances. More specifically, assuming that there is a distribution of natural assets, those who are at the same level of talent and ability, and have the same willingness to use them, should have the same prospects of success regardless of their initial place in the social system, that is, irrespective of the income class into which they are born. In all sectors of society there should be roughly equal prospects of culture and achievement for everyone similarly motivated and endowed. The expectations of those with the same abilities and aspirations should not be affected by their social class.[42]

Procedural justice requires that once such a goal is formulated the institutions of society be designed to assure that it is achieved (within practical limits). Therefore, the institutions of a free market that militate against such equality must be altered by political and social frameworks that work toward that goal. Excessive accumulations of property and wealth must be prevented and the education system, public and private, must be designed to lessen class barriers. The institution of the family prevents the achievement of fair equality of opportunity and consequently such principles as the difference principle must be adopted to adapt it to the design needed. Indeed, in Rawls's thinking, equal liberties and fair equality of opportunity imply that the better endowed can justly benefit from their advantages only if the least-advantaged gain from such inequality.

Equality of fair opportunity (which I equate with the worth of liberty in this sense) differs from the conventional sense of equality of opportunity in that it is not designed to work within the existing framework of free market liberal democratic institutions, but requires a variety of important changes in social structure, including those of the difference principle. Does it accommodate "affirmative action"? At one point the doctrine seems to conflict with it:

> I have not maintained that offices must be open if in fact everyone is to benefit from an arrangement. For it may be possible to improve everyone's situation by assigning certain powers and benefits to positions despite the fact that certain groups are excluded from them. Although access is re-

stricted, perhaps these offices can still attract superior talent and encourage better performance. But the principle of open positions forbids this. It expresses the conviction that if some places were not open on a basis fair to all, those kept out would be right in feeling unjustly treated even though they benefited from the greater efforts of those who were allowed to hold them. They would be justified in their complaint not only because they were excluded from certain external rewards of office such as wealth and privilege, but because they were debarred from experiencing the realization of self which comes from a skillful and devoted exercise of social duties. They would be deprived of one of the main forms of human good.[43]

Although in writing this passage Rawls had in mind the exclusion of the less-advantaged, symmetry of reasoning should lead to the same conclusion when the better-advantaged are discriminated against.

4. *The Just Savings Principle and Other Dynamic Concepts.* In the original position Rawls must extend his principles of fairness to include intergenerational justice by establishing guidelines for the accumulation of capital through saving. How much social overhead capital can future generations expect in justice from their forebears? In the original position the participants are ignorant of which generation they inhabit, that is, of the "stage of civilization" in which they will find themselves once they pass through the veil of ignorance. Because the amount of saving they will agree on is undoubtedly a function of their expectations of income level, the task of the decision makers is complicated by the need to hypothesize a set of income levels and specify a fair savings rate for each such level, and to integrate these changing rates into a just pattern over the future history of the society. At some point in that history, at a high level of income, such a fair rate would be zero on a net basis, so that capital thereafter is simply maintained and not augmented.

For any given hypothetical income level, the participants decide on this just rate by asking how much they would be willing to save if all other rates specified by them for other income attainments were adopted by the relevant generations. Rawls seems to have in mind an approximation to a simultaneous determination of the just savings schedule over the lifetime of the society through the use of some iterative scheme of reasoning. Being ignorant of their own generational identity, in effect the individuals give equal representation to all generations. Such ignorance, he asserts, leads them to adopt a zero rate of time preference in their determination of the principle of just savings rates, since discounting generational satisfactions on the basis of position in time may penalize the participants.

The dynamic interpretation of the difference principle is that the social minimum income set by it for the least-advantaged class be instituted at that value that maximizes the expectations of its representative person

over some future set of generations. Thus, if income inequality stimulates savings, and these savings benefit the least advantaged in future
periods, it might be presumed that a great deal more inequality would be
intruded into the income distribution at any particular time than the
static difference principle would contemplate. However, Rawls argues
that should such transfers reduce the prospects of the least-advantaged
of the generation whose savings are being determined, they would be
excessive, presumably on the basis of self-interest.

More important, Rawls does not think it possible to deduce the schedule of just savings over time but that it is possible to discern the principles on which it would be derived and to set some bounds on them.
However, Rawls's discussion of the just savings principles is not clear,
and indeed the principles and bounds are rather fuzzy. He declares that
the difference principle cannot be used to determine the just savings
schedule because future generations cannot benefit the least-advantaged of prior generations. What is implied is that an earlier generation
does not have the motivation to help the least-advantaged of future generations that it does its own generation, for that motivation, to be presented in detail below, is wholly one of self-interest. It is not, then, that
application of the difference principle would be unjust in some sense
other than that of Rawls who requires the derivation of the just from
rational self-interest in the original position; it is that decision makers
would not adopt it out of self-interest. In Rawls's dynamic context, the
difference principle's application in any particular own-generation is
constrained by the just savings passed on to the future, where those just
savings are determined in some unspecified manner. But this view of the
inapplicability of the difference principle to intergenerational justice
conflicts with the acceptance of a zero rate of time preference, as will be
shown in chapter 6.

In summary, then, the core of the principles of intergenerational justice is the set of savings principles adopted in the original position. But
the motivation that dictates—in Rawls's view—the two principles in the
static context cannot determine a savings principle, given generational
ignorance, a zero rate of time preference, and irreversible time. Somehow, Rawls asserts, the just savings principle will emerge, and its form will
be a constraint on the static difference principle, as indeed it is stated in
the Second Principle.

Assume with Rawls that in the veil of ignorance of the original position
the participants will adopt a zero rate of time preference, which is to say
that they will not distinguish between the satisfactions received in the
various generations wholly on the basis of distance from the present.
This springs from the ignorance of the participants concerning the generation to which they will belong, so that prudence dictates they treat all
generations as equally important with respect to their preferences inso-

far as time of consumption alone is concerned. Violating rationality in this sense, therefore, a positive rate of time preference violates justice, permitting earlier generations to take advantage of later. However, Rawls believes an "interest rate" would exist as a means of allocating scarce investment resources among uses and because of the downgrading of future satisfactions that would occur with (1) the rise in the living standards of those generations because of their increasing capital provision and (2) the progress of technology that may be expected to occur. Presumably, however, the information that incorporates these factors will not be available in the original position, so that the principle of savings that emerges must do so with a zero interest rate.

Throughout the discussion of the distributive shares received in both the static and dynamic frameworks of his theories, Rawls speaks interchangeably of organizing the economy with a market form or a socialist form that uses markets as allocative mechanisms and permits free choice of occupations, believing either is consistent with his principles of justice. But his difference principle envisions such interferences with a market economy's distribution and the principle of equality of fair opportunity implies such great constraints on individual enterprise that it is impossible to envision a market economy functioning effectively. His framework of reference is better described as a democratic socialism which uses markets to achieve efficiency of allocation when tax transfers and "adjustments in the rights of property" have effected the equality of fair opportunity and the difference principle.

The Rationale of the Principles

Why would a set of contractarian principals, enshrouded in a veil of ignorance, with no knowledge of their position in society, their prospects for success in that society, any probability associated with that position of success, their attitudes toward risk, their generational locus, or any other characteristic of the society or their own personalities that might bias their choice among alternative principles of social justice elect the First and Second Principles with the associated lexicographic orderings? Despite Rawls's initial attempts to interpret the context of the contractual negotiations as one of bargaining, clearly it is not. Each individual must consult his or her self-interest and each will be led within the confines of that isolated egoistic self-seeking to adopt the Rawlsian principles without any necessary interaction with other participants. The individual is playing a game against Nature, where Nature's set of strategies is a group of positions in a collection of alternative social states distinguished by level of material achievement among other factors.

How would such individuals go about selecting a strategy from a finite set whose content is the principles of social justice that will form the basic or background institutions of the society? The individual is without knowledge of the exact content of Nature's states, the probabilities of their occurrence, the payoffs that would be forthcoming from any of Nature's states given any of the participant's strategies, the relevance of those payoffs to the unknown goals in his or her rational plan of life, the form of his or her satisfaction function over such uncertain payoffs, and the nature of his or her attitudes to risk-taking.

The core assumption of Rawls concerning the state of mind of individuals in this position of seemingly numbing ignorance is *that they would act as if they were risk-averse even in the absence of their knowledge of their psychological attitudes.* As conservative, self-protective individuals, seeking to insure themselves against the dire potential of the worst states of nature, they would play a *maximin* strategy, designed to prevent Nature from reducing their liberty and their material status below a guaranteed floor. To protect themselves from others and from their own potential temptation to sacrifice self-respect for material goods, they would establish the First Principle of equal civil liberty and its priority over other principles of justice. Rawls argues that when individuals have no basis for estimating the probabilities over the likelihoods of Nature's states or his or her location in them, the marginal utility of primary goods above the guaranteed maximin minimum quota is viewed as declining rapidly, and where receipt of such primary goods in quantities below those of the maximin floor is viewed as disastrous, the individual would be led to elect the conservative maximin strategy. Each individual in the hypothetical state of ignorance would be led to such a strategy, and hence classic social contract unanimity would be achieved. To insure against Nature placing them in a state of material destitution with the attendant loss of self-respect, all would be led to identify with the least-advantaged group in the society and would seek to raise the expectations of that group as high as possible. Maximizing the minimum payoff would occur when all citizens received equal incomes or, if opportunities arose, when some inequality was permitted that allowed the floor income received by the least-advantaged to rise. Hence the Second Principle, which is ranked by participants above the need for efficiency. It is the validity of this line of reasoning hypothesized by Rawls for every rational participant in the original position that is at the center of the disputes that revolve about his theory. The critique of Rawls's work in chapter 6 will center about this rationalization.

Reflective Equilibrium

But Rawls does not rest his case for the principles of social justice at this point, especially in his later work. Rather, he believes that after derivation of the principles, decision makers initiate an iterative, interactive process of engagement with a body of pre-absorbed moral precepts of an intuitionist cast.[44] Interaction among the principles and these moral precepts, presumably occurring within the context of social debate, results in compromise or alteration of the original position principles or their imposition to override or alter the moral precepts until a reflective equilibrium is achieved among them. This new body of principles, in R. Dworkin's view, converts the model to a constructive body of ethical principles for a body of citizens similar in their choice of alternative theories in the original position and in the moral intuitions rather than discovering preexisting moral law—a view that corresponds to Rawls's present position.[45]

Reflective equilibrium introduces, therefore, absent precise definition of the content of the motivating moral precepts, a good deal of ambiguity into the Rawlsian final product. Indeed, I would suppose that a primary source of such intuitions derives from what I define as the ethos of liberalism as discussed in chapter 1 and to be elaborated further in chapter 7.[46] If it has the allegiance I believe it has and should have, it is difficult to see how any workable compromise between it and the original position propositions could be attained short of the evisceration of the difference and the fair equality of opportunity principles. Nonetheless, it must be viewed as an admirable attempt by Rawls to bring his abstract principles into a realistic context and to provide a framework for their operational usage consistent with an overlapping consensus.

The Institutional Implementation

After the extensive presentation of the derivation and motivation of the principles of justice, Rawls faces the difficult task of defining the institutions that would be necessary to implement the principles of reflective equilibrium as an effective, operational system of distributive justice. Indeed, Rawls makes it clear repeatedly that the purpose of the principles is to shape the background institutions of the constitutional democracy that incorporates them into its ethos. The society that is equipped to implement the potentially altered or subdued notions of equal justice, fair equality of opportunity, and the difference principle constrained by the undefined principle of just saving has (1) a constitutional protection of equal liberties, (2) a fair chance for education and culture through the subsidization of private educational opportunity and the establishment of a public educational system, (3) government guarantees of a social minimum receipt of primary goods through family allowances and payments on health insurance account or by negative income tax provisions, (4) corrective procedures to correct externalities and monopoly power of consequence, and (5) stabilizing institutions to maintain full employment.

Such institutions constitute a substantial role for government in the economic and distributive mechanisms, but Rawls attempts to maintain a neutrality in the type of economy most suited to effectuate such functions: "Throughout the choice between a private-property economy and socialism is left open; from the standpoint of the theory of justice alone, various basic structures would appear to satisfy its principles."[47] However, it becomes clear from Rawls's discussion that the use of markets in the society would be almost wholly allocative: the use of extensive taxes and transfer mechanisms to effect the difference principle would result in serious infringements on the right to proceeds from private property and substantial modifications of the receipts from sale of factor services on their markets, not excluding restrictions on the amounts of productive property owned by individuals. The envisioned society is one of democratic socialism using markets as efficient allocative mechanisms, but constraining them via tax and subsidy transfers from their distributive functions. Moreover, the state must determine an "interest rate" that allocates new investment efficiently among competing uses—certainly a function of such great social import that forbidding its determination to the free market goes far to eviscerate the capitalist anatomy.

Nor is it clear where the "social minimum" fits into the operational scheme to implement the difference principle, except as a resulting compromise in the reflective equilibrium. The pure original position principles of justice dictate equality of income as an initial position, modified by the difference and savings principles, effected by taxes on the more-advantaged to benefit the least-advantaged in a long-term sense. In what sense is such a distributive rule "setting a minimum"? From the theoretical discussion it involves the determination of the baseline receipts of primary goods payable to a large majority of the population. In no sense is it a "minimum" payable as a safety net. Indeed, "once the difference principle is accepted, however, it follows that the minimum is to be set at that point which, taking wages into account, maximizes the expectations of the least advantaged group."[48] It is not easy to understand the manner in which Rawls envisions the administration of the difference principle, nor the degree to which it will permit a variance in the distribution of primary goods.

The Feasibility of the Institutional Structure

Finally, given the definition of the principles and their institutionalization in the social structure, what are the prospects for their feasibility in providing the basis for an acceptable social process? What compromises or outright abandonments of the original position in the reflective equilibrium principles might have to be made to salvage their major outlines?

What Rawls terms the "stability" of the system or what might more accurately be called its "viability" hinges in his view on the moral development of individuals. He develops a theory of the development of that moral sense based on moral psychology and then faces the fundamental dilemma: in a society whose background institutions are shaped by the principles of justice, rational individuals will perceive that they can benefit by acting unjustly. What will restrain most individuals from doing so, and thus permit the society to function? Rawls's deontological answer is that the development of a sense of reciprocity of love and affection—a responding in emotional kind to treatment in the family and the circle of friendship—in the maturation process will extend to the society and lead individuals to forego such egoistic actions. Such development is to be contrasted with the notion of a sympathy for mankind that utilitarians depend on to confront the question. Rawls disputes the assertion that such a general altruistic feeling is general in societies, although his later attention to the moral person in a well-ordered society may well have altered his position.

In addition, an important feature of the Rawlsian principles of justice is their fostering of self-esteem via the difference principle and the principle of fair equality of opportunity. The lessened inequality and greater opportunities of such a social regime will eliminate much of the envy that is grounded in lack of confidence in the market economy and give effective meaning to the notion of "fraternity."

Finally, Rawls argues that a society characterized by the First and Second Principles has an advantage over one whose institutions are shaped by other theories of justice because there is a congruence of the right and the good. The good of the individual is the fulfillment of a life plan according to the principles of right the Rawlsian tenets define. The conception of the good springs from the notions of the right, so that the ends of the individual as well as the means of attaining them are solidly based on justice. In other theories, Rawls believes, and most importantly his major target—utilitarianism—a theory of the good is defined and the principles of right are subordinated to it. He feels that the individual is much more tempted to subordinate those principles when tempted by self-interest.

A SUMMARY

To keep the discussion of social justice in perspective, it is helpful to note that not all of the decisions an individual makes in the course of his living involve morality or justice. Indeed, it is more realistic to say that a small minority of them does. That subset of decisions involving justice is concerned only with those that have nonnegligible potential for a significantly harmful or beneficial impact on the welfare of others. The more close-knit the society, the more interdependent its citizens, and the more highly structured its institutions, the larger will be the subset as a proportion of all decisions. In the specifics of economic justice, the greater the complexity of economic interdependence and its implied need for citizen interaction and cooperation, the greater the need for a canon of equity principles to guide the design and functioning of the economic mechanisms.

Thinkers who have derived such principles and discern in them a strong emphasis on the obligations of individuals to assume an active responsibility for the welfare of others are featured in this chapter. I have isolated three such theoretical designs as influential intellectually and representative of their species. These include Kant's deontological search for imperatives that reason dictates to be principles of justice; the utilitarian's definition of such teleological principles by their capability of maximizing total or per capita welfare; and the Rawlsian derivation of such dictates from fearful prudence in a state of dense ignorance.

Kant is by far the most abstract of the theorists, grounding his theory in one characteristic of the human being—his reason—and abstracting from all other particulars of his or her situation or the nature of the world. The goal of the exercise is to construct the most *fundamental* principles of individual moral behavior that will aggregate into a body of principles for social justice binding in any society of human beings or indeed of *rational* beings—a distinction Kant makes frequently in his quest for generality. The result is, most importantly, a nonconsequentialist (i.e., a strict deontological) definition of morality that is based wholly on the motivation of the actor, and which prescribes action which the reasonable being would desire to become a universal law for all who act under the same circumstances. Such *categorical imperatives*, which afford no opportunity for the moral individual to ignore, include the duty of aiding others in their search for satisfactions, material and otherwise.

In the sphere of economic activity, the categorical imperatives imply the duty of conforming to voluntarily entered contracts, respecting private property, and more broadly treating others as moral beings who are ends in themselves as well as means for our own ends. Their economic welfare is of concern to every moral citizen and each is obligated to further the happiness of others. Those social functions that I have labeled *corrective* and *compassionate* fit within the Kantian ethic. One may quarrel with his notion that an action can be moral only if performed out of a sense of duty and contrary to the natural inclinations of the actor. Effectively, actions conforming to the categorical imperatives even when performed to obtain a higher sense of personal satisfaction produce effects with social equity consequences and constrain the individual's egoistic drives. Indeed, one might question whether those constraints may be excessive from the viewpoint of a social ethic reflecting the individualistic basis of society in the first sense of that word.

Utilitarianism is much less ambitious a theory of social justice, being satisfied with a search for rules of moral action on the premise that man's rightful goal in life is happiness and morality consists in facilitating its achievement in a social sense. Reason plays a role in discerning this social dimension by providing the insights of enlightened self-interest in one's relations with others. But so does the feeling of sympathy with one's fellows and the indulgence of man's social instincts. The corrective and compassionate functions are vitally enveloped by the utilitarian's goal of maximizing average per capita income, of necessity at the expense of the egoistic strivings of some individuals—perhaps most. This guiding social principle must suppress the egoistic goals of individuals to an even greater extent than Kantian principles, and must raise even more forcefully the question of balance between egoistic and social rights.

The Rawlsian exercise is Kantian in its ambition, methodology, and sourcing of principles, but much more explicit in its derived principles and their application. Also, as Rawls notes, the Kantian direction of principles determination is reversed in Rawlsian theory: social principles are derived directly as frameworks within which personal principles are to be integrated.[49]

Principles of justice that lead individuals to an extreme renunciation of egoistic strivings are derived, paradoxically, from motivations of the most selfish nature. Are such principles themselves derived ethically by forcing individuals to decide on them in a state of fearful ignorance? Would they indeed agree on the Rawlsian principles unanimously? If so, can they be asked to abide by their egoistic renunciations and sacrifice of rewards of self-expression in an operational context, outside the veil of ignorance? To what extent does the process of achieving reflective equilibrium invalidate the Rawlsian principles?

The questions that are raised are vital to our goal of defining an operational theory of social justice for capitalism, and they must be addressed to the theories of chapter 2 as well if we are to make progress. It is therefore, time to turn, in the next three chapters, to the critique of both sets of theories with the constructive purpose of defining an acceptable theory of economic justice for modern capitalistic society.

Chapter 4

A FRAMEWORK FOR JUDGMENT

THE DISTINCTION BETWEEN ECONOMIC ETHICS AND ECONOMIC JUSTICE

In chapter 1 *social equity* was defined to be a concept which is dichotomized into *social ethics* and *social justice*, leaving them to be distinguished later. The distinction that is now adopted follows John Stuart Mill's definitions of *duties of imperfect obligation* and *duties of perfect obligation*, which closely parallel Kant's notions of the hypothetical and categorical imperatives but are not identical to them.[1] I shall use social (and, more narrowly, economic) ethics to denote the former and social (economic) justice the latter. The concepts have been discussed in the treatment of Mill's utilitarianism in chapter 3, but it will be helpful to review them briefly in their present usage.

Economic ethics in this view is concerned with a set of principles to guide social and private actions that have moral implications and that establish obligations affording the agent a choice of time, place, and circumstances in which to obey them. The obligation to aid others in economic distress, to contribute to private charities, to perform volunteer work in civic causes, or to serve as mentor to the young in their professional advancement are duties that one is frequently entreated to perform as ethical responsibilities at times, places, and circumstances of one's choice and involving persons of one's election. The force of obligation is less than total in the sense that sanctions for nonperformance are not administered by the power of the state acting as society's agent.

Economic justice is administered with the support of such sanctions. It is applicable when social or private actions have impacts on individuals that threaten their lives, property, or well-being in such material ways that the duty to perform or not perform such actions is unconditional and failure to conform is punished by legal sanctions. Mitigating circumstances may exist, but the onus of proof lies on the individual and the judgment of their acceptability is within the province of legal authorities. The payment of taxes, avoidance of force and fraud in one's economic dealings with others, conformity to contractual obligations, respect of others' property rights, prudent fulfillment of fiduciary responsibilities, and so forth are matters of economic justice in this definition. In such matters others have the correlative right to demand that one fulfill one's duties unconditionally.

Adoption of principles of economic justice, therefore, imposes the obligation on the state to give statutory or constitutional standing to such principles and the authority to impose penalties for nonobservance of such economic obligations. The major goal of this work is to define an operational system of economic justice at the constitutional level rather than a total set of economic equity principles that would embrace ethics as well as justice.

The Necessity of a Bill of Economic Rights

A rather surprising feature of the American Constitution is that its economic prescriptions are minimal and generally confined to narrow specifics. Most particularly, the direct economic content of the Bill of Rights is confined to the Fifth Amendment protecting property from seizure without due process or compensation. The First Amendment's protection of freedom of speech, religion, press, assembly and petition, for example, does not extend to economic rights to acquire and transfer property, to engage without hindrance in occupations, or to equality in competition for reward. Further, it does not establish the obligation of government to provide basic necessities for those incapable of providing for themselves. The Founding Fathers, immersed in the agrarian, commercial, and pre-industrial manufacturing age, did not foresee the needs of a far more complex and interrelated society than the locally and regionally self-subsistent economies of their acquaintance. Their concern with economic issues was almost wholly restricted to the division of economic powers between the federal and state governments.

The point can best be made by briefly listing the entire economic content of the document, as presented below.

ARTICLE I. LEGISLATIVE BRANCH

SECTION 2. Direct taxes will be apportioned among the states according to population (excluding Indians and including slaves at .6 person each). [This was amended by Amendment 16 which excepted an income tax from this rule.]

SECTION 7. All revenue bills shall originate in the House of Representatives, but the Senate may make changes in such bills as in any other bills.

SECTION 8. Powers granted to Congress:

a. To levy and collect taxes, duties, imposts and excises, and to pay the debts of the United States. All duties, imposts, and excises shall be the same in all parts of the nation.

b. To borrow money on the credit of the United States.

c. To regulate commerce with foreign nations, interstate commerce, and commerce with the Indian tribes.

d. To establish uniform bankruptcy laws.

e. To coin money, regulate its value, and determine the value of foreign money circulating in the nation.

f. To set punishment for counterfeiting.

g. To establish copyright and patent laws.

h. To raise money to support an army with appropriations for not more than two years.

i. To make laws needed to carry out the responsibilities assigned by the Constitution. [The "elastic clause" forming the basis for much legislation not explicitly authorized in the Constitution.]

SECTION 9.   Powers denied to the Federal government:

a. Slaves will not be permitted to be imported after 1808, but until that time an import duty of no more than $10 per slave may be imposed.

b. No capitation or direct tax may be levied unless in proportion to population as determined by Census. [Amendment 16 provided that income tax was an exception.]

c. No tax can be levied on exports from one state to another or to abroad.

d. No preference can be given the commerce going through the port of one state over another nor can waterborne traffic between states be taxed.

e. All money spent by Treasury must have been appropriated and the accounts for receipts and expenditures made public.

SECTION 10.   Powers denied the States:

a. No state can coin money, issue bills of credit or allow other money than U.S. legal tender to pass, nor pass any law impairing the obligation of contracts.

b. No state can tax imports or exports except for fees for inspection without consent of Congress and, if given consent, the net receipts must be delivered to Treasury.

c. No state without consent of Congress can levy a duty on ships entering its ports.

ARTICLE V. SUPREMACY OF FEDERAL LAWS

1.   All debts contracted by the Confederation before the date of the Constitution will be assumed by the United States.

AMENDMENT 14. CIVIL RIGHTS GUARANTEED (1868)

1.   No state can deprive any individual of life, liberty or property without due process of law, nor deny to any person within its jurisdiction equal protection of the laws.

2.   Validity of the public debt of the United States incurred during the Civil War shall not be questioned, but no debt is assumed by the United States or any state for debts of the Confederacy or for claims for loss or emanicipation of slaves. They are null and void.

AMENDMENT 16. INCOME TAX (1913)

1. Congress shall have power to lay and collect taxes on incomes, from whatever sources derived, without apportionment among the states and without regard to the Census. [In 1895 the Supreme Court had ruled that an income tax law passed in 1894 was unconstitutional.]

AMENDMENT 24. POLL TAX PROHIBITION (1964)

1. The right to vote for federal office shall not be denied for failure to pay poll or other taxes.

The prosaic nature of most of these provisions, with the exceptions of the prohibition on the states' passage of legislation impairing contractual obligations and the protection of property by due process, contrasts dramatically with the political and civil protections of the Bill of Rights. The preamble contains no reference to economic goals, and from the body of the document one misses the vision of a sanctioned and protected economic liberty that one finds in its political content.

Congress thereby gains a much freer hand in economic policy than it has in the area of political and civil rights. But it also receives much less guidance and potential for resisting the selfish demands of highly organized and well-funded interest groups. An integrated body of rights and duties of individuals and the state, based on a corpus of principles of economic justice consistent with other social goals and the American ethos—a bill of *economic* rights—should be incorporated in the Constitution as both a constraint on and a support to congressional economic policy making.

The function of determining economic policy has, in the absence of clear constitutional authority, devolved on all levels of the judiciary, which have sought to resolve conflicts by extending clauses whose intent was political into the economic arena. Interstate commerce, due process, and the elastic clauses have been applied to issues of economic justice with questionable authority and highly debatable results. Explicit constitutional definition of the principles of economic justice that should guide economic policy will restore legislative power to its rightful situs and provide the judiciary with clearer principles for interpretation.

An Economic Contractarian Experiment

Hence, that which is sought in this work at its most ambitious are principles to guide the construction of a formal economic constitution which would codify the nation's most fundamental guarantees and protections of distributive rights. Such a document—a bill of economic rights—codifying the nation's principles of economic justice must be based firmly on the projection into the economic sector of the social and political concepts of freedom embedded in the American ethos and made explicit in the Constitution and its judicial interpretation. Most fundamentally, it must, in its formulation, define principles for determining the balance between both facets of individualism—the egoistic and the compassionate. Such principles must possess the flexibility inherent in the political Constitution, accommodating and shaping desirable shifts in the balance over time but constraining change within channels that protect inviolable egoistic and compassionate rights. It must, in short, define the charter of an American "compassionate capitalism."

The framework, then, is social contractarian, but one that rejects the desirability of or necessity for universal participation in defining the economic charter. In the spirit of the historical process that formulated the American Constitution, the following situation is defined and set of questions posed:

> Suppose a group of the most gifted intellectual and professional persons, with ideological commitments but no personal or career interests at stake other than those of the involved citizen, were to draw upon the best ethical theory available to write an economic constitution intended for adoption by the American society. What are the constitutive principles of economic justice that would guide their design of such a legal framework and how would those principles be made immanent in the more important legal provisions concerning distributive economic relations? How would such provisions reflect the compromises necessary for the coordination of ideological predilections along the spectrum of moral commitment, especially as those compromises bear upon the balance between egoistic and compassionate rights and obligations?

The contractarian paradigm is a *hypothetical* construct for the probing of the nature of a vital social foundation: the structure of the legal framework within which the society organizes its economic distributive institutions. It is in the nature of an intellectual experimental instrument as it was in social contractarian thought from Hobbes through Rawls. Still it has the additional advantage that it is closer to potential realistic achievement than these distinguished forbears, and indeed possesses an exemplification in the American constitutional framing in the late 1780s. With such a realistic relevance, the scheme is not without some hope of actual implementation in the future—a hope which gives added interest to the results of an experiment that does not need that hope to be valuable analytically.

For the achievement of its purposes, the constituting conditions in which the economic compact is derived permit some advantages over earlier usage. First, because the purpose of the exercise is not to search primitive reason to discern a set of natural rights and obligations, so it is unnecessary to seek unanimous consent from a participation that includes all reasonable persons. The principles deduced from such presumed rights and obligations are the moral and physical integrity of the individual and their projection in personal property. The hypothetical constituent convention is instructed to accept them as primitives beyond dispute and to interpret their implications in the light of the best relevant ethical theory and the body of institutions, values, and beliefs that have evolved historically into the American ethos.

Such defined tasks demand the finest intellectual and professional talent with knowledge and skills in social philosophy, jurisprudence, and policy formation. The criteria of selection must be openly meritocratic, and as far removed from the debasing activities of interest groups as practical democratic politics permits.

Second, once formulated, existing procedures and rules for amending the Constitution may be envisaged as means of gaining democratic approval for the document. Those rules reflect the type of formalized social and political ethos it is the purpose of this exercise to extend to the economic sectors, and they are therefore relevant to the American political process of consent. A ready-made, operational mode of testing assent that does not demand unanimity and need not substitute mere majority rule preexists the exercise.

Third, the experiment need not be conducted with a set of Rawlsian participants groping in a veil of ignorance concerning the nature of the society within which the sought-for principles must be incorporated as well as their own ideological leanings. The objectivity of the experts with respect to their self-interest is obtained in a credible manner and with less sacrifice of reality through the choice process. Unlike Rawls's original position, in framing the economic compact a relatively small number of expert participants whose freedom from self-serving is assured by their eminence can frame the basis for institutions in full knowledge of their intended context and free from the risk averse motivation of fear of the unknown.

The artifice of the social contract is used to address both the political and the philosophical questions that it was designed to probe. The first, historically, was the origin of state sovereignty and the consequent role and limitations of government power. The second was to discern the principles of justice to which rational men would assent in the broader task of forming a society. In the matter of economic justice the two purposes are closely allied, in that the execution of the corrective and the compassionate principles adopted by a society must fall largely to government with the use of state power because of the inherent dedication of the market economy to egoistic goal-seeking.

What questions, then, might the participants in such a constituent assembly pose to the body of ethical thought summarized in chapters 2 and 3 in seeking guidance in their task and in judging the relevance of such theory to *economic* justice? What inquisitive framework of reference might be generalized as a means of isolating alternative principles, judging logical completeness and consistency, gauging conformity to competing social goals, and assessing compatibility with those value and belief systems that I have denoted "the American ethos"?

THE CONCEPT OF THE GOOD EXPLICIT OR IMPLICIT IN THE THEORY

Theories of social equity differ in their conceptions of the objectives in private or social life that should be sought as *moral* ends of human existence. They bring into question both the individual's and society's quest for meaningful spiritual content in their actions and implicitly or explicitly define those criteria for choice that yield or should yield high or highest spiritual value. Of greatest interest to the present work, of course, are the implications of those criteria for private and social acts in economic life.

A series of questions can be addressed to each theory to better understand its structure and its relevance to the purposes of the hypothetical constituent assembly.

1. Does the theory explicitly or implicitly define the good as the ends toward which individual and/or social existence should be directed? If so, what is it?
2. If it does not, what types of such ends might it accommodate?
3. What is the subset of the ends derived from 1 or 2 that is relevant to economic actions?
4. How consistent are the proper ends so defined for the *individual* with such ends for *society*?
5. How does the theory derive the definition of the good?
   a. Is the set of criteria deduced from the rational faculty of man?
   b. Does the definition rest on some intuitive appeal of the good itself?
   c. Is the notion of the good derived in authoritarian manner (e.g., from religious notions of God's will or the sovereignty of the state)?
6. How well does the definition of the good conform to existing social institu-

tions and the needs of functioning social mechanisms? How difficult would it be to adopt such guidelines for a practical theory of economic equity with respect to the operation of such social mechanisms, especially the economic?

THE DEFINITION OF THE RIGHT IN THE THEORY

A second and more fundamental constituent of a theory of social equity is the concept of *right* that is presented. The right is a set of principles defining actions that receive moral sanction from a theory either from the prior definition of the good or as an independent derivation from the ethical theory. In utilitarianism, for example, the greatest happiness principle defines the good in human life and the right is obtained derivatively as that set of principles protecting the freedom of the individual to achieve private happiness or defining redistributive measures for the state to achieve the good in a social sense. On the other hand Kant derives the right in direct fashion in terms of the imperatives and the duties they impose on the individual. The good life led in conformance to duty is then implied by the right.

The core of an operational theory of justice consists of these principles that define proper private and social conduct. Philosophers may argue different viewpoints on the notion of the good life and the ends of man and yet be in fundamental agreement on the concept of the right. That is, a variety of beliefs concerning the good may coexist with a single notion of the right and, indeed, the good may be left undefined in some theories. But no theory can leave its principles defining proper action unclear and retain any pretence of usefulness.[2]

To examine these principles critically, the following questions should be addressed to theories of social equity.

1. What are the principles of the right that are derived in the theory?
2. Which of them are relevant to economic action?
3. How does the theory derive the definition of the right?
   a. Are the principles deduced from the rational faculty?
   b. Does the definition rest on some intuitive appeal of the principles?
   c. Is the notion of right action based on authoritarian prescription?
4. What is the relation of the right to the good in the theory?
5. Are the principles consistent with existing social institutions and the needs of functioning social mechanisms, especially the economic? How difficult would it be to adopt such principles for a practical theory of economic justice in the sense of conforming to or conflicting with the values necessary to energize the economic system and permit it to function effectively?

CONFORMITY TO MORAL BEHAVIOR

A theory of social ethics, having defined its principles of right action, must consider the effectiveness of the rewards and sanctions it implies or establishes to impose compliance. Most important, what is the bearing of this consideration on the necessity of enforcement using the authority of the state? This concern with the problems of economic justice has been discussed in the beginning of the chapter.

The following questions will aid in judging the theories with respect to the nature of the economic justice they establish.

1. In light of the theory, why should an individual faced with a choice elect to do what right action prescribes when it is against his or her self-interest?
2. Are the internalized rewards and sanctions plausible sources of a generalized enforcement?
3. To what extent does the theory threaten the sense of national cohesiveness?
4. Does the theory threaten an excessive need for external enforcement? That is, to what extent must such principles be the concern of justice rather than only morality?
5. What are bearings of the answers to 1 to 4 specifically for economic actions?

INTEGRABILITY WITH THE ETHOS

A last question is one that is the most difficult to answer yet one that must be addressed if our labors are to have any useful outcome: How well does the theory draw on and merge with the American ethos, assuming that the latter can be adequately defined?

Any society instituting a system of economic justice has a multiplicity of social goals, norms, mechanisms, values, and beliefs which act both as constraints on and enablers of systems of justice. Among these institutions are operating private and social mechanisms to perform decision-making tasks in the society. A system of economic justice must integrate into this ethos, adapting to it in some ways, forcing adaptations in it in others. No operational system of justice can be relevant if it is developed independently of the context within which it must function and without reference to its deeply rooted major features. The point may seem trivial, but it is frequently ignored by social philosophers whose concern with logical consistency and intuitive appeal has led them to ignore the broader social setting of their efforts. While it is true that the "ought" is distinct from the "is," and that the "ought" is not derivable from the "is," the "is" constrains the acceptability and operability of the "ought." Moreover, it is frequently difficult to separate constraints on the "ought" from dictation of its contents.

But what is the "American ethos," or this collective consciousness which defines the "representative" vision of social reality of the "typical" citizen? The concept is multidimensional, attributional rather than quantitative, definable wholly by subjective observation, and with components capable of interpretation only as central tendencies about which individual variances may be quite large. An object less accessible to analysis by scientific process would be difficult to imagine. Yet who would doubt not only its presence but its eminence among the forces that shape the nation's social, political, and economic processes, institutions, and policies? Measurability is not a prerequisite for existence nor simplicity of structure a necessity for strength of influence.

The ethos is a dynamic entity, in constant flux, subject to challenge and questioning, but absorbing change rather slowly over time. In the United States it is rooted in the historical experience of a people whose political institutions were shaped by seventeenth-century religious and eighteenth-century liberal thought, overlaid with waves of nineteenth-century religious evangelicalism and territorial expansion, the contradicting self-doubt of the slavery issue and the rise of modern industrialism, and shaken by the twentieth-century challenges of Marxism, fascism, and various forms of antirationalism. The threads of continuity are evident and basically intact over this three hundred-year period, but adaptation has occurred. However, bodies of thought that were foreign to the fabric, although they may have forced changes, were rejected when they demanded sharp breaks of a nonincremental nature.

What major themes in this ethos must a theory of economic justice confront in seeking integration? Which, that is, must be viewed as effective constraints on or substantial supports of such a theory, but capable at best of incremental adaptations? What ideational dedications in the national character define its elasticity in coping with notions of economic justice that are nonconformist to the status quo?

Without the intention of putting forward an exhaustive list, it is suggested that the following three are predominant. Their interrelationships are so complex that they are not mutually independent, but taken together they form a gestalt with the characteristics sought. They have been identified in chapter 1 as among the cultural reinforcements of the market mechanism, so that the amplification here will be limited to their relevance to the definition of rules of economic justice.

Individualism

In chapter 1 individualism was adopted as a primitive to screen out from consideration theories of social equity that do not rest solidly on the notions of the dignity and the moral inviolability of the individual. This choice of filter at the very start of the study is a witness to the dominance given this strain in the national ethos. It is the bedrock of governmental structure and policy, the foundation of the economic mechanism, the source of the citizen's civil protections, and an important underpinning of the mores and folkways that characterize interpersonal interactions. When its implications are violated in private or social relations, it instills a strong sense of contradiction that impels toward resolution and correction. It is so honored in the breach as well as the observance, and constitutes the dominant moral imperative of the American cultural persona.

By individualism I mean to denote and connote the principle that the individual is by virtue of his or her existence alone a moral entity with an inviolable claim on other individuals for the respect of physical and spiritual freedom, moral integrity, and the opportunity to manifest them as self-respect. Individualism in this sense is more fundamental than, but subsumes, *individuality*, which distinguishes the individual from others on the basis of a complex of physical attributes, talents, abilities, skills, knowledge, character and behavioral traits, and attitudes. Existence itself is the most basic claim that individualism establishes in a society that is forced thereby to respect the sanctity of human life, but those obligations extend far beyond this right to life.

Respect for the spiritual integrity of the individual requires that his or her will be given a radius of freedom that is bounded only by the coordinate radius of freedom that is reserved for others. *Freedom* from the will of others when that will is arbitrary in the sense of noncompliance with this limitation is thus an implication of individualism. Social mechanisms and institutions must be shaped in such manners as to minimize the restrictions on such individual freedom, and restrictions that extend beyond the need to protect the like freedom of others must be justified only on the basis of the highest social need.

The demand for freedom implies, therefore, that insofar as is feasible social mechanisms must incorporate the motivating forces of *voluntarism*. That is, individuals must be given the freedom to choose among alternatives following their own inclinations, and the social results of such actions must not be overruled except for compelling corrective or compassionate reasons. Collective decision making incorporating the decentralized voluntary actions of individuals is endorsed by the ethos as a manifestation of freedom which is itself grounded on individualism.

Historically, another projection of individualism is the right to acquire *property*, which is to obtain the power to exclude others from the possession or enjoyment of goods that are gained from voluntaristic social mechanisms whose results are untarnished by fraud or exercise of unacceptable power and whose use does not violate the freedom of others. The proprietary rights in one's own being project into such claims on one's capabilities which in turn project into proprietary rights to the rewards given by voluntaristic social mechanisms for such capabilities.

Individualism also implies the rightness of egoistic motivation in political, social, and economic decision making, providing it does not lead to violation of the same rights possessed by others or other implications of individualism. The acceptability of the individual's acting in his or her own self-interest permeates American culture as a dominant strand to the point frequently that its exercise becomes interpreted as a social duty or at least as a manifestation of one's self-respect.

The obverse of the rights that are sourced in individualism are the obligations that accompany them. The freedom to exercise free will in voluntaristic social mechanisms implies a responsibility for one's actions. Such duties are the primary obligation to provide for the material welfare of oneself and one's dependents; to honor contracts or other agreements made voluntarily; to respect the bounds to freedom of action implied by others' similar claims; to accept the rights of others to act egoistically and the property rights created by such action; and to respect the rights of others to the opportunity for self-respect.

This last obligation is present in the American ethos but is dominated by what was termed the *egoistic* strand of individualism whose nature was delineated in the forgoing discussion. It is the *compassionate* strain of the individualistic tenet and frequently conflicts with the expression of egoism. Its manifestation in the culture therefore often invokes a constraint on the much stronger drives grounded in egoistic individualism, and its proper bounds are therefore not as readily defined as those on rights and obligations implied by egoism's self-limitations. Nonetheless, however begrudged, individualism dictates that every person be given a reasonable opportunity to achieve the self-respect that derives in the ethos from acting successfully in voluntaristic social mechanisms under egoistic motivation, or, failing the ability to do that, be supported by society outside such mechanisms in a manner that conforms to those needs. But the coexistence of the compassion strand, with its implied sense of concern for others, does not always stand in opposition to self-interest. The strength of voluntary pro bono activity, of private charity, and of civic responsibility in the American ethos are witnesses to broad areas of peaceful synergism of the two strands.

In the current balance between the egoistic and compassionate strands in the ethos, the latter does not imply equality of income or wealth, but it does recognize the obligation to take steps to correct gross inequalities of opportunity to prepare for a successful social life. Also, a second type of equality that is promoted is what was termed *equality of competition for reward* in chapter 1. This involves the expectation that agents will be judged, when in competition with others, on the basis of relevant characteristics only. This facet of individualism was discussed in chapter 1 at some length and need not be repeated here.

The fuzzy boundary between the claims of the egoistic and the compassionate strands of individualism in the ethos, and the sensitivity of its location to the principles whose enunciation is the concern of a theory of economic justice, gives a primary focus to the task at hand. Any operational theory of economic justice must attempt to establish such a boundary with reasoned precision within the currently acceptable bounds the ethos permits and, ideally, to isolate the factors that determine the movement of those bounds over time in order to specify principles that should govern that movement. It is in these particulars that democratic governments become vulnerable to the political power plays of interest groups and are most likely in the distributive function to abandon principles piecemeal. The enunciation of firm guidelines and protections with constitutional authority, therefore, becomes the principal task awaiting the constituent assembly.

Pragmatic Rationalism

In isolating this second strand in the American ethos I mean to denote a mind-set that incorporates components that have been analyzed by such theorists as Veblen, Max Weber, and Schumpeter. They emerged as intellectual forces in the Renaissance, the Reformation, the scientific and technical revolutions that began in the sixteenth century, and the progress of industrial capitalism in the nineteenth and twentieth centuries. Their joint impulses are to establish the frameworks within which physical and social reality are interpreted by the majority of persons and to establish thereby important features of the value and belief systems and the policy institutions of the nation. They are cognitive filters in a sense, or unintentionally established visions of reality that give form and meaning to a nation's ideational artifacts.

To be more specific, the American ethos expresses a dedication to *rationalism* in private and social life. This has many facets, among which the following can be listed as important to the task at hand.

1. A *cause-and-effect* interpretation of phenomena which trains the mind to search for explanations that satisfy the reason. The capacity of

individuals who have developed the habit of employing this outlook in their daily employments to accept mystical explanations of past or present events declines as this view of nature spreads through all strata of society.

2. A *utilitarian* approach to social institutions which seeks their validation in their demonstrable usefulness rather than in the fact of their inheritance from the past culture of the society. A lack of regard or a disrespect for the past, or inherited authority, or tradition is a result. There is the threat of a consequent loss of the sense of historical continuity with the nation's past, or at least a diminution of its perceived importance in determining current social policy.

3. An emphasis on *rational calculation, planning, and foresight* in all life activities to attain defined goals. Activities tend to be viewed as time processes and such processes are valued in terms of duration and time shape of benefits. A kind of formal or informal cost benefit calculus becomes endemic, with close scrutiny of expected or achieved profit and loss, dollars and cents, and the bottom line.

4. *Efficiency* in executing goal-seeking programs receives a great emphasis in the rationalized society. Maximizing output for given input, minimizing time expenditure, "filling every minute with sixty seconds' worth of distance run," attain an importance much beyond that in other cultures. Information generation, transmission, and analysis as aids to the achievement of efficiency become important industries, and indices to summarize progress toward that end are valued instruments. An important emphasis is given measurement, numerate techniques, and scientific endeavor with important technological uses. Technological careers become highly favored in status and remuneration, and humanistic or artistic pursuits with no direct relevance to attaining measurable efficiency in some valued activity tend to become tangential. Striving to become the "best" one can be in one's career as a demonstration of one's efficient use of life produces an imbalance in treatment of living as "doing" rather than "being." As Weber noted, this leads to a dedication to one's career unknown in societies whose cultures permitted a more spontaneous, less time-aware, less goal-directed life.

5. One aspect of the planning-prone society is that of *routinizing* or *bureaucratizing* repetitive process in the desire to achieve efficiency. It was Weber who stressed this component of the rationality syndrome and analyzed its implications for suppressing spontaneity and innovation in great detail.

Pragmatic rationalism—process guided by formal or informal methods to attain practical goals in a consistently and continuously optimal manner gauged by quantitative measures and validated by the evidence of the senses—is a deep-seated trait in the American character. It has, of course, great relevance in the economic concerns of the nation, and its implantation is a prerequisite for the successful performance of a market economy. Indeed, its minimal presence seems necessary for acceptable results from alternative economic mechanisms. The long-term operation of the market economy has had a cause-and-effect relation to pragmatic rationalism, being both a beneficiary and active sculptor of such attitudes.

Materialism

Individualism's stress on personal responsibility for one's well-being and rationalism's impulses toward efficiency in the broad sense used above induce another element in the ethos: *materialism*. The American values material goods and well-being and orients many of his or her most crucial life decisions to attaining them. The choices of a career and the devotion of time to it, selection of a spouse, the circle of friends and acquaintances, the place of residence, one's leisure activities, and many other decisions frequently hinge on one's desire to maximize income. Status and authority are most frequently highly correlated with salary, and even within professions that deemphasize it, rank and prestige are nontheless tied to it.[3]

The monetary unit is the homogeneous unit of material welfare, and so the culture becomes thoroughly "monetized." The role of money in the American society extends far beyond its exchange and financial functions to become an index of desirability, a status symbol, and a social distancing instrument. Individuals are frequently willing to move thousands of miles, leaving close relations and friends, and disrupting the comforting familiars of their lives to better their money incomes by a few thousand dollars per year and the promise of promotion it affords.[4] Such mobility was generally unknown and unthinkable in other societies whose values are less affected by materialism.

Once again the market economy can be singled out as an important creator or reinforcer of such motivations. As a social mechanism the market is both a decision maker and an effectuator of those decisions. As a voluntarist institution the market must impose rewards and sanctions on participants to induce them to follow its allocation wishes and rewards and sanctions that do not depend on the power of the state. Effectively, the only reward it can use consistently is the prospect of greater money returns with the power and status associated with their receipt, and the only sanction their sacrifice. To function with reasonable efficacy, therefore, the market economy depends on a monetized value system and will actively seek to move that system in the needed direction.

For the market economy should not be viewed as a passive mechanism whose adoption has neutral implications for the society's culture. As noted in chapter 1, its core is a set of criteria for choice that are fostered by its very operation, and that operation will give rise to critics and defenders whose dialectic leads to long-term cultural changes that accommodate or constrain the market's functioning.

Sociologists and political economists have long debated the role played by the market economy in the ethos or culture of the liberal society, and this debate has intensified in the last decade, in part as a reaction to the antirationalist critiques of the New Left and its mentors. One school in that dispute urges the one-dimensional impact of the market's functioning on the values and norms of the culture. It is viewed as a dominant social mechanism which acts to substitute the impersonal values of the cash nexus for pre-existing charitable values in the society, and by "commodifying" and materializing the value system poses a threat of destroying a society's coherence and its integrating function for the individual.

The market may be viewed by this school as interacting with other social value and belief systems, but it is generally seen as overcoming any attempts to insulate society from its own cultural impellings or legal and institutional barriers to its cultural hegemony. It is little affected, therefore, by feedbacks from the defensive reactions of more passive social institutions and mechanisms. In recent years such scholars as Fred Hirsch and Michael Walzer have been prominent in presenting such views. Hirsch argues that values stressing cooperation and social responsibility have melted in face of the market's egoistic drives, and that the market's implantation of rational attitudes has converted such intimate relations as marriage and sexual relations to matters of contract and consumer preference.[5] In similar spirit, Walzer laments the seeming inevitability of the market's "imperialism" extending its hegemony over human relations, despite society's attempt to block such activities from its sway. Such "blocked exchanges" are doomed to failure as black markets or their equivalents arise to defeat the social buffers.[6]

Such notions of the unidirectional and irresistible impacts of the market's rationalizing and monetizing and essentially amoral values on the structure and content of the ethos are reinforced by the recent extension of egoistically based microeconomic theory. It has invaded such previously sociological turf as family structure, marriage, crime, education, and divorce.[7]

A second school features a two-directional interaction model of the market with other social value systems, such values both influencing the market's functioning and structure and being affected by them. It urges that the market economy is subject to rather strong and persistent cultural and social constraints, and that the term "market culture" is misleading in its absolutist implications.[8]

The bearing of this school's analyses is that economists, in their monopolization of market modeling, have at least implicitly given too much weight to the strength of rational self-interest in agent motivation and too little attention to the important constraining and conditioning cultural values in explaining behavior. It would impute a great deal more flexibility in the ethos to permit the injection of new elements of economic justice that conflict with the egoistic strand than the first school or my treatment above would indicate.

Sociologists would extend this list of elements in the American culture, but for the purposes of this work those featured above are reasonably exhaustive of the components that have relevance to economic justice. Most of the criticisms and defenses of the market society's impacts on social and individual values can be placed in one or more of the three categories. They must be confronted by any major economic policy proposal, notably if it implies distributive changes. Hence, an operational theory of economic justice must either conform to its imperatives or offer a well-reasoned argument that the ethos should and could change incrementally to accommodate the theory within the time span envisaged.

A SUMMARY

With the general outlines of the prominent theories of social equity discussed in chapters 2 and 3, it is time to propose the question: *What useful guidance can they give in the construction of a set of principles for economic justice in the United States?* A critical analysis of the theories in those chapters will be performed in chapters 5 and 6, and the framework of analysis to be applied to accomplish the task is the substance of this chapter.

A first need is to define more neatly the term "social justice" which has been used rather freely to this point. It is distinguished from social *ethics* through the adoption of John Stuart Mill's distinction between duties of perfect and imperfect obligation. Social justice is concerned with duties of the first type involving acts whose implications for the well-being of others are of such a prime nature that the state assumes the responsibility for overseeing their performance. Such duties therefore are imposed as legally enforceable obligations. Economic justice is that subset of such duties that is relevant to economic acts and the economic welfare of citizens. Social and economic ethics on the other hand are moral duties imposed on individuals more loosely with nonstatutory rewards and sanctions for their performance or nonperformance. Social (economic) justice and social (economic) ethics taken together form social (economic) equity.

The concern in this work is with principles of economic justice and therefore with principles that are encoded in their most general form in an economic constitution. As an intellectual experiment designed to give structure to the manner of derivation of these principles, I have defined a type of social contractarian situation in which select national intellectual talent is formed into a constituent assembly with the purpose of formulating such a bill of economic rights. What guidance would they derive from existing theories of equity? How would their discriminatory choices be guided in confronting the theories?

Four categories of questions that they might address to the theories have been proposed. They concern the concepts of the good and the right explicit or implicit in each schema, the nature of the enforcement process necessary to monitor performance, and the compatibility of the principles obtained from the theories with the American ethos. The most difficult question with the most problematical answers is the last, yet it is potentially the most demanding in terms of establishing the suitability of a theory of economic justice. Three broad categories of components in the American ethos that must accommodate the principles of economic justice have been identified: individualism, with both its egoistic and compassionate strands; rational pragmatism; and materialism.

With this structure of goals and methodology I proceed to the critiques of the theories of social equity to discern that which might be of value in the task of the constituent assembly.

Chapter 5

A CRITIQUE OF THE EGOISTICALLY
ORIENTED THEORIES

IN CHAPTER 2 three basic types of egoistic-directed theories of social equity were presented, with several variants of the contributory theories and the natural rights theories. The relevance of such theories to systems of economic justice in general and to operational systems of economic justice for the American society is not immediately apparent. It is time now to apply the framework developed in chapter 4 to each of the social equity theories of chapter 2 to seek helpful direction in the task of the constituent assembly.

A CRITIQUE OF THE CONTRIBUTORY THEORIES

I showed in chapter 2 that the laissez-faire marginal productivity theory of distribution which is inherent in the free market mechanism's functioning dictates that each agent in the economy draw from the annual social product an amount equal to the value of all of the factor services owned by the agent. Those factor services will be priced at their marginal revenue productivities, which reflect the strength of demand for the goods in whose production the factors are used, the scarcity of such services relative to cooperating factor services, and the ease or difficulty with which other resources can be substituted for the factor service in question. The Marxist contributory variant asserts that property relationships in the capitalist mode of production prevent income distribution from corresponding to what the actual contributory causation—average net product—would dictate.

Both contributory theories have the advantages for my purposes of being narrowly focused on economic justice rather than broader issues of social equity, as well as possessing rather simple structures. Let us examine those structures more closely.

The Concept of the Good

Both contributory theories are incomplete in the sense that they fail to develop from their internal axiomatic foundations notions of the ends toward which private and social living should be devoted. They are exclusively concerned with the derivation of principles of right, and will accommodate any notions of private or social good that do not challenge these principles.[1]

The marginal productivity theory of contribution is usually accompanied by a laissez-faire ideology that champions the goodness of maximizing individual freedom of action and choice, minimizing the radius of social corrective or compassionate actions to allow that maximization, and the desirability of permitting the individual to attain the highest material existence possible within the bounds of native talent and personal responsibility. Perhaps the most general term to describe the notion of good that frequently accompanies the theory (but is derived from external sources) is "a free choice of responsible life-style." Whatever it is, however, is of nonessential concern to the theory as long as it does not impinge on the principles of right action.

Marx's concept of the good life similarly must be pieced together from evidence outside of his contributory theory. From his early work—the so-called *Economic and Philosophical Manuscripts*—in which his theory of alienation is developed, one may formulate his notion of good as the fulfilled life from his criticism of what he viewed as its frustration in capitalism. The theme has been more fully developed by such neo-Marxist critics as the Frankfurt Institute of Social Research (Horkheimer, Adorno, Marcuse, Fromm, and Habermas), the New Left in America, and existentialism in France. The fundamental assumption is that the individual possesses a capacity for development in a variety of dimensions—the intellectual, the affective, the spiritual, the aesthetic, the athletic, material enjoyment—and so forth. The good life is the fulfilled life, or the enjoyment of existence enriched by the full or at least substantial development of all such facets of potential. Social institutions and mechanisms should be designed to foster such well-roundedness, or, minimally, should not interfere with such personal development. Capitalism (and especially American capitalism with its strong materialist, competitive, and consumerist orientations) was seen as *alienating* man from himself, from society, and from his products, thereby crushing out the opportunity for such meaningful living and fostering "one-dimensional man" with a life devoted to consumerism as a means of preserving the capitalist system.

In the purest sense of the Marxist contributory theory of economic justice, however, any theory of the good life that preserved the principles of just distribution would not violate its structure. Marxists and neo-Marxists, with their analytic visions of a holistic society in which no single element can be studied without considering its internal relations with all other elements, will deny this, and argue that the institution of the socialist society's contributory theory will imply the notion of the good as the unalienated life. But that linkage of a distributive method in a one-to-one correspondence to the ends of human existence is tenuous at best, and there is no reason to believe that a socialist economy, for example, which adopted Marx's assumptions about the origin of value could not also foster a concept of the good life that was thoroughly materialist or nonmaterialist.

The ends of social life are similarly indistinct as implications of the contributory theories, although their advocates are usually characterized by representative credos. In the case of the marginal productivity theorist the role of society is to provide for the basic security of the individual against domestic and foreign threats and to produce a rather restricted list of collective goods for individuals that private enterprise either cannot provide or can provide only inefficiently. And for average productivity adherents, the good social life is viewed as one of voluntary cooperation in which the individual can integrate in a satisfying manner with his or her fellows and full development of potential can be fostered. These positions are complements of the views of the individual good life, of course, and as the latter are fundamentally undefined by the theories themselves, so too are the former.

The Principles of Right

Purely and simply, the principles of right economic action that should be supported by legal sanctions are the principles of "just" distribution dictated by the causal impact of factor services on the value of the social product. That contribution is measured by marginal value productivity on the one hand or average net productivity of labor on the other. Proponents seek to convince by simply asserting some intuitively "obvious" or "provable" relation between factor supply and output, but are actually including the bases for deducing their propositions among the hidden axioms of their systems. In the case of the marginal productivity contributory theory the assumption is that the isolable contribution of any factor to the product is the amount of product that would be lost if a small portion of the factor service were withdrawn, all other factors held constant. An independent axiom asserts the justice of factor service reward in accordance with "social contribution" alone, supporting it by asserting its rational appeal and its intuitive acceptance as a principle of economic justice.

In like manner, the average productivity theory adopts similar postulates concerning the justice of reward by contribution and another axiom which simply asserts that all net value—the value of the social product after capital depreciation has been deducted—is contributed by labor service.[2] Marx and his economist followers have sought to give the latter axiom acceptability by denying its "ethical" foundation and urging its prima facie accordance with rational observation.[3] Philosophical support has been given through use of a bewildering array of interpretations discussed in chapter 2.

The primary hurdle to acceptance of contributory theories, even were one willing to accept contribution as the sole basis of distributive justice, is the philosophical unacceptability of the proposition that one can impute factor contributions in a "natural" or "causative" manner to the joint product of cooperating resources. To ask what proportion of the physical product of the steel plant was "actually" produced by the labor, capital, iron ore, scrap, coke, and air is to ask a question to which there is no operational answer. That is, there is no known experiment that can be performed to answer the query. Even in a Robinson Crusoe economy no credible response can be given to the origin of *physical* product, since Robinson's labor must be combined with nature's free gifts of resources to produce his goods. When the question is phrased in terms of *value* of product, perhaps it may be asserted with some confidence that all value is created by labor, since resources are free goods, and Robinson presumably would "value" goods according to the physical exertion required of his labor. But in an economy where labor is not the only scarce resource, value imputation becomes equally incalculable with physical imputation.

Physical and value production involve the application of a complex of factor services dedicated over some period of time to the production of a complex of products which achieve value through markets. What proportion of the four-door sedans that came off the assembly line at time t was produced by the labor applied at time $t-10$? What proportion was the result of the labor of time $t-30$? What of the contributions of the machinery at both points in time? How much of the output of trucks off the same line at time t was produced by the labor and capital resources of the stated dates? The inputs of resources are continuous over time and produce a continuous stream of output: to seek to isolate the contributions of each factor at each point of time is to ask how much of the wheat was produced by the sun, how much by the seed, how much by the rain, and how much by the soil? Converting the conundrum to a value basis is simply to complicate the task further by having to cope with the determinants of the market's valuation process.

But does not common sense say that one could approach the question by asking a simple question: if one withdrew all of the labor or all of the capital on a given day, how much would the product be reduced at time t? The first problem one faces is that the impact of the loss of the specified resource at a particular time could eventuate in any number of adjustments of output over time, depending on the production decisions taken by management. But abstracting from that—suppose for simplicity that each day's inputs contribute only to that day's outputs—the answer is that the withdrawal of any single resource in its entirety, holding all other resources constant, will generally reduce output to zero. We are confronted with the meaningless result that every factor service contributes 100 percent of the product!

Has not the economist neatly side-stepped this problem, however, by dealing with *marginal* products, obtained by reducing each factor service sequentially as all others are held constant at initial values? Does not the marginal productivity of the factor service truly index its contribution to product? But reducing the input of labor service slightly in time t–10 could impact the stream of product in a large number of ways, depending on management's production decisions, so that the marginal product impacts over a succession of periods could have a very large number of vector values. More fundamentally, however ingenious is the economist's method of measuring factor "productivity" in this way, and no matter how useful the concept is in determining efficient allocation of resources, and no matter how faithful its correspondence is to the market economy's valuation of factor services, marginal revenue products are no more successful in probing into final causation than other experimental methods.

The marginal physical productivity of a factor service—say labor—is a function of (1) its own quantity and (2) the quantities of all other factor services being held constant, given the technology being used. Marginal value (or revenue) productivity is, in addition, affected by the demand for the commodity being produced and the market structure affecting its pricing. If, when one reduces the supply of labor from 100 to 99 the amount of product drops by 1 ton if $1 million of capital is cooperating or by 1.5 tons if $2 million of capital is present, in what sense has one isolated the contribution of the one-hundredth unit of labor? Even more tenuously, can one say that the contribution of the 100 units of labor service with $1 million of capital is 100×1 ton = 100 tons, so that if the laborers receive this in wages they have received their "true" contribution?

Marginal physical and value productivities are invaluable concepts in modern economic theory in three important senses. If every firm adopts the fiction that the contributions of factor services are their marginal *value* products and hires quantities of them in accordance with those values, resources will be allocated in the perfectly competitive market economy in a definably *efficient* manner.[4] Also, if the firm follows the strategy of hiring such services in line with their marginal *revenue* products, the firm will maximize its profits in any market structure. And, from the last proposition, to the extent firms seek to maximize profits this is the manner in which they will determine their factor demand in reality, and hence the manner in which they will implicitly assign factor contributions. Nonetheless, the usefulness of the marginal concept does not nullify its fictitious nature as an indicator of total factor contribution. A clear way to validate this is to show that if every unit of factor were paid its marginal product and the amounts paid were summed over all factors, the total "contributions" would not exhaust the product except under special circumstances of technology.[5] Residual product is in general left after payment of marginal products and accrues to the firm as surpluses.

Marx's average-productivity-of-labor theory of contribution lacks even the semblance of validity possessed by the marginal-productivity-theory of contribution. Marx simply asserts that net value is the product of labor services, capital goods enhancing that product in a physical sense by their presence but contributing only their depreciation in product value. That depreciation is simply the proportion of the socially necessary congealed or dead labor that was used in the production of the capital good and that is yielded to the product of the current period. Living labor has the faculty of "energizing" dead labor in the form of net value creation, while the latter can only increase labor's physical productivity without enhancing value productivity in a net sense.

This interpretation of the results of factor cooperation in production gets Marx into a mare's nest of confused economic theory. The notion that a factor service can have a physical productivity but no value productivity can only be interpreted by a modern economist as implying that the factor is a free good—that is, a factor in excess supply even at a price of zero. Such an assertion about as rare a factor as capital in real economies is foolish with such silly implications as a zero interest rate. Allocating capital as if its price were zero and labor according to its average product would result in horrendously inefficient production patterns. Moreover, if all net value is proportionate to labor costs, and the wage rate is common to all firms but the ratio of capital goods value to labor costs is not the same throughout the economy, Marx himself realized that the rate of profit among industries could not tend to equality in a perfectly competitive market system, and that he was involved in a contradiction of real processes. If capital is nonproductive and consists simply of labor in another form, competition should bid the profits of the capitalist down to zero, eliminating this class immediately, not merely as the result of Marx's historic process. And finally, since all value in Marx's theory is determined by average socially necessary labor time, natural resources in their virgin state can have no value, since no labor was used in their production.

The conclusion must be that contributory theories which assert the justice of one distributive pattern or another on the basis of some scheme of factor imputation that purports to depict physical or value creation in cooperative enterprise are not credible. Such imputations may be valuable fictions in furthering other social or economic goals (such as efficiency) but they are mythological descriptions of the unobservable factor-to-product transformation.

Another line of criticism concerning the economic justice of contributory schemes concerns the implicit belief they express that the sole basis of right is factor contribution. There is an admitted intuitive attractiveness to the notion that an individual's return from society's product should be affected by the value of the contributions he or she makes to its production via ownership of factor resources. But are there not other legitimate intuitive principles that have important claims for consideration in any operational scheme of economic justice, even remaining within the category of egoistic principles? For example, some might find effort, or need, or ability to enjoy income, or desert in some sense equally or importantly attractive criteria for distribution.

Moreover, quite apart from the argument concerning the nonmeasurability of factor contribution there exists the question of whether contribution of social value should be calibrated in the market economy's scale of values. Assume for the moment that one rejects the argument that imputations are impossible to determine, and that one accepts the notion that the market's price for a factor service does indeed constitute a legitimate measure of each unit of that factor's value creation. Should a society seeking economic justice equate that return to *social* contribution? Does the $4 million-a-year baseball star who has the ability to hit a big league curve ball (or throw and control one) contribute eighty times as much to the social welfare as the $50,000-a-year cancer researcher? Should the society accept relative scarcity of skills in relation to demand for their product as the basis of judging just claims on social product? The scarcity of an Einstein's skills was nullified by the small and impecunious demand for his product, but were they less worthy of reward than those of the band leaders or crooners of his time?

In the section "The concept of the Good" it was indicated that contributory theories have no internally determined theory of the desirable ends of individual and social life and are consistent with a wide variety of such principles. The good does not follow from the right, nor is the right implied by a definition of the good. The two are essentially independent, although the ideologies that surround contributory theories or the large systems in which they are embedded usually do indicate predilections to specific visions of the meaningful life.

Incentives to Act in Accordance with the Right

Were the marginal productivity type of contributory theory to become the formal standard of economic justice in the American society—encoded in the hypothetical bill of economic rights to be adopted—it would be confronted with several difficulties of enforcement. The first would be the strong incentive of groups of individuals to act within the charter of political freedom to organize within the market mechanism to increase their returns above those that the competitive economy would permit. Labor union activity is the most immediately identifiable action whose purposes may well include the control of supply in order to lift the wage rate above a competitively determined level. The latter—the marginal revenue productivity of labor employment—is usually a nonobserved, hypothetical value whose legal enforcement would be extremely difficult. This is especially true because the freedom of individuals to organize into unions for economic and noneconomic protection, including the ability to strike to enforce their claims, is a legally enforceable right in the private economy. Nonetheless, such action in a regime of strict marginal productivity economic justice is a clear violation of that principle. If contribution is to be judged by an impersonal, competitive mechanism, giving a labor union the right to interfere with that mechanism for the self-advantage of its members is somewhat akin to permitting a party in a lawsuit to sit on the jury—a practice that would violate elementary notions of justice!

Union activity is not the only potential culprit, however, in violating contributory distribution principles. To judge from current levels of management compensation in American corporations, the same type of warping of salary and bonus levels away from market-determined returns is clearly operative. The mechanism is not formal, as in the case of unions, but informal practices involving compliant boards of directors indebted for their positions to those whose remuneration they review perform effectively.

These types of activities within the market mechanism are directly contradictory of marginal productivity distribution and would have to be eliminated if its regime is to be effective. Other types of market imperfections that conflict with it are more indirect in their impacts and probably could be tolerated. Monopsonistic purchase of resources by firms with the implied payment of prices that are less than what their marginal products would be in the absence of such power is sufficiently infrequent to be tolerated. Most raw materials face relatively competitive market conditions, frequently having their prices set in international auction markets, so that instances of price setting above the competitive level are rare. Cartels formed to attempt price setting have generally failed.

On the other hand oligopolistic pricing of goods sold to final users or to other firms is widespread and undoubtedly in excess of competitive prices, with far-reaching impacts on profits and returns to all resources throughout the economy. However, an operational theory of distributive justice must be defined for a realistic context, and realism demands that one accept the fact that oligopolistic market structure, with its mutually recognized interdependence of decision making and with its departures from perfectly competitive pricing patterns, be accepted as the prevailing form in the American economy. Norms and values and principles of economic justice must be framed with that fact of life in mind. Economists are too wedded to the perfectly competitive market model as a template against which to judge alternative economic mechanisms and imperfectly competitive models, in largest part because of its ease of analysis and manipulation.

In the real world distributive departures from contributory principles exist and will persist through the functioning of markets in which power is not atomized. It will be impractical to apply social corrective principles to attempt their remedy. Practically, a cost-benefit calculus will have to be applied to cases to determine which result in feasibly correctable abuses. Unfortunately, studies of the extent of monopolistic pricing effects in the U.S. economy have focused on *efficiency* losses and explicitly excluded distributive effects because of the difficulty of their measurement.[6] On these grounds the indirect effects of imperfectly competitive pricing on distributive justice are sufficiently threatening to the principle of contributory distribution as to warrant treatment as a major enforcement problem.

A far more serious problem arises outside that system itself and would be substantially lessened by the enactment of a bill of economic rights based on contributory principles of justice. It is frequently overlooked that agents' egoistic drives to maximize satisfactions or profits need not be confined to the economy. Economists, concerned with analyzing the implications of egoistic decision making within the market system, ignore the fact that in a democracy it is frequently more effective to work to attain one's selfish ends in the political arena through government-directed changes in the rules of the market game. Powerful blocs with narrow goals of substantial economic interest to their well-being can bring to bear on executive or legislative officials a pressure greatly out of proportion to their numbers, and effect measures with favorable distributive effects for themselves. The agricultural lobby can successfully obtain subsidies from a compliant Congress and executive through government-inspired distortions of market pricing or unilateral subsidy payments. Manufacturing industries through their trade associations can press for the passage of protective legislation to shelter their non-competitive facilities. Unions can succeed in obtaining quota restrictions or protective tariffs on imports that threaten the jobs of their members. And a host of other groups with egoistic interests in the distributive process—the aged, veterans, welfare recipients, wealthy taxpayers, and many more—are free to operate on government's susceptibility to the threat of loss of office in order to gain their ends.

But with the passage of a bill of economic rights this type of abuse of adopted principles of economic justice should ideally cease and in practical terms become much more difficult, whatever the nature of that body of principles. Constitutional prohibitions permit government officials to resist such self-seeking efforts and should inhibit the attempts, although experience leads one to suspect that a substantial amount of legal talent will be used to circumvent the intent of the principles.

In summary, the marginal productivity form of contributory theory could lead to prohibitive demands on enforcement powers, although their conformance to the self-interest of a substantial portion of the citizenry should lead to a substantial compliance. Indirect interferences with the criterion from the market's own functioning could threaten the defined justice of the system, and direct interferences, especially in the labor area, would force important exceptions to be permitted (given the political rights of workers to organize) or corrective action on the part of government (in the setting of management compensation).

On the other hand, adoption of the Marxist criterion of distributive justice would be incompatible with existing economic institutions and if enforced on them would rapidly lead to attempted evasions and underground activities that subvert the constitutional provisions. This will be discussed more fully below, but at this point one can assert that within the current and foreseeable shape of American institutions such an economic justice criterion would be as a practical matter unenforceable.

Compatibility with the Ethos

One strong supporting element in the marginal productivity variant of the contributory family is its compatibility with the dominant implication of individualism: the egoistic. As the dictate of an unimpeded market with respect to income distribution, it reflects the acceptance of the individual's striving for self-advantage, the freedom to act under its motivation, the voluntaristic nature of the individual's receipt from the social product, his or her responsibility for the achievement of material welfare, and his or her rights to own property and transfer the services therefrom. It is consistent also with equality of competition for reward.

With respect to the corrective and compassionate strands of individualism it is, of course, seriously deficient. As a completely egoistic principle of economic justice it takes no account of the demands of the social strain in the American ethos that requires some effort toward correcting power imbalances, equalizing opportunity, or providing in extenuating circumstances for the material basis necessary for life support and self-respect. However, the introduction of these elements into the principles of economic justice under such a regime could be accomplished via ac-

ceptable government programs financed by feasible taxation schemes. A
bill of economic rights that codified the marginal productivity contributory theory into law would unquestionably strengthen the egoistic strand
within the ethos, and thus make resistance to such taxation more strenu-
ous. But were the bill to establish formally the rights to social compassionate aid as well, there seems little reason to believe that it would be
unworkable within the context of the ethos.

The marginal productivity theory also is consistent with the tenets of
pragmatic rationalism that permeate the culture. Given its congruence
with the market's own efficiency-driven allocation processes it goes without saying that it satisfies the rationalizing and efficiency urgings of the
ethos and seems to validate its utilitarian nature. It possesses a surface
(but illusory) attraction of rewarding factor services according to their
contribution, which provides a false but attractive aura of cause-and-effect support to it as an institution.

It is also broadly consistent with a materialistic and monetized culture
in which individuals' life goals are dominated by strivings for material
welfare and security. This must be qualified, however, by the recognition
that the large variance in income distribution brought about by these
principles of economic justice would lead to a substantial undercurrent
of dissatisfaction among those whose gains in the market were in the
lower ranges of the distribution.

It is a quite different story with respect to an average productivity theory of contribution. If any favored resource receives its average product,
nothing remains to be distributed to the cooperating factors. No contributory theory has suggested that the favored resource be other than labor,
so that such theories assert the injustice of the owners of capital and
natural resources receiving any net return because those resources have
contributed nothing to value productivity. In an individualistic ethos
that views the right to own and transfer property as a projection of the
individual's right to self-protection and security, this principle is a serious challenge. It effectively abolishes private property in economically
relevant resources by denying their owners the ability to profit from
them. By favoring one class of resource owners over others—possessors
of human capital rather than other forms—it denies an important freedom: the voluntary acquisition of claims on future material benefit in
furtherance of meeting the responsibility of the individual to provide for
his or her material welfare.

Nor can the principle be said to foster necessarily the compassionate
strand inherent in the individualistic component of the ethos. Distributing the social product, industry by industry, to the workers in that industry would result in significant income inequality, since average productivity would vary with the presence of cooperating capital and natural

resources, assuming that pricing were done via a market mechanism. If the average productivity dictate were viewed as the average over all industries, so all workers received equal wages, inequality would be eliminated (at the expense of dreadful consequences for allocation efficiency) but this would reflect principles of economic justice other than the contributory. Also, it would seriously challenge the individualistic basis of current belief about the role of individuality and its reward in the earning of income. And it would still require governmental supplementary action to accomplish the provision of income to those who are unable to work.

As discussed earlier, contributory theories are seriously deficient in their claims on rational support. The marginal productivity theory offers some semblance of an operationally observable test for a notion of contribution, however ultimately unsatisfactory it is. An average productivity of labor contributory theory can only be supported by assertion and denies essential productivity to resources that can daily and plainly be observed to increase productivity. The allocative muddles which would result from pricing labor at its average productivity and other factor services at zero; of pricing the same quality of labor skills at different wages depending on the industry in which they are engaged or of pricing all labor regardless of skill at the same wage; and of destroying the incentive to accumulate capital or innovate new products and processes need little imagination. No market mechanism could operate with such irrational dictates, so that a command economy would be necessary whose core irrationality would be complicated by an inefficient allocation of resources by government economic direction attempting to force an irrational system to function with tolerable efficiency.

Such principles would be perfectly consistent with the materialist component of the American ethos, however. To the extent that property income was eliminated and income distributions with significantly smaller variances did result, however, the average productivity of labor principle of economic justice might well lessen the strength of this element, which many citizens might welcome as a by-product of the principle.

A Final Word on Contributory Theories

The notion of reward in proportion to contribution has a strong intuitive appeal to a nation whose ethos stresses egoistic individualism to the degree the United States's does. The fundamental problem that militates against its adoption as the sole or principal dictate of economic justice is the measurability problem. Because of the impossibility of separating out proportionate product by its causative factors in any observable manner, any purported theory that does so must rest on unfounded assertion. Ideological biases are easy to intrude, therefore, and may be hidden behind assertions that the factor imputation is "scientific" in an unspecified or fallacious sense.

In addition, the concept of contribution satisfies only one strand (albeit the dominant one) of the individualistic component of the ethos, ignoring the social responsibility toward those who need help through no fault of their own. It must be supplemented, therefore, by other principles that permit this dimension to be included in the adopted principles of justice. This supplementation, however, could be readily accomplished within economic frameworks that were successful in enforcing initial distribution by "contribution" but redistributed partially via taxes and subsidies.

Success within the current framework of the American society should be relatively assured in the case of the marginal productivity contribution theory, since the free market's efficiency drives lead it to this pattern when undisturbed. Some problems would be confronted in the labor sector in these regards, however. But the Marxist average-product-of-labor theory would require a complete restructuring of the society's institutions and mechanisms, not to mention the norms and values incorporated in its ethos. The hypothetical constituent assembly would undoubtedly rule it out of consideration.

Last, contribution theories are incomplete in the sense that their principle is based on definitions of the right without regard to a notion of the good. They are rather neutral with respect to the latter, therefore, and will accommodate any number of alternative definitions.

A CRITIQUE OF ENTITLEMENT THEORIES

Natural rights theories of the seventeenth and eighteenth centuries are largely of historical interest now. Based on the notion of the social contract and the necessity of a voluntaristic organization of society for emergence from a state of nature, they sought as a primary goal to identify the locus of sovereignty in the state and to define the limits of its authority. Of necessity that search forced them to confront the nature of human motivation and the grounds for honoring the preferences and goals that emerged from it.

Seeking to free such validation from a sole dependence on the divine nature of man—although never completely abandoning the notion—these theorists discerned certain claims that every individual had on his or her fellows that inhered in the will to survive and to protect the means of doing so. That discernment they felt was replicable by any rational person's exercise of his or her reason. It would lead the person to accept a number of rights that were so grounded in the nature of man and the universe. That bill of rights was the manifesto for the tenets of the liberal society that have been gathered together under the rubric of "individualism" in chapters 1 and 4.

I have begged the question of the origin of this complex of rights and obligations and assumed its existence as a primitive in the analysis. Philosophers have little regard now for the notion of natural rights, and the topic has little relevance for liberal societies that have enshrined the principles of political and civil rights in their fundamental law and their institutional structures. As noted in chapter 4, those principles have not been so clearly defined with respect to their economic implications, and it is the basis to fill that gap which this book seeks to build.

Nozick's entitlement theory essentially begins at the same point that this work does. Despite formal appearance, he does not really base the validation of his model on the existence of a set of natural rights and derive the legitimacy of the state, its minimal nature, and the implied principles of economic justice from them, at least directly. Rather, in my opinion, he stresses throughout his treatment the notion of *voluntarism* as the means of validating institutions and principles, and that basis for validation rests solidly on the assumption of the moral and physical inviolability of the individual. In this respect he follows Rawls in employing social contract theory to examine the philosophical implications of voluntaristic association and cooperation with respect to the principles of social organization.[7]

In the discussion of this family of theories, therefore, the critique will be confined to the modern versions exemplified by Nozick's entitlement theory. As interpreted here, it seeks to bring Locke's outdated theory of the origin of private property as the projection of one's labor into the free gifts of nature into a much more complex economic setting and to free it from the cumbersome assumption of the existence of a body of "natural" rights.

The Concept of the Good

Nozick does not derive his principles of economic justice from a prior notion of the good private or social life. From the strength of the voluntarism justification throughout his work one might infer that the good is a life that minimizes interference with the will of the individual, but any number of other assumptions that do not interfere with his principles of right will be consistent with his theory. The theory is a nonconsequentialist theory, so that the end result of following the principles of economic justice is of no relevance in judging the rightness of the principles and of secondary importance in judging the goodness of their operation.

The Principles of Right

As presented in chapter 2, Nozick's entitlements for individuals arise from economic process and are established by the voluntaristic nature of individual economic actions or the correction or compensation for such actions when voluntarism is violated by force or fraud. If the person acquires property or income via a voluntary transfer through inheritance or through market purchases or sales, or if he or she transfers such property or income to others via such actions, they are just. Where force or fraud is involved the actions are unjust and must be undone or redressed in some manner. No template of right can be applied to the results of such process to judge their justice or injustice: only the process by which the pattern of distribution was reached is relevant to its equity, and within that process only the degree of voluntarism of the agents involved.

One criticism of Nozick's principles applies more to his treatment than their nature. The third principle requires that if any acquisition was attained through the use of force or fraud the principle of redress must be applied, presumably through the power of the state. Since the institution of legacy is a legitimate means of transferring property justly, this redress must apply to acquisitions made by prior generations. Nozick accepts the principle as valid but spends little time concerning the question of how far back society must seek to judge the justice or injustice of current entitlements. Presumably, if one were to trace legacies back far enough few of them indeed would be found to be free of the taint of force or fraud. But how far back is society required in justice to go? Three generations? To Roman times? To Adam and Eve? What rate of time discount should be applied to the process of redress?

Obviously, this is a question that could stir a great deal of debate, and Nozick brushes it aside somewhat impatiently, opening himself up to the criticism that he is effectively accepting the status quo ante as just in judging current process. But this criticism is unfair. He does in fact recognize the need for *some* period of redress consideration, and were he to spend a great deal of time on the "proper" time period he would be sidetracked from his major task of attempting to establish the validity of his other two principles. It suffices for his theoretical purposes to indicate that the problem exists.

It is, in the final analysis, the concept of the rightness of *voluntarism* that drives Nozick's system, and its intuitive appeal rests on one's acceptance or rejection of it as the sole basis of economic justice. Most particularly, that which one receives for one's services or goods from others acting voluntarily through the market mechanism is a just entitlement, as is that which others voluntarily give one from their just acquisitions as gift or legacy. That legacy includes, besides material goods, the instillation of values, the love and guidance, and the educational attainment of the family into which one is born. Even more deeply it also comprises the abilities and talents that are passed down through the gene pool. To Nozick, the *individuality* of the person is intimately related to these non-material endowments, and as just entitlements they are the individual's justly acquired property which can be used to acquire more goods justly. For the state to tax away just acquisitions or the returns from such just acquisitions for redistributive purposes is to violate the voluntaristic basis of justice and the sanctity of the individual on which it rests.

This concept of voluntarism allows Nozick to escape the thorny problems associated with the assumption of natural rights as well as contributory theories, while at the same time emerging with very similar principles of justice. But in a realistic market society its definition leads to some practical problems. Given that most markets contain some degree of oligopolistic pricing power, does this warping of price away from its competitive level constitute force or fraud in the sense of unjust acquisition? Do labor unions similarly invalidate their members' earnings through the use of coercive force in the strike or boycott? Might one not view much of advertising and promotion that depends on false or misleading information as a form of consumer fraud? And to what extent is the offer of the unskilled or poorly educated worker to work for the minimum wage purely "voluntarist" when in fact no choice exists?

Do others' just rights ever preempt voluntarist acquisitions that do not involve force or fraud? Nozick addresses this problem in his discussion of his updated "Lockean proviso." The crucial factor in Nozick's concept of the conditions under which the principles of acquisition and transfer may be aborted in the social interest is whether or not others are denied usage of resources or knowledge whose benefits *they had previously been enjoying.* Hence, a perverse scientist who discovers a previously unknown cure for a dread disease but refuses to permit its use or prices that use at a prohibitive level may not justly be forced to make it available. On the other hand a storekeeper who raises the price of his wares in the wake of a catastrophe can be forced to supply them at normal prices because his or her customers had been enjoying their supply before the emergency.

One difficulty that this distinction raises is that, strictly applied, patents should not be restricted to any given time period. The provision of a previously unavailable good should yield an entitlement that is not subject to the action of the state under the Lockean proviso and hence should be capable of indefinite legacy to the inventor's descendants. Nozick's rather weak rejoinder to this challenge is to assert that because such a discovery today deprives future generations of making the same discovery and hence can be viewed as a type of Lockean proviso viola-tion, society is justified in placing a time limitation on the patent. This would presumably also apply to the scientist and the discovered cure. But when *future potential* usage in the absence of previous discovery or usage is included in the analysis, it is difficult to see what could not be brought under the definition. Every barrel of oil used today is a barrel that would have been used by some future generation, and if *would have been* is added to *have been* enjoying as a touchstone for the proviso, the principles of voluntaristic acquisition and transfer are in deep trouble.

Nozick's dedication to the minimal state and his desire to protect the individual against its unjust exactions surely lead him to too narrow an interpretation of social rights in relation to individual rights. Under his interpretation, such common procedures as condemnation and emi-nent domain are unjust exercises of the state's power except under ex-treme emergency. Surely any theory of economic justice that recognizes a role for the social corrective or compassionate functions would permit the state to force the reluctant scientist to make available at reasonable compensation a cure for suffering or death from a disease. The distinc-tion between whether or not individuals have enjoyed the use of some good or facility before it became private property seems a rather con-trived one, as is implicitly recognized in his treatment of patent rights.

The more rational distinction surely is whether the public interest—in Nozick's sense of the welfare of *individuals*—has such an overriding in-terest in the availability of the good that property rights can be overruled with just compensation. After all, principles of justice have to be distin-guished from ethics in any system of social life, and this is done on the basis of the overriding importance of some actions to individuals' health or life. Nozick's three principles (with the Lockean proviso) are defi-cient in failing to broaden the legitimate social corrective role from de-termination and correction of force and fraud to permit forced provi-sion of property for important social usage that cannot be limited only to extreme urgency.

Can any concept of the right be convincing if it takes no account what-soever of the consequences of the principles of economic justice it de-fines? What society could accept a theory of justice that permitted some of its citizens to literally starve to death in the absence of private charity on the grounds it is unjust to tax some to benefit others *in extremis*? Can any such exclusively egoistic interpretation of individualism provide an acceptable notion of just action? The answer must be sought in the com-parison of such finely spun webs of logical reasoning from narrow axio-matic bases with the ethos of a society in which it is designed to be ap-plied, and that will be done below.

As in the case of the contributory theories, Nozick is not directly and explicitly concerned with notions of the private or social good. However, the dominance of the voluntarism theme in his work and his explicit derivation of the form of the state that would emerge from voluntarism as the minimalist state might implicitly support the concept of the good life for the individual as one of maximum freedom of the will and the good society as that which minimizes interference with the individual. The "proper" goals of the individual in exercising his or her choices, however, are not determined, and are unrelated to the notions of justice except insofar as they might contradict those preeminent principles.

Incentives to Act in Accordance with the Right

Because Nozick's principles of economic justice validate the motivation and support the functioning of the free market mechanism, for the majority of individuals who act through the market to provide for their individual and dependents' needs external enforcement should not prove necessary. Such action may be required to prevent those incapable of such action from taking illegal steps to achieve an acceptable standard of living, since no claim in justice would exist on their behalf. Moreover, depending on the interpretation of monopoly power as a violation of the principle of acquisition, some corrective enforcement by the state might be necessary. Presumably, however, a benefit-cost criterion would be applied in such cases to eliminate excessive enforcement. In short, most citizens would find the principles of justice supportive of their accustomed values and norms in their everyday economic activities, but a significant minority would be disaffected and motivated by extreme need to disobey the law.

Compatibility with the Ethos

It follows from this compatibility with the market mechanism's operation that entitlement theory is a strong expression of the implications of the egoistic strand of individualism. The freedom of the individual to use his or her legacy of talent and familial provision to obtain material benefit, to acquire and be protected in the possession of property, and to obligate himself or herself in contractual agreements are reinforced by entitlement theory. But all acts of compassion are under the regime of economic ethics, not justice, which is to say they are duties of imperfect obligation. The compassionate strain of individualism in the ethos is completely denied as a just claim on individuals' egoistic entitlements, and notions of leveling inequality of opportunity are similarly unjust to the extent they reduce such entitlements without the consent of their recipients.

This is a serious deficiency in the relevance of the theory to the purposes of our hypothetical constituent assembly. It is not at all clear that participants in a social contracting exercise would be so exclusively egoistic in their motivation, or, indeed, would fail to provide a compassionate strain as a form of self-protection, and if the present interpretation of the American ethos is correct such compassionate regards would be taken into explicit account if the participants were acting within its value system. By not only failing to provide for such compassionate support of the deserving individuals who cannot earn sufficient entitlements but by ruling it to be positively unjust, Nozick's pure theory must be judged to be so fundamentally flawed that it should be ruled out of the realm of relevance. It demeans a significant portion of the society by denying the claim to life, improved opportunity, dignity, and self-respect.

On the other hand the entitlements theory is perfectly consistent with pragmatic rationalism and materialism, the other traits identified as important in the ethos. It is directly in the stream of individual self-seeking after the material, with rational planning over time to attain goals. As a supporter of the market's voluntaristic allocation process it implicitly endorses efficiency and materialistic motivation.

A Final Word on Entitlements Theory

There is much in entitlements theory that would make it attractive to the designers of a bill of economic rights. It is not encumbered by the specious rationalizing of the marginal productivity contributory theory, yet is most dependent on the free market mechanism to effect its principles of justice. It bases its justification on the notion of voluntary action, thereby placing its axiomatic foundation on the firm soil of the dominant strand in individualism. That foundation also assures that self-interest will coincide with the principles for the majority of the citizenry, minimizing the need for external enforcement. Its focus on the process of acquisition and transfer rather than its end results minimizes the need for the state to alter the market's results each period, forcing individuals' self-interest to diverge from justice principles and raising questions of effective enforcement.

But there are features of the theory that would make it unattractive to the designers of an operational theory of justice in the United States. The simplicity of structure and enforcement inherent in its nonconsequentialist principles are compensated by their indifference to the distributive consequences. The social strand of individualism is therefore completely rejected except insofar as fraud or force intrudes into economic relations, in which case corrective actions are sanctioned. But compassionate social action is not only neglected but positively denounced as unjust, both in its greater equalization of opportunity and its extension of aid forms. That not only is inconsistent with the ethos, but could lead to substantial difficulty enforcing the principles in the face of a strongly disaffected minority.

Finally, the Nozickean theory is unclear with respect to the conditions under which the voluntary acquisition of property and income becomes unjust by virtue of the application of force or fraud or because such acquisition interferes unacceptably with others' welfare. The acceptability of imperfectly competitive markets in a society whose principles of economic justice are so dependent on the untainted voluntarism of transactions must be highly sensitive to the balance of pricing power and symmetry of information on the part of all parties, as well as the potential for exertion of political power for private advantage. Also unclear, but implicit in the thrust of Nozick's argument about the Lockean proviso, the ability of the state to limit acquisition when social considerations make that desirable seems unduly restrictive.

These are serious reservations that militate against acceptance *in toto* of the entitlement theory. Yet it must be a serious candidate for providing substantial guidance to the design of an operational theory of economic justice in the American society.

A CRITIQUE OF JUSTICE-AS-FREEDOM THEORIES

As indicated in my explication of these theories in chapter 2, the most focused and fully developed of them is Friedman's and it will be analyzed as representative of the genre.

The Concept of the Good

This is the only egoistically oriented theory that defines its concept of the good explicitly and derives its notions of right from that definition. As presented in the discussion of "Friedman's Economic Ethic" in chapter 2, the good life of the individual is asserted to be that which maximizes the freedom of will and choice subject to natural and accumulated endowments and to the rights of others to like freedoms. The good society, and the state as its agent, constructs its institutions and mechanisms preeminently to allow the individual such free rein, to provide public goods for his or her welfare only to the extent voluntarist mechanisms

cannot, to reduce corrective actions to the minimum necessary to prevent excessive force or fraud, and to exercise its compassionate functions
in a constrained but nonetheless necessary manner.

In the exercise of its power the state is the major threat to the individual's enjoyment of such freedom, and social mechanisms must be designed to be voluntarist to the extent possible. Decentralization of power
becomes a crucial social concern, and the disjunction of political and
economic power a *sine qua non* of the good society. Moreover, the market
mechanism is more voluntaristic than the political mechanism as a decision maker, since the latter frequently is confined to a binary yes-or-no
type of choice, while the market allows a spectrum of preferences to be
satisfied when possible.

Private and social ends are compatible since the latter are defined
wholly to accommodate the former. In its relevance to economic matters, of course, the social good is achieved when individualistic economic
decision making is determined in a decentralized market mechanism
with atomized market power in every market, with individuals forced to
compare economic benefits with full social cost in their choices and to
bear the latter, with the collective economy functioning side-by-side with
the market mechanism to provide the relatively few collective goods the
market cannot. The relation between the individualistic and the collective economies is minimal. Where commutative or distributive justice
requires exercise of state power it must be done by functionaries who are
strictly controlled by legal guidelines and possess no discretion.

These definitions of the good are basically validated by a largely unex-
pressed appeal to the intuition. Such individual freedom as a *summum
bonum* is taken to be self-evident by consulting one's own feelings and
one's intuitive reaction to their historical violations. But such unconditional allegiance to freedom of will as in and of itself the dominant good
in private and social life is not beyond challenge on its own intuitive
ground and on the basis of its rational appeal. Is such freedom the ultimate end of existence or the means to even higher concepts of the good?
For example, should the state not constrain the individual from endan-
gering his or her own life (e.g., enforcing seat-belt laws, interfering with
attempts at suicide, requiring safety nets for death-defying acrobatic per-
formances, and so forth) or health (e.g., drug enforcement, inhibitions
on alcohol abuse, enforcement of safety conditions, and so forth) as
higher goods? John Stuart Mill argued that the individual who rationally
chose to end life by suicide cannot justly be prevented from doing so,
essentially on the basis of exaltation of liberty of action as the supreme
individual good. Yet are not such violations of the sanctity of human life
and dignity—quite apart from their social costs—such affronts to the
egoistic and compassionate strains of individualism as to warrant rejec-

tion on intuitive and rational (i.e., logically consistent deduction from axioms) bases?

Other analysts challenge this concept of good on the grounds that the average individual in the society is not equipped to cope with the extent of freedom thus thrust upon him or her. Erich Fromm believes that while freedom is a necessary component of the well-integrated personality, equally important is the need to be incorporated into a social body, perhaps at a cost of some loss of freedom of choice. Denying such individuals the security that accrues from guaranteed job security, or compulsory social security participation, or involuntary health insurance, as well as greater equalization of opportunity, Fromm asserts, may lead them to such defenses as conformism or such pathological organic philosophies as fascism to provide at least the trappings of social integration.[8] Is the good life one that thrusts so much freedom of choice on the individual with its attendant responsibilities when some comforting security is obtainable by some sacrifice of choice?

The Principles of Right

The principles of right derive from the concept of good. Those principles relate almost entirely to limiting state interference with the liberty of choice of the individual. In furtherance of these principles the state is enjoined from such activities as providing public education rather than subsidizing private education using a voucher system; enforcing civil rights statutes that overrule the individual's preferences however biased or prejudicial they may be; operating such services as the post office or national parks or Social Security plans that could be provided by private enterprise in efficient manners imposing their costs on those who elect to use them; licensing trades or professions as a means of screening incompetency; regulating private natural monopolies; enforcing zoning regulations or building codes; and taking corrective action in such commutative justice areas as antitrust regulation. The list could be extended, but the motivation of such principles is clear: the state, as the sole effective fulcrum for the exercise of power threatening the individual's liberty, must be restricted in economic as well as political and social matters to provision for the absolute minimum of public goods and corrective functions, relying to the maximum degree on private voluntarist mechanisms such as the market economy and honoring their decisions as reflective of individual preferences.

Some compassionate roles of government are permissible. Welfare payments to those who are incapable of providing support for themselves or their dependents are permissible rights, providing such relief is given in ways that do not sap the self-reliance or self-respect of the individuals involved. Even in such instances the maximization of individual free choice is important, and the ideal manner of ensuring it is to make such payments via a negative income tax that permits the individuals to spend the money in ways they elect. Redistributive measures to provide greater equality of opportunity, however, are not just: rather equality of competition for reward is stressed—a principle which is implied from the egoistic strand of individualism rather than its compassionate component.

Friedman's principles of justice, framed as they are to provide the nearly minimalist state, apply to a much broader social area than the economic. However, their applicability as principles of economic justice is quite extensive. They are designed to protect the individual, envisioned as acting within social mechanisms in which power is atomized and among which amplification of power is prevented by decentralization. Agents, therefore, are forced to follow implicit principles of right action in that they are prevented by the structure of the mechanisms within which they operate from interfering with the rights of freedom of others by significant exercise of power, and at the same time are protected against like actions by others. The perfectly competitive market mechanism is an outstanding instance of such an institution, of course, and the principles of justice are directly applicable to its operation.

The principles of right are derivative from the definition of the good, whose justification was based on the intuitive appeal of that definition. In an ultimate sense, therefore, the principles of economic justice must also be based on their appeal to the moral intuition, but given the acceptability of the notion of the good life it is possible to examine the rational basis for justifying them as the means of attaining the good life now lifted above argument. In that exercise some of the weaknesses in this theory of social equity become apparent.

The vision of the state as the sole potential power threat to the individual's freedom of action is an unrealistically restricted one. The market mechanism is simply not the antiseptically pure forum of exchange between agents with equalized power and symmetrical information envisioned in the derivation of the principles. Pricing power loci are quite strong in many important markets and are capable of threatening the freedom of anonymity discussed in chapter 1. Information and the ability to benefit from it are unequally distributed in such markets, and the ability to collect and sell such information to the uninformed much less feasible economically than advocates imply. Political power blocs, frequently but by no means always economically based, are also important threats to exercise disproportionate power in their own self-interest, and little can restrain them but the use of the power of the state to structure itself to inhibit them.

An operational set of principles of economic justice in the face of the frictional imperfections in the abilities of social mechanisms to organize atomistically must contain provisions for the corrective operations of the state. They are necessary to protect agents whose welfare is importantly threatened by the leveraged power of other agents and to provide at least basic information in the vital manners which are the concerns of economic justice. Can one really object to the requirement that brain surgeons be licensed by the state as a means of providing minimal information concerning their competence? Is this not an efficient manner of providing such information? Are not the costs of market processes eliminating the incompetent over the long run too great to object to such commutative action by the state?

Logically Friedman's system of economic justice should lead to quite strong protections of the rights of property, not only on the basis of its being a projection of the individual's property in self but as a means of protection against overweening state power. But Friedman's position, stated in the peculiar quotation reproduced in chapter 2 concerning the distribution of income in capitalism, is ambiguous. His position seems to be that property if not a creation of the state is subject to its rules of definition and rights to determine the benefits of its ownership. He implies that it is within the powers of the just state to overrule the market's distribution of social product and to redistribute income depending "markedly on the rules of property adopted." That the state could function with such broad powers in so important a social area, yet remain within the confines of his principles of economic justice, is so foreign to their uncompromising tenor in all other areas as to warrant the charge of logical inconsistency.

With the exception of the view of property rights, Friedman's justice-as-freedom theory and others in the same vein have the advantage of conforming to the structure and functioning of the institutions and social mechanisms of the liberal society. Although not egalitarian in the usual senses it is strongly supportive of democracy, and it is largely shaped to preserve the purported advantages of the free market mechanisms in preserving freedom as the foundation of its notion of the good life. It is a theory of economic justice designed to preserve the liberal— indeed the libertarian—society, and as such gives strong support to the mechanisms that are basic to the American society at the present time.

Incentives to Act in Accordance with the Right

As in the case of entitlement theories, justice-as-freedom principles of economic justice validate the motivations and outcomes of the free market. Incentives to conform to them, therefore, are for the most part identical to the incentives to accept the market's demands and judgments. For the greater part of the citizenry, therefore, no external enforcement by the state is necessary and, indeed, where other theories might see such state action as desirable, justice-as-freedom theories would not. With the commutative or corrective functions of the state so limited there might be expected to be a substantial dissatisfaction with the operation of some power blocs or with the state of information in many transactions, leading to a demand that greater state power be instituted. And finally, with a reduced compassionate program to provide greater equality of opportunity and relief to the disadvantaged, substantial disaffection might also occur in this area with attendant need to require external enforcement of the principles.

Compatibility with the Ethos

As is the case with their near cousins, the entitlement theories, these theories are in close correspondence to the dictates of the egoistic strand of individualism. That point hardly need be belabored. Their noncorrespondence—again in like manner to entitlement theories—is in their failure to allow except in the most grudging fashion the compassionate strain of individualism to enter their principles and their even stronger stand against the commutative role of government. They are a bit more willing to permit compassionate government action and a great deal more unwilling to allow commutative corrective action by the state than entitlement theories.

In von Mises's, Friedman's, and Hayek's versions efficiency in resource allocation is given great emphasis, so that the theories fit well into the pragmatic rationalism of the American society. The emphasis on the economic function and the market's efficient oversight of it makes the theories compatible with the materialism of that ethos as well.

In short, justice-as-freedom theories conform quite well to the ethos, most particularly the stronger strand in individualism, and offer strong ideological buttressing for its values, norms, institutions, and mechanisms. It is deficient, however, and seriously so, in its narrow conception of society's responsibilities to the individual in its corrective and compassionate roles. Its principles of right action would have to be supplemented and modified were it to be made operational.

A Final Word on Justice-as-Freedom Theories

The protection of the individual against the potential tyranny of the state must receive a strong priority in the liberal state, and in the light of historical experience has a powerful intuitive appeal as a guideline by which to design social institutions and mechanisms. But does it serve well as a sole criterion by which to shape the society's principles of justice?

More generally, can any theory of social justice that depends wholly on egoistic self-interest to define its principles of right ever deliver an acceptable blueprint for justice? Does not such a theory by exclusive attention to one strand of individualism deny the compassionate duties of society that must be included in that society's mapping of interpersonal relations? Can any operationally acceptable body of principles that relies on the atomistic, depersonalized anonymity of "ideal" social mechanisms, confining the interpersonal interactions that distinguish social from private actions to the linkages dictated by self-seeking in an uncaring nexus, ever adequately define individuals' duties to one another as moral beings?

Moreover, is not the rather simplified view of the exercise of power in the world as threatening only in its governmental guise misleading in describing the asserted aim of these theories of protecting the individual's freedom? A variety of power blocs exist in social mechanisms whose structures are not as atomized as the ideal mechanisms envisioned by these authors assume, and government may well be the only countervailing and protecting mantle the individual has. To deny the commutative as well as the compassionate roles of government in a modern liberal state is to ignore two centuries of the American experience and its reflection in the ethos.

Any potential to exercise power is a threat to the individual, and the state's power with its ultimate ability to coerce is the greatest threat of all. But powers can be controlled by law and state power can not only be controlled but can be channeled to conform to its own reason for existence: the protection and enhancement of collective individuals' welfares. It is granted, of course, that in its realistic functioning in a liberal society the task of preventing state power from being used to further the self-seeking of power groups is most difficult, which is indeed one of the reasons I have argued that an economic constitution should be forthcoming to constrain such efforts. But these imperfections are not sufficient grounds for deploring all but minimalist governmental commutative and distributive actions as unacceptable, while other power blocs are ignored on the unrealistic assumption that atomistic organization of social institutions prevents their formation for the most part and that competition among themselves makes their impacts negligible when they do arise.

Nor is it an adequate description of the licensing actions of governments to assert that they are invariably the creations of selfish vested interests designed to limit the supply of their services or to restrict competition or to enhance sales of goods or services. They serve to screen the qualifications of persons or goods in an important way when the welfare costs of such screening by the market would result in unacceptable burdens on individuals or the taxpayer. This is an efficient means of providing minimal information to a citizenry whose knowledge and means of improving it are limited by time, income, and the profitability of those whose interests dictate less than full disclosure. Asymmetry of information and the means of acquiring it must be perceived as of increasing importance as an imperfection in modern social mechanisms, particularly the market economy, and the corrective social function in these respects cannot be ruled out by a quasi-Marxist or populist charge that it is a tool of vested interests.

Notwithstanding these criticisms of justice-as-freedom theories, however, they would retain a great deal of attractiveness to a constituent assembly. Their conformity to the ethos—with the important exceptions noted above—is one source of that attraction as well as their support for existing institutions and mechanisms. But these qualities are also characteristic of the principles deduced from other egoistic theories considered, and perhaps more convincingly from the entitlements theory with its stronger support of the institution of private property.

A Critique of Bargaining Theories

In the discussion of bargaining theories in chapter 2, skepticism concerning their relevance to theories of social or economic equity was indicated. Designed as they are to discern candidate sets of imputations among limited numbers of participants acting under wholly egoistic motivation, such theories are not easily lifted into the macroconsiderations of social decision making. Their purpose, as perceived by their authors, is predominantly positivist rather than normative. As might be expected, therefore, they are most incomplete theories of social equity, and because I believe them to be irrelevant to the task of the constituent assembly, I will be brief in my critique of them.

The Concept of the Good

Bargaining theories profess no concept of the individual or social good that might play a role in defining principles of right action. As an extension of narrow microeconomic reasoning such guiding ethical principles are simply not relevant.

The Principles of Right

The principles of right action are straightforwardly the exercise of such bargaining power as one's initial endowment might confer to attain the solution that maximizes one's payoff subject to the relative strength of such bargaining power. It is most primitively egoistic, therefore, without pretension of a social dimension. Right action is argued on the grounds of the realism or acceptability of axioms within the context of power-constrained egoistic self-seeking: its justice in a social context is simply not relevant to the modelers' purposes. The appeal of the principle is that of the rationality of following self-interest and of recognizing the constraints on one's ability to influence others by virtue of one's bargaining power.

The relation between the good and the right obviously is nonexistent in the absence of the definition of the former.

Incentives to Act in Accordance with the Right

The right is defined as self-interest so that the need for incentives to conform to it is not necessary. No social dimension that might contain limitations on self-interest is present.

Compatibility with the Ethos

Compatibility with the egoistic strand of individualism becomes coincidence, and the motivation of the agents is certainly conformable to the rational pragmatism and materialism of the ethos. The theories are completely empty of any social concern, and it is therefore hard to imagine that were any such negotiation model lifted in ambition to determine the distribution of social product its results could begin to satisfy this strand of the ethos.

A Final Word on Bargaining Theories

The complete absence of a social dimension in these theories which are designed to analyze microeconomic problems implies that they are incomplete theories of social or economic justice. Much of social justice involves the alteration of individuals' differential bargaining positions, or the tempering of the outcomes that result from them. There is minimally no clear implication that any theory of social equity worthy of the name can emerge from motivation marked by egoistic self-seeking applying all endowed power to attain selfish ends.

A SUMMARY

The initial rational and intuitive appeal of egoistic theories within the context of the American ethos is a strong one: justice as market-determined contribution, as entitlements earned through voluntaristic payments, and as freedom of will strike powerful notes in a culture that glorifies the individual as the social unit of concern and imposes burdens of responsibility on him or her unknown in more organic societies. They not only are consistent with but rely heavily on the existence of the market economy as the distributive mechanism that enforces their principles of right. Although they do not specifically designate the satisfaction of individuals' material desires as the supreme goal of human existence, they can accommodate the strong strand of materialism on which the market economy depends. Finally, pragmatic rationalism with its emphases on the practical, the efficient, the utilitarian, the scientific, and the programmed are embedded in the derivation and validation of the theories of right action.

On closer examination, however, each of the theories reveals its blind spots and its inadequacies. In the case of the contributory theory its major shortcoming is the nonrational derivation of its pattern of distributive justice, and, more fundamentally, the nonderivability of any such pattern on the basis of its principle of right. But it also shares with entitlements theory and justice-as-freedom theories the failure to incorporate as internally derived principles of justice the obligations toward individuals that are asserted to be necessary by the social strand of individualism in the ethos. Each of them relies to an unrealistic extent on the purported atomistic structure, symmetrical information flow, and equal power potential extant in realistic markets to ignore or reject the need for social monitoring of commutative relations and corrective actions to prevent excessive force and fraud. And each denies or subordinates to an excessive degree the compassionate demands that arise from individual inadequacies and correctable inequality of opportunities.

Egoistic individualism simply cannot evolve an adequate theory of economic justice in a liberal society that asserts the need for a set of protective or meliorative rights for the individual to coexist with his or her private rights to freedom of will and action to fulfill responsibilities. But such a failure does not have to result in rejection of the principles of right derived by these egoistic theories. It can be corrected by supplementing these principles with a set of constraints that intrude the missing social dimension into an operational theory of economic justice as subordinated rights and obligations.

It is doubtful, therefore, that the constituent assembly can dismiss out of hand these egoistic theories. Besides the appeal of their principles, suitably supplemented, there is also Nozick's novel concept of principles of justice as rules of procedure rather than templates to apply to the outcomes of procedures. Can an operational theory of economic justice for America be wholly one of procedures or of outcomes, or is there some blending of the two that would be more acceptable to the ethos?

Is the ideal workable theory one that accepts the egoistic strand of individualism as one that should remain dominant in its principles, with the social strand subordinated as constraints, or should the emphases be reversed? To examine that question it is necessary to critique the socially oriented theories in the next chapter.

Chapter 6

A CRITIQUE OF THE SOCIALLY
ORIENTED THEORIES

THERE REMAINS the task of applying the framework of analysis developed in chapter 4 to the theories of social equity whose principles of right lean strongly in the direction of the compassionate strain of individualism. These theories have been presented in chapter 3, and reference will be made to those discussions in elaborating the points made in this chapter. The three theories included in this category are taken in turn: the Kantian theory, utilitarianism, and the Rawlsian theory of justice as fairness.

A CRITIQUE OF THE KANTIAN THEORY

Kant's moral system is at once the most profound and complexly structured of any of those systems being considering and the easiest to recast within the framework developed in chapter 4. Because of its complexity the implications it has for a theory of economic justice are best derived within that scaffolding.

The Concept of the Good

The highest good for the individual, and the only absolute or unconditional good, is a "good will," manifest in the actions of the person who chooses to perform duty for its own sake against the urgings of his or her natural inclinations and despite the consequences of those actions. Obedience to the rule of the categorical imperative when it is followed against one's self-interest or desires *and only when it is so performed* constitutes the moral life. The *summum bonum*, then, is to act in manners that one's reason dictates should be universalized in the same circumstances. Kant believed this rationally derived will to "legislate" a rule that should be binding on all to be the defining or unifying principle that underlies all moral law—the supreme idea of which all categorical imperatives are particular expressions.

However, besides this exalted type of good life a lower form is happiness, or acceding to the aims of the natural inclinations. Happiness results from obeying hypothetical imperatives that dictate actions to obtain further ends—in this case, that of satisfaction of inclinations. The search for happiness is recognized by Kant to be a legitimate end of human life, and indeed one is morally obligated to aid one's fellow man in attaining happiness in interpersonal dealings, especially when he or she is in distress.[1] But where such actions conflict with duty, the truly moral life dictates the route of choosing the categorical imperative.

Ethical theorists have long debated the meaning of the categorical imperative, whether the common man derives his notions of morality from such imperatives as Kant asserts, the relations between the First and Second Formulations of it, and the social consequences of Kant's notion of the individual good life. To what extent in a practical context might the individual be expected to confront challenges from the categorical imperative in the straightforward search for happiness? Were such moral actions envisioned as rather rare confrontations of conscience and desire, occasionally causing painful choices, or were they seen as daily challenges in a life resembling Pilgrim's Progress? Could such higher goods simply be viewed as a greater or qualitatively more satisfying form of happiness, and therefore capable of inclusion in a form of universalized utilitarianism? With respect to this last question Mill has rather severe views when some of the social consequences of following Kant's path of individual good are considered:

> Nor is there any school of thought which refuses to admit that the influence of actions on happiness is a most material and even predominant principle of morality, and the source of moral obligation. I might go much further, and say that to all those *a priori* moralists who deem it necessary to argue at all, utilitarian arguments are indispensable. . . . When [Kant] begins to deduce from [the First Formulation of the categorical imperative] any of the actual duties of morality, he fails, almost grotesquely, to show that there would be any contradiction, any logical (not to say physical) impossibility, in the adoption by all rational beings of the most outrageously immoral rules of conduct. All he shows is that the consequences of their universal adoption would be such as no one would choose to incur.[2]

If the field of action be narrowed to the economic, it becomes difficult to visualize the applicability of Kant's notion of morality to the individual's pursuit of the good. In one's economic actions within an ethos with a dominant strand of egoistic individualism, how does one pursue the good life in Kant's sense of following the call of duty? What dictates the choice among outcomes that would lead one to choose the route one wishes universalized?

The difficulties with applying Kant to economic equity problems seem insurmountable. For example, suppose a factory owner asserts the proposition "I will pay the unskilled more than the market-determined wage to increase their happiness" and wills that this be a universal law for all employers. Reason informs him that this will increase the welfare of those remaining employed, but will reduce the welfare of those among the unskilled who lose their jobs as a result. Reason also tells him that the total amount of goods and services available to society will be reduced and therefore the welfare of consumers would be adversely affected. Finally, it tells the employer that since he may not expect others to follow the path of generosity such action may make his product noncompetitive in price and force his bankruptcy.

Thus reason dictates a variety of outcomes that may lead him to conclude that social welfare would be reduced by such action and thus that the proposed universal law is rationally inconsistent. But must it? The consequences of the proposed action must be considered as a whole. In Kant one is bound to further the states of happiness of his or her fellow citizens. But which? In economic actions they are frequently conflicting. Does one follow a utilitarian course and maximize a macromeasurement of satisfaction? If not, what moral criteria does one use to judge the relative worths of different individuals' pleasures and pains? More important, perhaps, can one define the path of rational action independent of consequences? How would the businessperson define the universal law absent a weighing of consequences? Can Kant escape the need to be a consequentialist?[3]

Can Kant's theory function as a guide to individual morality in the economic realm when no one agent can perceive the impacts of his or her actions on others and, if he or she could, it is necessary to balance positive and negative impacts on happiness in some undefined rational manner? Is it not more relevant to defining the objectives and constraints of a society with government functioning in its role of agent for the social aspects of equity and receiving guidance in the manner stated above? Rawls points out that Kant's theory is a deontological theory in that the concept of right is prior to that of the good.

Should the employer view the incremental welfare of the employed unskilled of such overwhelming importance relative to the negative effects of the proposed universal application of the law that duty requires him to follow this self-destructive course? Can this be considered true economic equity? Can it be dependent wholly on reason independent of value judgments? Does reason dictate that he follow the course of duty without considering the high probability that others will not follow the course he has universalized? Is it reasonable and just to act as one wills all would act when reason also informs that few will so act? Or are economic decisions and actions largely to be ruled by the regime of hypothethical imperatives, and thereby to remain outside the realm of economic justice? Kant's guidance is most unclear in these matters.

The Principles of Right

Right action, whose principles derive from the notion of the good, consists in following the dictates of the categorical imperative. Kant derives it from man's rational faculty: his ability to foresee the consequences of his actions and to will those that—what? Formally, the criterion for the existence of a categorical imperative is that the universalization of its negative would result in a contradiction and interfere seriously with the functioning of any society. For example, were one to assert that he or she would make promises without the intention of keeping them and were such a maxim to be adopted universally, promises would not be accepted in the society. This would compromise its ability to function. On the other hand, suppose one asserted that one would never be kind to anyone, which universalizes to the maxim that no one is ever kind to anyone. This does not contradict itself and does not threaten the existence of society, since completely egoistic societies are conceivable (e.g., Nozick's minimalist state). Therefore, being compassionate does not constitute a categorical imperative.

How can pure logic dictate a path of universal economic action valid without regard to the state of the natural or social world and independent of consequences within a specific natural and institutional context? Must not that social organization be formed on rational principles derived prior to consideration of economic duty? And to what depth of perception in this featureless social landscape must the reason penetrate in defining the imperative? Must it foresee all implications and consequences in judging the desirability of its universalization? If so, how should it combine them into a decision aggregate?

In economic actions, those that the reason might lead one to endorse in a socialistic context might be rejected in a free market context. The extension of reward for useful innovations might be condoned in a free market economy on grounds of encouraging new discoveries and increasing social product, whereas it might be rejected in socialism as upsetting egalitarian distributions "merely" to increase efficiency. How can the reason choose among actions without consulting consequences and how can consequences be foreseen in an institutional vacuum? For example, a categorical imperative forbidding murder obviously contains death as a feature of the ruling state of nature. It is not independent of experience. If Kant is concerned only about the concept of right with respect to actions that are independent of the states of nature and that affect others in the same way in every conceivable society, must not the affected actions be a small or indeed an empty set?

The question of relevance arises, therefore, in addressing Kant's theory with respect to economic justice. To what extent can the categorical imperative in its First Formulation provide guidelines to just actions in a free market economy? It would presumably rule out the use of force or fraud in economic dealings, would protect the right of contract, but might well be nonsupportive of the institution of private property.[4] Its pronouncements with respect to the justice of such strategic economic institutions that dictate the structure of the just economy are ambiguous in that "reason" would not lead to clear paths of duty for individual action or social organization.

This ambiguity is even more apparent if the Second Formulation of the categorical imperative is examined within the context of economic action. It states: "So act that you treat humanity in your own person and in the person of everyone else *always* at the same time as an end and never merely as a means."[5] The derivation of this "restatement" of the First Formulation is not made clear by Kant, but can be constructed as follows. Individuals exist as subjects with wills to determine ends, and therefore are ends in themselves. Those ends must be the concerns of all as rational beings in the framing of universal laws. Hence, every person's ends must enter every other person's moral concerns and thereby gain recognition and respect from all others.

If one were acting within the liberal institutional environment with the stress on the rightness of egoistic action, must not one treat other individuals wholly as means for the economic mechanism to function? Or if one were imbued with the social desirability of efficient allocation of resources, would not one be led by reason to the same principles of impersonal, arms'-length treatment of other agents? Might the injunction be interpreted to mean not to treat rational beings *wholly* as means, and hence simply imply the compassionate strain of the individualistic strand of the ethos? The statement recognizes the necessity of treating others in part as means, but it seems to assert the need *in each action* to take into account the existence of the person as an end to some extent. But Kant says nothing about the degree to which one may use others as means, a failure which does much to lessen the relevance of his theory to economic justice.

Yet this is certainly a valuable derivation nonetheless, if supportable. Kant would then purport to have derived the basis for compassionate social action by universally applicable logic—a basis whose nature I have ignored by adopting the right to benefit from such action as a primitive. Man as an end in himself, possessing freedom to choose his own ends and the will to achieve them, must in logic be treated as moral subject not merely as an instrumental object. This precept requiring the respect of each for each certainly implies the necessity of the liberal, democratic political mechanism, as well as a social concern for the basic economic welfare of all.

But in the absence of greater specificity in giving guidance concerning how this principle shapes the mundane outlines of the society's economic allocation and distribution institutions, it remains a validation of uncertain range and intent. The extent of conformity of the Kantian theory to existing economic institutions therefore is not clear. The free market mechanism, as a wholly egoistically driven instrument, imposes a motivation on agents that is neither clearly supported nor opposed by the universalization precept. The injunction to give some recognition of individuals as ends does not necessarily rule out their role as means in individualistic economic dealings, but certainly raises a doubt.[6]

As noted above, the Second Formulation may be satisfied by the action of the state to institute corrective and compassionate monitoring and supplementation of the market economy's functioning, so that the theory conforms to and indeed supports existing liberal institutions. But Kant's striving for a theory of ethics based on pure reason without reference to natural or social bearings gives it a directionless irrelevance to the construction of an operational counterpart in economic justice.

Finally, and with greater exactitude, one can assert that the relation of the notion of right to that of good is that the former is the source of the latter. Kant's ethical theory is rule-driven—some would say, rule-obsessed—by man's duty to follow the dictates of reason implanted in Nature's purposes. Had her goal been that of permitting man to seek happiness alone as *the* good in life, she would not have endowed him with reason and the higher ends she envisaged for him. The appeal to a teleological intention embedded in human nature may or may not convince one of the proper ends of life, but it does define the direction of Kant's derivation of the good from the principles of right.

Incentives to Act in Accordance with the Right

The individual's incentive to act in accordance with the principles dictated by the categorical imperative is not very convincing, especially when the conflict between following the path of duty and that of self-interest may be quite severe. Kant's motivational basis is an asserted deeper satisfaction that the individual feels in so doing and participating in the "legislation" of universal laws. One of the prime difficulties encountered in the study of socially oriented theories and their applicability to the derivation of a theory of economic justice is the weakness of their arguments in this area of incentivization. The strength of the egoistic drives in a free market economy, buttressed by an ethos that gives high priority to this strand of individualism, makes it extremely doubtful that appeals to an overriding social preference can be effective. Kant's appeal to such potential is among the weaker apologia, in part because he devoted little time to developing the theme.

Depending on the uncertain extent of the domain of principles of economic justice dictated by the call of duty, enforcement could become a major problem. Because Kant's very definition of such a domain depends on conflict with "natural inclinations," were the universalized principles instituted in a framework of economic justice it would require extensive modifications in existing economic institutions.

Compatibility with the Ethos

The strength of the social strand in Kant's theory, as encapsulated in the Second Formulation of the categorical imperative, and as potentially productive of an extensive body of economic justice principles, may very well conflict with the ethos. But once more, the indistinct boundaries of economic justice that Kant's general theory of ethics permits us to discern does not allow a more specific discussion of that conflict. This same difficulty exists in viewing its relationship to the strand of pragmatic rationalism: it simply cannot be determined to what extent the principles would violate economic efficiency, for example.

On the other hand there would seem to be the possibility for coexistence with a materialistic culture. Happiness is viewed as a practical good for the individual, and the right of the individual to pursue happiness is uncontested. Presumably the materialist basis of much of that happiness would not be challenged. It is true, of course, that Kant viewed such a good as inferior to the higher call of duty, but that need not displace in his theory the predominant role of the search for lesser satisfactions in the typical individual's life nor the duty of each to help others to achieve such material satisfactions.

A Final Word on Kantian Theory

The most damning criticism of Kant's theory of social ethics in its relation to the task of defining an operational theory of economic justice is its generality. It is more in the nature of a methodology to derive principles of social or economic justice than an exposition of derivable principles themselves. To what extent such precepts derived from reason's discernment of categorical imperatives would interfere with the operation of a market economy, or demand the existence of an alternative economic organization, or depend for successful innovation on major changes in the American ethos, is unclear. As a direct and challenging source of alternative principles of economic justice that might be considered by the constituent assembly, therefore, it is not helpful.

Intriguing, however, is the potential implication of the Second Formulation of the categorical imperative for the operation of the market economy. Its injunction against the total use of rational beings as means if applied in the economic area could well rule out this mechanism of individualistic decision making. Factor services are treated impersonally in the market, not excluding labor services, and must be so treated to permit its efficient operation. In a broader social sense the liberal society views the individual as an end in him- or herself, but in the economic mechanism that treatment is suspended. Would the Kantian imperative establish principles that viewed this as unacceptable? Once more, it is not clear. The prohibition is not against ever considering the individual as a means, but rather not treating him or her *wholly* as such.

Kant's stimulating contribution to the task ahead is his attempt to ground the individualistic tenet of liberalism in reason. Man as a rational being has a will that dictates his ends. He is independent of the need for external forces to establish those goals. Hence, he is an end in himself, not a means to any further end, and he must be treated as such. We have treated such a view axiomatically, but if Kant's argument is accepted it makes the argument for individualism a stronger one.

A Critique of Utilitarianism

As the dominant individual and social ethic in various forms for two hundred years, utilitarianism has undergone continuous criticism, yet been successful in retaining its loyal following. At the present time there is a bewildering variety of utilitarian ethical theories, but they may be grouped into three categories for analytical purposes:

1. *Act-Utilitarianism.* The classic utilitarianism of Jeremy Bentham and John Stuart Mill falls in this category, asserting that any specific action is moral if and only if its consequences, adjudged over all interested parties, yields a net benefit at least as great as any alternative action or non-action available to the agent. Morality, in this interpretation, focuses on each potential action of an agent and requires an objective judgment concerning consequences. The goodness or badness of actions, therefore, must be judged by an agent acting under specific circumstances, taking into account global consequences.

In defining the consequences, ethical philosophers debate the question whether they must be (1) the *actual* consequences ex post facto of the action, (2) the *intended* consequences of the action ex ante facto, or (3) those consequences that are *rationally expectable* under the circumstances. In general, in this type of utilitarianism and in the forms to be defined, the latter two interpretations of consequences are most frequently envisioned.

2. *Rule-Utilitarianism.* Under this form of the theory, the responsibility of the individual to judge the morality of an action on an individual-event basis is eliminated, and such actions are taken to be moral if and only if such acts would have net beneficial impacts for society *if most persons were to act similarly under identical circumstances.* Hence, to return to the example cited in chapter 3, were an individual faced with the possibility of condemning an innocent person in order to prevent a riot that might claim many lives—an act that under act-utilitarianism would demand the sacrifice of the innocent party—the burden of decision would be lessened by the need to ask what social consequences would result if such actions were undertaken under similar circumstances in most but not all situations. Society might well dictate that sacrifice of the individual's civil rights to the expediency of the moment would under the conditions of a general rule be of negative utility to society and might condemn the practice when consideration of results were generalized.

3. *Universalized Utilitarianism.* This form of the doctrine is distinguished from rule-utilitarianism only in that the decision is made under the assumption that the action is adopted as a *universal* rather than a general rule. That is, would such an action if it were accepted by society in all cases when the circumstances were duplicated result in a positive net global result?

The purpose of both rule-utilitarianism and universalized utilitarianism is to remove the responsibility for moral decision making from the individual and to invest it in a set of social rules whose extraction assumes a general or universal acceptance under like circumstances. In this manner society can inject into moral decision making a broader social concern for consequences that the individual must consult in his or her actions, and infuse decisions with social norms and values.

The Concept of the Good

Under all types of utilitarianism, two assumptions underlie the definition of the good and the right: actions are good or bad in a moral sense depending only on their consequences, defined in any of the three ways discussed above, and the only acceptable definition of essential good is that of *pleasure.* The *consequentialist* and *hedonist* principles are therefore basic to its formulation as a social ethic.

The asserted existential good for the individual is that of maximum pleasure (when pain is treated as negative pleasure) and, since John Stuart Mill, for the society is the maximization of the sum of individual happiness for a population of given size. For Bentham, individual pleasure had several dimensions—duration, intensity, degree of certainty, and so forth—but it was perceived to be measurable with cardinal uniqueness and interpersonal comparability, so that summation over individuals was possible. Such sums were to be taken over equally weighted individual utility levels, and no qualitative adjustments were legitimate. For Bentham these assertions were axiomatic, subject to neither proof nor disproof, but supported by observation of human behavior and by the purported elimination of alternative concepts.

Mill adopts Bentham's notion of the good with the refinement that individual pleasures differ qualitatively as well as quantitatively, with more sensitive individuals capable of experiencing a higher form of "happiness" which may indeed require undergoing a certain amount of pain to acquire. Mill is not clear about the manner in which such qualitative characteristics will affect the summation of individual satisfactions to arrive at the social maximand, but such utilitarians as Sidgwick are insistent that unless they can be quantified they must not be permitted to intrude into the notion of social good.[7]

One may quarrel with some fervor about whether or not individuals do act to maximize their selfish pleasures and with greater vehemence concerning their willingness to factor others' welfare into their calculations. Bentham was prone to the belief that individual and social utility coincided naturally or could be made to do so artificially. Mill was more explicit in recognizing their potential conflict and the need to examine the forces that led the individual to subordinate personal to social utility. It should be noted that economists do not make either assumption in their analysis of consumer choice, despite some misleading language. "Utility maximization" is performed on a preference function that is used to summarize the choices a consumer would make *for whatever reason*, and is derived from information concerning such choices obtained from the consumer him- or herself. The economist simply uses such information to project the consumer's choices under hypothetical conditions on the basis of that information by using the *convention* of maximizing the value of that preference function subject to relevant constraints. It is the economist who is performing the maximization as a means of extracting revealed information or inferences from it in a convenient manner, but it in no way involves any assumption about the consumer explicitly or implicitly performing such operations.

If, in a different context, one meets objections to the notion that the individual is following other motivations in this or that instance with the defense that the individual derives a form of pleasure therefrom, however contrary to appearance the consequence may be, one runs the danger of converting the hypothesis to a tautology. If the agent is asserted to be choosing the action because it yields the maximum satisfaction from the set of alternatives simply by virtue of the fact that the act is chosen, then the assertion of pleasure maximization has no normative content. The agent can do nothing else but maximize satisfaction by definition.

But these concerns are beside the point when considering the doctrine as a social ethic, for then the "ought" replaces the "is" as the dimension of interest. In this respect Bentham and Mill are correct in arguing that the assertion of net pleasure as the ultimate individual or social good is not subject to proof but is an ethical value judgment. The only question one may legitimately raise is whether or not it is the ultimate good, or whether it is a means to a higher good which itself is incapable of logical examination. Mill, in accepting this proposition, but widening the concept of "proof" to evidence of the senses concerning behavioral motivation, discerning thereby that people desire pleasure and therefore that it must be a good, is confusing the "is" with the "ought." Desire and desirability cannot be so related: the fact that some people may derive pleasure from criminal acts does not make such pleasure desirable from a moral standpoint.

Hence, quarrels concerning concepts of the good life are disputes involving individuals' value judgments and become sterile when converted into arguments about ultimate ends that inhere in the natural order and are discoverable by reason. When defined prior to the definition of the right they are value judgments either more or less compatible with the intuitive notions of acceptable ends held by others.

The Principles of Right

The principles of right, therefore, derive from the notion of good. For the individual, right action consists in (1) choosing those alternatives that maximize individual utility after taking into account the positive or negative impacts on all interested parties, under act-utilitarianism, or (2) following the rules dictated by rule- or universalized utilitarianism indicated above.

The objections to the notion of right as defined by act-utilitarianism have already been stated. It imposes on each individual the burden of discerning the utility he or she derives from each action, the identities of all of the persons affected by such acts, the utilities or disutilities accorded to each such person, and the aggregate utility as a sum. It is doubtful that the typical individual has the capability or the time to probe so extensively into social impacts to identify relevant parties, not to mention determine utility increments in a manner that yields meaningful summations. Further, considering only the individual action of each agent, were he or she capable of such calculation, decisions would then be without the broader social impacts implicit if such actions were made generally or universally. And finally, one must always allow for the likelihood that individual self-interest would warp decisions away from those that truly maximized the social utility of his or her acts. It is unrealistic, for example, not to expect the individual to weight the impacts of his or her decisions on relatives or friends more heavily than the impacts on others—nor is it clear that it is socially desirable to eliminate this bias were it possible.

When the individual is spared this travail with the implantation of rules based on general or universalized behavior, some of the pitfalls implied under act-utilitarianism can be avoided. The potential for act-utilitarianism to violate fundamental civil rights and intuitive notions of justice has been noted above. The assertion by Mill (quoted in chapter 3) of the distinctive nature of the disutility suffered by individuals when rules of justice are violated is an indication of his discomfort with this aspect of the doctrine, and his argument might well be construed as one to remove such consequences from the felicific calculus and introduce them as constraints on the maximization of more routine forms of utility.

Attaining a similar end through rule-utilitarianism or its universalized form involves the establishment of a rule-making authority and a set of weights over social consequences that do not derive from individual pleasure. It is not clear, for example, in the case of the vengeful mob and the innocent scapegoat, on what quantitative basis the rule maker would arrive at a net social disutility were such sacrifices generalized or universalized. Such social implications would be derived from considerations that transcend sums of utility conceptually existent in particular instances. Use of these two reinterpretations of utilitarianism, therefore, effectively introduces principles of right action that are not based in an identifiable sense on pleasures and pains of individuals, by intruding "overriding social considerations" into the principles of right. Again, constraints reflecting such considerations are one manner of doing so.

Nor do these procedures give unambiguous guidelines for the determination of such principles. Consider, for example, the individual who decides that the cost in time and inconvenience involved in voting yields more negative pleasure than casting of the ballot yields positive pleasure. Consequently, he or she does not vote. Were such action generalized or universalized, however, democracy would be unworkable. Therefore, suppose the rule-making authority assesses a fine against all nonvoters sufficiently large to induce most or all individuals to vote. But is it socially desirable to force uninformed or disinterested voters to cast ballots, perhaps spitefully? Should the policy not be to force or induce *interested and informed* individuals to vote, and to *discourage* others? But how does the rule-making authority establish rules that permit this fine discrimination? Rewards for voting might encourage the unqualified more than the qualified, and be unnecessary for most voters. And is it a wise manner to establish principles of right on the assumption that a particular action is generalized or universalized when in fact it will not be? Act-utilitarianism makes no such assumption in permitting the uninterested voter to opt out of the polling and may thereby attain a socially more desirable consequence.

Taken more broadly, utilitarianism possesses the advantages of deriving principles of right from a simple and intuitively plausible motivation: the maximization of social good, where good is defined as the receipt of pleasure by human beings (and possibly extends to all sentient creatures). But that simplicity begins to vanish when intuitive principles or social norms enter into the computation of social utility as essentially external constraints on personally defined pleasures. Might Bentham and Mill have been right in believing that such social norms are best inculcated in the education of the individual and the sanctions or rewards of public opinion, accepting some failure to conform to them as inevitable and less costly to suffer than correct? How much of utilitarianism survives when the simple sum of individual pleasures, simply conceived, is replaced by notions of social utility derivable wholly in intuitive fashion from the preferences of rule makers over social values and norms whose choice is arbitrary in itself?

How relevant is the principle of right to economic behavior and how well does it conform to the market mechanism? Its most direct implication for the direction of economic motivation is in the distributive area and that implication is in direct conflict with the distribution dictated by the market's energizing motivation. As a decentralized system, there is no social welfare function that the market is attempting to maximize, although in its ideal, never-attained form it does achieve several necessary conditions that would hold in a command economy where such a function is being purposively optimized.

It most certainly does not achieve a distribution of income that can make any claim to maximizing average individual utility or total social utility defined in less clear fashion. Individual agents act wholly selfishly taking into account only those effects of their actions that register through the market on parameters of importance to their decision making. Most impacts on others are negligible, become negligible on an individual basis when dispersed over large numbers, or are treated as externalities. As a theory of economic justice, utilitarianism's strong social dictates are unattainable in the market's operations and must be imposed by substantial governmentally imposed alterations of the distributive mechanism on a continuous basis if the market economy is to be continued in use as an allocative tool.

An important decision field for government in the economic arena would be the need to take account of externalities that may have no impacts in the small, in that particular individuals affected are not identifiable, and yet which may be hypothesized to have important impacts in the large. For example, egalitarian income policies that may be indicated on the basis of straightforward summation of individuals' utilities, including identifiable externalities, may lead to reduced employment or inefficiencies in production. It is difficult to see how utilitarianism—a consequentialist philosophy—could discern the potentials of such actions or governments could quantify them to offset the sums of individual utilities. Presumably policymakers would have to step outside the formal utilitarian methodology and enact constraints on distributive decisions in an intuitionist manner. As was shown in chapter 3, John Stuart Mill seems to have foreseen some need to restraint the felicific calculus on grounds of "overriding social concerns," but went no further in expositing methodology.

It is important to note that social concerns at the core of utilitarianism's principles of right do not imply egalitarianism of income or of satisfaction and indeed may run counter to the compassionate dictates of the ethos. Suppose, for example, that the utilitarian were to choose between the following two income distributions on the basis of maximizing average income:

	Income Distribution	
	Distribution 1	*Distribution 2*
Individual 1	100	200
Individual 2	100	75
Individual 3	100	30
Average	100	101.67

The utilitarian acting to maximize per capita income would opt for the second distribution, despite its extreme inequality when compared with the first, and the potential distress of Individual 3 within it.

Incentives to Act in Accordance with the Right

Doubt can be entertained whether individuals in different strata of an individualistic society would be drawn in enlightened self-interest or charity to the greatest collective happiness principle as the expression of moral and legal obligation. Man's rational self-interest has not consistently led him to paths of social obligation and certainly cannot be shown to have induced him to embrace the extended greatest happiness principle. Similar statements are justified in judging the effects of education and institutions in moving men toward such nondiscounted accounting of their neighbors' feelings.

Mill's ultimate appeal to the social sentiments of man is consistent with many principles of morality and justice.[8] It is not a support for utilitarianism but rather an argument for *some* body of moral principles and *some* definition of those to be encompassed by legal protection. Indeed, this is merely to say that if society is to exist some desire to cooperate must develop and must effect some structure for coexistence. However, the principles of right yielded by utilitarianism may offend intuitive concepts of justice in two respects: extensive redistribution of income may be necessary to effect the necessary per capita income maximization and some persons may be left in great poverty. As indicated in the example above, neither income egalitarianism nor the expression of social compassion is an inherent implication of utilitarianism's principles of right. The strains on enforcement, therefore, could be quite severe.

These assertions may seem debatable in view of the quotations from Mill reproduced in chapter 3, since at times he seems to assert that everyone has "an equal claim to the means of happiness"; however, such statements are qualified by the needs of "social expediency."[9] His notions of "social expediency" are not stated and might very well include concerns about the impact of economic equality on efficiency, as will be elaborated upon below. Equality of "treatment" certainly has the appearance of embracing income equality, but strict application of the greatest happiness principle defined in Mill's terms could lead to large income inequalities, as illustrated in the tabular example above. Additional assumptions concerning individuals' abilities to enjoy happiness are necessary to establish it as a support for equal treatment in this sense.

Confusingly, however, Mill asserts that individuals have an equal claim to happiness and to the means of happiness except insofar as "the inevitable conditions of human life and the general interest in which every individual is included" set limits to that principle. At the same time, Mill urges that these conditions should be strictly construed. Exactly what those conditions and the general interest are with respect to their role in moving the desirable income distribution away from equality is unclear. Do they permit the role of incentives and efficiency to dictate inequality, and if so, how much? Does the equality condition exclude persons who choose not to work and hence not to contribute to the social stockpile?

At another point Mill seems to respond negatively to the last question:

> If it is a duty to do to each according to his deserts, returning good for good as well as repressing evil by evil, it necessarily follows that we should treat all equally well (when no higher duty forbids) who have deserved equally well of *us,* and that society should treat all equally well who have deserved

equally well of *it*, that is, who have deserved equally well absolutely. This is the highest abstract standard of social and distributive justice; towards which all institutions and the efforts of all virtuous citizens should be made in the utmost degree to converge. . . . It is involved in the very meaning of Utility, or the Greatest Happiness Principle. That principle is a mere form of words without rational signification, unless one person's happiness, supposed equal in degree (with the proper allowance made for kind), is counted for exactly as much as another's.[10]

Participation in the production of society's goods would seem to be a precondition for benefit. But to what extent? What determines "equal" desert? Effort? Intensity of effort? Value of effort in some utility sense? In another context, Mill discusses two theories of product distribution in a cooperative industrial effort: a contributory theory and one of equality for equal effort. Only social utility can decide which theory of justice should rule, he asserts, but they do not have the same implications for income distribution nor does either result in equality of satisfactions or income.

But strictly interpreted the claim that all persons have equal claims to happiness and the means of attaining it is not consistent with Mill's significant departures from Bentham's views on the interpersonal nature of utility and the capacity for its enjoyment. Mill argues that individuals do have differential capacities to derive happiness from economic means, and in making these important distinctions concerning the heterogeneity of pleasures and the qualitative differences of such utilities among men, destroyed Bentham's critical assumption for the operationalism of the doctrine in the policy field concerning the intra- and interpersonal measurability of utility. This is certainly not an argument for equality of income shares nor even of equal utility, somehow calibrated, nor does it give support to the notion that men will support such equality out of their purported sense of social cohesion. Maximization of social utility argues for higher incomes for those capable of experiencing these more deeply satisfying sensations in order to overcome the implicit suffering. But an alternative argument could be made for rewarding them with less income to compensate for the more deeply satisfying pleasures they obtain from their activities. In any event, the greatest happiness principle and its requirement that marginal utilities be equalized would not give presumptive preference to income equality in Mill's system.

One of the significant efforts to incorporate Mill's differentiation of satisfaction potential among individuals, and yet salvage the egalitarian implications for income distribution in Bentham's theory without adopting the untenable assumption that all persons have equal capacities for enjoyment, was made by Abba P. Lerner.[11] He made two relevant assumptions about individuals' satisfactions: first, that they were "similar" for all individuals, and second, that as a function of income they revealed diminishing marginal utility. The term "similar" was not clearly defined, but among other attributes was meant to permit ranking satisfaction levels among persons. Effectively, Lerner assumes that utility is cardinally measurable and interpersonally comparable, but that the functions are not capable of observation.

Interestingly, Lerner's proposition is true for an *ex ante facto* distribution of income, or one in which an *original* distribution is being considered, but is not established for an existing *ex post facto* distributive move from an existing distribution. Operationally, the latter situation is the more relevant condition, that is, redistribution decisions on the basis of a theory of economic justice. Indeed, it is within this context that Lerner chooses to motivate his theorem, and I shall consider his presentation first using figure 6.1. Suppose that a society had a *fixed income* (so that incentive effects of different distributions are assumed absent) of $200 to distribute between $n=2$ individuals, A and B, whose marginal utility of income functions are graphed as AA' and BB'. A's income is measured on the horizontal axis from left to right and B's from right to left.

As the functions are drawn, A has a higher capacity to enjoy income than B, but their marginal utilities (were they observable) would be equal at the value S where the distribution is [$150, $50]. At this point social utility as a Benthamite sum of individual utilities would be maximized.

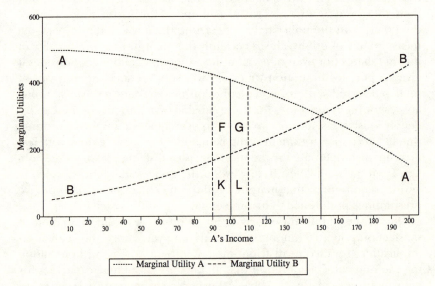

FIGURE 6.1. Marginal Utility of Income—A and B

But, absent the ability to observe these functions, Lerner proposes that the equal distribution [$100, $100] would maximize expected social utility. Suppose that distribution were in effect. If a small quantity of income (e.g., $10) were transferred from *B* to *A*, or from the person with lesser enjoyment capacity to the person with more, the latter would gain *G+F* in utility and the former lose *F*, for a net social gain of *G*. Were the transfer to go in the opposite direction, from the one with greater to the one with lesser capacity, the gain would be *K* and the loss *L+K*, for a net loss in social utility of *L*.

However, in fact it is impossible to know which individual's capacity for enjoyment is higher and which is lower, so that a $20 transfer from one to the other may represent a gain or a loss in social utility. In the absence of any knowledge about the distribution of individuals' capacities, Lerner adopts the principle of insufficient reason and assumes that the probability of a movement in either direction is .5. Hence the expected value of the change in social utility is

$$E(U) = .5G + .5L$$

which is nonobservable, but given diminishing marginal utility of income for both parties, *L* will be larger than *G*. Hence, *dE(U) < 0, and the movement away from income equality will lead to a decline in expected social utility.* Therefore, Lerner concludes, such a distribution maximizes expected social utility and recommends itself on a probabilistic basis as the just distribution under utilitarian definitions of the good and the right.

But Lerner's argument does not prove his proposition. What it establishes is the unwisdom of moving from *any* initial distribution of income. For if such an arbitrary point were chosen on the horizontal axis of figure 6.1, either to the left or the right of the true maximum at [$150, $50], *L > G*, so that a redistribution away from that point would reduce expected social utility.

The reasons for this result are not hard to find. The argument is simply a variant of the well-known proposition that for a person with diminishing marginal utility of income a fair bet at any point on his or her utility function will not be taken because the potential utility loss is greater than the potential utility gain. Society in Lerner's analysis is simply being placed in the situation where it is not profitable to gamble on an uncertain outcome in redistribution because of universal diminishing marginal utility of income (the sum of strictly concave individual utility functions).

Let the *total* utility functions of *A* and *B* be plotted as a function of *A*'s income receipts between $0 and $200. Each is a strictly concave function and their vertical sum, depicting social utility, will also be strictly concave, reaching a maximum at [$150, $50]. Beginning at any arbitrary

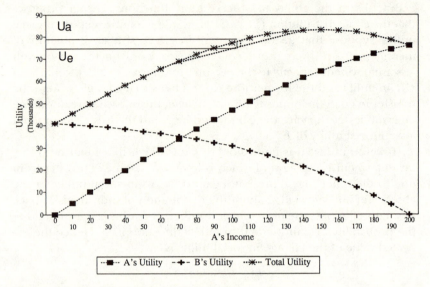

FIGURE 6.2. A and B Utility and Total Utility

initial point on the horizontal scale, say at [\$100, \$100] as in figure 6.2, construct a lottery with a .5 chance of a [\$75, \$125] distribution and a .5 chance of a [\$175, \$25] distribution. Its expected income distribution is the same as the initial distribution, but the expected utility value of the lottery (U_e) is less than the utility of the initial distribution (U_a). Society's risk aversion reflects that of its citizens, and movement from the initial position would result in a loss in social welfare.

However, Lerner's proposition does hold when income distribution is being established *ab ovo*. Suppose the \$200 in social income were to be distributed between *A* and *B* with utility functions

(1)
$$1.\ U_A = 1 - e^{-.1Y_\alpha}$$
$$2.\ U_B = 1 - e^{-.5Y_\beta}$$

where

(2)
$$Y_\alpha + Y_\beta = 200$$

In Lerner's conditions of ignorance, expected social utility is

(3)
$$E(U) = .5[(1 - e^{-.1\theta(200)} + (1 - e^{-.5(1-\theta)(200)})]$$
$$+ .5[(1 - e^{-.1(1-\theta)(200)} + (1 - e^{-.5\theta(200)})]$$

because when the shares $[\theta, 1-\theta]$ are distributed it is uncertain whether the share went to *A* (with the higher marginal utility of income schedule) or to *B*. The first order maximization condition is, then

(4)
$$\frac{dE(U)}{d\theta} = .5[20e^{-20\theta} - 100e^{-100(1-\theta)}]$$
$$+ .5[-20e^{-20(1-\theta)} + 100e^{-100\theta}] = 0$$

whose solution is $\theta = .5$. Both utility functions being strictly concave, $d^2E(U)/d\theta^2 < 0$ and a true minimum is achieved.

If one perceives the problems of defining principles of economic justice for the United States as involving a redistribution of income from status quo patterns, therefore, rather than specifying a distribution in perfect plasticity, Lerner's theorem is of doubtful operational relevance. One is not assured, even on probabilistic basis, that moving toward income equality will increase social utility.

One concludes that a convincing case can be made that utilitarianism is not inherently a body of theory that will yield principles of economic justice that moderate the income inequalities implied by egoistic theories. Nor is the social strand of individualism explicit in the principles. Social cohesion could be threatened on both counts, therefore, especially were Mill's rather meritocratic version taken literally.

Compatibility with the Ethos

It follows, therefore, that utilitarian economic justice could violate the individualistic component of the ethos by failing to comply with both of its strands. Redistribution of income to attain a per capita utility maximum would overrule the market economy's initial dictates, thereby confronting the egoistic values of the society. And the needs of greater equality of opportunity and support obligations for the unfortunate are also potentially neglected. The socially oriented nature of utilitarianism therefore springs from the organic manner in which it treats social income, distributing it in a manner that ignores the personal consequences of maximizing a global magnitude,[12] not from a compassion-driven goal.

In essentially ignoring the implications of its income distribution procedures on incentives and economic efficiency, the theory also runs a substantial risk of contravening the pragmatic rational content of the liberal value system. No doubt some compromise could and would have to be made with this social goal were such principles to be established, but the latter are strongly violative of productive efficiency.

However, the doctrine gives strong support to the materialist accents of the value system. By stressing pleasure or happiness as the supreme goal of individual life and its maximization as a social goal, the worthwhileness of the material is certainly given a central position in its norms.

A Final Word on Utilitarianism

Utilitarianism now denotes a spectrum of theories of social equity, differentiated by the act-specificity or the rule-specificity of its strictures as well as by supplementary but crucial assumptions concerning the similarity or dissimilarity of individuals' capacities for experiencing pleasures. All of them, however, share a teleological structure in that they define individual and social good as the maximization of some form of physical or psychological sensation, and derive their principles of right and justice from those definitions. Economic justice, therefore, in its distributive phases, consists in enforcing the rules necessary to maximize the sum of individual pleasures dependent on economic activities, subject perhaps to rules that constrain the optimization within the domain of political and civil rights for the individual.

The core of dispute about the desirability of utilitarian precepts of economic justice for any society is centered on the assumption that income distribution should be shaped by a desire to equate the marginal utility of income of individuals. Where this goal is compromised, by rules that intrude other social goals, for example, utilitarianism becomes an eclectic theory with large intuitive content.[13] Substantial redistributions away from the market economy's pattern must be anticipated, therefore, and great faith tends to be put in the operation of diminishing marginal utility of income to assure that such reshuffling results in more economic egalitarianism. That result, however, is by no means a firm conclusion when differential capacities are taken into account: differences among individuals in the rate at which marginal utilities decline (the second derivative of the total utility function) could well dictate enhanced inequality.

The doctrine also bears the burden of being nonoperational, in that the uniqueness of utility measurement that it depends on is not possible, which goes far to cancel the advantage it offers in simplicity of structure. Government policymakers would have to make judgments of the form "I believe that A is receiving less pleasure than B because I would prefer B's situation to A's." While such judgments may be acceptable and necessary for decisions that involve incremental adjustments of distributions dictated by other principles, it delivers up to "wise men" much more power than desirable in a liberal society when global distributive decisions are at stake.

Utilitarianism clashes rather violently with the egoistic strand of individualism, and may indeed do so with the compassionate component. Economic justice based on its precepts would require substantial enforcement if the market economy is used to allocate resources, to the extent that it might well be unenforceable. Moreover, the efficiency of the allocation process could be severely affected. The materialistic thread in the ethos, however, should be reinforced by the emphasis given economic welfare in its definition of the good.

As a theory of social ethics, utilitarianism harbors a substantial antagonism between its urges to protect the individual and its inherent organicism. The maximization of a social aggregate when the distribution of that aggregate among persons is ignored and determined by capacity for enjoyment of pleasure may be questioned both on consequentialist grounds and the moral sufficiency of the distributive criterion. On these bases, too, the appropriateness of the theory as a guide to social justice in a liberal society is questionable.

A CRITIQUE OF RAWLSIAN RATIONAL PRUDENCE

As a social ethic whose design was much influenced by the Kantian rational approach and whose intent was to challenge utilitarianism's doctrines, Rawls's theory of justice as fairness holds a special interest for the purposes of this book. Has Rawls succeeded in avoiding the imprecision and questionable relevance of the Kantian theory to economic justice in a liberal society, while using its method to derive rationally appealing precepts of economic justice? Does he also succeed in building into the theory principles of right that incorporate the social dimension at the same time that they allow full exercise of the egoistic strand of individualism? Have we arrived at a socially oriented theory that can give practical guidance to the constituent assembly?

The Concept of the Good

Rawls's concept of good for the individual is a rather noncommittal one: the good life is one that is led following a rational plan that conforms to the principles of right. It would be difficult to imagine any theory designed for appropriateness in a liberal society which would derive a concept of individual good that could not be fit into such a description. This concept would permit such definitions as the maximization of material welfare or the radius of free choice, subscription to the performance of duty, or the hedonist search for happiness. The simple reason, of course, that Rawls asserts such a vague notion of the end of individual existence is that it was not the vital core of his theory. Rawls's theory of rational prudence is a deontological theory in which the good is independent of the right. The exclusive focus of the theory is on derivation of the principles of right, and consideration of the good is something of an afterthought. Its exact definition is unimportant as long as its pursuit does not violate the principles of right.

Moreover, the social good is simply the aggregate—not the sum—of individual good. Society has no independent concept of the good which it seeks to impose on individuals or to strive for in support of or in opposition to the efforts of individuals to follow their plans.

In short, therefore, Rawls gives short shrift to consideration of the existential ends of the individual, merely asserting that they should be sought in some rational manner over time following the fairness principles. The derivation of these principles of right are an all-but-exclusive concern of his theory.

The Principles of Right

Those principles—as summarized in his final formulation and reproduced in chapter 3—are derived as a product of rational prudence in a state of fearful ignorance. Rawls goes to extreme lengths to obtain the equivalent of a "disinterested observer" in each participant in the social contracting process. The First Principle and First Priority Rule are affirmations of civil and political rights and their placement outside of the economic mart. They are elegant statements of the implications of individualism in a liberal society and as such are beyond dispute. The focus therefore is on the meaning, derivation, and social impacts of the Second Principle and the Second Priority Rule.

Objections have been made to the "unrealistic" nature of the original position as a means of deriving operational principles, but I believe this is misplaced criticism. Rawls has every intellectual right to ask his readers to perform a mental experiment designed to eliminate inclinations to bias judgments in the direction of their known advantages or disadvantages. This is an imaginative use of social contract theory that permits every person to engage singly in a constitutive process—or a Kantian "legislative" function—and to explore the principles which an uninformed self-interest would lead him or her to adopt. However, whether all or a majority of such participants would be led to the principles that Rawls asserts, whether such principles conform to existing social mechanisms or would require changes in their structure, and whether the principles and any revised mechanisms would be consistent with the American ethos are separate questions.

Serious questions arise about the validity of Rawls's attempt to deduce the nature of the decision-making process from which unanimous agreement would be achieved by participants behind the veil of ignorance. First, and perhaps inevitably, some doubt exists about the extent of the imperfect knowledge individuals possess in that state. The "general organizational facts" concerning the society that are known include the size of society, its level of economic attainment, and its institutional structure. Such data could very well lead participants away from the adoption of Rawlsian principles, as will be argued below.

A second criticism is that although every participant is ignorant of his or her attitudes toward risk, he or she will act in extremely risk-averse manners by identifying with the least-advantaged class and adopting the conservative maximin strategy to protect against income being reduced below a floor value and to raise that floor value as high as possible. Implicitly, this must suggest that each individual acts as if the economy functions at subsistence levels, or that the probability of it being in that state is menacingly high. But if they do know the level of economic attainment, this need not be true, and if they do not, in a state of ignorance the likelihoods of any particular income level are not available and the adoption of a "worst-state" assumption could be excessively pessimistic.

Besides, there is a simple way the participants could protect against this fearful ignorance. In his discussion of the determination of the just savings rate, Rawls asserts that this element in the dynamic principles of justice is a function of the level of income attained by any generation and must be determined on the basis of assumptions about those levels. Hence, the principles of economic justice are partially determined by income levels. Why should this not also be true of the static principles of justice? The degree of conservatism behind individual participants' decision making would vary with assumed per capita income levels.

Why would they not then draw up *conditional* principles of justice from which the effective set could be chosen once the level of income was known? On the basis of Rawls's own reasoning, were the participants to hypothesize that the average income level were $50,000 per year, they should certainly act in a less conservative manner than if they hypothesized that it was $15,000 per year. The acceptability of Rawls's principles of economic justice hinges on the assertion that in the absence of such knowledge and that of their attitudes to risk persons would act *as if* they were extremely risk-averse. That they would so act in itself is debatable, but that they would not follow the procedures he himself suggests they must in considering intertemporal justice seems incredible. And if they do, the effective rules of justice that would emerge for an affluent society would differ greatly from Rawls's.

The rational support for adjusting all social mechanisms and institutions to benefit the least advantaged and to provide fair equality of opportunity weakens substantially as income levels rise from subsistence to comfortable to affluent. No doubt the need for compassionate treatment for the least-advantaged would continue to exist, but the difference principle might well be abandoned in favor of Pareto optimality, and *fair* equality of opportunity—which requires substantial institutional changes, not excluding forbidding of "excessive" accumulations of property and wealth—might well become more conventional equality of opportunity.

The capacity to enact such conditional rules of economic justice also casts serious doubts on the rational legitimacy of the Second Priority Rule. Efficiency might become of much higher priority than Rawls is willing to concede and the difference principle (or its probable successor, the Pareto principle) might gain a more prominent role than fair equality of opportunity were level of affluence considered.

Third, Rawls's attempt to use his framework to deduce principles of economic justice in an intertemporal or intergenerational setting results either in failure to derive such principles in the case of a just pattern of savings or in highly questionable results, as in the case of his conclusions concerning the nonapplicability of the difference principle. As noted in chapter 3, the task of the participants is a daunting one. They must assume sequentially they are members of particular generations, decide somehow on a fair savings rate for each hypothetical level of income available to that generation, then tie those rates together into trajectories of savings alternatives in a rational and just plan for a period of unspecified time or until that rational plan indicates that the just rate of net savings is zero.

One important indication of the inappropriateness of the veil of ignorance in determining just savings patterns is the Rawlsian deduction that self-interest would lead participants uncertain of their generation to adopt a zero rate of time preference, if in fact this will happen. Economists are fairly in agreement that the postponement of consumption by one generation for the benefit of future generations inflicts a true psychic cost on the savers and in voluntarist economies would lead to compensation. Indeed, given the productivity of capital, the resource that limits its accumulation and keeps the interest rate positive is this reluctance to save. To the extent that justice dictates some reward for the provision of a scarce factor, therefore, the adoption of a zero price for its supply seems inequitable, permitting later generations to take advantage of earlier, so to speak. Moreover, it is unclear that ignorance of one's generational identity would lead rationally to a zero rate of time preference. Each participant must hypothetically assume he or she is in a particular generation at a hypothetical array of income levels: it is unclear why, with such specific identification, participants would not consider the psychic cost of sacrificing consumption for generations (at least two, Rawls says) whose benefits they will not hypothetically share.

The amount of saving in each generation is then determined on the basis of principles of justice that Rawls asserts are derivable but does not derive. Given such levels of savings time-phased over the planning period, an interest rate will emerge ex post facto determined by the state of technology existing at the time. Presumably another schedule of potential environments must be hypothesized which somehow forecasts the states of technology in order to obtain interest rates for use in allocating hypothetical savings levels over time. Also, although he dismisses positive time preference as a factor, Rawls believes that interest rates will reflect the downgrading of future satisfactions that occurs with increasing affluence of those generations. This is unclear as it implies an impacting of the rate of interest by a positive time preference factor which Rawls has previously eliminated in his analysis.

In determining just savings rates Rawls asserts that the difference principle cannot operate because future cannot benefit prior generations. For every hypothetical generation in the original position's planning period, straightforward application in an environment with zero time preference would dictate that a given generation should save as long as such savings benefit the least-advantaged of all future generations more than it hurts the least-advantaged of the hypothetical present generation. Rawls realizes, of course, this would imply a large savings rate for all generations prior to the generation that attains a steady state capital equipment, and that in turn would imply a great degree of income inequality to the extent it facilitates savings. But he seems to imply that self-interest would lead each hypothetical generation to favor its own least-advantaged class at the expense of future least-advantaged for the same reason that participants identify with that class in the static analysis. However, this is merely to say that the present generation would discount the satisfactions of future generations at some positive rate, or that a positive rate of time preference would emerge after all. Indeed, the nonapplicability of the difference principle in the intertemporal setting sets that rate of discount at infinity. The inconsistency in Rawls's position is clear.

But is the rate of time preference determinate at any level in Rawls's framework? In the original position his planning time *is* reversible, as each hypothetical generation makes decisions sequentially and then iterates until a satisfactory trajectory of just savings is somehow determined. Would not each successive hypothetical generation seek to burden prior generations with high savings rates, reflecting perhaps negative time preference, undoing those prior decisions to save much less if anything? After several iterations of these walks through time, would participants throw up their hands and impose a zero rate of time preference as Rawls asserts? If so, this would lead to the applicability of a dynamic difference principle, as indicated above. Or would the participants accept the indeterminacy implicit in the exercise and adopt other principles of justice? In short, rational self-interest would lead to indeterminate principles of intergenerational justice and must be supplemented by other principles from frameworks other than Rawls's. The latter is simply unworkable in the dynamic version of the original position.

Rawls's effort to derive a complete theory of social equity that incorporates a comprehensive framework of economic justice, and to do so within an imaginative social contractarian generator, is as impressive in its achievement as in its ambition. But nonetheless, one is left with troubling reservations about his methodology and its application. With regard to the latter, basic questions arise concerning the adoption of principles he imputes to participants on the basis of their self-interest, and therefore of the rational validity of his principles. The more important of those shortcomings have been discussed above.

But Rawls's methodology also raises a question which was posed several times in chapter 5: can an acceptable theory of economic justice that incorporates society's obligations to its unfortunates be based wholly on egoistic self-interest? In other instances the question was raised because egoistically oriented theories neglected such duties; in the case of Rawls it is because egoistic rational prudence is asserted to embrace them to the exclusion of other obligations. Is it just to signalize *any* class as favored to the exclusion or subordination of the interests of others? Though one must admire the intellectual *tour de force* by which Rawls derives such exclusive benevolence from its antipodal motivation, does fearful ignorance serve as an adequate base to reach such extreme principles of right?

Incentives to Act in Accordance with the Right

Although it is not entirely clear the degree to which the difference principle would permit inequality of income in the Rawlsian society, there is an upper bound beyond which Rawls believes that it threatens the First Principle. Certainly there is a strong flavor of egalitarianism in his presentation, and one is entitled to assume that substantial redistribution away from the market economy's determination would be necessary. Moreover, instituting fair equality of opportunity would require fundamental changes in property accumulation, the educational system, and perhaps the family itself. Although Rawls asserts that his theory of justice is consistent with both capitalism and socialism, he seems to contemplate the use of the former to allocate resources but substantial state intervention in the distribution process.

Once through the veil of ignorance to their places in the social and economic structure of the developed liberal society, individuals for the largest part would find their situations more advantageous than their fearful expectations in the state of ignorance. It must be anticipated, therefore, that substantial pressure would exist to repeal the enacted

principles of economic justice to permit a greater role for more egoistically accommodating laws. Despite Rawls, it is difficult to conceive of a
functioning schizoid economy that is capitalistic in its allocation decisions and egalitarian socialist in its distributive decisions. Within a liberal
ethos and the present institutional structure of American society, the
direction of the motivation to change cannot be in much doubt.

What then will be the incentives for individuals to conform to the
principles of economic justice? Rawls does not assume the existence of a
general empathetic benevolence in individuals, but his explanation remains rather Millian in tenor. The individual, he believes, progresses
from childhood to adulthood through a succession of psychological development phases based on the reciprocity of affective relationships that
mature into a regard for the welfare of others. Further, individuals are
"just," he believes, in that they are desirous of living according to fair
principles, and would be motivated by that feeling. Moreover, the principles themselves inspire a sense of fraternity among members of society
which also serves as an inspiration to accept the laws even when they
conflict with personal advancement. Also, as the society functions for a
time under such laws, the difference principle and the principle of fair
equality of opportunity serve to reduce the differentials among earned
incomes and thus to lessen egoistic pressures.

One need not be cursed with the stunted soul of an economist to have
doubts about the strength of such social motivations in the face of egoistic drives. They are weak reeds indeed to lean on in instituting such
completely nonegoistic principles of justice as those Rawls desires to em-
place. He himself realizes that given the imperfections of human nature,
some compromises with those principles will be necessary and at points
his description of the envisioned compromise society is close to that of
the enlightened liberal variety. As noted in chapter 3, it guarantees constitutional rights to equal liberty, establishes public education and subsi-
dizes private, extends minimum welfare payments to families in need,
corrects externalities and monopoly power, and guarantees full employment. Even allowing for the necessary extensions a Rawlsian philosophy
would insist on—especially the setting of the minimum support level at
that value that, with earnings, "maximizes the expectations of the least
advantaged group"—the stated outlines seem implicitly to admit the
difficult enforcement problems his pure principles would require.

Compatibility with the Ethos

The notion that superior talents and abilities should benefit all individuals in society rather than their possessors is incompatible with the
egoistic strand of individualism, interfering with current notions of the
entitlements due individuality. The enactment of that notion into dis-

tributive law would require substantial changes in the content of the American ethos that go far beyond the incremental. Further, the extreme emphasis Rawlsian principles give the compassionate strain also violates current notions of distributive fairness, essentially requiring all social policy to be formulated with the goal of maximizing the expectations of the least-advantaged. Such an extreme focus of social purpose on one rather ill-defined social segment is a revolutionary revision of the priority currently given this component of the ethos.

With respect to pragmatic rationalism one must be most concerned about the effects of the principles on economic efficiency. They remove the incentives of the individual to acquire skills and to apply full measure of dedication to effort, given the constraints placed on income and property accumulation. In the intertemporal setting, by eliminating positive time preference and treating savings as essentially costless except insofar as they reduce the welfare of the least-advantaged class of the current generation, an uncertain and inefficient method of determining savings and consequently the interest rate raises deep questions about the rationality of the growth process in a Rawlsian economy, or, indeed, its very determinateness.

Finally, for all Rawls's desired development of broader social affective relations, his principles give every prospect of being neutral in their impacts on the materialist bent of the ethos. The emphasis on the material components of the primary goods with which he is concerned does not appear to be much less than that currently engrained in the ethos.

A Final Word on Rawlsian Rational Prudence

Rational prudence theory is a complete theory of economic justice in that it explicitly addresses each of the four categories of questions used in this work to unify the critiques of both forms of those theories. Like Kant's system, and with greater precision, it seeks to derive pure principles of economic justice through the use of man's disinterested reason. Similar to the Kantian theory also, it imposes the duty of obeying right principles against one's self-interest on the basis of a love of just living, expressed somewhat less forcefully than Kant's prescription in the notion of the good life. As the "invisible hand" in the market economy, self-interest leads to a socially benevolent result unintentionally but effectively.

The set of criticisms that has met Rawls's formulation centers on his simulation of the decision making of the average participant in his original position. That rational self-interest in a state of dense ignorance will lead to the choices he asserts under static conditions is subject to question. By Rawls's own admission they do not lead to determinate results in a dynamic setting, and indeed contain inherent contradictory tendencies in that state.

Of the six theories examined in depth, except for the Marxist contributory variant the Rawlsian results in the greatest conflict with current institutions and the ethos in American society. Its pure principles of right if enacted into law would require the economic mechanism to become essentially socialistic with some bow toward inequality under strict conditions and within an upper bound. Within the tradition of socialism it would belong to that genus which specified a favored class and oriented its goals and policies to maximizing the welfare of that class. Those are momentous changes to recommend on the basis of uncertain deductions about human decision making in a dense state of ignorance. Within the body of liberal thought one may well question whether such "infracaninophilism"[14] can be truly termed "democratic."

Rawls writes "the decision as to which form of regime [a market economy with widely distributed ownership of productive resources or liberal socialist] is best for a given people depends upon their circumstances, institutions and historical traditions."[15] I view this stance as one that can be taken only after the propositions of the original position have been modified by compromises with the ethos of a community in reflective equilibrium. A regime dedicated to the Difference Principle and fair equality of opportunity could not simultaneously subscribe to individualistic liberalism in the purely egoistic or dualistic individualist forms. The society those Rawlsian propositions define in their pure form is one of democratic socialism, with somewhat Utopian foundations and lingering capitalist institutions especially in allocation matters.

On the extreme left, this implication is supported by the objections that orthodox Marxists have to original position Rawlsian principles. They view them as reflective of bourgeois society ignoring and therefore perpetuating class conflict in false consciousness; retaining the priority of individual "rights" that is blind to their unequal benefits and suppressive of communitarian obligations; failing to establish equal rights in the workplace; and Utopian in that Rawls does not provide a theory of transition from the "injustice" of capitalism to the "justice" of the principles.[16] It is in their view, therefore, somewhat short of a communist system.

Peffer, as a moderate Marxist, believes Rawls's reflective equilibrium concept is not acceptable but does accept most of the original position principles as a potential core of Marxist justice with some modifications. Peffer doubts the practicality of Marxist distributive principles in a communist society, even if affluence characterized it, but he does share Rawls's belief that the principles could provide justice in a class-divided society. Peffer's modifications to Rawlsian principles are:

1. Explicit provision of an income floor below which no individual would fall. Peffer is, therefore, as confused as I as to how this would integrate in a Difference Principle society.[17]
2. Equal (approximate) equality of the *worth* of liberty as well as strict equality of liberty, which would bound inequality.
3. The Difference Principle must include social bases of self-respect as well as material.
4. Democracy must be extended to the social and economic spheres, especially to the workplace, as well as the political.

I believe the first three of the "modifications" are explicitly or implicitly in Rawlsian original principle propositions, the first in the Difference Principle, the second in Rawls's definition of *fair* equality of opportunity, and the third at least implicitly in Rawls's emphasis on self-respect and its broader social base. Only the fourth I believe lies outside the Rawlsian precepts and it in Peffer's interpretation would mount a Marxist challenge to private ownership of property.

This last requirement, I think, might well rule a moderate Marxist just society incompatible with Rawlsian principles, as they certainly would be for an orthodox Marxist society. But on the other hand Rawls in his later work does not subscribe to the protection of property that is basic to individualistic liberalism:

> Liberties not on the list, for example, the right to own certain kinds of property (e.g., means of production) and freedom of contract as understood by the doctrine of laissez-faire, are not basic; and so they are not protected by the priority of the first principle.[18]

This proscription and the denial of the right of the individual to benefit from the valuation of his or her talents by the voluntary actions of others infringes the individualistic and dualistic notions of individuality and makes the Rawlsian principles inapplicable to American society. Rawlsian justice derives from a vision of the democratic egalitarian socialist community, lying somewhere between the democratic socialist and the Marxist society in its precepts of justice.

It is doubtful therefore that a constituent assembly would find much guidance for *economic* justice in Rawls's principles. His First Principle is simply a restatement of the eminence of political and civil rights which already exist as ideals in American society. The Second Principle, by focusing so intently on the obligations of society under the compassionate rights of the individual as recognized by the ethos, serves the practical purpose of helping to direct attention to such duties. But those matters are better approached directly rather than obliquely through a rather labored egoism.

A Summary

In the realm of economic justice, the contributions of the socially oriented theories of social equity to the task of devising an operational legal framework conformant to existing institutions and deeply ingrained norms and values are meager. In these respects their faults are serious and not subject to correction by supplementation.

Act-utilitarianism, which has been treated as utilitarianism's purest variant, dictates a social objective function which is unacceptable within the American ethos for a variety of reasons, most importantly for its denial of the propriety of egoistic individualism and, quite possibly, of compassionate individualism. The function is, besides, incapable of definition, and if instituted as a guide to social policy would yield far too much judgmental power to policy formulators. Rule-utilitarianism shares these faults but avoids some of act-utilitarianism's excesses by permitting a method of in-building the norms and values of the ethos to a greater extent. In doing so, however, it approaches the status of an intuitive theory departing from the social goal of the purer form of the doctrine more and more as such constraints are added to the decision process.

Kantian rationality is also a poor guide to our task for several reasons. Like utilitarianism it is a nonconsequentialist theory in distributive matters, with the troublesome features such a characteristic possesses for practical policy in a liberal state. But it is also an uncertain guide because "reason" in the absence of instruction in the degree of impact interdependence to be taken into account and the weighting given to each component does not yield uniquely specified rules of action. As a methodology for thinking through the desirability of suggested rules of economic justice it may have some value for the hypothesized assembly. Moreover, the Second Formulation, however strictly nonapplicable to the economic allocation process, injects a general caution into such deliberations that has great attraction to a liberal society in formulating the broader outlines of corrective and compassionate rules of justice. But as a generator of specific precepts of the economic right it is deficient.

Rawlsian rational prudence is a consequentialist theory, but the template it holds up for the judgment of economic justice is unsatisfactory in terms of the rationality of its derivation; it has revolutionary implications for economic institutions, norms and values; and, because of the weakness of the incentives of individuals to conform to its dictates, it would be difficult to enforce. It is therefore ill-conceived to give much valuable specific guidance in the formulation of rules of economic justice within a society whose interpretation of individualism places greatest emphasis

on the right of egoistic purpose and the propriety of benefiting materially from one's distinctive individuality. But the theory has an indirect
value, as does Kant's, in serving to keep the corrective and compassionate strand of individualism within the view of our hypothetical framers of
the bill of economic rights and obligations, preventing its submergence
under the weight accorded egoism in the American ethos.

Chapter 7

THE BASES FOR ECONOMIC
JUSTICE IN AMERICA: PHILOSOPHY,
RIGHTS AND OBLIGATIONS,
AND POLICY

THE DEFINING OVERVIEW: A FRAMEWORK FOR
ECONOMIC JUSTICE

We have reached the point in our presentation where we can pose the three questions whose answers constitute the goals of the inquiry:

1. What philosophy of economic justice is most appropriate for American society, given its values, norms, and governing mechanisms and their capacity for change in the foreseeable future?
2. With this philosophy serving to provide guidelines, what rights and obligations of the individual should be formalized in constitutional law to define applicable bounds for economic policy?
3. In the light of this bill of individuals' economic rights and obligations, what guidelines for policy formulation and administration are to be recommended?

In a sense we are joining Kant's "Kingdom of Ends" as a "legislator" of universal laws, and the burden of responsibility is awesome. Obviously, the subjective component of any such exercise is great but inescapable. This is especially true in the present case because rules of economic justice must conform to the American ethos, or change it within desirable and tolerable limits, and both the concept and its ability to yield to change are highly judgmental. That requirement therefore violates Kant's intention of forcing decisions on universal laws to be the product of reason alone. Whether or not that is possible is another question. Nor does the situation satisfy the requirements for a Rawlsian objective observer, at least in the sense of forestalling ideological bias whether or not self-interested.

In view of this highly personal nature of the analysis one is compelled to explain as carefully as possible the basis of one's choices, and to make explicit intuitive value judgments. In one guise or another such judgments must enter any theory of equity, but one does have the obligation to make them clear and explicit.

An Operational Theory of Economic Justice

The Necessity and Desirability of the Market Economy

Any acceptable theory of economic justice must make substantial concessions to the egoistic strand of the individualistic component of the ethos. I believe this is not only necessary but is morally desirable. American individualism incorporates the freedom of the individual to maximize self-interest within voluntarist frameworks as the most basic tenet in its informal principles of economic justice. Violations of this code are opposed vehemently, and are generally allowable (albeit reluctantly) only in the name of compassion or corrective principles. One important implication of this is that the only acceptable economic mechanism for individualistic decision making is a market mechanism, with limited interferences in its operation by government tolerated but deplored. No system of economic justice that does not start with the distribution dictated by the market and modify that scheme in directions required by the justice principles to relatively minor extents will be accepted by the society, nor should it be in my own value scheme. Excessive encroachments are and should continue to be viewed as limitations on freedom that is grounded in the dignity and responsibilities accorded each person in the liberal society.

This may seem to be an argument that no theory of economic justice that changes the status quo is acceptable, and hence that our whole exercise is wasted effort. While the emplacement of such constraints on our study does rule out the adoption of the more radical socially oriented theories in toto, it does not follow that substantial portions of their recommendations may not be emplaced to alter the market's dictates. *But it is true that the crucial decisions that must be made in the economic justice area concern exactly the degree, nature, and rationalization of these alterations in the name of the socially compassionate or corrective.* This observation narrows considerably the focus of my search for guidelines from the alternative theories.

The argument for use of the market mechanism as the primary and final allocator of resources for the most part is strongly reinforced by rational pragmatism. The logic of the market's allocation is relatively straightforward and sensed if not fully understood by the citizenry, even when its operation bruises self-interest. Efficiency in that allocation process is widely accepted as a socially desirable property of the economic mechanism and the market's superiority in its attainment generally applauded, although frequently with inadequate definition of that concept and an incomplete acceptance of some of its deficiencies. Moreover, every other aspect of rationalism that was discussed in chapters 1 and 4 is supported by the operation of such an economic system. The worker confronts the cause-effect duality daily so that the outlook becomes trivial; utilitarianism is the hallmark of decision criteria, reinforced by competitive pressures; science and technology are integral forces internalized within the market; profit and loss as rewards and sanctions energize it; and the planning and programming functions infuse firms' decision making.

Last, the market conforms wholly to the notion of the importance of the material in life. Its use by the economy as the very means by which it tempts resources into the uses it dictates helps to implant this component in the ethos and reinforces it daily. It is the lubricant that permits the system to function, without which it would soon lock resources into obsolescent patterns that would make it unacceptably inefficient. And the very end of the market economy is to provide the goods and services that meet the material desires of the masses of the population, at once stimulating and satisfying those material longings.

Some Alternative Theories Eliminated

The market's distribution of income cannot be justified in equity terms by a contributory theory of economic justice, for reasons detailed in chapters 3 and 5. Marginal productivity pricing of resources is a necessity for efficient allocation, however, and by its conformity to the rationalism component of the ethos provides some support for its acceptability. But this is independent of its acceptability in terms of equity, since compatibility with the ethos is a constraint on acceptability, not a positive endorsement.

The marginal productivity theory is supported by those who view the market economy primarily as a means of extending and protecting the freedom of the individual—an aspect of the egoistic strand of individualism in our framework—and the distribution of income that results from its operation is not justified independent of its necessity in performing that primary task. One should not denigrate the importance of such freedom of choice in a liberal society; indeed, I have stressed its importance in the individualism that inheres in the American ethos. The point is simply that putting such great stress on the free market's role in commutative justice neglects consideration of distributive justice. In the purest forms of such theories, *any* distribution of income resulting from the market's operation must be accepted by society as right because it is a necessary consequence of protecting the primary desideratum in social equity: freedom of choice and contract.

Justice-as-freedom theories have the additional disadvantage of defining the maximization of freedom of choice as the sole or the primary goal of social justice. The adoption of this value judgment leads to a view of the state's role in economic and social justice which does not reflect the values of the American ethos or modern liberalism in general. The state's power to protect individuals against persons who threaten their lives or welfare in serious ways extends to the individual him- or herself who wills such self-harm or whose ignorance endangers him or her seriously. The social corrective strand of individualism is slighted or deplored in such theories as Friedman's and Hayek's out of an excessive fear of state power, ignoring of the costs of competitive correction if such corrections will in fact occur, and expressing an unrealistic faith in the availability and symmetry of information in a market economy. Such justice-as-freedom theories therefore do not offer a philosophical basis that is sufficiently flexible to allow the social dimension of individualism to be incorporated as a comfortable supplement.

The Attractiveness of Entitlements Theory

However, Nozick's entitlement theory is an intuitively appealing theory of distributive justice in a liberal society when it is supplemented to constrain its excessive egoism and accept the dictates of social equity; that is, when it is based on dualistic individualism rather than egoistic. The distribution of the market economy meets a necessary condition for justice because, assuming the lack of force or fraud in prior or present acquisitions, the *process* from which the distribution is a fallout is just. That justice is based on the voluntarism that characterizes the mechanism and is reflective of the egoistic individualism that quite properly infuses the liberal society. The freedom of the individual to choose on both the supply and demand sides of markets, and to dictate the disposition of that which he or she justly obtains *validates* the distribution directly. One does not have to justify it indirectly by asserting that capitalist process maximizes the highest individual good in life and thereby makes distribution fallout inviolable.

Further, entitlements theory is just in permitting the expression of the individuality of the person, when that term encompasses the gifts from man or nature that he or she receives as legacy. Justice requires an even-handed treatment of natural and man-made bequests to the individual. Both yield material and immaterial economic benefits to their possessor and neither form should be discriminated against as is currently done in American tax policy. Rawls's position in this regard is a consistent one, in that he argues that both forms of bequest should benefit all (in a close-knit society) or the least-advantaged (in the absence of close-knittedness). But it is manifestly unjust to the individual to confiscate for social purposes his or her justly acquired property at death, diverting it from those to whom he or she wills it. It would be equally unjust to deny them the right in life to provide a differentially advantageous education to their children, or to deprive those children of the right to use and benefit from genetic advantages gained through the gene pool. Such restrictions impinge unacceptably on the protection of precious individuality in an individualistic society.

Performance of obligations in fulfillment of social compassion should be financed on the principle of equal sacrifice from the economically relevant results of both forms of legacy: the income that flows therefrom. "Reshuffling the deck" between generations by exactions from material legacies is an unjust discrimination between legacy types and a violation of the rights of those who acquired the property to transfer it in accordance with their wishes. To remove through taxation the benefits derived from differential abilities and talents solely because of their existence is to interfere intolerably not only with individuality but voluntaristic transfer, and so also by extension is the confiscation of inherited material advantages. Compensation for inherited disabilities, where income falls below socially determined minimum levels, is the proper concern of the compassionate facet of dualistic individualism and should be financed by the more fortunate through taxing the fruits of differential advantages through income levies in a just manner. Forcing such benefits to be shared equally treats individuals wholly as means to achieve the happiness of others, violating the Kantian dictate against contravening the dignity rooted in individualism.

The Need for Supplementation: The Compassionate Function

The major deficiency in entitlements theory is its inability to incorporate principles of economic justice that recognize the rights of individuals who are not capable through their own efforts of earning a minimum livelihood through the market mechanism or that define the obligations of government to act as social agent in their behalf. Any theory of economic ethics that relies wholly on voluntarism in defining its principles has no potential for inclusion of the compassionate strand of individualism and its proponents may—as in the case of Nozick—take peculiar pride in its incapacity. But since the time of Locke natural law theory—in whose inspirational wake the American concept of dualistic individualism was born—has recognized the absolute right to life of individuals innocent of the taking of human life, and that ethos has broadened the concept over time to include the right to the opportunity for dignity and self-respect. Dominant indeed is the right of individuals to maximize self-interest within voluntaristic mechanisms and the obligation to employ self-effort to provide the material provision for themselves and dependents. But the compassionate obligations of society are an important, if subordinate, constraint on egoistic actions.

Included in such social obligations is the desirability of effecting such relief partially through improving the opportunity for more remunerative self-effort. Increasing educational opportunity in one form or another is the most important element in the program with ancillary enabling measures (e.g., day care facilities for children). The phrase "equality of opportunity" is an unfortunate description of such obligations for several reasons. Equality for the sake of equality is not prima facie a desirable or achievable goal if my interpretation of American individualism is correct. Neither, then, is movement toward equality when inspired wholly to get closer to that goal. It would require significant restrictions on market-determined entitlements which would be perceived as unjust deviations from these dominant principles of right. Given differential natural abilities it is impossible to equalize opportunity for success in voluntarist mechanisms, and compensation for lower genetically derived capacities is best adjudged on a needs basis and distributed via the compassionate relief payments discussed above.

The liberal society, of necessity organized and coordinated through voluntarist mechanisms, is neither painless nor costless, and such burdens are not borne equally by all citizens of the community. Responsibility for the material welfare of one's family in an economy subject to rapid change and sudden obsolescence of occupation, requiring increasing educational preparation and basic ability, imposing burdensome costs for such basic needs as education and health care, and suffering recurrent phases of recession is a rather awesome charge on the individual. Without destroying the voluntarist basis of its organization, and with it the individualism inherent at its core, the liberal society can neither eliminate such costs nor distribute them equally among all citizens. It can, however, acting within the bounds of the compassionate strand, render assistance in bearing them through support of minimum income standards and the provision of opportunities to enhance the rewards from self-effort.

In this belief dualistic individualism is in strong disagreement with Rawls's doctrines of (1) permitting individuals to benefit from differential abilities only to the extent such departures from income equality benefit the least-advantaged, and (2) fair equality of opportunity. Both principles I believe are undesirable denials of the dominant strand of egoism in American individualism, and as such unjust to those exercising their individuality for their own advantage. The questionable derivation of the principles, their unenforceability in the environment of the ethos, and their interference with economic efficiency have been discussed in chapter 6. Rawls's belief that the market economy could function under the heavy redistributive exactions required of his principles is rather fanciful. His principles of justice would require a stress on egalitarianism and social organicism that exceeds that of many democratic socialist schemata and could be instituted only in an ethos that tolerated such deemphasis of or redefined individualism and that was ready to sacrifice substantial efficiency to permit such principles.

In saying this one must admit to some uncertainty as to the exact meaning of "fair equality of opportunity" in Rawls's principles, as he himself does. In distinguishing it from conventional equality of opportunity, however, he indicates that it would require substantial changes in existing educational, legal, and political institutions, not excluding the possibility of altering family relations in unstated ways. Society in his view is obligated to make extensive efforts to alter the present methods of providing access to education and political office, among other primary goods or the means to them. The implication is that funding such programs would draw heavily on others' incomes that are already oriented strongly toward the egalitarian in his envisioned society.

Affirmative action programs to correct injustices are also unjust violations of the right of equality of opportunity for reward. This position—most surprisingly—disagrees with the views of Nozick and seems to agree with Rawls by implication, as noted in chapter 3. Correcting past and present injustice by reverse discrimination imposes severe burdens on a small group of victims and violates what is effectively viewed as a right by the ethos and the logic of individualism. Corrections of instances of force and fraud—especially when such injustices affect large numbers of persons—should be effected through income adjustments and, more appropriately, provision of educational opportunities, with the burden of such programs falling on all citizens through income tax levies. Where the injustice is not one of past unjust treatment but present discrimination against persons of superior or equal merit, broad gauge class actions are again inappropriate and the corrective functions of government should be employed.

The Need for Supplementation: The Corrective Function

This corrective function is a legitimate constraint on the egoistic strand of individualism and forms an integral part of its social component. It monitors the commutative relations of agents in the society as they relate to economic justice and takes action to correct violations when they reflect use of undue force or fraud, when potential actions taken with an eye toward self-advantage have potentially grave consequences for the welfare of others, or when an asymmetry of information exists which can inflict damages of such magnitude on the unknowing. The entitlements theory, in recognizing the importance of an absence of force or fraud in defining voluntarist and therefore just actions, permits a scope for this function that Nozick was not eager to exploit. His narrow and ambiguous interpretation of the updated Lockean proviso has been criticized in chapter 5. But it is not a necessary implication of entitlements theory. Indeed, corrective principles become a rather integral part of its validation of just acquisition and transfer.

The corrective function of the state in a theory of economic justice springs from a frank recognition of deficiencies that are active or potential in a realistic market economy with respect to equitable treatment of individuals. It is analogous in the concerns of equity to recognized efficiency disabilities that inhere in the market's allocation processes. It cannot provide public goods, for example, or produce them with acceptable efficiency, nor can its voluntarism finance their provision. Equity requires that the corrective function of *taxation* be executed in manners conformant to fair distribution of burden. Externalities—or instances in which costs or benefits do not register through market prices and hence are ignored in allocation—cause injustices and, where such individual inequities are sufficiently threatening to life or welfare, should be corrected by state measures to internalize them.

In instances where selfish motives may lead to actions that seek profit at the potential expense of others in terms of health or economic well-being, where judged sufficiently important, state corrective or preemptive action in the form of testing, or licensing, or information provision, or prohibition is appropriate in equity. Monopolistic pricing power has equity as well as allocative implications in a society whose norms and values are formed by the American ethos, and where its necessity is dictated by efficiency considerations or when it is a substantial burden on buyers the state has an obligation to regulate or correct it.

In exercising the corrective function the state must be concerned to act only when *significant* threats to life, health, and economic welfare are at issue and where the costs of effecting corrections do not outweigh benefits. In realistic markets some power over price is possessed by firms as a general rule, and it would be foolish to attempt to eliminate it if significant inequities were not involved. Externalities are also widespread, but it is infeasible to correct all through state action and probably inefficient to correct most completely. Friedman is correct, also, in warning against the use of state corrective action by selfish interests for the advantage of incumbents: licensing of trades whose malpractice would involve relatively minor impacts on public welfare is an example (e.g., barbers).

A compromise with values other than those of economic justice must be made in the case of labor unions as well. By strict interpretation their exertion of control over supply to exact higher compensation is an exercise of monopoly power and in general with significant adverse consequences for the economic welfare of consumers. As such it is economically unjust and should be outlawed. However, as a human resource in a liberal economy, labor has political rights that are interpreted as including the right to bargain collectively and to use the strike if necessary as a tool in such bargaining. Unions serve other sociological needs of laborers as well. In this case, the dictates of economic justice must be waived in the interests of other social priorities. But union practices that transgress the bounds of narrowly protective practices—secondary boycotts, or job protection through restrictive hiring practices or import tariffs or quotas, for example—should be the subject of governmental corrective action.

The most important corrective function of government in terms of its strength of impact is in the state's means of diverting resources away from the market economy to provide for those economic functions that individualistic mechanisms cannot. This, of course, is taxation. Justice in taxation is a most complex subject and is hotly debated by advocates of one set or principles or another. The set of basic tenets in this area consistent with a dualistic individualism theory of economic justice revolve about two principles:

1. When employed as a general revenue levy divorced from the provision of specific goods or services enjoyed by identifiable individuals, all taxation should be based on income as the best available index of ability to pay;
2. Income should be taxed at progressive rates to permit a closer approximation to equal sacrifice.

The first of these principles incorporates two notions of equity. The first is the projection of the principles of entitlements theory: the individual acting through the voluntarist market mechanism is forced, at least ideally, to pay the true social cost of producing a good or service. The allocative efficiency of that principle, which forces the buyer to compare incremental benefit with social cost, is well known. But a rather elementary interpretation of economic justice also is effective in this case, namely, that cross-subsidization of one buyer by another not exist. The price is an "equity price" as well as an "efficiency price."

In the public sector several complications arise in defining an "equity price" that are not present in the unregulated private sector. Production under conditions of declining costs leads to a result where the marginal cost or "efficiency price" does not cover full average costs, and where subsidization from general tax revenues would involve cross-subsidization of users by the general public. Therefore, the equity price in this interpretation would be average cost, for it would eliminate such penalization of nonusers for the provision of benefits to users. Society, if it chose this route, would sacrifice efficiency for equity.

The peak-load problem, in which non-peak-load users "piggy-back" on capacity installed to meet the needs of peak-hour users, is another instance. Efficiency dictates that all capacity costs be loaded onto the peak-load user as the causative agent, and that the non-peak-load user pay only the marginal noncapacity costs that could be avoided in the absence of his or her demand. But equity considerations might well dictate that if a user gains benefit from a service he or she contribute something toward cost on the basis that enjoyment of benefits entails some obligation of payment toward the cost of provision.

Prevention of cross-subsidization is an attractive principle of economic justice in the financing of governmental services that are provided to identifiable individuals in identifiable quantities. Where such impositions result in devastating financial burdens, such as cases of catastrophic illness, government's role should be that of an insurer if private insurers do not voluntarily offer protective policies. Those governmental rates in equity should provide for the full costs of service to avoid cross-subsidization. On the same basis, they may also be mandatory on the individual if nonpurchase would force others to subsidize the services provided nonpayers. Where payments for such governmental services would not be possible for some individuals whose earnings via free market entitlements would be deficient, corrections should be made in the manner recommended for goods purchasable through the market: income payments on the basis of need.

The second concept involved in the first principle is that of determining the best index of capacity to pay taxes for the provision of governmental services and for administration of the compassionate strand. Individuals' incomes are the best approximation to this ability since they measure the potential flows of benefits over a period of time. The extent to which receipts of income in kind—the services of owned homes, the costs of company-provided fringe benefits, and so forth—are included is left open for policy determination. Alternatives to income taxation are less attractive on grounds of justice. The taxation of expenditure introduces a bias in favor of saving, which benefits higher income earners at the expense of lower, and also biases the rate of saving from what voluntarist mechanisms would have established in the absence of the tax system. Wealth, as opposed to or in addition to income, might also be chosen as a tax base, but it is of value to the possessor only as it yields flows of tangible or intangible income. The latter flows are better indices of the value derived by the individual over a period of time.

The second principle, dictating progressive income taxation, derives of course from the notion of diminishing marginal utility of income. The satisfaction derived from income rises less than proportionately to income, so equal sacrifice dictates the higher income individual pay proportionally larger amounts of taxes. This is a qualitatively defensible proposition despite the nonmeasurability of utility with cardinal degrees of uniqueness, and should be accepted as a principle of corrective equity.

A Summary of the Guiding Philosophy

Using the framework explained in chapter 4 and employed in the critiques of chapters 5 and 6, let us summarize briefly the principles of economic justice recommended by dualistic individualism. The assertion of this work is that they constitute a complete and consistent theory of economic justice that may be used to formulate a body of fundamental rights and obligations of individuals as well as an operational policy program in the areas of distributive and corrective economic justice.

1. *The Concept of the Good.* The theory is nonspecific in its treatment of the ends of individual life. By accommodating a wide spectrum of individual definitions of the good life it provides for the diversity of aims that one would expect in a liberal society stressing the rightness of individual freedom of choice, giving free rein to individuality, and placing great responsibilities on individuals as well. Some persons may view the *summum bonum* of existence to be full enjoyment of the material life, others may seek Millian happiness, others a Kantian path of duty. Within the bounds of noninterference with the similar rights of others to choose their goals in life, and within the constraints of their material and nonmaterial legacies and the rightful goals of the state, freedom of choice of life-styles and goals is guaranteed.

The goals of the state are more tightly circumscribed, as is to be desired in a liberal society. Maximizing the per capita happiness in a society is an unacceptable definition of the social good in the theory because it transgresses the principles of right protecting the individual in his or her search for material benefit through voluntarist economic relations with others. Its redistributive implications are incompatible in these respects with the theory. On the other hand the state's role in the individual's life is viewed as more extensive than that dictated by the justice-as-freedom school. Its just functioning requires greater constraints on the individual's freedom to choose in the way of corrective action to prevent substantive harm to others and a greater compassionate role with the necessary funding reducing many incomes below market-determined levels.

2. *The Principles of Right.* These principles are the core of the theory and are derived from the dualistic interpretation of individualism. Voluntarism—the notion that the individual is competent to make eco-

nomic choices and should have the right to effect them and to benefit from such action—forms the basis for the judgment of rightful conduct. Acquisition and transfer of goods and services, within and between generations, as long as a degree of force or fraud that compromises the voluntarist nature of the transaction was not employed, is just and should form the basis for initial distribution of income. Just acquisition encompasses the receipt of genetic or environmental advantages or disadvantages from which the individual benefits or suffers.

The principles of distributive justice that emerge from a pure Nozickian entitlements theory of this type, however, are procedural and nonconsequentialist. As such they are not wholly satisfactory in that they fail to provide for the individualistic rights of individuals that cannot be protected within voluntarist mechanisms. These rights are the right to social provision of measures guarding against the use of excessive force or fraud that would destroy the voluntarist nature of acquisition and transfer, and that provide a standard of living permitting the maintenance of dignity and self-respect by those who cannot provide sufficient income to reach such levels through the market economy. The corrective and compassionate functions of the state are grounded in individualism as important protections against circumstances that are vital to personal welfare and are beyond individual control.

But the principles of individualism dictate rightful administration of both social functions. Individuals receiving aid by virtue of the compassionate component of individualism acquire it justly and should thereby have full control over its transfer. This dictates that almost all such assistance should be delivered in the form of income, preferably by anonymous negative income tax mechanisms. Recipients then will transfer it in accordance with their preferences and the need to face "equity prices" that cover full social costs without cross-subsidy, in the same manner as others in the society. Governmental corrective actions should also be conducted in ways that minimize interference with voluntarist transfer and its terms. In taxation this implies the use of a progressive income tax.

As indicated in the discussion of the good, the definition of the principles of right is independent of concepts of the good. As such the theory is deontological in the decoupling of the good and the right rather than relating them derivatively.

3. *Incentives to Act in Accordance with the Right.* In being formulated to conform to egoistic self-interest for the largest part, and in finding their expression in the voluntarism of the free market economy, the principles of right in their major expression are self-enforcing. This certainly must be a major recommendation of them.

Similarly, the principles guiding the corrective function of government should be supported by the majority of individuals. But they will encounter the egoistic purposes of a minority who, with the energy of actual or potential income enhancement to motivate action, will oppose such functions. Such opposition should be confined within tolerable limits largely within the domain of policy making. The exception to this minority opposition to corrective policy is that of income taxes. As a contravention of the egoistic self-interest of all individuals, resistance to it in a liberal society must be expected to be quite strong. This will be especially true to the extent their purpose is to fund compassionate programs, given the majority interest in their deemphasis. Also, the principles, by stressing the substitution of income taxes for a variety of presently hidden indirect taxes, will increase the visibility of such exactions on the individual's material welfare.

This must be of concern to a voluntarist society. By its strong emphasis on the rightness of egoistic action, the ethos subordinates compassionate concerns despite its acceptance of them. This will be reinforced when taxes to support them are made more visible. I believe it is unrealistic to appeal to a Millian sense of social responsibility, or a Rawlsian notion of fraternity, or a Kantian reason-based sentiment of duty for a strong motive to accept such direct assaults on egoistic well-being. They may render some help, but the primary enforcer of these principles of right must be the sanction of legal action against nonconformance.

4. *Compatibility with the Ethos.* Little further need be said concerning the conformance of the theory to the individualism component of the ethos. In our view it is a closer approach to that core of liberalism than either the purely egoistic or the socially oriented theories presented and analyzed in chapters 3 through 6.

As a market economy ethic it is also fully compatible with materialism and rationalism. It certainly accommodates definitions of the good life as one that includes a substantial role for the material, although it is not constrained to that view alone. To put it in its most neutral assertive mode, nothing in the principles endangers the allocative motivation that the market mechanism requires for efficient operation.

Finally, similar statements are appropriate to the pragmatic rationalist component. It stresses the necessity of utilitarian validation of institutions and social mechanisms and adopts an equally pragmatic view toward rational planning of economic and political process. As compared with wholly egoistic theories it compromises somewhat with the priority given efficiency by its inclusion of the social dimension, but nonetheless that social goal is given a very high position in the scale of values.

A BILL OF ECONOMIC RIGHTS AND OBLIGATIONS

Instituting such principles formally in a bill of rights and obligations appended to the political Constitution would fill a gap in that largely political document. It would also provide Congress and the executive branch, increasingly sensitive to the pressures of interest groups, with guidance and external constraints. The susceptibility of legislators facing increasingly expensive campaigns and the threats of well-organized single-issue constituents has increased in recent times. The result, especially in the area of distributive economic policy, verges on the irresponsible. Nor is the executive branch a model of resistance to claims of special privilege in economic matters. Both branches of government could benefit in terms of the furtherance of a more just economic program if the judicial branch were given the same type of constitutive power that it possesses in the political sphere to gauge the conformance to principles of justice of congressional legislation and executive orders.

To stimulate debate, therefore, the following articles in a bill of economic rights and obligations to protect the individual in a liberal society are suggested to incorporate formally dualistic individualism in the nation's system of economic justice.

Article 1. The Right to Entitlements

The basic privilege conferred by the philosophy of dualistic individualism is the right to acquire and transfer income and wealth when such transactions are executed through voluntary exchange mechanisms without force or fraud after the just levies of government are enforced against it. Voluntarism is the key to just economic actions in the philosophy recommended—a voluntarism constrained by the natural and property legacies of the individual and by the just claims of governments. The egoistic strand of individualism dictates the necessity of voluntaristic institutions and ultimately endows such actions with the imprimatur of equity. The typical importance of such transactions to the individual's welfare converts them to matters of economic justice.

The fundamental economic protection of the individual, and the obligations that follow from that protection in matters economic, are contained in the following article:

ARTICLE 1

SECTION 1.   *Individuals shall be protected in their right to engage in transactions when all parties enter into such transactions voluntarily, bound only by constraints of natural and property or income endowments and the legality of the actions.*

SECTION 2.   *When such transactions result in binding contractual commitments they are enforceable at law.*

SECTION 3.   *Income and property acquired or transferred through such transactions shall confer the rights to exclusive use and exclusion inherent in private property.*

The required legality of the actions incorporates the government's right to monitor the use of excessive force or fraud among other restrictions that are forbidden. Income endowments also include government enhancements given in furtherance of the compassionate component of individualism.

Article 2. The Establishment of the Market Economy

A philosophy of economic justice based on the voluntarism of economic actions must be administered by economic mechanisms that maximize its exercise. In the political sphere the only acceptable institution, therefore, is political democracy, and it is guaranteed by the Constitution. Where state economic action is required, policy formulation within a democratic framework executed, where possible, through the private economy is the appropriate mode on the same grounds. Where individualistic decision making is at issue, the only mechanism that can assure that voluntarism and thereby validate economic actions as just is the free market economy. Its establishment in constitutive terms is as appropriate for economic structure as political democracy is as a governmental mechanism. The following provision, therefore is suggested:

ARTICLE 2

SECTION 1. *The integration of interactive individualistic economic decision making will be effected through market mechanisms when feasible. Their ability to function without interference, subject to the exercise of the proper corrective functions of government, is guaranteed.*
SECTION 2. *Further, in legislating to provide public goods and services, Congress shall effect such provision through market mechanisms when feasible.*

This article is meant to establish formally the right of markets to function in manners free of governmental interference that is not in furtherance of its just corrective function, and to force the federal government to purchase necessary goods and services through the free market process rather than producing them internally, whenever such production is unnecessary.

Article 3. The Obligation of Self-Support

Individualism places squarely on the shoulders of each person the responsibility to provide for his or her own material needs as well as those of legal dependents. That charge should be an explicit one in constitutive principles:

ARTICLE 3

SECTION 1. *Nothing in these articles shall be construed as lessening the responsibility of every individual to exercise all reasonable effort to provide for the material welfare of self and legal dependents through existing economic institutions.*

SECTION 2.   *Congress shall establish standards for the award of income supplements under Articles 4 and 5 which include guarantees that such reasonable effort is being expended.*

The article is self-explanatory and places responsibility for assuring that recipients of income supplements are deserving. Such programs as work-fare, for example, would be a legitimate requirement where appropriate.

Article 4. The Right of Provision

Basic to the individualistic core of liberalism is the sanctity of the human being as a unique individual with an inviolable claim to the respect for his or her physical and moral being and the opportunity to experience the self-respect due the dignity of that being. The compassionate strand of individualism stressed in the philosophy presented in the Section "An Operational Theory of Economic Justice" guarantees the provision of the materialist basis for that quality of life. The following article formalizes that obligation:

ARTICLE 4

Except in periods of armed conflict, the absolute claim to life of all individuals not judged guilty of wilfully taking human life is recognized. The material basis for maintaining it at a level that affords the opportunity to live in dignity and self-respect in the society is guaranteed, when the individual, acting in good faith, is unable to provide that provision in whole or in part.

This assertion of individual rights recognizes the prerogative of society to ask individuals to risk their lives in time of war and to inflict capital punishment in the instance of wilful murder. With those reservations it guarantees material support of individuals unable to provide for their material well-being acting in good faith through voluntarist economic mechanisms. The requirement that the supported level be such as to permit the achievement of self-respect and dignity implies that the legislated level of support should rise with the affluence of the society.

Article 5. Reducing Inequalities of Opportunity

A second charge of government in fulfilling the compassionate duty of society toward its disadvantaged is to act within the limits of social affluence to reduce the inequalities of opportunity that occur in birth and nurture to restrict the economic opportunities of individuals. Actions such as those providing prenatal health care, child nutrition, day care for working families, decent housing, and so forth, are best provided under income supplements set forth in Article 6. Educational and occupational training programs to enhance the acquired endowments of income potential are the primary tools of aid that is extended conditional upon its use in such investment in human capital. The formal obligation of government to provide such help is the purpose of the following article:

ARTICLE 5

SECTION 1.   *Congress is charged with the obligation of determining manners in which inequalities in opportunity that occur naturally and in nurture can be lessened by programs designed primarily to increase the earning potential of disadvantaged individuals in voluntaristic social mechanisms.*

SECTION 2.   *The extent of such programs shall be limited by the affluence of the economy, and the designation of criteria to determine those persons to be benefited shall be made by the Congress.*

Article 6. Provision in the Form of Income

Extension of the individualism principles of respect for the competence of persons to exercise free choice and to act in their own best interests dictates that material support by the state, where necessary, be accorded in the form of general purchasing power. In addition to permitting individuals to purchase in accordance with their needs and preferences, and to accord them the respect the recipients deserve, such a policy forces them to make choices in face of full equity prices, placing them on the same footing as their fellow citizens and avoiding inequitable cross-subsidization. Using income as the instrument of aid has the additional benefit of neutrality in respect to the price system with accompanying efficiency benefits, and forestalls interest groups from using such aid for their own profit (e.g., food stamps or housing benefits).

Such aid (rendered under Article 4) must be distinguished from payments designed to lessen the inequality of opportunity through such means as education and training (provided by Article 5). It also should be made in purchasing power, but its expenditure may be limited to goods or services that serve the purposes intended.

The suggested provision is the following:

ARTICLE 6

SECTION 1.   *All assistance rendered to individuals in fulfillment of the charges of Article 1 shall be accorded as direct income supplements in the form of general purchasing power over all commodities in the economy.*

SECTION 2.   *All payments in kind, supplementary subsidies to third parties, or protective measures against imports to support employment, are prohibited.*

SECTION 3.   *Assistance that is given to lessen inequality of opportunity can be restricted to expenditures on goods and services that serve to achieve that purpose.*

This is admittedly a rather broad-gauged prohibition against many forms of relief to the unfortunate that are rendered in indirect manners and that may result in subsidization of third parties, inequitable charges against taxpayers, and inefficient resource allocation. The word "direct" is meant to prohibit such means of extending income relief as agricultural subsidization through price supports and acreage or output limitations. The article also denies Congress and the executive the ability to employ tariffs or quotas to inhibit or prevent the entry of foreign goods in order to protect jobs in the United States.

I distinguish between benefits in kind that are meant to alleviate poverty by whether or not their payment in lieu of cash lessens significantly the burden on taxpayers. Education vouchers, for example, are designed to aid the recipient in a manner that will relieve or preempt future burdens on the taxpayer, and the society has a just demand on the recipient that they be used for that purpose. On similar grounds I believe a strong case can be made for compulsory retirement contributions by all persons, and that their payment by the poor should be taken into account in setting support levels.

On the other hand food stamps, school lunch, or housing subsidies force the recipient to a lower level of economic welfare by restricting the individual's ability to substitute among goods according to tastes and needs. Such subsidies do so without large benefits to taxpayers, who by paying a subsidy in cash would permit the recipient to receive more benefit at the same or lesser cost. Such in-kind programs are often designed to benefit nontarget groups, such as farmers interested in reducing government food stockpiles that depress support prices. Finally, to use these programs to force recipients to spend in patterns deemed desirable by the government demeans recipients by implying their incapacity to make rational decisions or to be concerned for the welfare of their dependents.

An additional advantage of Article 6's equity implications is that it forces the amounts of all such payments to the deserving poor to be explicit and readily subject to taxpayer surveillance. Also, it places the availability of such relief wholly on a needs basis rather than benefiting categories of citizens who are not eligible for such aid on the basis of income, as is the case in present agricultural subsidization.

Article 7. Equality of Opportunity for Reward

As interpreted in this work, American dualistic individualism infers the right of individuals to compete in all economic endeavors wholly on the basis of qualifications relevant to the performance of those endeavors. Discrimination on other grounds violates economic justice in this interpretation. When such discrimination is intended to correct past instances of force or fraud, recourse should be had to income compensation tied to measures designed to lessen inequality of opportunity. When meant to correct current discriminatory practices not related to relevant characteristics, government corrective action is appropriate.

ARTICLE 7

SECTION 1.   *Congress shall take no action intended to discriminate among individuals or groups of individuals in any activity when the grounds for that discrimination are unrelated to characteristics that are relevant to the performance of that activity.*

SECTION 2.   *Further, such discrimination is forbidden to all individuals when acting in capacities that affect materially the obtaining of gainful employment, whether directly or indirectly.*

The provision is intended to prevent the passage of affirmative action legislation, or the favoring of unionized labor in contracting, or the fostering of minority small business, or favoritism granted veterans, and so forth, in the award of government contracts or in measures that constrain private economic priorities in these manners. Beyond that, it forbids individuals from so discriminating, and is meant to include such activities as education whose effect on employment opportunities is indirect but important.

Article 8. Freedom of Choice of Occupation

Among the more important aspects of voluntarism is the freedom of the individual to choose his or her profession or occupation without hindrance, unless the consequences of incompetence in such pursuits threaten substantial material harm to the physical or financial welfare of injured parties.

ARTICLE 8

SECTION 1.   *Governmental authorities shall pass no law restricting by licensing or other means any individual's entry into a profession or occupation unless the effects of incompetent performance in such occupations are potentially harmful to the physical or financial well-being of others in a substantial manner.*

SECTION 2.   *In the case of such potential harm government authorities have a responsibility to test or in other ways establish standards for entry or to take other corrective or preemptive action.*

The article establishes a positive obligation for governments to fulfill their corrective responsibilities when necessary in the area of occupational practice. This reflects the social strand of individualism, as developed in the discussion—a strand of obligation denied by justice-as-freedom theorists. The criterion of substantial harm must be defined by public officials, but constitutional restrictions of their actions permit a review of such decisions by courts, and hence cannot be wholly arbitrary.

Article 9. Correction of Force and Fraud

The other component of government corrective responsibilities is the monitoring of commutative economic procedure to protect parties from the exercise of force or fraud when such usage is potentially harmful to individuals' physical or financial welfare or where the offense is so blatant as to constitute an unacceptable contempt for the dignity of others or exploits an inescapable asymmetry of knowledge. Public authorities are obligated to act to protect potential victims in such cases. The following article gives them such a charge formally:

ARTICLE 9

It shall be the responsibility of the proper governmental officials to take appropriate action against those who practice force or fraud in economic dealings when such action is potentially damaging to victims' physical or financial welfare in substantial manners, when the practice is blatantly contemptuous of the moral integrity of individuals, or when it exploits an inescapable asymmetry of information.

The article is broad enough to permit criminal action against violators, or orders to cease and desist, or publication of information to correct information gaps.

Article 10. Just Taxation

Justice in taxation must take into account the right of the individual to dispose of that which was acquired through the market economy without force or fraud, even in its disposition after death. It must also seek to distribute the burdens of taxation among individuals in such manner as to equalize such burdens. Once property has been justly acquired it should not be subject to taxation except to the extent that it generates a flow of goods and services. All taxes directed by governments to the raising of revenue should be derived from a progressive income tax against individual incomes, where business profits are imputed to stockholders for tax purposes and other forms of imputed income are included in consumers' incomes as governments see fit and proper. Profit taxes on business should be eliminated as double taxation of individuals. Property taxes, too, as taxes on wealth are unjust exactions.

Such requirements do not exclude the levying of excise taxes to discourage use of potentially harmful commodities, to internalize the costs of externalities, or to accomplish other government goals of a corrective nature.

A suggested wording is the following:

ARTICLE 10

SECTION 1. *All taxation levied solely or primarily to obtain revenue for government operations shall be in the form of a progressive income tax on market-realized or imputed individual incomes. This shall not be construed as preventing the governmental use of fees for goods or services received by identifiable beneficiaries.*

SECTION 2. *All taxes on wealth or its growth in value are forbidden as are all taxes on inheritances or estates.*

SECTION 3. *For tax purposes the undistributed profits of economic entities shall be imputed to owners or shareholders.*

SECTION 4. *Nothing in this provision shall be construed as denying governments the right to levy indirect taxes on commodities in fulfillment of their just corrective functions.*

This provision would require a major revision of the tax structure at all levels of government, but I believe it would create a more equitable and more efficient tax system conformant to the principles of dualistic individualism. The best index of ability to pay and of the advantages rendered to individuals by the existence of a society is in the flow of potential and actual goods and services enjoyed over a period of time. Requiring income taxes to be progressive intrudes some inefficiencies into the economy to be sure, but I believe the gains in economic justice are well worth the burden.

A POLICY PROGRAM FOR ECONOMIC JUSTICE

With a completed philosophy for economic justice and a statement of the individual rights and obligations that emerge from it there remains the task of designing a program of policy actions that will institute the principles. References have been made to such policies earlier in the chapter, so the discussion can be brief.

Policies to Implement Article 1

Article 1, which establishes the right of acquisition and transfer of income and property, the right of contract and its binding nature, and property rights, needs no new policy implementation as it is well-established in statutory and common law. The article is designed to give constitutive status to such law.

Policies to Implement Article 2

The primary policy implications of these provisions are to reinvigorate the federal government's acquisition process in requiring competitive bidding whenever feasible; to out-source for the obtaining of supplies currently produced by government owned-government operated (GOGO) facilities when noneconomic reasons do not dictate otherwise; and privatizing such existing government or quasi-governmental monopolies as the postal service and Amtrak. The hope would be that such actions would serve as an example to states and municipalities to follow suit, contracting out for such services as refuse collection, road maintenance and repair, parks administration, and the like.

Policies to Implement Article 3

Congress is given the obligation of establishing criteria to assure that individuals applying for receipt of aid under compassionate programs are expending every effort to support themselves that may be reasonably expected of them. Recently enacted work-fare provisions are important steps in providing this assurance, and greater provision for child care availability to ensure the opportunity of single parents to work is another. Limitations on asset holdings have been in existence for some time and do not need enhancements. Given the expansion in compassionate programs that the enactment of the recommended principles of economic justice would imply, and the movement toward even greater emphasis on means-testing than at present, it would be more important in the future than the present to screen applicants closely for eligibility.

Policies to Implement Article 4

Article 4 establishes formally the obligation of the federal government to provide income supplementation to all those who meet the criteria of Article 3 and whose income falls below some minimum limits set by Congress. Those income floors should vary with the needs of the families aided and should be established as proportions of some measure of central tendency of per capita personal income. In this manner they will rise with both nominal and real incomes over time, and will preserve some balance between the incomes of those who earn it through the market economy or government employment and the less advantaged.

Chapters 10 and 11 suggest that median personal incomes of the various family or household sizes in the first category be used as the bases against which to apply the percentage multipliers. Arthur Okun's suggestion that 50 percent of average income might be taken as a feasible support level is an alternative proposal.[1]

This article's requirements should be applied to *all* recipients of aid uniformly: Social Security, agricultural subsidy recipients, Medicaid and Medicare patients, food stamp eligibles, veterans, the unemployed, and so forth. Such aid should be based wholly on needs as determined in a uniform manner by Congress—steps which will avoid the inequitable differentials with which different groups are treated and which will eliminate those who benefit from such programs without true income deficits.

Policies to Implement Article 5

This article recognizes the need for a second compassionate program to provide greater opportunities to succeed within the market or governmental economies when income deficits indicate the need for aid and the individual reveals the potential to benefit from such help. Most of that aid is envisaged to be educational and instructional, teaching the individual new skills, making him or her more competent in using existing skills, retraining those whose skills have been obsolesced by the market, compensating for failure to learn basic skills in youth, and so forth. The need criterion must be fulfilled in terms of falling below the income criteria discussed above, and the aid received must be tied to pursuit of the program agreed upon.

Friedman's voucher plan seems the optimal manner of rendering such assistance. This would be an extension of the suggested program from educational aid in the primary and secondary levels to the types of educational rehabilitation in later life referred to above. Such a program stimulates competition among private suppliers of such services and permits the recipient to choose among the suppliers on the basis of quality and conformance to personal preferences and needs.

These policies would produce a marked expansion in the government expenditures for "welfare programs," but would have the advantage of offering the prospect for future reduction in expenses of income supplementation. Moreover, it would be a vital means of aiding individuals to attain the level of self-respect and dignity guaranteed by Article 4.

Policies to Implement Article 6

The provisions of Article 6 are vital to the reform of social equity inherent in present methods of distribution support payments. Currently such programs are a hodge-podge of legislation with no coherent core concept of purpose or justice, many enacted at the behest of powerful interest groups. Many who are worthy of compassionate aid in the form of income supplements or equality-of-opportunity support are denied access to such programs, while others who meet no needs criterion benefit from them. By enforcing the income criteria of Article 4 to assure need and by rendering that aid in the form of general purchasing power for supplements and vouchers for educational support, a unifying principle will be introduced that recognizes the purposes of compassionate assistance and treats individuals uniformly in terms of those purposes.

Such means of assistance would replace *all* other forms of income support currently being rendered. Payments to the aged to supplement their retirement incomes from other sources would replace Social Security as a means of gaining retirement income. This would place aid to the retired on a needs basis as a current charge against the national product, rather than continuing to foster the charade that a reserve is being built over the working lifetime of the individual that is "invested" in government security "trust funds." Individuals would be responsible over their lifetimes to provide any excess over such floor levels of retirement income by private retirement or insurance programs. Funds for the support of the aged, by being provided from progressive income taxes, would distribute the burden of supporting retirees on the same uniform basis that Congress has determined is equitable for general government expenses in voting income tax schedules.

Medical insurance should be provided by policies issued by private insurers and purchased by individuals from their incomes. The cost of such insurance obviously must enter into the determination of the proper income floors established to implement Article 4. Individuals failing to insure themselves in this manner should be provided necessary care but be charged in later periods to recover the costs of that care. Cases of catastrophic illness, where insurance has not been obtained or when private insurance is not available, may be rendered by rare government programs of insurance subsidized from general revenues with the equitable distribution of burden implied.

Agricultural subsidy programs acting through price supports, crop limitations, export subsidies, and so forth, would be eliminated and all such support would be put on an income-needs basis and implemented by income payments. Current programs distort prices to the consumer, encourage output and the use of dangerous pesticides and fertilizers that turn land into chemical landfills, hide from taxpayers the true costs of the policies, and reward farm families out of proportion to need. In the longer run, the income subsidy program would encourage a movement out of farming into areas whose output is valued more highly and which increase the efficiency of society. This could be enhanced by educational aid designed to retrain farmers for other jobs when practicable, although movement off the farm would probably occur mainly as generational changes. Job protection in other forms would likewise be eliminated.

Restriction of foreign imports through tariffs, quotas, or "voluntary export agreements" would give way to income payments for unemployment and retraining. The major advantage in such instances is to prevent the inflicting of an unjust and inefficient burden on consumers to protect outmoded jobs and plant investment: charges of $60,000 a year in higher prices to consumers to protect $15,000 a year jobs would be eliminated. Another casualty of this type would be programs that subsidize firms to locate in areas that market forces have determined are uneconomic, so that where such artificial insemination results in birth a continuing subsidy may well be necessary to ensure viability. Far better than fighting the eroding forces of spatial economics is the provision of income supplements and retraining of workers with encouragement to migrate to areas of greater opportunity.

Housing subsidies, frequently in whole or in part funded by rent controls that inflict inequitable burdens on landlords and encourage the subdivision of housing into units with unhealthy occupation density, would be eliminated in favor of income payments to recipients of compassionate aid. The long-run effect of such a program would be to stimulate the construction of new housing in the lower income brackets. Undeniable distress would occur in the short run as rents were bid up, and income payments would have to take such increased costs into account. But in the medium and long terms new residential housing should occur in large cities that have seen very little construction in recent years for the low-to-medium income housing needs.

A list of subsidization programs for the middle classes would also be eliminated in the interests of fairness and equity. Foremost among them is the ability to write off interest costs on mortgages in the payment of income taxes, which would be eliminated in the interests of tax equity. Such aid is extended without consideration of need, and as such is inequitable within the context of dualistic individualism principles of economic justice. It is also inefficient as it encourages the overbuilding of housing space, using up scarce savings which could be alternatively invested in more productive activities.

The article, then, calls for a major restructuring of economic policy insofar as it concerns distributive justice. The use of income as an indicator of need and a means of correction simplifies the present patchwork of unfair exactions and benefits and eliminates much of the discretion possessed by Congress that is so shamelessly exploited by powerful interests. In general, as a supplementary benefit, moving to a needs basis and an income instrument improves the efficiency of the economy as well as providing a clearer measure of the costs of compassionate aid for the public understanding.

Policies to Implement Article 7

Affirmative action programs of all types would be the casualties of this article if enacted. The argument has been given above: such policies seek to correct past injustices that are really beyond correction by placing the burden of their enforcement on individuals who did not cause such injustices. It would be illegal to hire preferentially on these grounds, to award contracts for these reasons, to establish quotas for admission to educational institutions, and so forth. Where individuals can be identified as having suffered directly from such injustice, compensation is due on the grounds of justice. Where such identification cannot be made, income supplements and educational allowances where appropriate are the route of just action. Where violations of the article occur, the corrective function of government should inflict penalties and right the wrongs. In no case is the use of reverse discrimination an equitable means of effecting redress.

Policies to Implement Article 8

The policies that implement Article 8 establish the right of governments to regulate entry into professions whose malpractice has great potential for harm for others or for the practitioner. Hence the licensing of physicians and other health care personnel, lawyers, electricians, plumbers, and so forth, is protected. It would outlaw, however, government restrictions on trades and professions that do not have such potential whose enactment is in many cases due to the pressures of interest groups. The statute would forbid private agencies from restricting the entry of persons into fields, notably union activity designed to ensure favoritism in hiring or to induce scarcity and higher wages.

Policies to Implement Article 9

The provisions of this article are meant to confirm and establish formally the corrective rights of government now being exercised. Hence, such supervisory and licensing functions as those exercised over new drugs by the Food and Drug Administration, the Federal Aviation Authority, the Occupational Safey and Health Administration, the Environmental Protection Agency, and so forth, are established in constitutive fashion. The broad powers of the Justice Department to monitor economic activities for excessive force or fraud, including in the former term the use of monopoly pricing power, exclusion of competition by noncompetitive means, tacit or overt collusion and so forth by firms, are recognized. And publication of information by such agencies as the Department of Commerce to inform consumers of product safety or effectiveness also is protected.

The only qualification is that the use of force or fraud be of "substantial" importance to public welfare or that the actions be blatant in their disregard for such welfare. In cases of antitrust action particularly this would require some effort at a benefit-cost analysis of the alleged mal-practices and would recognize that some degree of control of price in most markets is so common as to constitute the normal. Such a require-ment probably would mean an alteration of the guidelines currently used to screen such actions as mergers and acquisitions.

Policies to Implement Article 10

Article 10 mandates revolutionary changes in the tax structures at fed-eral, state, and local government levels. Except for taxes that are levied against commodities or firms to internalize externalities, or to discour-age usage of harmful goods, or to cover the legitimate costs of monitor-ing imports, or to pay for government services whose benefits are re-ceived by identifiable individuals, all taxes would be raised by progressive income taxes. Efficiency may in fact dictate that the Internal Revenue Service collect such taxes for all levels of government, permitting state and local taxes to "piggyback" on federal collections.

It may be judged equitable to impute income received in kind in the total taxed. The rental value of owner-occupied houses may be such a charge. Certainly the value of medical benefits received from employers should be included, since it is unfair to tax the income of those who bear such expenses from income and permit those who benefit from em-ployer programs to escape taxation. Scholarship aid rendered parents by firms or educational institutions should be included. Other fringe bene-fits may well belong in taxable income and would be considered in for-mulation of the policy.

Such extensive definition of the tax base in terms of income received is accepted by the principles defined above to be the best index of ability to pay that has intuitive acceptability and is practicable of measurement. Its usage excludes capital gains taxes as unwarranted and unjust exac-tions against wealth whose income is taxable as dividends received. Those capital gains are in largest part either the compensation for infla-tion or capitalized future dividends that will be taxed when received. Relief from double taxation of corporate income is achieved by eliminat-ing income taxes on businesses and imputing the undistributed income to stockholders in the year earned. Inheritance and estate taxes are abol-ished on the grounds that they are unjust interferences with the transfer of income that was justly earned and taxed when earned. And sales taxes or expenditure taxes are forbidden because they are regressive and un-fairly burden the nonsaver to the benefit of the wealthy.

Progressive taxation is also mandated to distribute the burden more equitably—that is, more evenly in terms of sacrifice. With identifiable services enjoyed by identifiable individuals paid for in full by those bene-

ficiaries, the income taxation program becomes one of applying equitable principles for the provision of government services that are non-
identifiable in terms of beneficiaries or that are dispensed in fulfillment
of compassionate responsibilities of government. Income as both an
index of absorption of the benefits from other-than-compassionate government programs and as ability to pay recommends it as a basis of
collection. The generally accepted diminishing marginal utility of income—despite an inability to measure it or its rate of decline—dictates
progressivity.

Finally, such a tax structure—especially of the unified form when the
federal government collects for all levels of government—permits the
citizenry to obtain a clear measure of the burdens of governments, and
to judge as voters the priorities to be given government activities. The
hodge-podge of direct and indirect taxes now inflicted on taxpayers
hides—and is intended to hide—the extent of taxation. The open and
above-board provision of such information to those who bear the burdens is in itself an important aspect of economic justice.

A Summary

This chapter has attempted to provide a consistent philosophy of economic justice that meets intuitive standards of justice and that reflects
the relevant and desirable components of the American ethos. The two
criteria are not independent, of course, but the first is challengeable
more directly than the latter. Nonetheless, the theory rests solidly on the
individualistic component of that ethos, reflecting the dominance of the
egoistic strand in that component, but incorporating the compassionate
and corrective strands as well in a substantial manner. Fundamental to
both the egoistic and social strands of this component are the notions of
the sanctity and dignity of human life, the importance of its being led in
an individualistic manner, and the rightness of both individual and state
actions that support the needs implied by these beliefs. The guiding req-
uisites that emerge from these concepts and that must shape the principles of economic justice are *voluntarism, compassion,* and *correction.*

Throughout the construction of that theory in this work I have tried to
keep in sight the goal of producing an *operational* set of principles that
could be instituted within the governing ethos, recognizing its ability to
sustain changes within bounds in the medium run. A first demonstration
of the ability of the theory to perform that practical function is in the
definition of the principles in constitutive form as a proposed bill of
economic rights and obligations that would expand the scope of the
Constitution to protect the individual's *economic* rights and define his or
her obligations as well as *political* and *civil* rights. The result, which is

offered in the spirit of stimulating debate, is a set of ten articles which provide a formal definition of the principles of economic justice which I believe should constrain Congress and the executive branch in the formulation of economic policy. Such a statement with constitutional force is badly needed in the face of gathering evidence that members of Congress and the executive branch have found it increasingly difficult to resist well-organized and amply funded pressure groups in their quest for selfish advantage in distributive policy.

Finally, major policy implications of the bill have been outlined. The greatest changes foreseen in current policy are in two areas: the manner of raising revenue at all levels of government and the extent of compassionate aid to less-advantaged individuals as well as the methods of dispensing it. Both sets of changes are capable of being instituted within the ruling ethos, perhaps over a transitional period of three decades or so. As pointed out in the discussion of Nozick's entitlement theory, however, no theory of economic justice can be advocated as a basis for social equity independent of its consequences.

To judge the past and present states of distributive patterns in the United States, to forecast changes in those patterns that would occur over the next decade or two if existing policies were retained and extended, and to estimate the impacts on those distributive patterns if the policies recommended in this chapter were introduced, chapters 8 through 11 present an empirical analysis of income distribution in American society.

In these chapters the discussion will be limited to the practical implications of redistributive policies within the framework of current institutions. Chapter 8 discusses some definitional and substantive issues that arise in measurement of income inequality. Chapter 9 presents an extensive view of income distribution currently in the United States. In chapters 10 and 11 analyses are undertaken to judge the feasibility within the American ethos of various levels of income support in the short- and long-run periods respectively in the confines of dualistic individualism.

PART III

The Patterns of Income Distribution in the United States

Chapter 8

MEASURING INEQUALITY: A MENU OF
PROBLEMS AND CHOICES

THE CONSEQUENTIALIST PERSPECTIVE

The discussion of chapter 2 asserted that no theory of economic justice could be acceptable as an operational alternative without some concern for feasibility within the context of the ethos. However desirable a pattern of distribution dictated by an abstract scheme of justice might appear were it to be instituted in some perfectly plastic social matrix, its placement against the backdrop of existing values, beliefs, norms, and mechanisms could lead to rejection or substantial alteration on account of incompatibility. In individualist and materialist societies especially, the redistribution of incomes away from the market-dictated status quo must be expected to be a particularly wrenching policy experience.

With this injunction in view, chapter 9 presents a vista of the inter-family and interhousehold income distribution patterns in the nation during the postwar period. Chapter 10 forecasts changes in such patterns that are likely to occur in the next five years or so if support levels were set at various percentages of the relevant median incomes. Chapter 11 continues the feasibility analysis by extending the time horizon thirty years into the future to project incremental tax burdens to support three vulnerable groups whose social demands dominate the costs of poverty.

In each chapter the investigation is limited to the redistributive burdens inflicted by implementation of the compassionate policies of dualistic individualism discussed in chapter 7. The aim is limited to assessing the feasibility of such programs within the constraints of the ethos and existing institutions. The more far-reaching implications of the policies in those programs are ignored in the belief that their imposition in largest part can occur only after the thirty-year period is over.

The purposes of the analysis of Part 3, therefore, are quite restricted: they are (1) to judge the order-of-magnitude of net impacts on income-earning units in the middle- and upper-income brackets that proposed policies to aid the lower quantiles would imply, and (2) to speculate on the ability of the ethos to permit such changes in the short and long terms. These are not unambitious goals, it is acknowledged, but their accomplishment does not depend on a degree of measurement accuracy that is currently unattainable from the data nor on the mastery of the body of extremely sophisticated and intricate analysis practiced by those who devote their careers to the derivation and interpretation of such data. The goals of this work can be accomplished within rather wide tolerance bounds.

Nonetheless, some introduction to the difficult problems encountered in devising usable measures of inequality and to the difficult and often data-dictated choices they require must be presented as a preliminary to the material of chapters 9 through 11. To do so it will be necessary to present some technical material, but readers with little interest in the development of the arguments supporting the analysis may skip them if the literary presentation seems sufficiently clear.

Finally, the definition of poverty adopted in a theory of economic justice must be determined within the body of principles established by that theory and its feasibility must be judged within the confines of a society's affluence and its ethos. Ready-made definitions, therefore, are not relevant. However, the official U. S. government definitions of poverty are widely used and some knowledge of them is necessary to interpret existing data and analysis. Therefore, they will be discussed briefly later in this chapter.

THE MEASUREMENT OF INCOME INEQUALITY: BASIC PROBLEMS

A first preliminary task of the analysis, then, is to discuss the problems of measuring income inequality, to present currently employed techniques, and to discuss the advantages and disadvantages of alternative methods.

Problems of Measurement and Definition

To assess the complexities of compressing the distribution of incomes among recipient units in the United States in a given year into a single index figure, consider the many dimensions of the measurement that must be taken into account.

1. *The Recipient Unit.* Which is the proper demographic unit to adopt for income receipt? Given the availability of data, the following field of choice presents itself:

   a. Household. The Bureau of the Census, the major source of distribution data, defines the household as *all persons occupying a housing unit,* the latter defined as *a separate living quarters with either a separate entrance or separate cooking equipment.* For example, in 1981 there were 82,368,000 households in the nation, of which families constituted 60,309,000, single-person households 18,936,000, and households consisting of unrelated individuals 3,123,000. The Census category *unrelated individuals* comprises the last two categories listed.

A major difficulty with the household as a meaningful unit for analysis of distributions in both static and dynamic studies is its nonhomogeneity with respect to numbers of individuals and structure. It includes single individuals or one-person households, any number of unrelated individuals with any number of income earners, as well as families (to be defined below) with any number of income earners and members. Hence, the unit lumps together single individuals in the labor force; persons not in the labor force but being supported by other income earners or by transfer payments wholly or in part (e.g., students, widows, retirees); groups of unrelated cohabitants with any intragroup pattern of earnings (e.g., migrant workers, young roommates in the middle-income brackets living together to lower costs, one- or two-earner cohabiting couples sharing life without benefit of clergy); and family units of all types and income sources.

In analyzing the distribution for any given year, obviously it is difficult to arrive at normative judgments of household welfare when household units can vary in number of members, age, numbers of earners engaged in part-time or full-time employment, and so forth. Putting income receipts on a per person basis may help somewhat, but this fails to capture the economies of scale that larger households gain through joint tenancy. When studying the distribution over a period of time, changes in household structure can interfere seriously with meaningful comparisons. In the United States, for example, between 1947 and 1984, the proportion of families with no working member rose from 5.4 percent to 15.1 percent, reflecting the decline in retirement age over the period and the increasing number of families headed by women.

These are substantial structural changes that must be taken into account when comparing family-based distributions in the postwar period. In addition, the age at which persons marry has climbed significantly in the postwar period, the number of children per family has declined, and the proportion of married women in the labor force has skyrocketed. Measures of distributive inequality must be interpreted with these complicated and multidimensional structural alterations in mind.

b. Family. The Bureau of the Census definition of the family is simply *two or more people who are living together and who are related by blood, marriage, or adoption*. As noted in the discussion of households, families constitute about 73 percent of such units. Limiting analysis to families achieves greater homogeneity among units than including other component households, but the discussion of households indicates that families still constitute a diverse group in terms of size, structure, number of income earners, ages, dependence on transfer payments and so forth.

And the trend toward greater heterogeneity over the postwar period has included an increase in two-earner families, the rapid rise of families headed by someone over 65, and, most important, more female-headed families.

c. Tax Returns. An income unit which is employed when dealing with Internal Revenue Service data is based on tax returns, frequently measuring the adjusted gross income on federal tax returns. The disadvantages associated with such data are legion: not all members of the families who earn income file tax returns, for those who do tax-free income and transfer payment income is excluded, and realized capital gains and losses are included. The extent of the coverage bias, therefore, is unknown, and this unit must generally be used only to supplement results from the use of data for the other two recipient units.

2. *The Income Concept.* Another dimension of the problem of measuring inequality is the definition of income. In the discussion of adjusted gross income above it was noted that its adoption as the datum of concern when tax returns are used implies various inclusions and exclusions that may not be desirable from given analytical perspectives. Because of the predominance of Bureau of the Census data the definition of "money income" it uses is much more important. Nonetheless elements of arbitrariness enter into its choices. Included in the concept are:

1. Wages and salaries
2. Self-employment net income
3. Dividends and interest
4. Royalties and net rental income
5. Social Security and welfare payments in cash
6. Pensions
7. Miscellaneous income, such as alimony

Excluded are:

1. Inheritances
2. Tax liabilities
3. Gifts
4. Capital gains or losses
5. Fringe benefits
6. Food stamps
7. Value of government services received (e.g., schooling for children, police protection)

The exclusion of gifts raises problems in the analysis of lower quantiles of the income distribution, because frequently young single persons who are separated from their families are receiving support from family members. The cases of students and young unrelated individuals who receive aid from parents are important instances. Far more important, however, is the exclusion of fringe benefits and food stamps from the Census income data. Ignoring the receipt of ever larger amounts of employment compensation in the form of fringe benefits over the postwar period, in the form of medical and dental insurance, life insurance, pension payments, automobile usage, and the like, can understate seriously the value of incomes received and distort comparisons over time.

Exclusion of in-kind payments to the impoverished, most notably food stamps, health care, and housing subsidies also distorts the calculation of inequality measures and the comparison of such data over time. If they were included, should the imputed income received by consumers from durable consumer goods also be entered? Notably, should owner-occupiers' incomes be raised by the imputed rental value of their homes? Should the housekeeping services of women in the home be valued as family income? If these in-kind receipts were included, how should they be valued? Should food stamps be valued at their cost to the government or at the value households would pay to receive them? Should fringe benefits be costed at the expense to employers or at the valuations of their recipients?

Should capital gains and losses be excluded from the income concept? Some economists would argue that income should be viewed as the maximum amount a household can spend during the year without reducing its net worth. This would include its money income, fringe benefits and all transfer payments somehow valued, including inheritances, and the change in the net value of assets. In the literal sense, this last category would include net capital gains that were not realized during the year. Obviously, inclusion of that portion of gains that was realized would capture at least a fraction of this net value.

In-kind income also consists of received government services. Police protection, fire protection, refuse disposal, public education, and so forth, are enjoyed by many in the lowest quantiles of the income distribution at no or little charge in fees or taxes. Does the value of these receipts belong in measured income when distribution data are used to make welfare comparisons? If so, where does one draw the line? The cost of educating one's children may indeed have an important claim for inclusion, but do such intangible benefits as fire protection or environmental protection or street maintenance lend themselves to valuation as welfare enhancements rather than parts of the background environment of daily life in a modern society?

The exclusion of tax liabilities seriously distorts the distribution data. Only if one is willing to equate such tax payments with equivalent services received by paying households can one view such exclusions with equanimity. With rather steeply progressive income taxes such equation is not intuitively appealing. Hence, the income distribution is biased downward in the lower quantiles and positively in the upper quantiles with such omissions when the federal tax burden is considered. However, there is some evidence that when all taxes are included the tax structure may indeed become regressive, as will be discussed in the analysis to follow. In any event, it seems clear that it would be desirable to correct the Census income data for tax payments to obtain a clearer perception of the degree of inequality in distribution.

Finally, a problem with both survey and complete enumeration data on income distribution is that of underreporting. The underground economy, barter systems for the exchange of goods and services, and unreported cash transactions are serious distortions in such data. In some analyses attempts are made to correct for such biases, but it is not clear to what extent they are successful.

3. *The Period of Measurement.* One of the most important decisions to be made by an analyst of income inequality is the time dimension of analysis. A static snapshot in time captures an important aspect of inequality in depicting current patterns of income receipt and the welfare associated with it, especially the extent of current poverty in the lower quantiles. Moreover, those current occupants of such ranks will continue in such straits for some periods into the future. The income patterns are quite persistent in the short and medium run.

But over the longer run there will be substantial individual unit mobility among the quantiles as persons age and gain education, experience, skill, and seniority until their incomes peak and they approach retirement. The typical member of the labor force begins at low wages as an entrant and follows an earnings path over time that rises to a maximum in his or her fifties and then begins a decline until retirement. The static distributions do not capture this dynamic. Most units in the lower quantiles today will over their lifetimes move through the middle brackets and perhaps into the upper quantiles, then drift backward somewhat to end their working careers.

Hence, proper judgment of the welfare implications of income distributions must take these *life-cycle* considerations into account. The market economy and its institutions reward productivity and seniority in this fashion, and the judgment of the justice of their rewards system must incorporate its time pattern. The typical young single person or married couple in the lowest quantile today will progress rather steadily into comfortable circumstances in the future, substantially conditioning any judgments concerning inequity that might be raised from a time-slice analysis alone.

In a *static* sense, income equality implies that every recipient unit receive the same income year by year—a pattern no society has achieved in the past, however egalitarian its professed strivings. Moreover, the desirability of attaining it may be seriously questioned when efficiency or equity itself are addressed. On the other hand, movements toward a more equal distribution in the *dynamic* sense, defined as the equality among recipient units of life-cycle income, is at once more feasible in terms of the American ethos and may satisfy a larger number of theories of economic justice. As Paglin writes:

> A very substantial part of the traditional area of inequality (one-third to one-half) is simply a function of the diversity in the ages and size of families and the lifetime income pattern typical of a technically advanced society. Such inequality does not represent a limitation on lifetime opportunities, nor is it a quintessential evil to be obliterated if our society is to be considered just and humane.[1]

Paglin's quantitative estimates are derived from a mathematical decomposition closely allied to analysis of variance and have been subjected to a great deal of challenge on a number of grounds (see point 2 of the section below on the Gini coefficient), but the thrust of his argument is convincing.

Nonetheless, after having said this, one must recognize that for a substantial and growing portion of the population permanent occupancy of the lowest income quantiles is the reality. This is true of a proportion of households headed by a person 65 years or older, although Social Security has done much in recent years to raise this group above poverty levels. More serious is the plight of those female-headed households with children, especially in minorities. In 1984, for example, 43 percent of all black families were headed by women as opposed to 13 percent of white families. Fully 50 percent of all black families under age 35 were headed by a woman, 75 percent of whom had never married. Most disturbingly, 54 percent of black children were in families headed by a woman.[2] The growth of these categories in the postwar period—in part the effect of poorly designed welfare policies that encourage family breakup—is one of the major concerns of those analysts who discern the emergence of a permanent underclass decoupled from the economy and doomed to lifetime poverty.

Such problems can be as readily hidden by static analysis as revealed by it. Some evidence exists that over the postwar period a rather remarkable stability in the distribution of income by quantiles, when income is defined according to some concepts, has existed, at least before in-kind welfare payments are included, with the lowest 20 percent (quintile) of households receiving about the same proportion of total income over the period. The patterns of income distribution offer little indication of the causation or changes in its structure that underly it: the sociological and cultural stresses on minority families; the high rates of educational dropout among the impoverished and their effect on unemployment or low-income persistence; the existence of racial, sex, or religious discrimination in the workplace; changes in attitude toward or capability for early retirement; cultural factors that encourage the persistence of high incomes in wealthier families over generations; and so on for a rich variety of determinants.

At a more profound level intellectual challenges even more difficult to answer are presented. To what extent does the distribution reflect genetic versus acquired differential abilities? How does one measure "ability" independent of success in the market? Where in the process of acculturation does the poverty child with ability become alienated from the society?

THE MEASUREMENT OF INCOME INEQUALITY: ALTERNATIVE MEASURES

Sen distinguishes between two types of measures of income distribution inequality: *positive* measures which are neutral with respect to normative significance and *normative* measures based on some explicit welfare concepts.[3] In a work concerned with theories of social justice, normative judgments are undertaken within a comprehensive philosophical schema of necessity more complex than what can be incorporated in simple welfare concepts guiding measurements. My interest therefore centers on positive measures.

As will be clear from the discussion of measurement problems to this point, the very notion that it is possible to encapsulate interpersonal, interhousehold, or interfamily income differentials in a single measure is rather fanciful. Indeed, my analysis will focus more on vector comparisons of shares of different measures of income received by variously sized quantiles. But measures of inequality, suitably conditioned by their content limitations, can provide some insight in denoting temporal patterns or in comparing different regions' or nations' distributions. Three positive measures are most commonly used and will be presented below.

The Coefficient of Variation

Suppose we have a society of n individuals with incomes x_i, $i = 1, \ldots, n$, and we are interested in the dispersion of those incomes as a gauge of inequality, since the concept of inequality is one of dispersion of individual incomes about some measure of central tendency. A common measure of the dispersion of values about the *mean* value is the second moment about the mean, or the *variance*:

$$\sigma^2 = \frac{\Sigma_i (x_i - \mu)^2}{n}$$

where μ is the mean income. The variance is the mean of the squares of the income deviations from the mean.

Squaring such deviations gives greater-than-proportionate weight to deviations farther from the mean. An absolute deviation that is twice as much as another receives four times the weight, not double, in the calculation of the variance. Thus, because σ^2 rises rapidly as the absolute spread of a distribution rises, it is extremely sensitive to inequality. However, a transfer of $50 from a rich person to a person with no income may have the same impact on the variance as the same transfer to the same person who has a larger prior income. If one believes that a measure of inequality should be reduced more by an equal transfer of income to a poorer than a richer person, this may appear to be a disadvantage of the variance as a measure.

But the most serious drawback of the variance is that its value is sensitive to the units in which income is measured. If one used dollar units of income σ^2 would be much larger than if one measured income in thousand-dollar units, even though the same income distribution is being measured. To use another example, it might be that horses are much more uniform in weight (i.e., cluster closer to their own mean) than dogs, but the variance of horses will be much larger than dogs simply because the weights are larger. To correct this bias we can make the measure relative by taking the square root of the variance as a proportion of the mean:

$$V = \frac{\sigma}{\mu}$$

This is the *coefficient of variation*.

Now, for example, if everyone's income rose 100 percent, V would not change. Those interested in incorporating normative judgments in inequality measures might object to this property, on grounds *either* that the measure should rise with absolute income levels to reflect the ability of the society to correct inequality with less sacrifice *or* that it should fall because inequality is less painful at higher absolute income levels. As a positive measure, however, this neutrality is an advantage because relative differences among recipients are more relevant to most equity issues and mean income levels can be used where absolute income considerations are concerned.

However, using the square of deviations (rather than some other even integer exponent) is arbitrary and unsupported by any logic based on the purposes of the measure or the structure of income distributions. Other measures with less specialized methodology may then be investigated.

The Gini Coefficient

The most frequently used measure of income inequality is the *Gini coefficient*, which yields a "pure" number ranging from 0 (for static equality of incomes) to 1 (for "perfect inequality"—all income received by one unit). The basis for the measurement is the *Lorenz curve* which graphs cumulative proportions of income received by recipient units (on the vertical axis) against cumulative proportions of those units (on the horizontal axis), when recipients are ranked in ascending order of income received. To illustrate, table 8.1 reproduces the distribution of family incomes in 1984 as percentage shares[4] of total family income received by quintiles of family units, ranked from lowest (first) to highest (fifth) quintile shares.

TABLE 8.1
Census Family Income Distribution, 1984, by Quintiles

Quintile	Income Share (y_i)	Families Shares (z_i)	Cumulative Income Shares	Cumulative Family Shares
1st	4.7%	20.0%	4.7%	20%
2d	11.0	20.0	15.7	40
3d	17.0	20.0	32.7	60
4th	24.4	20.0	57.1	80
5th	42.9	20.0	100.0	100

Source: U.S. Bureau of the Census, *Current Population Reports*, series P-60, no. 149, table 4.

In figure 8.1 the cumulative shares of income are graphed against the cumulative income recipient units, z_i, and the five points are connected to form the piecewise linear Lorenz curve L. The 45° line, E, depicts what the Lorenz curve would be if the distribution were characterized by static equality, with each quintile receiving 20 percent of family income. The L curve would be smoother, of course, if the quantile "mesh" selected for listing the distribution were finer (deciles or percentiles, for example).

A visual image of the degree of inequality can be obtained by comparing the degree of departure of L from E. The Gini coefficient simply computes the ratio of the area captured between L and E to the area

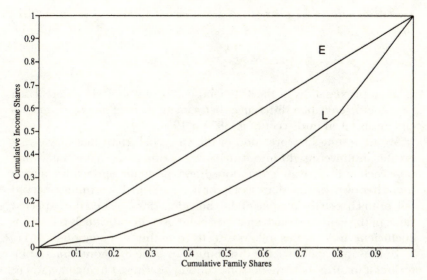

FIGURE 8.1. Family Money Income Distribution, 1984

lying under the E line and bounded by the axes. This latter area—the denominator of the Gini coefficient—is simply .5 (i.e., $1 \times 1 \times .5$). If L coincides with E—so that perfect equality rules—the Gini coefficient is 0. The line of perfect inequality is the horizontal axis from 0 to 1 where it is joined by the right-hand vertical axis. This would be approached if all income were received by one household, and the Gini coefficient would approach 1.

The precise calculation of the Gini coefficient measure of inequality can be made in the most straightforward manner from the following formula:

(8.1)
$$G \quad = \quad \frac{\sum_i \sum_j |x_i - x_j|}{2n^2\mu}$$

$$= \quad \frac{\sum_i \sum_j |y_i - y_j|}{2n}$$

$$= \quad \frac{\sum_i \sum_j Max(0, y_i - y_j)}{n}$$

where n is the number of quantiles, μ is the mean of quantile incomes, x_i is total quantile income in quantile i, and y_i is quantile i's income share. From the last expression it is seen to be the average of the nonnegative differences between individual units' income shares. To facilitate interpretation of (8.1) assume that $n = 5$ and that these individuals share a total income of $1 distributed as indicated in table 8.1. Then (8.1) yields

$$G = \frac{1.796}{5} = .3592$$

as an approximation to the U.S. Gini coefficient in 1984. (The actual Gini coefficient when differences between all pairs of family income recipients is taken into account is .385 for 1984.)

An interesting interpretation of the Gini coefficient that may give a greater intuitive insight into its meaning is due to Graham Pyatt.[5] Suppose each individual after a random draw is given the option of retaining his or her own income share as a floor beneath which it is unnecessary to fall, or to choose the income of the individual drawn. Then the expected value of the gain from such an experiment over all individuals is the Gini coefficient. Indeed, this follows directly from the last equation in (8.1).

To illustrate, consider the distribution in table 8.1, continuing to interpret it in terms of a five-person economy sharing $1 in income, where the individuals are listed in ascending order of income shares. The probability of drawing any one of the five individuals to benefit is .2. Then, assuming a specific individual is being considered, the possible gains of that individual times the probability of that gain are as indicated in table 8.2.

TABLE 8.2
The Results of the "Pyatt Game"

Individual 1	0 + .063 + .123 + .197 + .382 =				.765 × .2 =	.1530
Individual 2	0 +	0 + .060 + .134 + .319 =			.513 × .2 =	.1026
Individual 3	0 +	0 +	0 + .074 + .259 =		.333 × .2 =	.0666
Individual 4	0 +	0 +	0 +	0 + .185 =	.185 × .2 =	.0370
Individual 5	0 +	0 +	0 +	0 +	0 = 0 × .2 =	0

Expected Gain = 1.796 × .2 = .3592
Gini Coefficient = Expected Gain = .3592

The straightforward Gini coefficient, based as it is on the Lorenz curve, has certain limitations that should be kept in mind in its interpretation. In comparing income distributions between two years for the same nation (or region, etc.) or between different nations (regions, etc.) in the same year, when one Lorenz curve lies wholly inside the other, one can assert unambiguously that the outer curve represents greater static inequality than the inner. When the curves intersect, however, the Gini coefficients do not give clear-cut signals.

TABLE 8.3
Hypothetical Intersecting Lorenz Curves by Deciles

Deciles	Income Shares (y)		Cumulative Income Shares	
	Year 1	Year 2	Year 1	Year 2
1st	.03	.06	.03	.06
2d	.05	.07	.08	.13
3d	.06	.08	.14	.21
4th	.08	.08	.22	.29
5th	.08	.08	.30	.37
6th	.10	.08	.40	.45
7th	.11	.08	.51	.53
8th	.12	.10	.63	.63
9th	.17	.16	.80	.79
10th	.20	.21	1.00	1.00

Consider, for example, the hypothetical data of table 8.3, listing distributions of incomes share for households in Years 1 and 2 by deciles as well as their Lorenz curve coordinates. The Gini coefficients are .278 for Year 1 and .208 for Year 2, indicating a movement toward greater equality in the latter year. But closer study of the data reveals that although the lowest three deciles and the tenth increased their proportionate shares, the middle fourth through ninth either lost or remained constant in share. Thus, the unidimensional Gini coefficient masks this divergent movement. As is clear from figure 8.2, the Lorenz curves intersect to depict these ambiguities graphically.

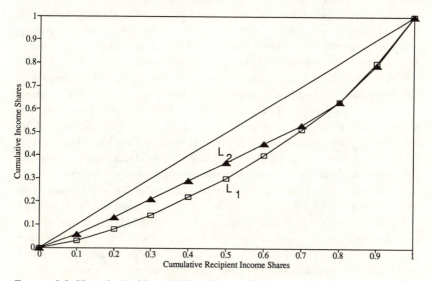

FIGURE 8.2. Hypothetical Intersecting Lorenz Curves

The reason for such behavior of the Gini coefficient inheres in the large weights given to lower quantile shares (see the last column of table 8.2). Another formula for the Gini coefficient is the following: where $y_1 \leqslant y_2 \leqslant y_3 \leqslant \ldots \leqslant y_n$.

(8.2)
$$G = 1 + \frac{1}{n} - \frac{2}{n}(y_n + 2y_{n-1} + 3y_{n-2} + \ldots + ny_1)$$

Suppose dy_n in income share is taxed away from the highest income earner and given to individual 1, the lowest earner. Then, from (8.2),

$$dG = (\frac{2}{n})(1 - n)\, dy_n$$

That is, the Gini coefficient falls by a large amount because the lower income recipients are weighted much more heavily than higher in the income scale. In table 8.3 the increased income shares of the lower recipients in Year 2 outweigh the equally large reductions of the middle of the array and the increase of the highest earner. In a normative sense many analysts regard this weighting scheme as an appropriate one, since it values redistributions disproportionately in favor of the lower brackets. As a positive measure, however, it constitutes a defect in judging such redistributions from the objective viewpoint of equality regardless of the benefiting quantile. This property of the Gini coefficient should certainly be kept sight of in interpreting comparative Gini measures.

1. *Decomposition of the Gini Coefficient and Life-Cycle Income.* Let us now abandon the simplifying assumption that each quantile contains only one recipient and recognize that each of the n contains k_i units, $i = 1, 2, \ldots, n$. Within each quantile, or income share group, there is a distribution of shares with mean share μ_i. The question arises, therefore, whether one can define the k groups of recipient units on a basis other than income shares—ascending order of age of the head of the family, for example—and decompose the Gini coefficient into that portion of the inequality in income shares that is criterion-related (e.g., age-related) and that portion that is "unexplained" by differences in criterion status. More generally, is it possible to determine what portion of inequality originates *within* the k groups formed by the classifying variable or attribute and what proportion arises from differences *among* the groups? Can these two sources of variation be neatly separated?

To be able to do so with respect to age of household head would have great relevance to the distinction between static and life-cycle income inequality. With success one could organize recipient units into groups by ascending age brackets, compute the differences among the groups' mean income shares, and ascribe such differences to age differentials and life-cycle causes, leaving residual income share differences to be explained by non-life-cycle causes. The Gini coefficient that was based wholly on this residual variation, which incorporated the variance of income shares within the groups, might then be a truer measure of the inequality about which society should be concerned.

Unfortunately, it is in general not possible to perform such a dichotomization of the causation behind the Gini coefficient. The reason is best seen by using Pyatt's interpretation of the Gini. Assume that we have indeed classified the income share data into k groups defined by age brackets of head of household, and that these groups are arranged in ascending order of average income. Assume initially that for each group's income share distribution the maximum share is less than the minimum share in the distribution of the group that follows it in the ascending sequence and that the minimum share is higher than the maximum share of the group that precedes it. In this case, the within-group distributions have no "overlap," and every member of a group in computing the potential net gains from the "Pyatt game" described in table 8.2 would have potential positive gains only from all households with greater income share in his or her own age group and in all age cohorts above him or her in the ascending sequence. The pattern of potential gains for each individual would show the "upper triangularity" revealed in table 8.2, with all entries below the main diagonal at zero. Every individual can improve income share only by (1) moving up within the distribution of his or her own group or (2) moving to a higher mean income bracket.

In this case it is possible to break the variation neatly into that associated with nonage causes within the own-group and that *positively* associated with higher groups. But now suppose the conditions stated above did not hold: overlapping occurs because some individuals in group k could improve their income share by exchanging incomes with some individuals in group $k-1$. Now the unidirectional between-group variation is destroyed and it is possible to gain by moving in either direction of the ranking. Positive terms now appear beneath the diagonal of the gains matrix. Income share can now be improved by (1) moving up within the distribution of the own-group, (2) moving to a higher ranked (by mean income) age bracket, or, disturbingly, (3) moving to a lower ranked age bracket. The association between age and income share is muddied, and all of the nonage factors cannot be viewed as being captured by the within-group variation. There is a third component to be added to the age- and non-age-determined differentials: an age differential that is not associated with greater experience and skill but with lower.[6]

To effect a decomposition, continue to assume that the age groups are arranged in ascending order of their average incomes, μ_i, $i = 1, 2, \ldots k$.

Further, assume for the moment that all individuals in group i earned μ_i, so that intragroup income share variation is eliminated. Then compute the "age-Gini" based on the variation among the group means (weighted by age-group population shares and interpreted as a Pyatt game). This "between-means" average expected gain can be interpreted as that amount of the total or Lorenz Gini coefficient that is determined by position on the life-cycle curve, since, by assumption, no other variation exists in the data but that which is associated with such position.

But consider now the fact that within each age group income shares do vary among themselves, and, ideally, for reasons that have nothing to do with age since all recipients in group i are the "same" age. Measure the "within age group" variation over all groups by use of a Pyatt game: obtain the average of the expected gains of every individual *in a given age group* were that individual to compare income shares with every other individual *in the same age group.* Summing these measures over all groups and averaging gives the portion of the Gini coefficient associated with nonage factors as captured *within groups.*

When income brackets within age groups do not overlap, these two components—the age-Gini and the nonage Gini—should add to the Lorenz Gini. But the Lorenz Gini captures *all* expected gains among individuals, including expected gains made by individuals comparing incomes with persons in lower income brackets. If overlapping age-group distributions exist, some individuals in a higher bracket would gain when compared with some individuals in lower brackets, and neither the age-Gini nor the nonage Gini will capture this portion of the Pyatt game average gains. This "interaction" Gini component escapes capture in the suggested decomposition. *In a purely statistical sense, then, the "between-groups" and "within-groups" decomposition of the Lorenz Gini is not exhaustive when distribution overlaps occur among groups, and certainly such overlaps are a general occurrence.*

2. *Paglin's Decomposition.* Paglin, beginning from the rather uncontroversial position that the true measure of "nonfunctional" and potentially unjust inequality is a departure from life-cycle equality rather than static equality sets out to measure such a departure and to base a Gini coefficient on it (the *Paglin Gini*). His seminal article stimulated a great deal of controversy on three different fronts—the conceptual, the statistical, and the interpretive—and it is important to discuss each of the debates.

a. Conceptual Debate. First, as noted above, the disputes about the *conceptual* framework are rather muted, with something of a consensus among economists that troublesome social inequality is that which is measured from the life-cycle curve rather than from the static equal-income-by-quantiles norm (as depicted by the 45° line on the Lorenz diagram). Some differences within this broad agreement have arisen, however.

Danziger, Haveman, and Smolensky argue that a better base from which to judge income inequality from a justice standpoint would be a distribution of life-cycle income norms based on a "collective judgment" of the needs of different age groups, much as U.S. poverty definitions are set. They argue that the age-Gini determination in Paglin's decomposition is made by using the static distribution of a single year's data and that the means of such age group income shares vary from year to year.[7] Such life-cycle norms should have policy content and continuity in their view. Paglin argues that it is preferable to use norms that reflect market judgments, productivity, and political decisions (such as Social Security benefits), not expert-determined "needs" alone. From the viewpoint of the goals of the current investigation I find considerable common ground with Paglin: the needs approach ties notions of justice to a particular philosophical viewpoint that may not be acceptable to others (and happens not to coincide with the one adopted in chapter 7). It is better to abstract as far as possible from such normative judgments when searching for a measurement that should be neutral in its moral implications. However, Danziger, Haveman and Smolensky certainly are entitled to this viewpoint as a derivation of a well-articulated theory of economic justice, for then the measure is normative. One can sympathize at least with a desire for a greater stability of the age-income profile over time.

Minarik, on the other hand, believes the age-class determination of income norms should be further differentiated by educational level within each age group, suggesting also that other determinants within groups might be distinguished as causing significant differences in group shares: sex and race of household head, for example. It is unreasonable to argue that all members of an age group should have the same mean income in the face of such differences, Minarik asserts. Also, society may be interested in the adjusted distribution of earned income in addition to total income, because since some families have no earned income at all, the life-cycle adjusted earned income measure of inequality might be much larger than for total income including transfers.[8]

Paglin's response to these suggestions is that his decomposition is one that aims at distinguishing those forces operating on income distributions that are essentially inescapable and functional from those, like education, in which choice plays an important role. Education indeed is one of the major programs available for lessening the inequality that remains after life-cycle considerations are subtracted out. This inescapability argument does not, of course, answer the suggestion that sex and race should also be discriminants within the life-cycle categorization. But they are causes for nonfunctional discrimination in income receipts which are among the most blatantly unjust sources of residual inequality within an ethos that prizes individualism so highly and whose isolation the decomposition is designed to accomplish. To mix them with life-cycle causes is to mix functionally "justified" and "unjustified" causes, which, along with "inescapable" versus "escapable" causes, should form the basis of the distinction.

Paglin's response, therefore, is that life-cycle income determinants are both *functional* in a voluntarist, individualist society with a strong emphasis on the economically rational and efficient and impose an *inescapable* pattern of earnings (before policy measures are employed) given their existence. For my purposes, the best decomposition is that which separates out those factors associated with predominantly just impacts on distribution from those that have significantly unjust implications, with "just" and "unjust" defined explicitly by the theory of economic justice presented in chapter 7. Within this framework life-cycle income determinants are fundamentally just and ethos-conformant and impose a broadly socially desirable pattern of earnings. Residual unjust aspects associated with age can be adjusted rather straightforwardly within the income subsidization programs of the compassionate motivation of individualism. Educational distinctions are functional but within the framework unjust to the degree they reflect correctible inequality of economic opportunity. Sex and racial identifications are inescapable but unjust to the extent they lead to inequality of fair competition for reward.

Kurien suggests a similar purpose of decomposing income distributions with a view toward isolating "just" from "unjust" or socially desirable or acceptable from undesirable.[9] His is the distinction between those sources of inequality reflecting "choice" versus those reflecting "opportunity." Presumably, the first would aggregate inequalities arising from situations in which all individuals had the same opportunities but freely made choices entailing differential income receipts and the second where all individuals did not have the opportunities to make such choices. Paglin points out the difficulty of separating out choice from opportunity and suggests it is probably insurmountable. Is there any situation in which all individuals begin with equal opportunities to make a given choice? (Certainly aging is one case in which they have equal nonfreedom to make a nonchoice!) When is choice not constrained by opportunity? However, those factors which cause unequal opportunities that have *significant* impacts on income distribution *and* are correctable by socially acceptable means are a feasible subset of the whole and would have to be identified by the dualistic individualism theory of economic justice.

My quarrel with Kurien's criterion for determining the decomposition of the Gini, in addition to the difficulty of disentangling decision circumstances, is that "just" is not coextensive with "choice" nor "unjust" with lack of opportunity. One's denial of opportunity to become a nuclear physicist or corporate executive or professional baseball player may be quite just if one lacks the intelligence or talent to master those skills—that is, if discrimination occurred solely on the bases of relevant characteristics. One's free choice of actions under conditions of uncertainty may result in income consequences that a theory of justice may view as unjust. As noted in Part 2, no theory of justice can wholly ignore consequences. One of the major purposes of the compassionate strain of individualism is to protect the individual from the consequences of actions freely chosen. Economically just and unjust actions and policies must be judged within the guidelines of a much more comprehensive and sophisticated theory than Kurien's suggestion permits.

No decomposition of measures of inequality is going to accomplish its purpose completely. Age of household head, after all, is simply a surrogate for many different factors that cause rather consistent differences in income receipts at different stages of life. Some of them may be judged to have unjust consequences by one's theory of justice: forced retirement, deterioration of youthful appearance, discrimination in favor of youth by employers seeking to reduce benefit costs, and so forth, are likely candidates. But most of these factors would be accepted by the dualistic individualism theory of economic justice: differential educational attainments or skills associated with maturity, growth and lessening of physical capabilities, returns to investment in human capital, changes in choice patterns of work and leisure, and so forth. In my view the latter forces strongly dominate the former and do so in age groupings to a degree found in no other single criterion. Hence, I would agree with Paglin and most other economists—including those who criticize Paglin on other grounds—that the use of age-of-household head as a decomposition criterion is a valuable means of investigating the degree of *potentially* unjustifiable income inequality and superior in these respects to other suggested criterion attributes.

b. Statistical Debate. Second, the *statistical criticisms* of Paglin's methodology are by far the most well-founded and damaging. As noted earlier, an exact decomposition of the Lorenz Gini coefficient is rendered impossible because of the existence of overlaps among the age-cohort distributions, and this has been known for some time.[10] In terms of the allied techniques of regression analysis, if one regresses income on age-of-household head the Lorenz Gini is analogous to total variance, Paglin's Age Gini is the "explained variance" accounted for by a nonlinear estimating equation, and the Paglin Gini—which is simply the Age Gini subtracted from the Lorenz Gini—is the equivalent of the "unexplained variance" embodied in the scatter of the observations about the equation. This latter includes both the intragroup scatter and the interaction terms occurring because individuals in an age group with a lower mean income earn more than some individuals in a group with a higher mean incomes.[11]

This inability to perform a dichotomous decomposition is recognized by all parties, including Paglin. But he, in effect, merges the interaction variation with the within-group variation by simply subtacting the intergroup Gini (Age Gini) from the Lorenz Gini, and treats this residual as the inequality unexplained by age factors.

c. Interpretive Debate. The debate rages about the *interpretation* that Paglin gives this residual Gini. He believes the interaction variation to be primarily the reflection of intragroup variation and therefore to be fittingly added to the direct measure of that variation. In his view it arises primarily because of high-achievement individuals who are differentially more able than their fellow age-group contemporaries for reasons unrelated to age and associated skills. Hence, although the procedure is statistically impure, Paglin believes they should be grouped with those inequalities that are not associated with life-cycle factors. This is admittedly a strong assumption based largely on intuition, and his critics have been quick to cite exceptions. Intragroup variation (before the inclusion of the overlap interaction) may capture productivity differentials which are "functional" in Paglin's sense. More important, from the aims of this study, they may be judged to be just by the dualistic individualism theory of economic justice. On the other hand, all of life-cycle differentials may not be just. Kurien points out, for example, that currently older age groups' incomes reflect the years of skill achievement lost in World War II service, unanticipated gains in longevity, and changes in the abilities and attitudes of children to support parents in old age. Such factors are not related to the "functional" or just causes of life-cycle differences.

Further, some of the "acceptable" life-cycle factors are not captured by the year-by-year computation of the Age Gini. If two individuals are in occupations commanding equal lifetime incomes in the market economy, but the time profiles of those earnings are different, the cross-sectional decomposition will capture these differences in intragroup variation, distorting the Paglin Gini's depiction of age-adjusted inequality.[12]

To these interpretive difficulties must be added those arising from the ambiguities of the interaction variation. Extreme outliers in the age-group distributions may reflect mixtures of age- and nonage-related factors. Age brackets used to define groups tend to be rather wide, and thus high achievers in one bracket may be close in age to low achievers in the higher bracket. Moreover, age may correlate rather poorly with acquisition of experience and skill, since they may be obtained in accelerated fashion by greater investment in human capital. Placing all interaction variation in the "nonfunctional" category of inequality would overstate potentially undesirable inequality. On the other hand much of the interaction effects may spring from sex or race discrimination which are both nonfunctional and unjust in terms of the dualistic individualism theory of justice.

But these points are reflections of the earlier acceptance of the inability to obtain a decomposition that performs its task perfectly with respect to one criterion or another, even when the statistical problems in doing so are eliminated. Like many economists, I am convinced that in eliminating inequalities arising from life-cycle factors we are presenting a more accurate picture of economic inequality. Unlike Paglin's critics, I am also ready to accept the fact that his residual inequality is predominantly the result of nonage causes and that it should be looked at closely with the view of eliminating or reducing it within the limits of just policy. It should be studied more closely in terms of demographic and sociological factors to reduce distortions that are the inevitable result of imperfect methodology interacting with grouped data. But its use in the Paglin form eliminates more distortion than it causes; the age-related criterion is a better discriminant for purposes of economic justice than other feasible alternatives; and its basis in the widely used Lorenz-Gini measure of inequality makes it readily interpretable, partly because of the well-known deficiencies of that measure.

Theil's Entropy Measure

The last nonnormative measure of inequality I shall consider is Theil's entropy measure.[13] Its primary interest for my purposes is that it does offer the possibility of an exact decomposition of inequality into inter- and intragroup components. The price one pays for that admitted advantage, however, is the loss of an intuitively appealing interpretation of the measure and the absence of a convincing rationale for the applicability of the concept that underlies it.

The core notion of the measure is that of Shannon's entropy concept in information theory. Suppose the probability of an event's occurrence is judged to be y_i. Should it occur, how much "information" is conveyed about the phenomena being scrutinized? Presumably, the new light shed on a situation will be a function of the degree of "surprise" event i's occurrence entails. If $y_i = .01$ its *nonoccurrence* will not cause much shock nor alter one's viewpoint on the phenomena under analysis. But its *occurrence* will convey some sense of surprise and perhaps prior misperception, so its information content will be great. Hence, information is taken to be related inversely to the probability of occurrence. A convenient function to represent this relation is

$$I(y_i) = ln(\frac{1}{y_i})$$

In a probabilistic sense, then, the expected informational content of all events can be defined as

(8.3)
$$I(y) = \Sigma_i \, y_i \, ln(\frac{1}{y_i})$$

$I(y)$ attains its maximum value when all events i are equiprobable, in which case it equals $ln \, n$, where n is the number of events (and $y_i = 1/n$, $i = 1, 2, \ldots, n$).

Theil adapts this reasoning to the measurement of income inequality by letting n be the number of recipient units and y_i the proportion of income received by unit i. When equality holds in the static sense, so that $y_i = 1/n$, Theil then subtracts $I(y)$ from this maximum for his measure of inequality:

(8.4)
$$T = ln \, n - \Sigma_i \, y_i \, ln(\frac{1}{y_i})$$

Hence, $0 \leqslant T \leqslant ln \, n$. A pure number may be obtained by dividing T by $ln \, n$ if one is not concerned about decomposition.

Suppose, now, we worked with grouped data, classifying individuals into classes by age of household head, and let the groups be symbolized $j = 1, 2, \ldots, k$, with y_j the proportion of income received by group j. The Theil measure can be decomposed into intra- and intercohort variation by the following formula:

(8.5)
$$T = \Sigma_j \, y_j \, ln(\frac{y_j \, n}{n_j}) + \Sigma_j \, y_j \, (ln \, n_j - I_j(y))$$
$$= \Sigma_j \, y_j \, ln(\frac{y_j n}{n_j}) + \Sigma_j \, y_j \, T_j$$

where $I_j(y)$ is the entropy equation (8.3) for cohort j and T_j is the Theil measure for cohort j. The first term in (8.5) is intercohort inequality and the second term is intracohort inequality.

Despite the attraction of the exact decomposition that the Theil measure permits, one apparent disadvantage is that T is not a pure number but varies with the size of population. Two responses to this criticism can be made. First, as noted above, division by $ln \, n$ will convert T to a pure number varying between zero and one. Second, as Theil shows, T is invariant when income shares are distributed in the same *proportions* to the same *proportions* of populations. Thus, if $n = 2$ and $y_1 = 0$ and $y_2 = 1$, or if $n = 200,000$ and $n_1 = 100,000$ with $y_1 = 0$ and $n_2 = 100,000$ with $y_2 = 1$ with equal distribution within the second cohort, or if $n = 1,000,000$ and $n^1 = 500,000$ with $y_1 = 0$ and $n_2 = 500,000$ with $y_2 = 1$ with equal division within the cohort, T will have the same value. The difficulty, however, is that interyear comparisons will feature changing distributions within classes and among them. Recourse to the division by $ln\ n$ will sacrifice the decomposition capability, the primary advantage of the Theil measure.

More fundamentally, however, the problem of interpreting the meaning of T intuitively limits its value as a measue of inequality. Why should $I(y)$ have any validity as a measure of equality? Why this specific form? How does one move in a convincing manner between the justification of $I(y)$ in communication theory and income distribution matters? Theil has attempted to provide such an explanatory transition, but it is highly abstract and unconvincing.

THE MEASUREMENT OF POVERTY

Poverty is a level of income receipt plus wealth holdings endured by income units which is judged by a theory of economic justice to be inconsistent with the individualistic right of persons to life within a context of comfort sufficient for the opportunity to maintain health and self-respect. As such it must be defined within the guidelines of a theory of economic justice to be meaningful. In the case of the dualistic individualism theory the truly discriminant criterion is that of "self-respect" and such definitions can be safely left to policymakers subject to judicial review. However, the poverty measure must be one that is *relative* to a society's affluence, perhaps defined as some percentage of median or mean incomes for families of similar demographic makeup. Subject to feasibility conclusions, for working purposes in chapters 9 and 10 several percentages of median income will be analyzed as the necessary level of income below which poverty is suffered.

The Official U.S. Poverty Levels

A widely quoted set of poverty definitions is that derived by Mollie Orshansky in 1963 at the Social Security Administration and, after some modifications and simplifications, still employed officially by the U.S. government.[14] It must be characterized as minimalist definition in the context of the dualistic individualism theory in three respects. First, it is an absolute rather than a relative standard, in that it is adjusted upward only for inflation through use of the all-items Consumer Price Index, thereby ignoring increases in real income. Second, the notion of providing opportunity for self-respect does not enter into its composition. And third, its basic floor income levels are driven by estimated food requirements in a Department of Agriculture "economy food plan."

Using this food plan the cost of providing basic nourishment to families of various sizes and types was computed as a base. The cost was then tripled to obtain a poverty line for such family types on the basis that food constituted about one-third of family expenditures. Until 1980 there were 124 poverty thresholds identified, but these were then simplified by eliminating distinctions between farm and nonfarm and male- and female-headed families.[15] These poverty thresholds and the implications for redistributive policy within a context of economic justice will be explored in detail in chapter 10.

A SUMMARY

The measurement of income inequality confronts the analyst with a number of troublesome choices. Which definition of income is the relevant one for the task at hand: money income before tax; money income after tax; money income plus in-kind income (and if so, which forms of in-kind income); personal income; adjusted gross tax income; or any of a variety of others? Which is the proper recipient unit: family, unrelated individuals, both, individual taxpayer? Should the analyst be interested in a static cross-sectional inequality or a life-cycle age-group classification? Should one's measure be as neutral with respect to values as possible, or should it incorporate normative values, and if so, which?

For my purposes money income (including money transfers) for families on the one hand, and for unrelated persons plus families on the other, are the best available units and income concepts for the feasibility study to follow. Inclusion of in-kind income opens up a host of questions concerning which forms of such income are properly included or excluded as well as the valuation of such benefits. The income concept implicit in most discussions of the topic are money incomes, including money transfer payments, and possibly including the money value equivalent of in-kind payments for the *most basic* needs: food, housing, medical care, and the like. Where the data are available these extended concepts will be employed. Similarly, income after all taxes would be most welcome as a supplement, but such data are available only rarely.

Also, life-cycle income more closely conforms to the appropriate sense of inequality for this study than static income levels. The pattern of income receipts over time in a market economy reflects directly the operations of a market economy whose existence is identified as basically conformant to the dualistic individualism theory of economic justice and to the ethos within which it must be embedded. However, life-cycle inequality ignores extreme static inequality in a society, even if everyone in it had equal lifetime incomes, when the lower quantiles live in unacceptable poverty as defined in chapter 7, even for short periods. When one recognizes that many of the families or individuals in those lower quantiles do not follow the representative life-cycle progression pattern, the ignoring of static inequality becomes even more unjustified. Hence, chapters 9 and 10 will be concerned with both dynamic and static inequality.

The interest in life-cycle income intensifies the debate concerning the appropriate measure of inequality. It is of course recognized that no single index measure can characterize all of the many facets of inequality in a society's income distribution. Having said this, however, which measure is least distorting? A positive measure is most appropriate for a study that is deriving its justice norms independently of the three positive measures studied—the coefficient of variation, the Gini measure, and the Theil measure. Primary emphasis will be placed on the Gini measure because its interpretation is most straightforward and it can be given a visual interpretation on a Lorenz diagram.

However, the alleged advantage of the Theil measure in providing an unambiguous decomposition of the inequality measure when considering dynamic life-cycle analysis does not outweigh its difficulty of interpretation. It is accepted that Paglin's decomposition of the Gini measure is impure statistically, but I am more convinced than his critics that the aggregate nonage residual inequality isolated by his method is an acceptable measure of inequality that is "unexplained" by the life-cycle pattern. Ideally, therefore, we would adopt the Gini measure and employ Paglin's decomposition when data is available and it is appropriate.

Chapter 9

THE DISTRIBUTION OF INCOME
IN THE UNITED STATES
IN THE POSTWAR PERIOD

INTRODUCTION

The discussion of chapter 8 is a chart of the minefields that await the unwary explorer of income distribution terrain. A primary lesson of the caveats expressed in that chapter is that no single measure can encapsulate the multidimensional concept of inequality, so that any approach with the prospect of an adequate depiction must be multifaceted. In this chapter, therefore, an effort is made to display and interpret the data in a variety of forms with two goals in mind: first, to obtain some realistic picture of the profile of inequality in the present U.S. society and its evolution from the recent past and second, to isolate problem areas that could threaten the feasibility of the policies implementing the compassionate strand of the dualistic individualism theory of economic justice presented in chapter 7.

The "recent past" is taken as the post–World War II period. That conflict was a watershed between the extreme depression of the 1930s and the prosperous years that have followed since its end. The period has permitted a variety of experiments in government policies to alleviate inequality that were not possible in prior periods. A continuous concern for melioration of the condition of the poor is a persistent theme that unifies the period, even when that concern was not actively indulged in policy and was voiced as opposition protest. And finally, the period has seen some remarkable cultural, geographic, and demographic changes that are unique historically and whose impacts can only be gauged by a study of the data over the period as a unit.

CROSS-SECTIONAL OR STATIC DISTRIBUTIVE ANALYSES

The Distribution of Family Income: An Overview

1. *All Races, Unadjusted.* As an introduction table 9.1 reproduces in detail the family distributions of Census-defined money income for all races in the period 1947–1987, where the chosen "quantile"—the percentage unit of family groupings—is the quintile.

TABLE 9.1
Census Family Money Income Distributions, All Races, 1947–1987,
by Quintiles and Top 5 Percent of Families, with Gini Coefficients

Year	Quintiles					Top 5%	Gini Coefficient
	1st	2d	3d	4th	5th		
1947	5.0%	11.9%	17.0%	23.1%	43.0%	17.5%	.376
1948	4.9	12.1	17.3	23.2	42.4	17.1	.371
1949	4.5	11.9	17.3	23.5	42.7	16.9	.378
1950	4.5	12.0	17.4	23.4	42.7	17.3	.379
1951	5.9	12.4	17.6	23.4	41.6	16.8	.363
1952	4.9	12.3	17.4	23.4	41.9	17.4	.368
1953	4.7	12.5	18.0	23.9	40.9	15.7	.359
1954	4.5	12.1	17.7	23.9	41.8	16.3	.371
1955	4.8	12.3	17.8	23.7	41.3	16.4	.363
1956	5.0	12.5	17.9	23.7	41.0	16.1	.358
1957	5.1	12.7	18.1	23.8	40.4	15.6	.351
1958	5.0	12.5	18.0	23.9	40.6	15.4	.354
1959	4.9	12.3	17.9	23.8	41.1	15.9	.361
1960	4.8	12.2	17.8	24.0	41.3	15.9	.364
1961	4.7	11.9	17.5	23.8	42.2	16.6	.374
1962	5.0	12.1	17.6	24.0	41.3	15.7	.362
1963	5.0	12.1	17.7	24.0	41.2	15.8	.362
1964	5.1	12.0	17.7	24.0	41.2	15.9	.361
1965	5.2	12.2	17.8	23.9	40.9	15.5	.356
1966	5.6	12.4	17.8	23.8	40.5	15.6	.349
1967	5.5	12.4	17.9	23.9	40.4	15.2	.348
1968	5.6	12.4	17.7	23.7	40.5	15.6	.348
1969	5.6	12.4	17.7	23.7	40.6	15.8	.349
1970	5.4	12.2	17.6	23.8	40.9	15.6	.354
1971	5.5	12.0	17.6	23.8	41.1	15.7	.356
1972	5.4	11.9	17.5	23.9	41.4	15.9	.360
1973	5.5	11.9	17.5	24.0	41.1	15.5	.356
1974	5.5	12.0	17.5	24.0	41.0	15.5	.356
1975	5.4	11.8	17.6	24.1	41.1	15.5	.358
1976	5.4	11.8	17.6	24.1	41.1	15.6	.359
1977	5.2	11.6	17.5	24.2	41.5	15.7	.364
1978	5.2	11.6	17.5	24.1	41.5	15.8	.364
1979	5.2	11.6	17.5	24.1	41.7	15.8	.365
1980	5.1	11.6	17.5	24.3	41.6	15.3	.365
1981	5.0	11.3	17.4	24.4	41.9	15.4	.370
1982	4.7	11.2	17.1	24.3	42.7	16.0	.381
1983	4.7	11.1	17.1	24.3	42.8	15.9	.382
1984	4.7	11.0	17.0	24.4	42.9	16.0	.383
1985	4.6	10.9	16.9	24.2	43.5	16.7	.389
1986	4.6	10.8	16.8	24.0	43.7	17.0	.392
1987	4.6	10.8	16.9	24.1	43.7	16.9	.392

Source: U.S. Bureau of the Census, *Current Population Reports,* series P-60, no. 162, table 12, 42–44.

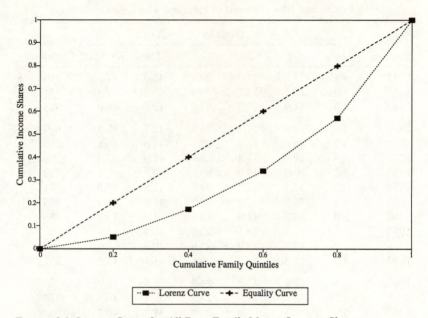

FIGURE 9.1. Lorenz Curve for All-Race Family Money Income Shares, by Quintiles, 1987

Two characteristics of those distributions impress one immediately. The first is the degree of inequality that currently prevails in American society, even when money transfer payments are added to private earnings. In 1987 the lowest 20 percent of family income recipients received less than 5 percent of the total, while the highest 5 percent obtained about 17 percent, or almost four times as much. The lowest 60 percent of families received one-third of total family income, the highest 40 percent two-thirds. And the highest quintile received about 44 percent of the total. Recently the Gini coefficient is almost .40 on the scale of static inequality that rises with inequality from 0 to 1. Because of the sensitivity the coefficient has to changes in the lower quantiles, its relative stability is testimony to the failure of the least well-off to make relative progress over the period. However, in interpreting this fact normatively, the important structural changes in family structure, especially with respect to the number of families headed by single women, must be considered.

Figure 9.1 is the first of three charts to give rather vivid graphic displays of static inequality. It depicts the Lorenz curve for the money income distribution for families in 1987, and, by the convexity of the curve, conveys the marked departure from the line of static equality. Figure 9.2 presents the same distribution as a pie chart, in which the dominance of the fifth quintile (Q5) is revealed most graphically, and figure 9.3 is a bar chart.

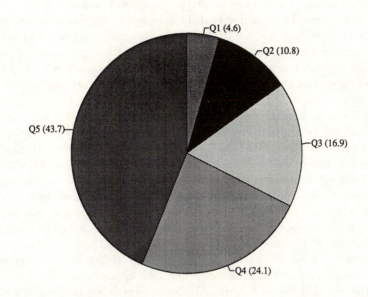

FIGURE 9.2. All-Race Family Money Income Shares, by Quintiles, 1987

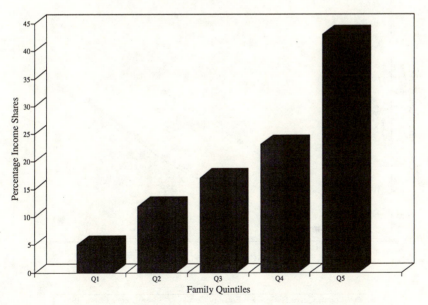

FIGURE 9.3. All-Race Family Money Income Shares, by Quintiles, 1987

Moreover, as pointed out in chapter 8, a good deal of this inequality can be explained and justified within the context of a voluntarist society: age characteristics, years of schooling of income earners, number of earners per family, and a large student population, are some of these explanatory factors. At this point, however, I am simply denoting outstanding surface characteristics, and inequality must certainly be listed as one of them.

The second characteristic revealed by a study of table 9.1 is the essential stability of the pattern over this forty-one-year period. Figure 9.4 makes the point graphically by superimposing the 1947 and 1987 Lorenz curves for family incomes and revealing their near-coincidence, despite the forty years that separate them. As will be shown, this impression is somewhat misleading, since it masks the existence of a slight trend toward more inequality, especially in the post–Vietnam War period, although the Lorenz curves in the figure give some evidence of it. Nevertheless, the 1987 share data differ from those of 1947 a percentage point or so at the most, despite the rather extensive changes in transfer policies and otherwise over what is a rather lengthy period of time. The Gini coefficient also moves by only .016 points, revealing no dramatic shift one way or another.

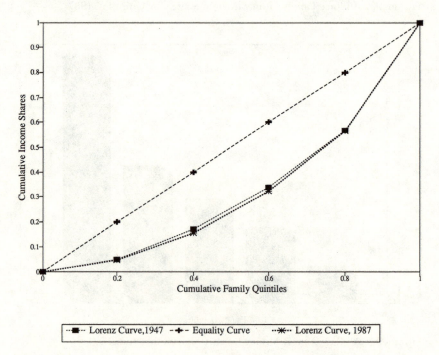

FIGURE 9.4. Lorenz Curves, All-Race Family Money Income Shares, by Deciles, 1947 and 1987

TABLE 9.2

Descriptive Trend Lines Fitted to Quintile Family Money Income Shares
and to Gini Coefficients, 1947–1987

	Gini	1Q (y_1)	2Q (y_2)	3Q (y_3)	4Q (y_4)	5Q (y_5)	Top 5%
C	.37501	4.95334	11.99411	17.01334	23.00870	42.98139	17.61205
	(121.25)	(34.78)	(158.60)	(190.41)	(159.51)	(162.39)	(79.38)
t	−.00124	−.05648	.05499	.19910	.20086	−.33935	−.30785
	(−1.82)	(−1.81)	(6.29)	(6.27)	(3.92)	(−3.61)	(−3.90)
t^2	−.00002	−.00663	−.00217	−.01610	−.01651	.02149	.02134
	(−.63)	(3.63)	(−10.29)	(−4.90)	(−3.11)	(2.21)	(2.61)
t^3	.000002	−.00014	—	.00051	.00054	−.00067	−.00073
	(2.65)	(−4.79)		(4.12)	(2.71)	(−1.82)	(2.37)
t^4	—	—	—	−.000006	−.000006	.000009	.000009
				(−3.87)	(−2.40)	(1.98)	(2.48)
R^2	.809	.663	.891	.847	.632	.838	.754
$\bar{R}^2$	.794	.604	.885	.830	.591	.820	.727
SE	.005	.249	.169	.132	.212	.390	.327
DW	1.18	1.75	.989	1.52	2.09	1.37	2.02
μ	.365	.05	11.92	17.53	23.87	41.63	16.04
σ	.012	.40	.50	.32	.33	.92	.62

Source: Table 9.1.

Notes:

1. t = years from origin year (1947 = 0)
2. Student's *t*-values in parentheses below coefficients
3. $\bar{R}^2 = R^2$ adjusted for degrees of freedom
4. SE = standard error of estimate
5. DW = Durbin-Watson statistic
6. μ = mean of Gini or income share series
7. σ = standard deviation of Gini or income share series

Of course, second thought suggests that small *percentage point* changes
can be significant *percentage* changes. The falls in first and second quintile (1Q and 2Q) shares over the period are 8.0 percent and 9.2 percent
respectively. But other quintile changes in ascending order are only .6,
4.7, and 1.2 percent, and the Gini's rise is 3.5 percent. One can at least
be excused the impression that even though the changes are more disturbing than initially perceived, and that such changes move in the
direction of greater, not lesser, inequality, they are not dramatic in
magnitude.

However, a closer analysis of the data of table 9.1 reveals more complicated patterns and gives some cause for concern on grounds of economic justice. In figures 9.5 to 9.11 descriptive trend lines were fitted to
the Gini coefficients and to the income shares of 1Q through 5Q and of
the top 5 percent of family recipients. The estimating equations of best
fit were third- and fourth-degree polynomials reproduced in table 9.2.

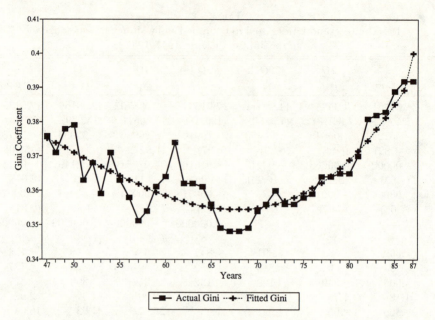

FIGURE 9.5. All-Race Family Money-Income Gini Coefficients, Actual and Fitted
Trend Line, 1947–1987

The coefficients of multiple determination confirm the visual evidence
from the figures that rather good descriptive fits were obtained.

Figure 9.5 reveals a U-shaped pattern for the Gini coefficient, declining (with implied decrease in static inequality) from 1947 to 1968, then
rising steadily with a steeper upward slope than the prior period's negative slope. Table 9.3 counts the number of positive, negative, and zero
year-to-year movements in the Gini coefficient for intervals within these
periods to give a deeper qualitative interpretation of these overall
changes. The difference in slope magnitudes in the earlier period is sustained by the data in the first row category of table 9.3. The strength of
the positive movements period is largely the result of a string of rapid
increases in the Gini coefficient during the recessionary periods of
1948–1949, 1953–1954, and 1957–1958. The cyclical impacts on inequality are quite apparent in this period, rising in recessions and declining in
periods of prosperity. The latter type of movement is particularly evident
in the Vietnam prosperity of 1961–1968.

Three recessions had similar positive impacts on the Gini in the later
period, as revealed by the rises in the coefficient in 1969–1972, 1974–
1977, and 1980–1982. But the strong succession of increases from 1982
to 1986—a period of extended prosperity—is countercyclical and is as-

TABLE 9.3

Direction of Year-to-Year Changes in Gini Coefficients and
Quintile Money Income Shares, All-Race Families, 1947–1948

| | | Changes | | |
Variable	Period	Positive	Negative	Zero
1. Gini Coefficients	1947–1968	8	11	2
	1969–1987	13	1	4
2. 1Q Share	1947–1952	1	3	1
	1952–1973	10	9	2
	1973–1987	0	6	8
3. 2Q Share	1947–1960	7	6	0
	1960–1987	5	13	9
4. 3Q Share	1947–1957	10	2	1
	1957–1976	5	7	7
	1976–1987	1	6	4
5. 4Q Share	1947–1957	4	6	10
	1957–1970	5	5	3
	1970–1987	8	4	5
6. 5Q Share	1947–1970	10	11	2
	1970–1987	10	4	3
7. Top 5%	1947–1975	11	14	3
	1975–1987	8	3	1

Source: Table 9.1.

cribable in large part to the structural changes occurring in the U.S.
economy.

Figure 9.6, which traces the percentage of income received by first
quintile recipients, mirrors the movements in the Gini rather well in the
path of income shares of the lowest quintile. The smooth trend reveals
a decline in the period 1947–1952, followed by a steady rise from 1952 to
1973, and a steep fall thereafter. The recessionary periods 1948–1949,
1953–1954, 1957–1958, 1969–1970, 1974–1975, and 1980–1981 are
clearly reflected in declines in income shares. Table 9.3 presents the
record of qualitative changes in the periods 1947–1952, 1952–1973, and
1973–1987 which are distinguished by inflection points in the trend line.
The first and third periods clearly depict domination by worsening factors, but the second period does not show the strong dominance of improvements that the trend line discerns. This is largely the result of the
inclusion within this period of three recessions.

Movements in the shares of the second quintile are presented in figure 9.7. The trend line shows a slow rise from 1947 to 1960 and a steep

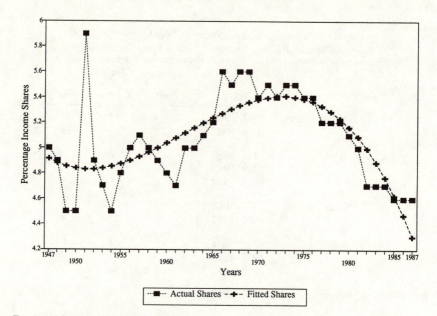

FIGURE 9.6. First Quintile Shares, All-Race Family Money Income, 1947–1987

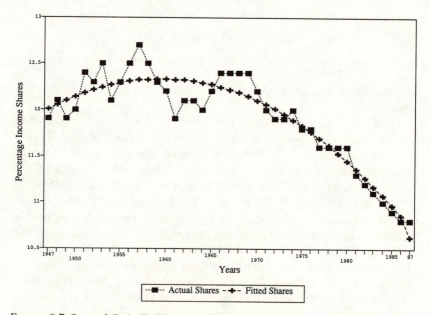

FIGURE 9.7. Second Quintile Shares, All-Race Family Money Income, 1947–1987

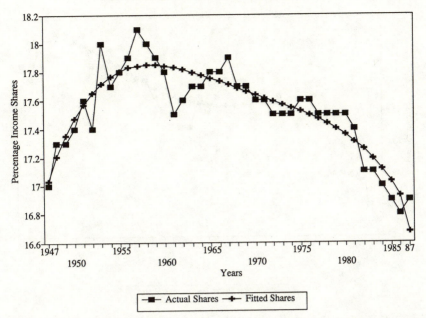

FIGURE 9.8. Third Quintile Shares, All-Race Family Money Income, 1947–1987

decline in the period 1960–1987. The six recessionary periods in the postwar years are reflected clearly in the year-to-year declines, and the qualitative volatility of the changes is recorded in table 9.3. As in the analysis of 1Q shares, these qualitative measures are more decisive for the later period of decline than for the earlier one of expansion, repeating the evidence given by the absolute values of the slopes of the trend line. However, the decline in received shares begins as early as 1959 for 2Q.

Broadly speaking, then, the income shares of the lowest 40 percent of families rose during the 1940s and 1950s, declined and then recovered previous levels during the 1960s, then fell in the 1970s and experienced an accelerated fall in the 1980s.

This pattern of change is also repeated for the middle 20 percent of the family incomes (i.e., 3Q), as shown in figure 9.8. The trend line rises rather steeply until about 1957, then falls continuously over the remainder of the period, accelerating from 1976 to 1987. The qualitative changes of table 9.3 confirm this pattern. One interesting feature of this "middle class" is that cyclical movements in the shares are much less pronounced than in the 1Q and 2Q classes, and indeed changes are often countercyclical. Only in the recession of 1980–1981 was a sharp decline recorded. Nonetheless, the long downward slope of the shares

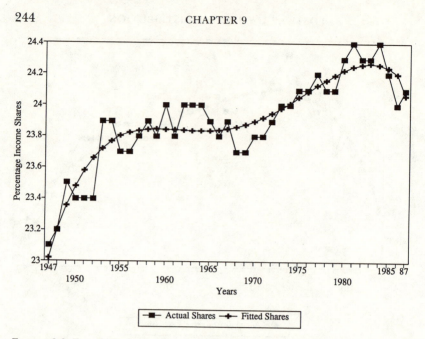

FIGURE 9.9. Fourth Quintile Shares, All-Race Family Money Income, 1947–1987

trend is quite clear in figure 9.8, as is the acceleration in the Reagan years.

It is of course in the upper quintiles that the necessary mirror reflex movements must occur. In figure 9.9 the trend line for 4Q reveals a period of rapid rise from 1947 to 1957, a plateauing from 1957 to 1970, and a continuation of the upward trend to 1984. Table 9.3 distorts somewhat the pattern of the first period through its inability to take quantitative changes into account, but supports the trend movements in the last two periods. Cyclical movements are either counter to the changes in gross national product or quite small in a cyclical direction, with the dramatic exception of 1976, which resulted in a drop of a full percentage point for this class.

Figure 9.10 reveals a simpler and somewhat different pattern for the highest quintile. Comparison of both the actual movements and the trend line fittings with figure 9.5 shows a remarkable conformance. This is somewhat surprising because in chapter 8 it was pointed out that the weighting of movements in the lower quantiles was much greater in the calculation of the Gini than the weights given the upper quantiles. However, the U-shaped function is repeated in figure 9.10, with a rather symmetrical decline from 1947 to 1970, a rise from 1970 to 1987, and with accelerated increase from 1980 on. Note that the rise in the percentage

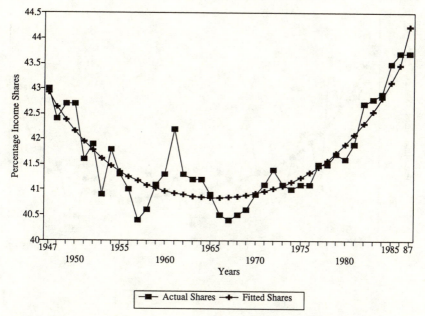

FIGURE 9.10. Fifth Quintile Shares, All-Race Family Money Income, 1947–1987

share of 5Q predated the Reagan administration, starting in the Vietnam War period about 1967. Table 9.3 is broadly confirming. Importantly, all of the recessions reveal countercyclical movements in the shares: the top 20 percent of income recipient families increase their relative shares during recessions.

Not surprisingly, the top 5 percent of the families follows the actual and trend lines of the top 20 percent quite closely, as comparison of figures 9.10 and 9.11 reveals. The latter graph shows that the top 5 percent extended the period of decline to about 1975, but then recovered even more sharply than the quintile within which it is embedded. Once more, table 9.3 confirms the visual impression. And finally, countercyclical movement is once more the rule.

The fourth and fifth quintiles, then, reveal quite different patterns of adjustment through the postwar period. The improvements in the shares of the first decade of the postwar period experienced by 1Q, 2Q, and 3Q were also obtained by 4Q, so that they occurred largely at the expense of 5Q. During the next 15 years 1Q continued to benefit at the expense of 2Q, 3Q, and 5Q, while 4Q moved sideways. Finally, the rise in the last 15 years enjoyed in 4Q and 5Q occurred at the expense of shares of all three of the other quintiles.

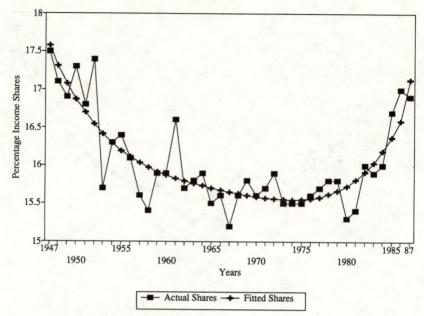

FIGURE 9.11. Top Five Percent Shares, All-Race Family Money Income, 1947–1987

2. *All Races Adjusted.* The unadjusted data of section 1 should be modified somewhat by such considerations as tax burdens, size of family, and receipt of in-kind income and fringe benefits. Table 9.4 makes such estimates for the year 1984. The adjustments result in a significant lessening of inequality. Figure 9.12 compares the quintile shares for the unadjusted and the total adjusted income of item 5 in table 9.4. The computation of estimates of unadjusted and adjusted Gini coefficients from the grouped data reveals a fall of 22 percent from the unadjusted to the adjusted figures (.359 to .280)—a substantial decline of inequality. Figure 9.13 displays the Lorenz curves for the two distributions, and the failure of the curves to intersect as well as the substantial gap between them gives another visual impression of the importance of the adjustment. Finally, table 9.5 provides some basis for belief that inequality of adjusted income has been rising since since 1979.

These data are extremely fragile, however, being results of a simulation model built on many value judgments. They should be accepted as hypotheses, not validated truth.

3. *Whites and Blacks, Unadjusted.* Table 9.6 reveals, for selected years in the postwar period, the quintile distributions for whites and blacks (or,

TABLE 9.4

All-Race Family Money Income Distribution, Corrected for Taxes,
In-Kind Government and Private Benefits, and Family Size, by Quintiles, 1984

	Quintiles				
	1st	2d	3d	4th	5th
1. Current Population Survey Definition (pretax, cash only, table 9.1)	4.7%	11.0%	17.0%	24.4%	42.9%
2. Current Population Survey Definition less Taxes	5.8	12.3	17.8	24.1	40.0
3. Current Population Survey Definition less Taxes plus Medicare, Medicaid, and Food Stamps	7.2	12.2	17.8	24.3	38.7
4. Current Population Survey Definition less Taxes plus Medicare, Medicaid, and Food Stamps, and Employer Fringe Benefits	6.7	12.3	17.6	24.3	39.1
5. Item 4 Adjusted for Differences in Family Sizes across Quintiles	7.3	13.4	18.1	24.4	36.8

Source: Frank Levy, *Dollars and Dreams* (New York: W. W. Norton, 1987), 195. The estimates were derived from the Urban Institute's Transfer Income Model (TRIM2) which uses the Current Population Survey data base. Tax estimates include federal income and payroll taxes, state income taxes, state and local sales taxes, and state and local property taxes. Because TRIM2 cannot estimate private fringe benefits, they were projected by applying the estimates in T. M. Smeeding, "Alternative Methods for Valuing Selected In-Kind Transfer Benefits and Measuring Their Effect on Poverty," U.S. Bureau of the Census, Technical Paper No. 50, U.S. Government Printing Office, March 1982, for 1979 to the 1984 data. See Levy, *Dollars and Dreams,* appendix D, 223–226 for further details on the derivation.

more accurately, all races other than white). Figure 9.14 displays the 1987 Lorenz curves for both races, and figure 9.15 reproduces the complete profiles of their Gini coefficients over the period with fitted trends.[1]

Tabular and graphic displays reveal two marked differences between the two family money income distributions. First, black inequality tends to be markedly greater than that of whites. In figure 9.14 the former curve lies outside the latter for 1987, and hence is unambiguously more

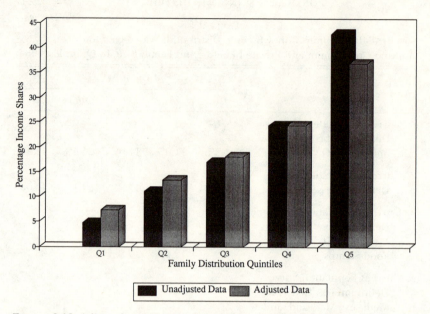

FIGURE 9.12. Adjusted and Unadjusted All-Race Family Money Shares, by Quintiles, 1984

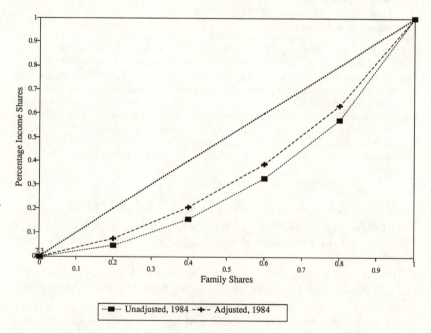

FIGURE 9.13. Adjusted and Unadjusted Lorenz Curves, All-Race Family Income, by Quintiles, 1984

TABLE 9.5

The Adjusted All-Race Family Income Distribution over Time, by Quintiles

	Share Received by Quintile				
	1st	2d	3d	4th	5th
1949 Upper Bound Estimate	5.8	13.1	18.6	23.2	39.3
1979 Adjusted Estimate	8.7	14.5	18.0	24.8	34.0
1984 Adjusted Estimate	7.3	13.4	18.1	24.4	36.8

Source: Levy, *Dollars and Dreams*, appendix D, 223–226.
Note: Figures include adjustment for family size.

TABLE 9.6

Census Family Money Income Distributions, White and Black Races, Selected Years, by Quintiles, with Gini Coefficients, 1947–1987

	1st		2d		3d		4th		5th		Gini	
Year	W.	B.	W.	B.	W.	B.	W.	B.	W.	B.	W.	B.
1947	5.5	4.3	12.2	10.4	17.0	16.1	22.9	23.8	42.5	45.3	.366	.406
1950	4.8	3.5	12.4	10.3	17.4	17.6	23.2	25.2	42.2	43.4	.369	.404
1955	5.2	4.0	12.7	10.4	17.8	17.8	23.7	25.6	40.8	42.2	.353	.381
1960	5.2	3.7	12.7	9.7	17.8	16.5	23.8	25.2	40.7	44.9	.353	.417
1965	5.6	4.7	12.6	10.8	17.8	16.6	23.7	24.7	40.3	43.2	.346	.388
1970	5.8	4.5	12.5	10.6	17.7	16.8	23.6	24.8	40.5	43.7	.346	.392
1975	5.7	4.7	12.6	10.1	17.6	16.7	23.9	25.1	40.7	43.3	.350	.392
1980	5.6	4.1	11.9	9.5	17.6	16.0	24.0	25.5	40.9	45.1	.355	.418
1985	5.0	3.6	11.2	9.1	16.9	15.7	24.1	25.1	42.9	46.4	.379	.432
1987	5.1	3.2	11.2	8.5	17.0	15.3	23.8	24.8	42.9	48.3	.379	.455

Source: U.S. Bureau of the Census, *Current Population Reports*, Series P-60, no. 162, 42–44.

unequal in its depicted distribution, and the same pattern would be revealed for every year in the period, as the large differences in the Gini coefficients, graphed on figure 9.15 and listed in table 9.6, confirm. Moreover, the trend lines on figure 9.15 reveal that the gap has been getting larger since about 1970, although both curves reveal the U-shape obtained in figure 9.5 for all families. There was a slight tendency for the black distribution to become more unequal in 1947–1951, but this receded until about 1970—the later years of the Vietnam conflict—after which, in tandem with the white distribution, inequality increased.

A second interesting feature of the distributions is the greater susceptibility of the black distribution to recessionary periods in 1947–1970 and the lessening or elimination of that differential response pattern during the years since. In general, the difference in volatility of the two distribu-

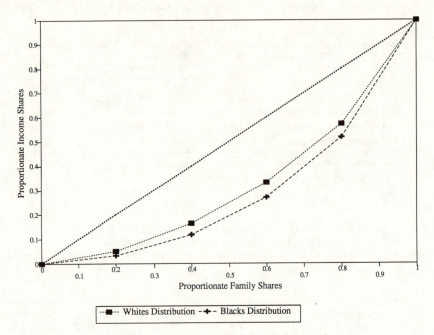

FIGURE 9.14. Lorenz Curves, White and Black Family Money Incomes, by Quintiles, 1987

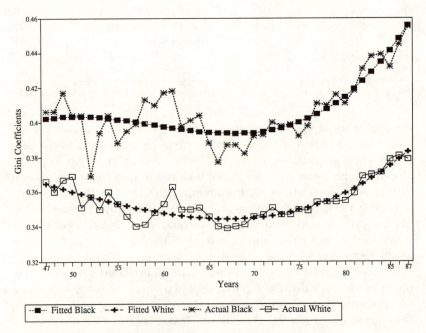

FIGURE 9.15. Gini Coefficients, White and Black Family Money Incomes, Actual and Fitted Race Ginis, 1987

tions in the earlier period and its lessening in the second are striking. The greater attainment of skill levels and experience by blacks, their increasing representation (especially for women) in the service industries, the continuation of the urbanization of blacks that started in World War II, and the lessening of discrimination are registered in this melioration.

For 1987, the highest black quintile earned 48.3 percent of family income, compared with white families' share of 42.9 percent. The fourth black quintile is also a full percentage point above its white counterpart. These black upper classes have made substantial progress absolutely and relatively since 1980. But the lower three quintile shares are 1.7 to 2.7 percentage points below those of white quintiles and have been in decline since about 1970. In pre–World War II years this could have been explained by the concentration of blacks in poorly paid agricultural employment in the South. But the shift out of agriculture to urban areas occurred in the war years and their immediate aftermath. The increasing numbers of female-headed households in the black community, the large proportion of elderly persons in the lower quintiles, the relative lag in educational attainment, the structural shifts in American industry from heavy metal-bashing industries, and the increasing technical prerequisites for newer employments play major roles in explaining these differences.

The Distribution of Family Income: Detailed Characteristics

One leaves the postwar overview of family money income distribution with several conclusions:

1. Over the entire period the distribution of family income for all races has been quite unequal in a static relative sense.
2. However, the relative distribution has been stable over the period, with some tendency to reduction of inequality from 1947 to about 1970 and increasing inequality since then as registered in declining percentages in the lower two quintiles and rising percentages in the upper two, as well as rising Gini coefficients.
3. Cyclical response to the business cycle in the period has been marked, though somewhat dampened since 1970.
4. Nonwhite inequality is significantly greater than that among white families, with greater shares in the upper two quintiles and lower relative receipts in the lower three.
5. Nonwhite and white Gini coefficients reveal the same U-shape with minimum reached about 1970.
6. Some evidence exists that although black inequality fluctuated with greater amplitudes in the period to 1970, it has diminished substantially in cyclical responsiveness since that time and appears to be about the same as white cyclicity.

TABLE 9.7

Family Money Income Distribution, All Races, 1987, by Income Classes,
with Relevant Family Characteristics (1987 Dollars)

Classes	1 % Fam.[a]	2 $\bar{Y}$ Ratio[b]	3 $\bar{Y}$/Family Member[c]	4 Persons/ Family	5 Earn.[d]	6 Mean Age[e]	7 Mean Schooling[f]
Under $2,500	1.80	.02	.02	2.94	.55	39.2	10.7
2,500–4,999	2.62	.10	.11	3.03	.56	40.0	10.2
5,000–7,499	3.61	.17	.18	3.06	.69	45.5	9.7
7,500–9,999	3.74	.24	.26	2.97	.84	49.3	9.9
10,000–12,499	4.55	.31	.33	2.94	.99	50.0	10.3
12,500–14,999	4.45	.37	.41	2.87	1.09	50.4	10.8
15,000–17,499	4.85	.44	.48	2.91	1.23	49.1	11.0
17,500–19,999	4.67	.51	.55	2.95	1.30	49.1	11.5
20,000–22,499	4.92	.58	.61	2.99	1.41	47.6	11.6
22,500–24,999	4.27	.65	.67	3.08	1.55	47.3	11.9
25,000–27,499	4.64	.72	.74	3.06	1.57	46.3	12.1
27,500–29,999	4.25	.78	.80	3.13	1.66	45.3	12.3
30,000–32,499	4.80	.85	.81	3.17	1.71	45.2	12.3
32,500–34,999	3.81	.92	.91	3.21	1.80	45.2	12.6
35,000–37,499	4.39	.99	.97	3.25	1.80	43.8	12.9
37,500–39,999	3.43	1.06	1.04	3.24	1.92	44.7	13.1
40,000–44,999	6.83	1.16	1.10	3.32	1.99	44.6	13.2
45,000–49,999	5.52	1.29	1.23	3.33	2.06	45.3	13.4
50,000–59,999	8.28	1.49	1.41	3.36	2.18	45.4	13.8
60,000–74,999	6.83	1.81	1.66	3.47	2.38	46.2	14.3
75,000 and over	7.77	2.96	2.69	3.50	2.42	48.3	15.3
All Classes	100.00	—	—	3.17	1.65	46.4	12.4

Source: U.S. Bureau of the Census, *Current Population Reports,* Series P-60, no. 162, table 13, 45.

[a] Percent of total families (65,133,000).

[b] Ratio of class mean income to mean income of all families ($36,568). Median income was $30,853.

[c] Mean income per family member as a ratio to value for all families ($11,525).

[d] Number of earners per family.

[e] Mean age of head of household.

[f] Mean school years completed by head of household in families headed by householder 25 years of age or older.

1. *All Races Unadjusted.* With the overview developed to this point it is possible to concentrate on recent, detailed, absolute measures of income distribution that are directly relevant to the feasibility study of chapters 10 and 11. Consider, therefore, the all-race family distribution for 1987 broken down into twenty-one income classes, together with relevant family characteristics, in table 9.7.

Income ratios in table 9.7 are expressed on mean family income as a base, but because such means are greatly affected by the extremely high incomes in a positively skewed income distribution, they are biased upward as a representative measure of family income. It is preferable to use the median family income level as such a measure of central tendency—that is, the level above and below which 50 percent of family incomes lie—because it is a measure of location unaffected by the values in the distribution. In 1987 the median family income level was $30,853, or about 84 percent of the mean level.[2] From columns 1 and 2 of table 9.7, about 20.9 percent or 13,369,000 of families of all races received less than 50 percent of median family income, or, using column 4, approximately 39,677,000 persons.[3] With similar calculations, the estimate of the number of families receiving less than 60 percent of median family income is 17,918,000 or about 27.5 percent of U.S. families, with 52,894,000 individuals. In round numbers, then, about 21 percent of families received less than 50 percent and 28 percent of families less than 60 percent of median family income in 1987.

To formalize the associations between family income by classes and potential causal variables, multiple regression analysis is employed. Surprisingly, perhaps, family size is not negatively associated with income class, but tends to rise with income, reflecting the large proportion of families headed by single women and retirees in the lower income classes. Income per family member in column 3 of table 9.7, therefore, tracks mean family income quite closely. The gross correlation coefficient between mean class income and mean persons per family is .887, confirming visual impressions.

Moreover, mean numbers of persons in the family parallels the mean numbers of earners, with a gross correlation coefficient of .868. Potential collinearity recommends elimination of one of the two as an explanatory factor in a regression and, because the relative variance of the number of earners—measured by the coefficient of variation—is about six times that of number of persons, the former variable was chosen for retention as a better representative of family structure.

Skill and experience of earners are reflected in mean schooling and age and were expected to be important explanatory variables. Visually, education seems strongly associated with income class and some support is given the hypothesis by the gross correlation of .937 between it and mean income. On the other hand the mean age of householder is not linearly associated with mean income by virtue of the retirement hump in the lower income classes and the tendency for income to decline in the post–50 age groups. Indeed its gross correlation coefficient with mean income is only .115 and its coefficient of variation only .06, leading one to expect rather large standard errors for its regression coefficients.

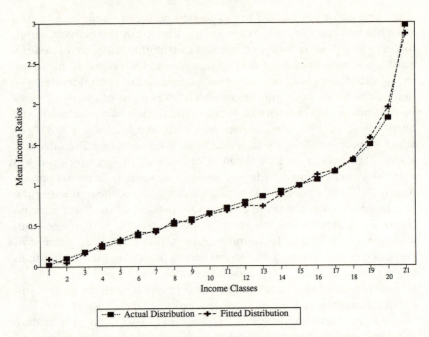

FIGURE 9.16. All-Race Family Money Income as Ratios of Income Class Means to All-Family Mean Money Income, 1987

Nonetheless, because mean age exhibits no collinearity with schooling and by virtue of its importance in the definition of life-cycle income equality, it was decided to include it as a regressor variable.

The initial choice of explanatory variables on which to regress mean income of classes, therefore, was mean number of earners per family, mean years of schooling of householder, and mean age of householder. Unfortunately, however, the earners and schooling variables are highly correlated—$r = .964$—and this resulted in highly volatile regression coefficients when both variables were included. The schooling variable was more highly correlated in a gross measure than number of earners and seemed also more likely to include the causal forces of the latter than vice versa. Therefore, number of earners was eliminated. Finally, mean schooling was included as a quadratic variable by including the square of its values as a regressor.

Figure 9.16 depicts the excellent fit of the regression, plotting the actual data and the fitted equation, whose values and parameters are the following:

$$\text{MEANIN} = 6.449 - 1.565 \text{ MEANSC} + .081 \text{ MEANSC}^2 + .028 \text{ MEANAGE}$$
$$\phantom{\text{MEANIN} = } (6.73) \ (-10.60) \qquad\quad (13.49) \qquad\qquad (5.28)$$

$R^2 = .992$ Standard Error of Estimate = .068
$\bar{R}^2 = .990$

where *t*-values are parenthesized and where:

MEANIN = mean income ratio of each of the 21 classes listed in table 9.7
MEANSC = mean years of school completed by householder
$MEANSC^2$ = square of MEANSC
MEANAGE = mean age of householder

All regression coefficients are statistically significant at the .05 level, including mean age of class, whose underlying association with mean income is revealed on a net basis. Finally, the correlation matrix reveals little collinearity, except, of course, that between the two schooling regressors:

	MEANIN	MEANSC	$MEANSC^2$	MEANAGE	Means	Standard Deviation
MEANIN	1.000	.937	.956	.116	.83	.68
MEANSC		1.000	.998	−.042	12.04	1.51
$MEANSC^2$			1.000	−.034	147.21	37.09
MEANAGE				1.000	41.09	2.90

The treatment of mean age as linearly related to mean income is a violation of the theoretical shape of the life-cycle earnings profile, which tends to rise to a peak in the 35- to 44-year age bracket and then fall to retirement. The inclusion of a quadratic age regressor ($MEANAGE^2$) did yield the proper shape but yielded nonsignificant regression coefficients for both linear and quadratic terms, peaked at the late age of 68 years, and did not improve the fit. The median age of householders in the income classes is not sufficiently sensitive as a measure of age differentials among individuals, and hence the linear relationship between age and income was retained.

On the other hand, the quadratic relation of years of schooling completed by the head of household yields a hyperbola with minimum at 10 years of completed education, which, from column 7 of table 9.8, is close to the lower bound of observed data. Hence, the relation shows mean incomes rising over years of schooling and therefore falling only for classes 2 and 3, which contain large numbers of retirees whose schooling reflects past standards and families headed by single women who are forced to drop out of school before completing high school.

Schooling and age, therefore, serve as excellent predictors of family income, with the recognition that schooling incorporates much of the causal influences of number of earners per family and the ratio of non-earners to earners. The result supports the arguments in chapters 6 and 7 concerning the importance of stressing educational attainment in less-

TABLE 9.8
Family Money Income Distribution, Whites, 1987, by Income Classes,
with Relevant Family Characteristics (1987 Dollars)

Classes	1 % Fam.[a]	2 Y Ratio[b]	3 Y/Family Member[c]	4 Persons/ Family	5 Earn.[d]	6 Mean Age[e]	7 Mean Schooling[f]
Under $2,500	1.35	.01	.01	2.86	.65	41.2	10.7
2,500–4,999	1.86	.11	.11	2.93	.63	40.8	10.2
5,000–7,499	2.93	.17	.19	2.95	.71	46.3	9.8
7,500–9,999	3.20	.24	.27	2.78	.84	50.9	9.9
10,000–12,499	4.18	.31	.34	2.83	.96	50.9	10.3
12,500–14,999	4.36	.37	.43	2.78	1.06	51.2	10.9
15,000–17,499	4.73	.44	.50	2.82	1.19	50.0	11.1
17,500–19,999	4.57	.51	.57	2.86	1.25	49.9	11.5
20,000–22,499	4.86	.58	.62	2.94	1.37	48.1	11.6
22,500–24,999	4.28	.65	.68	3.02	1.51	47.6	11.9
25,000–27,499	4.76	.72	.76	2.99	1.52	46.4	12.1
27,500–29,999	4.44	.78	.81	3.08	1.64	45.8	12.3
30,000–32,499	4.94	.85	.86	3.13	1.69	45.3	12.4
32,500–34,999	3.94	.92	.93	3.15	1.75	45.6	12.7
35,000–37,499	4.54	.99	.97	3.21	1.78	44.0	12.9
37,500–39,999	3.62	1.06	1.05	3.19	1.89	44.8	13.1
40,000–44,999	7.22	1.16	1.12	3.28	1.96	44.8	13.2
45,000–49,999	5.80	1.29	1.26	3.26	2.03	45.4	13.4
50,000–59,999	8.83	1.49	1.42	3.32	2.16	45.5	13.8
60,000–74,999	7.25	1.81	1.67	3.43	2.36	46.2	14.3
75,000 and over	8.35	2.98	2.73	3.46	2.40	48.4	15.3
All Classes	100.01	—	—	3.12	1.67	46.9	12.6

Source: U.S. Bureau of the Census, *Current Population Reports*, Series P-60, no. 162, table 13, 45.

[a] Percent of total white families (56,044,000, or 86% of total families).

[b] Ratio of class mean income to mean income of families *of all races* ($36,568). Median income was $30,853.

[c] Mean income per family member as a ratio to value for families *of all races* ($11,525).

[d] Number of earners per family.

[e] Mean age of head of household.

[f] Mean school years completed by head of household in families headed by householder 25 years of age or older.

ening the inequality of opportunity and in chapter 8 with respect to age and life-cycle income patterns in discussing the ideal concept of equality.

2. *Whites and Blacks, Unadjusted.* If the data of table 9.7 are presented separately for whites and blacks, some of the deeper aspects of family money income inequality are revealed. First, table 9.8 presents the breakdown of white family income by the same twenty-one classes as

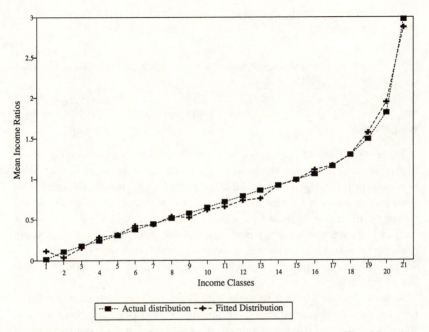

FIGURE 9.17. White Family Money Income as Ratios of Income Class Means to All-Family Mean Money Income, 1987

those used in table 9.7 with the same family characteristics featured. Because the intention is to compare the mean income ratios of white and black families, the values for mean income and per capita mean income of income classes have been divided by the mean income for all-race families.

Because white families constitute about 84 percent of all families, one must expect that the same regressors that fitted the all-race data so well would work equally well with white families. That is, indeed, true, as comparison of the following regression equation and parameters with their counterparts for all families reveals. Comparison of figures 9.17 and 9.16 attests visually to the similarity:

$$\text{WMEANIN} = 6.595 - 1.594 \text{ WMEANSC} + .083 \text{ WMEANSC}^2 + .027 \text{ WMEANAGE}$$
$$(6.56) \; (-10.44) \qquad\quad (13.33) \qquad\qquad\quad (4.97)$$

$R^2 = .991$ Standard Error of Estimate = .068
$\bar{R}^2 = .990,$

where the names of the variables are self-evident from the previous display and the correlation matrix, mean variable values, and standard deviations are almost identical and the t-values are quite close. The gross correlation coefficients and variable means and standard deviations are also very similar:

	WMEANIN	WMEANSC	WMEANSC²	WMEANAGE	Means	Standard Deviation
WMEANIN	1.000	.936	.956	−.007	.83	.68
WMEANSC		1.000	.998	−.176	12.07	1.50
MEANSC²			1.000	−.165	147.75	36.85
WMEANAGE				1.000	41.09	2.90

Figure 9.17 almost duplicates figure 9.16, with the estimating equation underestimating slightly the actual data in classes 9 through 14 and over-restimating it for classes 19 and 20. For both figures mean income ratios tend to rise linearly for the first seventeen classes and then show a steep progression in the highest four classes. Educational levels for these last four classes are the same in both charts—between 13.4 and 15.3 years completed—and age levels are at most one-tenth of a year higher for the white families in these classes when compared with their counterparts for all families.

From columns 1 and 2 of table 9.8 about 18.7 percent of white families, or 10,469,000, containing about 29,735,000 persons, received less than 50 percent of the median income of all-race families, comprising 17 percent of white family population. This implies that about 78 percent of the all-race families and 75 percent of such family members in this category of income receipt are white, compared with their 86 percent shares of the total number of families and 85 percent of family population. Further, about 24.5 percent of white families, or 13,708,000, earned less than 60 percent of all-race median family income, encompassing 38,911,000 persons and 22.2 percent of white family members. This reveals that 76.5 percent of all families and 73.6 percent of family members receiving less than 60 percent of median family income are white. Table 9.9 presents the family income distribution data for black families.

About 43.5 percent of black families have incomes less than 50 percent of median family income for all U.S. families, or 3,119,000 families with 10,323,000 persons, constituting 41.2 percent of black family population. Hence, about 23.3 percent of all families in this category of income receipt are black and 26 percent of all family members in this bracket are black. These percentage figures compare with family and population percentages of 11.0 and 12.1 respectively. Black families, therefore, are overrepresented in this threshold income category by about 100 percent.

Fully 50.9 percent or 3,654,000 black families, with a total population of 12,131,000, or 48.4 percent of black family population received less

TABLE 9.9

Family Money Income Distribution, Blacks, 1987, by Income Classes, with Relevant Family Characteristics (1987 Dollars)

Classes	1 % Fam.[a]	2 $\bar{Y}$ Ratio[b]	3 $\bar{Y}$/Family Member[c]	4 Persons/ Family	5 Earn.[d]	6 Mean Age[e]	7 Mean Schooling[f]
Under $2,500	4.97	.03	.04	3.04	.36	34.9	10.6
2,500–4,999	8.51	.11	.10	3.22	.44	38.7	10.3
5,000–7,499	8.65	.17	.16	3.34	.64	43.1	9.7
7,500–9,999	7.78	.24	.22	3.47	.82	45.0	9.8
10,000–12,499	7.08	.31	.29	3.34	1.10	46.9	10.0
12,500–14,999	5.39	.37	.36	3.37	1.28	46.8	10.2
15,000–17,499	6.33	.44	.41	3.36	1.46	45.1	10.9
17,500–19,999	5.43	.51	.47	3.41	1.63	45.3	11.5
20,000–22,499	5.70	.58	.56	3.24	1.64	44.7	11.8
22,500–24,999	4.32	.65	.58	3.54	1.80	44.9	11.5
25,000–27,499	3.73	.71	.61	3.69	2.00	46.1	11.8
27,500–29,999	3.20	.78	.70	3.57	1.91	41.0	12.0
30,000–32,499	3.90	.85	.79	3.43	1.93	44.6	11.4
32,500–34,999	2.72	.92	.76	3.85	2.34	41.5	11.7
35,000–37,499	3.18	.99	.87	3.59	2.08	42.3	12.5
37,500–39,999	2.15	1.06	.88	3.82	2.32	42.9	12.8
40,000–44,999	4.19	1.16	.96	3.83	2.42	44.0	12.3
45,000–49,999	3.27	1.29	.99	4.15	2.54	44.1	12.5
50,000–59,999	4.01	1.49	1.24	3.82	2.50	44.7	13.2
60,000–74,999	2.95	1.81	1.49	3.85	2.68	45.8	13.0
75,000 and over	2.52	2.62	2.04	4.07	2.90	45.1	15.0
All Classes	100.00	—	—	3.49	1.50	43.7	11.3

Source: U.S. Bureau of the Census, *Current Population Reports*, Series P-60, no. 162, table 13, 45.

[a] Percent of total black families (7,177,000, or 11% of total families).

[b] Ratio of class mean income to mean income of all all-race families ($36,568). Median income was $30,853.

[c] Mean income per family member as a ratio to value for all all-race families ($11,525).

[d] Number of earners per family.

[e] Mean age of head of household.

[f] Mean school years completed by head of household in families headed by householder 25 years of age or older.

than 60 percent of median family income in 1987. Therefore, 20.4 percent of all families and 22.9 percent of all family members in this category were black. These figures are again roughly double their percentage representation in the population.

The comparisons in the very low income classes—the first four of which include all families earning less than $10,000 in money income per year—are much more unfavorable to blacks. Almost 30 percent of black families fall into these classes, compared with only 9.32 percent of white families. Of the 7,666,000 families of all races in these ranks, 5,223,000 were white and 2,146,000 were black. Thus, 68 percent was white and 28 percent was black.

The estimating equation that bests tracks the mean incomes of the twenty-one classes in the distribution of table 9.9 includes as independent variables schooling and number of earners per family, a departure from the regressors used to fit the white family distribution. The regression coefficients, t-values, and parameters are the following:

$$\text{BMEANIN } -9.315 - 1.780 \text{ BMEANSC} + .083 \text{ BMEANSC}^2 + .469 \text{ BEARNER}$$
$$(5.00) \quad (-5.84) \qquad\qquad (7.00) \qquad\qquad (5.79)$$

$R^2 = .973 \qquad$ Standard Error of Estimate = .112
$\bar{R}^2 = .968$

where the variables are mean income, mean years of schooling completed by the head of family, the square of that variable, and the mean number of earners in families in each income class.

The correlation matrix does reveal some multicollinearity, casting some suspicion on the exactitude of the regression coefficients:

	BMEANIN	BMEANSC	BMEANSC²	BEARNER	Means	Standard Deviation
BMEANIN	1.000	.937	.950	.889	.81	.62
BMEANSC		1.000	.997	.888	11.64	1.31
BNEABSC²			1.000	.871	137.20	31.50
BEARNER				1.000	3.60	2.45

Multicollinearity may be the reason the schooling values define a hyperbolic relation over income classes that reaches a maximum at 10.7 years—about 1 year too high to judge from column 7 of table 9.9. This leads to the underestimates by the regression equation for income ratios in the first two income classes.

Figure 9.18 displays the estimates against the actual mean income ratios, with one change: the estimate for the first class was a small negative value and it has been changed to zero. The very low actual mean incomes for the first four classes lead to a downward bias in estimates for the fifth through the eleventh class, but overall the fit is a good one.

Figure 9.19 contrasts mean income per family member in 1987 for white and black families in the twenty-one classes, where income is expressed once more as a ratio to mean per capita income for all-races. The discrepancy tends to be quite small in the very lowest classes, but then rises with incomes until it becomes 35 percent higher for whites in the highest income class.

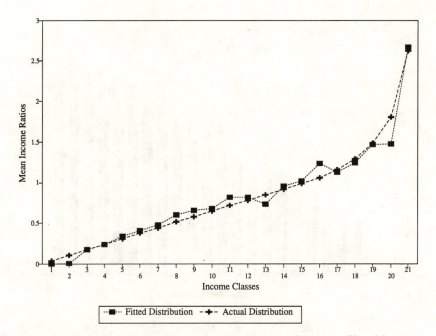

FIGURE 9.18. Black Family Money Income as Ratios of Income Class Means to All-Family Mean Money Income, 1987

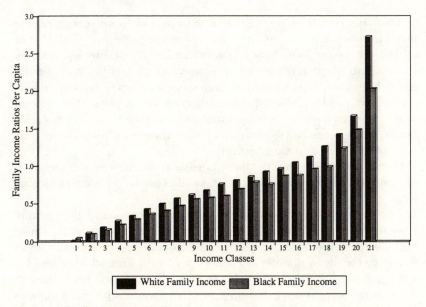

FIGURE 9.19. White and Black Family Money Per Capita Income as Ratios of Income Class Per Capita Means to All-Family Mean Money Per Capita Income, 1987

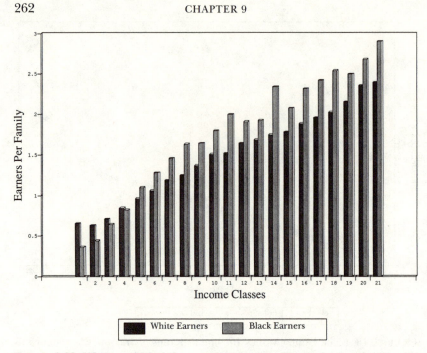

FIGURE 9.20. White and Black Income Earners Per Family, by Income Classes, 1987

These discrepancies are magnified in impact when one compares the mean number of income earners in each income class and finds that in all but the lowest four classes (where families headed by black single women and black aged are concentrated) black families have significantly larger numbers of earners than white families. This is an important aspect of black family poverty: despite the fact that they expend more effort in terms of average number of income earners, per capita family incomes are consistently lower than those of whites. Figure 9.20 presents these data in bar chart form.

Part of the explanation for these persistent differences over classes in per capita family income is that black families are larger in every income class, as shown in figure 9.21.

But these two factors—larger numbers of earners and larger families—tend to cancel out in all but the lowest four classes, as shown in figure 9.22. This chart traces the mean number of persons per family as a ratio to the mean number of earners per family for each class and for white and black families. There it can be seen that for classes 5 through 21 both races are remarkably close in this measure, with black families actually having a small advantage in all but three classes. On the other hand this chart points up in dramatic contrast one of the major problem

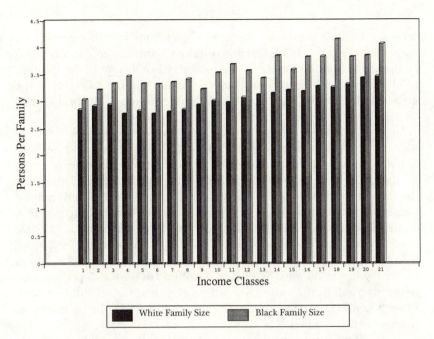

FIGURE 9.21. White and Black Family Sizes, by Income Classes, 1987

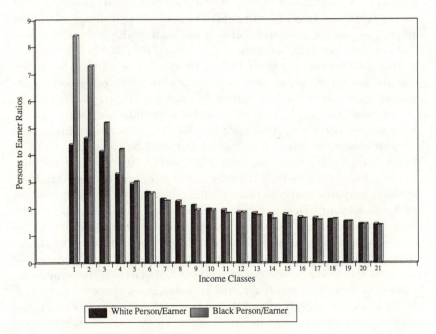

FIGURE 9.22. White and Black Family Persons to Earners Ratios, by Income Classes, 1987

areas in attacking economic inequality: black families in the lowest four classes have extremely high ratios of family members to earners when compared with white families. This is largely a reflection of the number of black families headed by unmarried females and may also reflect the greater tendency for retirees in black families to live with working relatives.

In 1987, 16.29 percent of all U.S. families were headed by a female with no husband present. Within that total, 12.91 percent of white families were in this category, but 42.83 percent of black families were so designated. Hence, almost 29 percent of all female-headed families in the United States were black. The penalty this inflicts on a family may be judged with the following data: for all races, the median income of a family headed by a woman was $14,620; for whites, the figure is $17,018; but for blacks the median income is only $9,710.[4] As reported in chapter 8, in 1984 fully 50 percent of all black families whose household head was under the age of 35 were headed by a woman, of whom 75 percent had never married. In the nation as a whole 21 percent of all children were in such families, but 54 percent of black children were being reared in female-headed families.[5]

In these statistics we have focused on one of the major demographic factors dictating income inequality in an individualistic economy. The plight of the black family has received a great deal of attention in the last twenty years, and the consequences of its continuing disintegration with respect to income inequality present the society with one of its major tasks on compassionate account.

Years of schooling completed by the head of household and his or her age are two variables that have been demonstrated to be important explanatory factors in income distribution patterns. Figures 9.23 and 9.24 present comparative data for white and black families on mean age and schooling of householders in each income class respectively. In the lowest four classes, the mean age of black householders is rather markedly lower than that for white counterparts, and the difference remains important for classes 6–10. Thereafter, the gap between ages tends to lessen. Comparison with the differential per capita income differentials of figure 9.19 indicates that the age differentials have no apparent relation to such earnings. Another interesting observation from study of figure 9.24 is that mean white and black educational differences almost disappear in the first four classes, are rather small in favor of whites for the next seven classes, and become substantial in most of the remaining classes. In these data, it is really only in those classes whose mean schooling is in excess of high school that substantial differences between the races are registered. Later in this chapter, where more detailed educational comparisons are made between the races, it will be seen that these

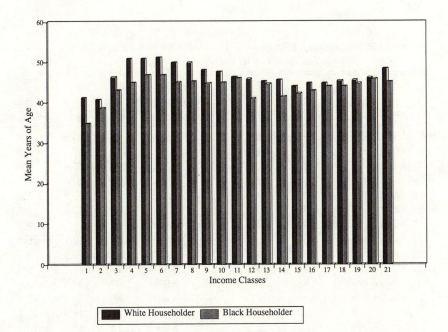

FIGURE 9.23. White and Black Family Householder Mean Age, by Income Classes, 1987

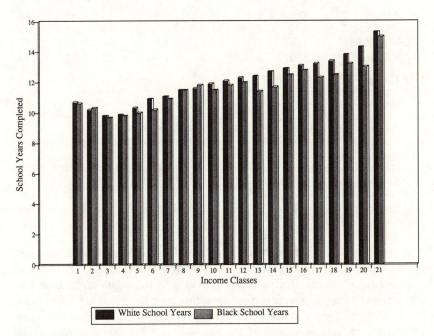

FIGURE 9.24. Mean Years of Schooling, White and Black Family Householders, by Income Classes, 1987

TABLE 9.10

Family Money Income Distribution, Hispanic Origin, 1987, by Income Classes,
with Relevant Family Characteristics (1987 Dollars)

Classes	1 % Fam.[a]	2 Ȳ Ratio[b]	3 Ȳ/Family Member[c]	4 Persons/ Family	5 Earn.[d]	6 Mean Age[e]	7 Mean Schooling[f]
Under $2,500	3.38	.03	.03	3.14	5.79	35.8	8.8
2,500–4,999	5.17	.11	.10	3.47	5.12	37.4	7.8
5,000–7,499	7.32	.17	.15	3.52	4.90	41.4	7.8
7,500–9,999	7.06	.24	.21	3.65	2.97	40.0	7.7
10,000–12,499	7.69	.30	.25	3.91	2.00	39.8	7.8
12,500–14,999	6.98	.37	.33	3.57	1.69	42.0	8.8
15,000–17,499	5.99	.44	.39	3.60	1.31	41.3	9.3
17,500–19,999	5.67	.51	.42	3.83	1.33	42.1	9.4
20,000–22,499	5.84	.58	.50	3.64	1.04	40.9	9.8
22,500–24,999	4.34	.65	.53	3.88	1.19	41.2	9.9
25,000–27,499	4.75	.71	.57	3.97	1.09	40.3	10.0
27,500–29,999	3.71	.78	.65	3.80	.85	40.1	10.1
30,000–32,499	4.19	.85	.68	3.98	.88	38.8	11.1
32,500–34,999	3.05	.92	.76	3.86	.74	43.4	10.1
35,000–37,499	3.42	.99	.81	3.87	.80	40.2	11.7
37,500–39,999	2.22	1.06	.83	4.07	.94	39.2	11.6
40,000–44,999	4.75	1.15	.96	3.81	.80	39.8	12.1
45,000–49,999	3.60	1.29	1.02	4.02	.72	40.8	12.7
50,000–59,999	3.16	1.49	1.14	4.15	.73	41.5	12.6
60,000–74,999	3.66	1.80	1.25	4.59	.65	43.7	12.8
75,000 and over	2.92	3.01	2.35	4.06	.42	47.1	14.1
All Classes	100.00	—	—	3.79	1.33	40.7	9.9

Source: U.S. Bureau of the Census, Current Population Reports, Series P-60, no. 162, table 13, 45.

[a] Percent of total families with Spanish householder = 4,588,000.

[b] Ratio of class mean income to mean income of all families ($36,568). Median income was $30,853.

[c] Mean income per family member as a ratio to value for all families ($11,525).

[d] Number of earners per family.

[e] Mean age of head of household.

[f] Mean school years completed by head of household in families headed by householder 25 years of age or older.

mean measures of school years completed by head of household mask rather large differences in secondary school attainments. In terms of rendering assistance in equalizing opportunity through educational programs to reach the lowest four classes, however, the need is race-neutral.

3. *Hispanic Origin, Unadjusted.* A last family group to be analyzed is one that may include members of any race—that whose head of household is of Hispanic origin. Its income distribution is presented in table 9.10.

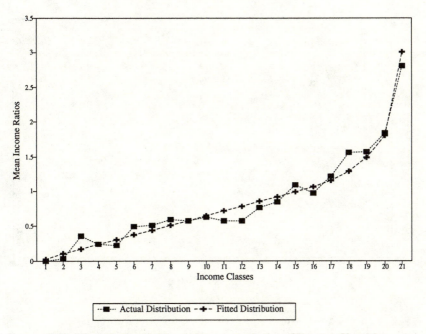

FIGURE 9.25. Hispanic Family Money Income as Ratios of Income Class Means to All-Family Mean Money Income, 1987

The most interesting variation in table 9.10 from its counterparts for all-race, white, and black distributions is the "inverted" earners profile in column 5. Among Hispanic families, low-income classes have very large numbers of earners that decline steadily as incomes rise—a pattern exactly contrary to that of all other family groups. Impoverished families in this community employ large numbers of their members, then elect to reduce this intensive employment as incomes rise. The mean number of earners per family—1.33—is less than that for black families—1.50—but these summary measures hide a distinctively different pattern of family behavior.

The fitted values to the actual data, plotted on figure 9.25, were obtained from the following regression equation:

$$\text{SMEANIN} = -.709 -.626 \text{ SMEANSC} + .043 \text{ SMEANSC}^2 + .080 \text{ SMEANAGE}$$
$$(-.58)(-3.33) \qquad\qquad (4.77) \qquad\qquad (5.22)$$

$R^2 = .969$
$\bar{R}^2 = .963$ Standard Error of Estimate = .131,

where the variables, as in previous regressions, are mean income expressed as a ratio to all-family mean income ($36,568), mean years of school completed by head of household, mean years of school com-

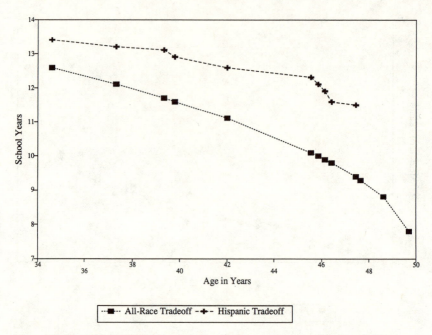

FIGURE 9.26. All-Race and Hispanic Family Money Income Trade-offs Between Age and Years of Householder, 1987

pleted squared, and mean age of the householder. As in the case of the regression for black families, the small negative projection for the lowest class was set equal to zero. The fit is a good one, and the regression coefficients are all significant at the .05 level. The coefficient matrix is the following:

	MEANIN	SMEANSC	SMEANSC²	SMEANAGE	Means	Standard Deviation
SMEANIN	1.000	.911	.933	.709	.83	.68
SMEANSC		1.000	.996	.478	10.29	1.89
SMEANC2²			1.000	.502	109.21	40.05
SMEANAGE				1.000	40.80	2.30

Straightforward multicollinearity does not loom as a problem with respect to age and schooling.

Once again years of schooling completed and age of householder serve to predict mean income rather accurately. Relatively speaking, school years completed plays a more determining role vis-a-vis income determination for Hispanic families than does age, when the regression equations for all-race families and Hispanic families are compared. This can be seen from figure 9.26, which plots the trade-offs between age and

TABLE 9.11

A Comparison of Mean Age and Schooling of Householders,
Earners, and Persons per Family, for Races and
Hispanic Origin, 1987

		Mean Values		
Variable	All-Races	Whites	Blacks	Hispanic
Age (years)	46.4	46.9	43.7	40.7
Schooling (years)	12.4	12.6	11.3	9.9
Earners/Family	1.65	1.67	1.50	1.33
Persons/Family	3.17	3.12	3.49	3.79
Persons/Earner	1.92	1.87	2.33	2.85

Source: Tables 9.7, 9.8, 9.9, 9.10, with sources cited there.

school years completed by the householder over the age of 25 for all-race
and Hispanic families when the income ratio is held constant at 1. That
is, the curves show all combinations of median age and median school
years that yield the all-family mean income of $36,568. The curves have
been truncated to conform to the age domains listed in tables 9.7 and
9.10 for the two family types.

The slopes of the Hispanic curve are shallower than those of the all-
race graph: in the age range from 34 to 45 small amounts of education
compensate for rather large age changes. Only in higher age groups
does the trade-off approach that for all families. The trade-off curves also
project that to earn the mean all-family income the Hispanic householder of any age had to have substantially more schooling, or, for any
level of schooling completed, required years more of experience.

The Hispanic family is disadvantaged in most respects when compared with all-race, white, and black counterparts. Table 9.11 lists mean
values for five variables of importance in the determination of family
welfare, and in each of them Hispanic families are the most penalized.
The mean Hispanic householder at 40.7 years of age would require,
from figure 9.26, about 13 years of completed schooling to obtain the
mean all-race family income, compared with the mean all-race householder's need for about 9.5 years. Yet the Hispanic householder averages
only 9.9 years of completed schooling. Moreover, the mean family size of
the Hispanic household is about 20 percent larger and the number of
income earners about 19 percent lower than in the case of the average
all-race family. Hence, the ratio of family members to earners is 37.5
percent higher. On all accounts, therefore, the Hispanic family must be
addressed as an important target for compassionate income policy.

From table 9.10, it can be estimated that about 38.6 percent, or
1,772,000 Hispanic families, receive less than 50 percent of all-race me-

TABLE 9.12

Comparisons of Families and Persons Receiving Less Than
Specified Thresholds of Median All-Race Family Money Income,
as Percentages of Group Totals, by Races and Hispanic Origin, 1987

	Family Groups			
Classes	All-Races	White	Black	Hispanic
Below 27.7% ($10,000)				
Families	11.8%	9.34%	29.9%	22.9%
Persons	11.2	8.59	28.2	21.1
Mean Persons per Family	3.00	2.87	3.29	3.49
Below 50% ($15,427)				
Families	20.9	18.7	43.5	38.6
Persons	19.2	17.0	41.2	35.8
Mean Persons per Family	3.05	2.84	3.31	3.59
Below 60% ($18,512)				
Families	27.5	24.5	50.9	45.9
Persons	26.2	22.2	48.4	41.0
Mean Persons per Family	3.02	2.83	3.32	3.60

Source: Tables 9.7, 9.8, 9.9, 9.10, with sources listed there.

dian income, accounting for 6,225,000 persons, or 35.8 percent of Hispanic family persons. Fully 45.9 percent, or 2,105,000, received less than
60 percent of all-race median income, or 7,115,000 persons comprising
41 percent of Hispanic family members.

4. *Unadjusted Family Incomes: A Summary.* In general, the greatest single
"explanatory" variable for family income distributions is the years of
schooling completed by the head of household. In the case of all-race,
white, and Hispanic families, a second significant regressor variable is
found to be age, functioning as a surrogate for acquisition of skill, seniority, and experience. For black families, however, a better regressor is
number of earners per family, due in large part to the very low numbers
of such income recipients in the lowest four income classes. The pattern
of earners per family in the Hispanic community was distinctly inverse to
that of other groups analyzed, especially that of blacks.

Table 9.12 summarizes important measures with relevance to a concern for economic justice and the policy implications of its social strand.
It lists the numbers of families and family persons as proportions of relevant group totals with family incomes less than 50 percent and 60 percent of all-family median income by race and origin. The major foci of
distributive policy measures become rather clear with this information.

The first four income classes in the classification used in the analysis
incorporate families receiving less than $10,000 in annual money in-

come. For the weighted average poverty thresholds in 1988, and with interpolation between amounts for three and four member families, the poverty threshold for 3.3 member-families was $10,232 and for 3.5 member-families was $10,764. These family sizes are the means for blacks and Hispanics in those four classes. Hence, we are dealing with families below the extremely conservative government poverty guidelines. About 30 percent of black and 23 percent of Hispanic families with 28 and 21 percent respectively of their total family members lived below those thresholds.

Almost 44 percent of black families and 39 percent of Hispanic families received less than 50 percent of all-race median money income of $30,853 in 1987, compared with about 19 percent of white and 21 percent of all-race families. That level of income is about $15,427 for families that average about 3.31 members for blacks and 3.59 for Hispanics, and hence maximum incomes per capita of $4,661 and $4,297 respectively. These per capita income figures are 40 percent and 37 percent of all-race median per capita income of $11,525.

If the threshold is raised to 60 percent of all-race family income the same problem areas reemerge. About 51 percent of black families with 48 percent of their population members received less than $18,512, with per member incomes under $5,576. In Hispanic families, 46 percent fell below this threshold with 41 percent of their population. Per member incomes were below $5,128 in 1987.

The feasibility of any proposed theory of economic justice in American society should be discussed within these brackets of roughly 25 to 60 percent of median income. The lower bound accords roughly with current poverty lines, and the upper bounds accommodate a high degree of compassion within an individualist ethos. On the basis of the outlines provided by table 9.12, adoption of policies conforming to these brackets would involve extending compassionate aid to between 12 and 28 percent of all American families, with disproportionate amounts to minorities. Between 30 and 51 percent of all black families would be benefited and between 23 and 46 percent of Hispanic families, compared with 9 to 25 percent of white families. In absolute terms, between 7,816,000 and 18,237,000 families of the total of 65,133,000 would receive compassionate aid encompassing between 24,777,000 and 57,812,000 persons, or between 10 percent and 24 percent of the entire American population.

The Distribution of Nonfamily Income

To this point the analytical focus has been placed on the distribution of family income to the neglect of nonfamily households or unrelated individuals. In 1987, 72 percent of households were families, so that the em-

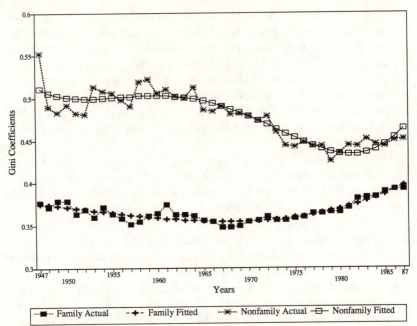

FIGURE 9.27. Gini Coefficient Profiles for All-Race Families and Unrelated
Households, Actual and Fitted Values, 1947–1987

phasis is well-placed, but it is not possible to neglect the 28 percent of
remaining household units in a study of inequality.

1. *All Races.* Income inequality among unrelated individuals is consistently and significantly greater, as measured by the Gini coefficient, than
for corresponding all-race, white, and black families. However, all three
of the unrelated individual Lorenz curves intersect that for all families,
introducing an element of ambiguity into the comparison. Figure 9.27
presents the actual and fitted data for unrelated individual Gini coefficients in the postwar period, along with the same data for all-race families as reproduced from figure 9.5.[6] The curves for unrelated individual
Ginis are seen to be substantially above those for all-race families.

The rather steady decline in inequality among unrelated persons from
1960 to 1980 is highlighted by the trend line for their data in the figure,
and by comparison with the all-race family trend line it is seen to have
been a contrary movement to the drift upward in the family Gini coefficient in that period. The latter reflects the falling retirement age for
householders in families and the rise in the number of families headed
by single women. The drift upward in the post–1980 period parallels the
family curve, however. In 1987 the difference between the unrelated individual and family Gini coefficients was about .06 points—a substantial
amount.

TABLE 9.13

Distribution of Census Money Income by Quintiles,
All-Race Families, All-Race Unrelated Individuals, and
White and Black Unrelated Individuals, 1987

	Income Shares			
	1	*2*	*3* *White*	*4* *Black*
Quintile	*Families*	*Unrelated*	*Unrelated*	*Unrelated*
First	4.6%	3.6%	3.9%	2.7%
Second	10.8	8.8	9.0	7.7
Third	16.9	15.0	15.2	13.5
Fourth	24.1	24.2	24.1	24.6
Fifth	43.7	48.4	47.8	51.5
Mean Income	$36,568	$16,872	$17,581	$11,996
Median Income	30,853	12,559	13,338	8,094

Source: U.S. Bureau of the Census, *Current Population Reports*, Series P-60, no. 162, table 12, 42–44, and no. 166, 19–22.

Further, the unrelated individuals' Gini coefficients are in general more volatile cyclically than families' over the period, although in the recessions of 1953–1954 and 1969–1970, the Gini tended to move down. Finally, the extremely high 1947 value, reflecting the transient conditions of veterans' demobilization and transition from wartime production, should be ignored.

Table 9.13 compares the distribution of money income by quintiles for all families, all unrelated individuals, and for white and black unrelated individuals in 1987. It also presents mean and median incomes for such groups. A comparison of all-race families and all-race unrelated individuals in columns 1 and 2 reveals the greater tendency toward inequality displayed in figure 9.27. The lower 40 percent of unrelated individuals receive only 12.4 percent of total unrelated persons' money income compared with 15.4 percent of total family income for families. On the other hand, the upper 40 percent of unrelated individuals obtain 72.6 percent versus 67.8 percent for families. These imbalances are explained in large part by the large number of nonearning or low-earning students and other young persons receiving partial or total support from relations, as well as the large number of retired and semiretired persons in the group. In 1987, of the 24,919,000 nonfamily households, about 85 percent consisted of individuals who lived alone. Hence a large majority of these households had one income earner at most, and many of them held only part-time jobs. Median income, therefore, was only 41 percent of that for all-race families.[7]

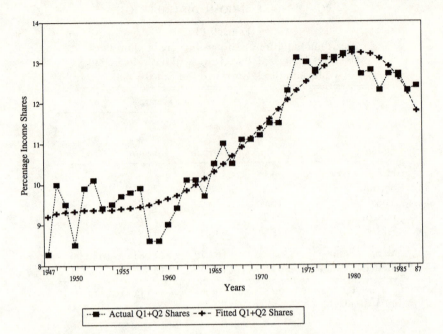

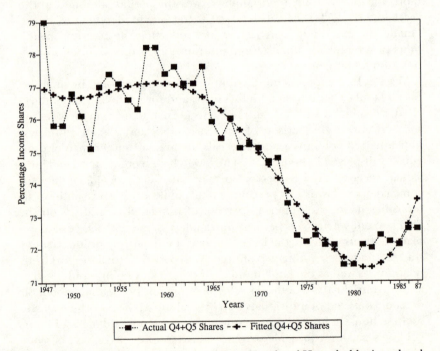

Until 1980, however, there was some slight tendency for the lowest 40 percent of the unrelated individual households to gain share at the expense of the upper 40 percent. Figures 9.28 and 9.29 display the path of income shares over the postwar period for these two groups on exaggerated scales. The rise in the former group from about 10 percent in 1948 to about 13 percent in 1979 is highlighted, while the second group declined from about 76 percent in 1948 to 71.5 percent in 1979. After 1979, however, the by now familiar and general movement toward greater inequality is reflected in the sharp downward movement in the income share of the lowest 40 percent and rise in the share of the highest 40 percent.

Table 9.14 displays the distribution of money income among unrelated individuals for all races, whites and blacks in 1987, in both absolute and relative terms. As noted, the median income for all races—which can be used as a base to gauge distributive performance for all nonrelated groups—was $12,559, or about 41 percent of all-race family median income. Considering that the mean number of persons per family was 3.17, on a per person basis this compares quite well with family income.

Figure 9.30 condenses the income classes into six groups and shows the percentage frequencies for the distribution for all races. The distribution of retirees and the very young is especially important in interpreting the data in table 9.14 for all races and its condensed version in figure 9.30, and it is presented below in condensed-group detail:

	Percentage of Age Class		Percentage of Income Class	
	15–24	*65 and Over*	*15–24*	*65 and Over*
$0–$3,999	40.4	20.5	27.8	20.7
$4,000–$6,999	12.3	25.4	12.4	53.4
$7,000–$9,999	10.6	15.1	15.1	45.1
$10,000–$17,499	22.0	25.5	16.7	40.3
$17,500–$29,999	11.9	9.1	9.7	15.5
Over $30,000	2.8	4.5	3.2	11.0
Total	100.0	100.0		

From table 9.14, about 40 percent of all-race unrelated individuals earn less than $10,000 per year. The age composition of these three classes provides the explanation for their poor showing: over 42 percent of these persons are 65 years of age or over and about 17 percent are under the age of 24. Fully 63 percent of unrelated individual households in this latter age bracket fall in these three classes. Only 27 percent fall within the prime earning ages of 25–54. In class 4, earning between $10,000 and $17,500, the very young and very old account for 57 percent of the individuals, but prime-earning-age occupants have grown to 43 percent. The composition of group 5—$17,500–$30,000—contains only

TABLE 9.14

Money Income Distributions for Unrelated Individuals 15 Years or Older,
All Races, Whites, and Blacks, by Income, 1987
(Levels in thousands of persons)

Income Classes	All Races		Whites		Blacks	
	Levels	Ratios	Levels	Ratios	Levels	Ratios
<$2,000	1,845	.056	1,339	.047	417	.106
2,000–2,999	679	.021	508	.018	143	.036
3,000–3,999	1,067	.032	796	.028	242	.061
4,000–4,999	2,038	.062	1,492	.053	502	.127
5,000–5,999	1,802	.055	1,494	.053	275	.070
6,000–6,999	1,883	.057	1,601	.057	250	.063
7,000–7,999	1,529	.047	1,378	.049	126	.032
8,000–8,999	1,359	.041	1,160	.041	171	.043
9,000–9,999	1,136	.035	1,022	.036	87	.022
10,000–12,499	3,041	.093	2,681	.095	300	.076
12,500–14,999	2,189	.067	1,870	.066	263	.067
15,000–17,499	2,374	.072	2,114	.075	220	.056
17,500–19,999	1,673	.051	1,496	.053	150	.038
20,000–24,999	3,112	.095	2,765	.098	294	.075
25,000–29,999	2,241	.068	2,008	.072	196	.050
30,000–34,999	1,583	.048	1,421	.050	132	.033
35,000–49,999	2,211	.067	2,005	.072	146	.037
Over 49,999	1,100	.033	1,045	.037	28	.008
Totals	32,862	1.000	28,195	1.000	3,942	1.000
Median Income	$12,559		$13,338		$8,094	
Mean Income	16,872		17,581		11,996	
Year-Round Full-Time Workers						
(Percent)	42.4%		43.0%		38.3%	
Median Income	21,534		21,916		18,220	
Mean Income	24,914		25,421		20,428	

Source: U.S. Bureau of the Census, Current Population Reports, Series P-60, no. 162, table 38, 152–157.

25 percent of the oldest and youngest categories and 66 percent prime age group earners. Finally, for those earning over $30,000, about 3 percent are 15 to 24 years of age, 11 percent are over 65, and 73 percent lie between 25 and 54 years of age.[8]

In 1987 for all races only 42.4 percent of unrelated individuals over the age of 14 were full-time, year-round workers, excluding the armed forces, as noted in table 9.14. The prime-earning-age groups—25–34, 35–44, and 45–54 years of age—had percentages of 68.8, 66.6, and 61.1

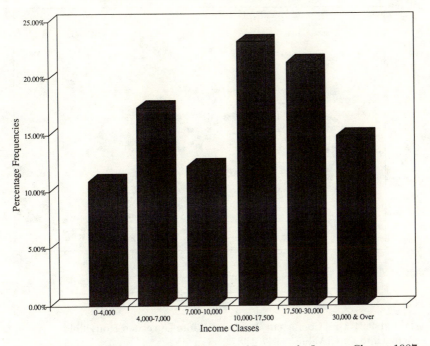

FIGURE 9.30. Money Income Shares, Unrelated Persons, by Income Classes, 1987

respectively. Age groups 15–24, 55–64, and over 65 years of age showed 42.9, 35.8, and 3.6 percent in full-time employment. In the latter two classes the effects of early retirement and current timely retirement are quite apparent, raising serious questions of whether the nation will be able to afford extended end-of-career leisure in such generous amounts, given the likely costs of the compassionate strand in the economic ethic. In all categories median incomes for the full-time workers were substantially above those for the age groups as a whole, as shown below:

Age Group	Median Income of All Members	Median Income of Fully-Employed
15–24	$9,450	$14,984
25–34	18,226	21,874
35–44	20,692	25,773
45–54	17,545	24,188
55–64	11,529	20,476
65 and Over	8,205	20,616

Note that peak earnings for unrelated individuals tend to occur in one's late 30s and early 40s, although the decline in earnings in the ages 45 to 54 is not drastic. The potential rise in national productivity from

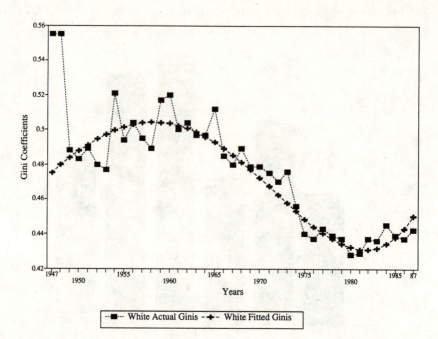

FIGURE 9.31. Gini Coefficient Profile for White Unrelated Households, Actual and Fitted Values, 1947–1987

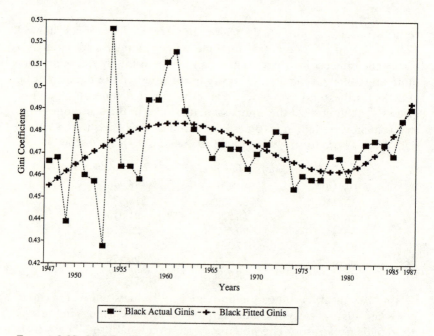

FIGURE 9.32. Gini Coefficient Profile for Black Unrelated Households, Actual and Fitted Values, 1947–1987

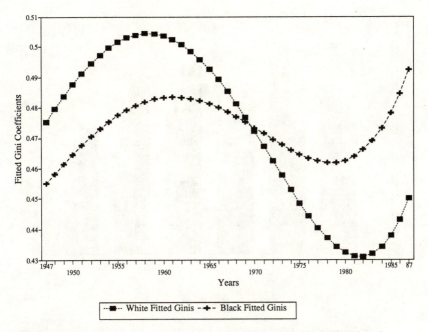

FIGURE 9.33. Fitted Gini Coefficient Profiles, White and Black Unrelated Households, 1947–1987

delaying retirement in age group 55–64 and encouraging employment for the able-bodied in the 65 and older class is striking. Of course, the reduction in social burden from such policies is twofold, in that the national product is increased at the same time that individuals leave the rolls of those receiving governmental aid.

2. *Whites and Blacks.* Figures 9.31 and 9.32 present the actual Gini coefficients for white and black unrelated individuals respectively over the postwar period, with fitted trend lines to discern basic movements in the measure.[9] The patterns of movement are similar: both sets of Gini coefficients tended to rise from 1947 to about 1960, then declined to about 1980, and rose steeply thereafter. These basic tendencies are highlighted in figure 9.33, which plots the fitted trend lines for the two series. Until 1960, the blacks' Gini coefficients were somewhat smaller than the whites', but from 1960 to 1980 the latter's declined substantially below the former's and remained lower till the end of the period. In 1987, unrelated blacks' Gini coefficient was .490 and whites' was .442. Among unrelated persons, therefore, blacks' income distribution is more widely dispersed than whites' at present, reversing the relationship that ruled until 1970. Rising dropout rates from school and underreporting of underground income are likely reasons for this.

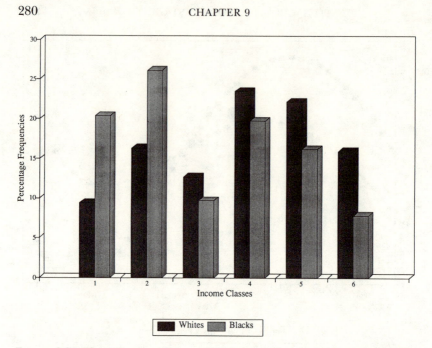

FIGURE 9.34. Money Income Shares of White and Black Unrelated Households, by Income Classes, 1987

Table 9.14 presents a clearer elaboration of the nature of this inequality difference between the races. It lists the distributions of white and black unrelated persons as percentages of their respective total numbers over eighteen income classes in 1987. The contrast highlights of the two distributions are accented in figure 9.34 by condensing the number of classes to six, formed by successive triads of the eighteen in the table. The data reveal that the major differences can be found in the heavy concentration of blacks—relative to whites—in the lowest two classes and their relative underrepresentation, enlarging as the classes rise in income, in the highest four classes of figure 9.34. They translate into the wide discrepancies between the percentage frequencies in the first two and last three classes of the figure. These tend to average, in the eighteen classes of table 9.14, about 4.6 percentage points of over-representation in the poorer classes and 3.2 percentage points of under-representation in the highest groups. The differences in the percentage frequencies of the fifth through fifteenth classes tend to be substantially less. These "extremes disparities" define the nature of racewise income inequality among nonfamily households, in the same manner as they do for family distributions.

TABLE 9.15

Full-Time, Year-Round Employment Rates for Unrelated Individuals over
the Age of 14, Age Distributions for Whites and Blacks,
and Median Incomes, 1987

Age Group	Employment		Age Distribution		Median Income	
	Whites	Blacks	Whites	Blacks	Whites	Blacks
15–24	46.0%	36.4%	13.7%	10.0%	$10,204	$ 6,084
25–34	70.6	59.5	25.0	24.2	19,080	13,573
35–44	68.1	59.2	13.1	16.4	21,603	13,239
45–54	64.3	44.7	8.7	12.6	18,974	11,715
55–64	37.0	30.8	9.9	14.6	12,570	8,005
65 and Over	3.7	2.7	29.6	22.2	8,706	4,990
Average	43.0	38.3			13,338	8,094

Source: U.S. Bureau of the Census, *Current Population Reports,* Series P-60, no. 166 (Washington, D.C.: U.S. Government Printing Office, 1989), table 18, 73–77.

This characteristic distributive pattern of differences between white and black income recipients is reflected in median incomes for the two populations. For all unrelated individuals over the age of 14 the median incomes for whites is $13,338 compared with $8,094 for blacks. However, for those individuals in full-time, year-round employment the difference narrows to $21,916 and $18,220 respectively, revealing a major source of the inequality to lie in differential full-time employment rates. Table 9.15 presents these rates for both races disaggregated by age classes.

The employment differentials are both substantial and puzzling. Age distributions cannot explain them, since, from the table, in the low-earning groups—the very young and the very old—blacks have smaller percentages than whites, and in the prime-earning-age groups—35–54—they have more. This repeats a pattern noted in the family distributions. Differentials in years of schooling completed and racial discrimination are suggested as primary determinants of the differences in employment rates and earnings within those employments. Figures 9.35 through 9.41 display these departures graphically for white and black unrelated persons of both sexes 15 years and older and for decennial age cohorts.

The overall educational differentials between the races is depicted starkly in figure 9.35. Blacks are significantly underrepresented in the ranges of post–grammar school education. The percentage of blacks with a high school diploma or above is only 82 percent of whites' percentage; the percentage for a college diploma or above is 50 percent; and for postgraduate education it is 42 percent. On the other hand the gap, though remaining positive, narrows considerably for lesser educa-

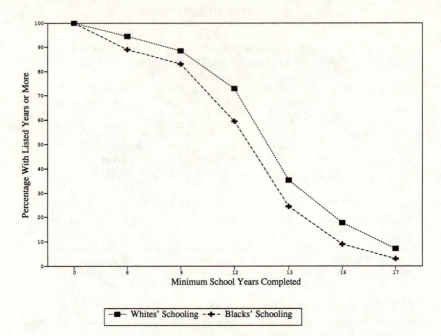

FIGURE 9.35. Years of Schooling, White and Black Unrelated Households for Individuals 15 Years or Older, 1987

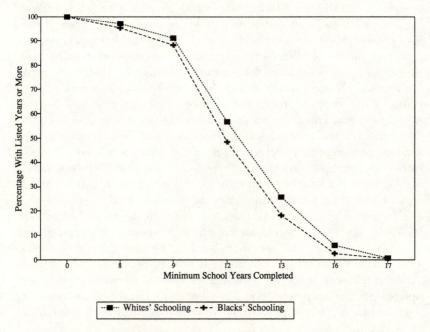

FIGURE 9.36. Years of Schooling, White and Black Unrelated Households, for Individuals 15–24 Years, 1987

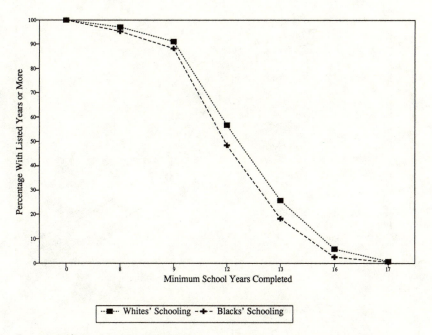

FIGURE 9.37. Years of Schooling, White and Black Unrelated Households, for Individuals 25–34 Years, 1987

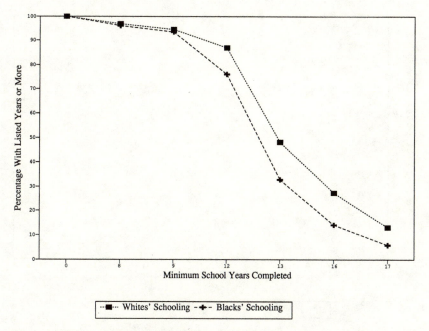

FIGURE 9.38. Years of Schooling, White and Black Unrelated Households, for Individuals 35–44 Years, 1987

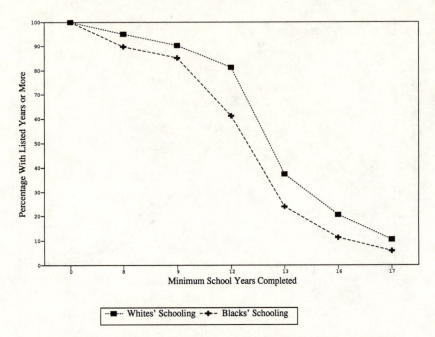

FIGURE 9.39. Years of Schooling, White and Black Unrelated Households, for Individuals 45–54 Years, 1987

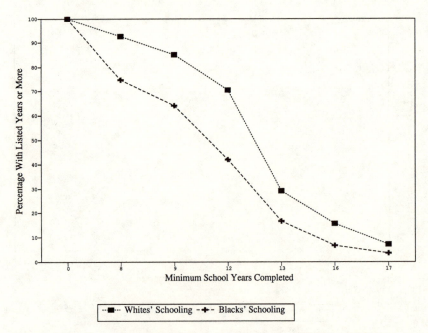

FIGURE 9.40. Years of Schooling, White and Black Unrelated Households, for Individuals 55–64 Years, 1987

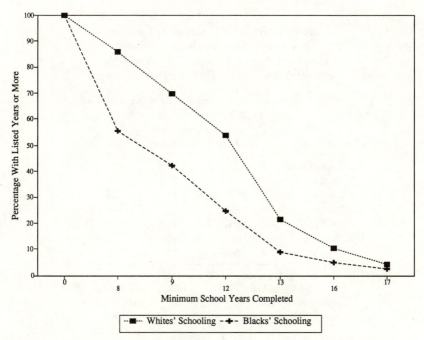

FIGURE 9.41. Years of Schooling, White and Black Unrelated Households, for Individuals 64 Years or Older, 1987

tional achievements: for example, for a grade school education or more the difference is only 6 percent lower than whites'. Rather clearly, the attainment of a high school diploma is the level at which significant racial achievements register, and the disadvantage for blacks intensifies at higher and higher levels.

Table 9.16 lists the education level differentials for whites and blacks in 1987 by age groups for those with a high school education or better and for those with a college education or better. In the younger age groups the increasing improvements in opportunity for blacks is revealed through the narrowing of these differentials in the age groups 15–24 and 25–35 years. In the first of these brackets the percentage of blacks receiving a high school education or better rises to 85 percent of whites' percentage, and for a college degree or better 45 percent. These differences narrow even further for the 25–35 year cohort at values of 94 percent and 49 percent respectively.

The differential for those with a high school education or more narrows monotonically as one rises from the oldest age class to the 25–34-year-old group. Blacks' proportions as percentages of whites' mounts continuously from 46 percent to 94 percent in this bracket. There is a

TABLE 9.16
Differentials in Years of Schooling Completed
and Median Incomes, White and Black
Unrelated Persons 15 Years of Age and Older,
with Black Attainments Expressed as Percentages
of Whites', 1987

Age Group	High School Diploma or More	College Diploma or More	Median Income
15 and over	82%	50%	61
15–24	85	45	60
25–34	94	49	71
35–44	87	51	61
45–54	75	54	62
55–64	59	42	64
Over 65	46	47	57

Source: U.S. Bureau of the Census, Education Attainment in the United States: March, 1987 and 1986, Current Population Reports, Series P-60, no. 428 (Washington, D.C., 1988), table 1, 3–16; and Series P-60, no. 162, table 18, 73–77.

discouraging fall to 85 percent in the 15–24-year-old class, however. The pattern correlates rather well with the median incomes for blacks as well as the employment percentages for blacks in table 9.15, as well as the median income differential percentages in table 9.16, most relevantly for the preretirement ages between 15 and 54 years.

For college diploma thresholds the differential profile rises from the oldest cohort to the 45–54-year-old group, but then declines steadily over the remaining four age groups. The changes in both directions are not as dramatic as those for the high school level: indeed, their relative stability over the age structure is striking and a bit discouraging in terms of hopes of closing the education gap between the races. In general, blacks achieve a college, graduate, or professional education at a frequency of only 50 percent that of whites.

3. *Hispanic Origin.* The category of "Hispanic origin" lumps together at least five groups of individuals with quite disparate social, economic, and educational backgrounds. In 1988 there were 19,431,000 persons in this population grouping, consisting of 62.3 percent Mexican, 12.7 percent Puerto Rican, 5.3 percent Cuban, 11.5 percent Central and South American, and 8.1 percent others of Hispanic origin.[10] They constitute 8.1 percent of the population but are growing in size rapidly: between 1980 and 1988 the Hispanic population grew 34.4 percent, compared with a

TABLE 9.17

Differentials in Years of Schooling Completed
and Median Incomes, White and Hispanic Persons
15 Years of Age and Older, with Hispanic
Attainments Expressed as Percentages
of Whites', 1987

Age Group	High School Diploma or More	College Diploma or More	Median Income
15 and over	66%	39%	65%
15–24	72	40	89
25–34	69	40	70
35–44	66	35	62
45–54	51	43	60
55–64	50	39	63
Over 65	39	22	66

Source: U.S. Bureau of the Census, *Education Attainment in the United States: March, 1987 and 1986, Current Population Reports*, Series P-60, no. 428 (Washington, D.C., 1988), table 1, 3–16; and Series P-60, no. 162, table 18, 73–77.

non-Hispanic population growth rate of 6.6 percent. They will become, therefore, an increasingly significant minority with problems that bear heavily on the tasks we are studying.

In a previous section I have analyzed income data for Hispanic families, but similar data for unrelated persons of Hispanic origin is not available. In 1987 about 18 percent of such households consisted of unrelated individuals, containing in excess of 1 million persons. From fragmentary data their economic situation seems to lie between whites and blacks. For example, in 1987 median income for unmarried households was $12,033, compared with $15,696 for whites and $9,667 for blacks.

Hispanic educational levels do not reflect this conclusion, however. Table 9.17 reproduces the counterpart for Hispanics of the data in table 9.16 for blacks. It lists percentages of Hispanics who have completed high school or higher education and the percentages of those who have college educations or more, by age groups, as percentages of whites' percentages in these categories. The comparisons in every instance are less favorable than those of blacks in table 9.16, and usually by significant margins. Only 80 percent as many Hispanics as blacks have attained a high school diploma, and 78 percent college and postcollege schooling. But the rate of rise from older to younger cohorts is strongly and continuously positive. Also, a somewhat stronger tendency than exists in the

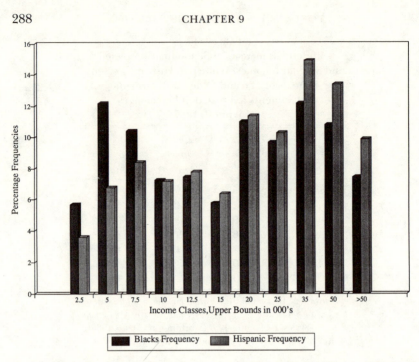

FIGURE 9.42. Money Income Distributions for Black and Hispanic Unrelated Households, 15 Years of Age or Older, by Income Classes, 1987

black data is revealed in Hispanics' progress in advanced education through the age classes, although as in the case of blacks it seems to plateau in the younger groups.

Nonetheless, Hispanics' median household money income in 1987 was 12 percent higher than blacks and the relative frequencies in the Hispanic distribution more concentrated in the middle and higher brackets. Figure 9.42 displays the two distributions. In the first four income classes which yield money income less than $10,000, the Hispanic frequencies are less than those of blacks. In every other class they surpass blacks', especially in the three highest classes, yielding incomes above $35,000.

The Hispanic median income levels for the age groups are recorded in the last column of table 9.17 as percentages of respective white values, and can be compared with their counterparts in table 9.16. With the exception of the youngest and the oldest cohorts, the values for Hispanics and blacks are comparable. The better performance for the 15–24-year-old age category is due in large part to the larger number of earners in this group for Hispanics relative to blacks; in the oldest category it may be due in large part to transfers from the stronger family support systems among Hispanics. In any event, Hispanics' deficiencies in educational

TABLE 9.18

Percentage Money Income Distributions for Unrelated Individuals 15 Years or
Older, by Race and Sex, and by Income Classes, 1987
(in thousands)

Income Classes	All Races		Whites		Blacks	
	Males	Females	Males	Females	Males	Females
<$2,000	5.7%	5.6%	4.6%	4.9%	11.3%	9.8%
2,000–2,999	2.0	2.1	1.8	1.8	2.9	4.4
3,000–3,999	2.6	3.8	2.2	3.3	4.9	7.5
4,000–4,999	4.4	7.8	3.6	6.7	9.2	16.7
5,000–5,999	3.7	7.1	3.3	6.9	5.7	8.4
6,000–6,999	4.2	7.0	4.0	7.1	6.1	6.6
7,000–7,999	3.3	5.8	3.5	6.1	2.5	4.0
8,000–8,999	4.0	4.2	3.6	4.5	6.4	2.0
9,000–9,999	2.7	4.1	2.9	4.2	1.8	2.7
10,000–12,499	9.2	9.3	9.3	9.7	8.5	6.6
12,500–14,999	6.2	7.1	6.1	7.1	6.7	6.6
15,000–17,499	7.4	7.0	7.9	7.2	5.0	6.3
17,500–19,999	5.2	5.1	5.2	5.4	4.4	3.2
20,000–24,999	10.6	8.5	11.2	8.6	7.8	7.0
25,000–29,999	8.2	5.6	8.6	5.9	6.1	3.8
30,000–34,999	6.0	3.8	6.2	4.1	4.6	1.9
35,000–49,999	9.3	4.5	10.0	4.7	5.1	2.2
Over 49,999	5.3	1.6	6.0	1.8	1.0	.3
Totals	100.0	100.0	100.0	100.0	100.0	100.0
Median Income	15,666	10,689	16,664	11,137	9,555	6,493
Mean Income	19,855	14,289	20,935	14,805	13,580	10,235
Year-Round Full-Time Workers (Percent)	52.3	33.8	53.9	34.1	44.3	31.6
Median Income	23,345	19,704	23,878	19,947	18,769	17,442
Mean Income	27,116	21,973	27,789	22,329	21,540	18,701

Source: U.S. Bureau of the Census, Current Population Reports, Series P-60, no. 162, table 18, 73–77.

attainment are not as punishing when compared with blacks although, as with blacks, they are highly determinative with respect to income within the race or origin category. Some presence of greater discrimination in the job market against blacks is therefore suggested.

4. *Sexes.* As a last analysis of cross-sectional income distribution in the United States I shall consider distinctions in income receipts by sex, often distinguished by race or origin as well. Table 9.18 presents income distributions by sex for all races, whites, and blacks for unrelated individ-

uals 15 years of age or older in 1987. The data are given as percentages of the total numbers of each sex group that fall within the eighteen income classes distinguished in table 9.14. Median and mean incomes for all persons in the group are also given, as well as the percentage of the totals employed in full-time jobs and their median and mean incomes.

Figure 9.43 presents the distributions of white and black males using only nine income groups obtained by combining successive pairs of the more extensive classification of table 9.18. Once more we encounter the "extremes disparities," that is, extreme differences between the races in the three lowest income classes and the three highest. The middle three classes reveal a closer conformance.

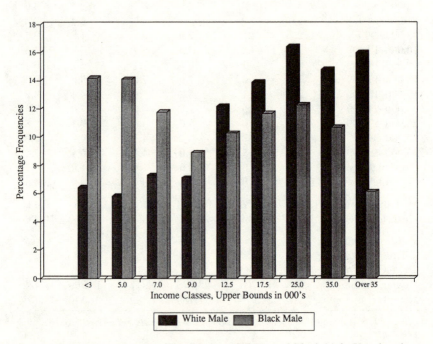

FIGURE 9.43. Money Income Distributions, White and Black Male Unrelated Individuals, 15 Years or Older, by Income Classes, 1987

The lower three groups in the figure consist in large part of the very young (15 to 24 years of age) and the very old (over 65) for both whites and blacks. The percentages of persons in those groups that fall in these two age brackets are the following:

Income Class	Age 15–24		Over 65		Total	
	Whites	Blacks	Whites	Blacks	Whites	Black
	(%)		(%)		(%)	
Less than $3,000	24.6	37.8	5.4	6.1	30.0	43.9
$3,000–$4,999	22.5	9.2	26.2	26.3	48.7	35.5
$5,000–$6,999	19.4	14.3	33.9	32.7	53.3	47.0
Combined (<$7,000)	24.6	20.9	22.3	21.0	46.9	41.9

About 25 percent of whites in these three income groups and 21 percent of blacks are in the lowest age class and, roughly, equal percentages are in the oldest age bracket. About 47 percent and 42 percent respectively of those unrelated persons over the age of 14 who earn less than $7,000 are found in these age groups.

The median income for all unrelated persons of both sexes and all races in 1987 was $12,589 ($21,534 for those fully employed). About 39 percent of white males earned less than this total median income, but 59 percent of black males were below this threshold.

Figure 9.44 depicts white and black female distributions by the same nine income classes used in figure 9.43. When compared with the male distributions two differences are noticeable. The dramatic disparities are in the two lowest income classes, with the $3,000 to $5,000 class showing black concentrations almost 2.5 times that of whites. The second difference from the male distributions is the greater concentration of females of both races in the lowest three income classes. This is especially true of blacks. About 31 percent of white females are found in these three classes with incomes below $7,000, and over 53 percent of black unrelated females are located in them.

Income Class	Age 15–24		Over 65		Total	
	Whites	Blacks	Whites	Blacks	Whites	Black
	(%)		(%)		(%)	
Less than $3,000	42.4	22.7	20.0	19.3	62.4	42.0
$3,000–$4,999	12.3	5.3	57.1	65.0	69.4	70.3
$5,000–$6,999	12.0	2.5	66.8	47.1	78.8	49.6
Combined (<$7,000)	16.6	10.2	53.4	47.9	70.0	58.1

Interestingly, the age structures of these three classes differ significantly between the races. With white women the bulk of these persons are the aged over 65: over 53 percent are in this group, most of them in the $3,000 to $7,000 income bracket. But about 17 percent of the occupants of the three classes are aged 15–24. Hence, 70 percent of these impoverished classes consist of very young or very old white females.

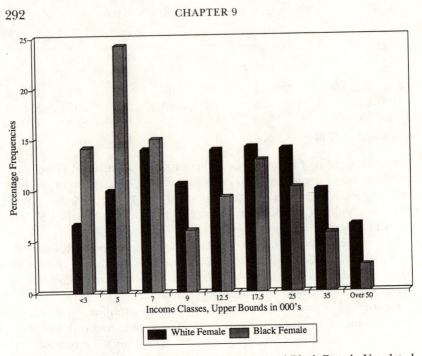

FIGURE 9.44. Money Income Distributions, White and Black Female Unrelated Individuals, 15 Years or Older, by Income Classes, 1987

For blacks only about 10 percent of these classes are the very young, and they are highly concentrated in the first class. About 48 percent, however, are the aged, found mainly in the $3,000-$7,000 bracket. A total of 58 percent of the persons in these three classes is, therefore, made up of black youngsters and oldsters. The discrepancy for the very young reflects the larger number of full-time students among whites. It is the concentration of the aged in these classes for blacks that weights the distribution so heavily downward.

For white unrelated women, the first income class is dominated by persons in the 15–24 year bracket and the second and third by those over 65. In the younger category only about 59 percent have high school diplomas or higher educations and 6 percent have a college diploma or more. In the older category only 55 percent have reached the high school diploma threshold and 10 percent have a college education or better.

For blacks the very young form only about 10 percent of the numbers in these lower three categories, compared with 17 percent for whites. The black aged in these classes are about five times more plentiful than the young. For this over-65 age group only 29 percent have high school diplomas or more and only 6 percent have a college education or

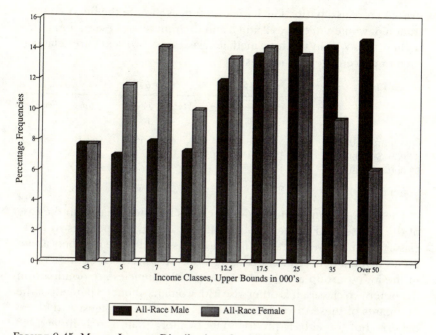

FIGURE 9.45. Money Income Distributions for All-Race Male and Female Unrelated Individuals, 15 Years or Older, by Income Classes, 1987

higher. For the youngest class 52 percent have the high school diploma or better—not far different from the whites' 59 percent—although only 2.7 percent have the higher level of attainment compared with whites' 6.1 percent attainment. Rather clearly, the large differentials between whites and blacks in the first two income classes in figure 9.44 reflects primarily the concentration of aged blacks with relatively low educational attainments rather than a dominance of young persons.

Last, median income for all unrelated black females is only about 58 percent of white females, which is essentially the same as the difference for similar categories of males. However, for year-round full-time workers, black median income is 87 percent that of white female workers, somewhat above the 79 percent for the male categories. But 69 percent of black unrelated females are below the all-race, both sexes median income, compared with 55 percent of white unrelated females. This is considerably below the 59 percent and 39 percent figures for black and white males determined above.

Consider now the male–female income disparities holding race constant. Figure 9.45 condenses the data for all-race males and females in table 9.18 into the nine classes used for figures 9.43 and 9.44. Once more the differences appear in the extremities, although the first class in figure 9.45 reveals a parity. The large differences show in the heavy concentration of women in classes 2 and 3 and their underrepresentation in the highest two. Within the intermediate classes the two sexes are relatively even in percentage frequencies.

Income Class	Age 15–24		Over 65		Total	
	Males	*Females*	*Males*	*Females*	*Males*	*Females*
	(%)		*(%)*		*(%)*	
Less than $3,000	31.7	31.4	5.4	19.1	37.1	50.5
$3,000–$4,999	19.6	10.7	25.9	8.9	45.5	69.6
$5,000–$6,999	17.7	11.0	33.3	64.5	51.0	75.5
Combined (<$7,000)	23.1	15.6	21.5	52.1	44.6	67.7

The composition of these poorest classes is quite different in the case of the two sexes. For males, about 45 percent of the persons in these classes are in the youngest or the oldest classes, with the numbers about evenly divided between the two age groups. Relatively few of those males in the lowest group are the elderly whose frequencies are dominant in the other two classes. It is otherwise with women. About 68 percent of the occupants of these three income classes are in the youngest and oldest cohorts, but the elderly predominate by more than 3 to 1. Indeed, 43 percent of all unrelated females over 64 years of age are found in these three income groups compared with 34 percent of males.

Also, 43 percent of all unrelated females in the 15- to 24-year-old cohort are located in these three classes, compared with 35 percent of males. These percentages compare with a total of unrelated females of all ages in these three groups of 33 percent and a total of unrelated males of all ages of 23 percent. Hence females in the youngest age group are underrepresented in these three income groups and the elderly are significantly over represented, while males are proportionately present in both categories. Hence, the elderly unrelated female population constitutes a distinct focus of income need.

The education profiles play their role in explaining these differences between the sexes. Among males over the age of 64, 12.8 percent had college degrees or postgraduate education, compared with 8.0 percent for females. About 54.8 percent of males had at least a high school diploma, compared with 51.4 percent of females. At least as important, however, was the differential in those employed at full-time employment: 5.8 percent for males and 3.0 percent for females in this elderly age category.

Finally, about 42 percent of unrelated males fall below the median income for all unrelated persons compared with 57 percent of females. The median income for all unrelated males was $15,666 and for females was $10,689, although for fully employed persons these median incomes

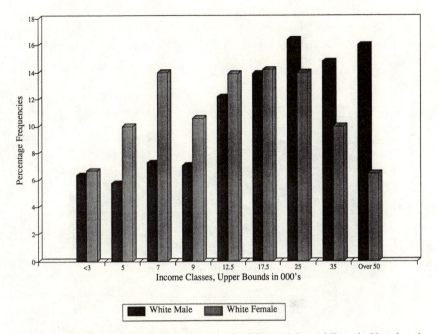

FIGURE 9.46. Money Income Distributions for White Male and Female Unrelated Individuals, 15 Years or Older, by Income Classes, 1987

rose to $23,345 and $19,704 respectively; females' median income in the first case was only 68 percent of males, but this rises for fully employed females to 84 percent.

White male and female distributions repeat the same basic patterns as all-race male and female distributions, as would be expected given the predominance of whites in the latter. Figure 9.46 depicts the distributions.

A rather marked comparative difference between the white and black male–female distributions is the tendency for the latter to be more equally configured than for whites. The dramatic inequality for blacks is in the second class, where almost one-fourth of unrelated black females are concentrated compared with 14 percent of males. The constitution of the lowest three classes in this category is given below:

Income Class	Age 15–24		Over 65		Total	
	Males	Females	Males	Females	Males	Females
	(%)		(%)		(%)	
Less than $3,000	37.8	22.7	6.1	19.3	30.0	42.0
$3,000–$4,999	9.2	5.3	26.3	65.0	48.7	70.3
$5,000–$6,999	14.3	2.5	32.7	47.1	53.3	49.6
Combined (<$7,000)	20.9	10.2	21.0	47.9	46.9	58.1

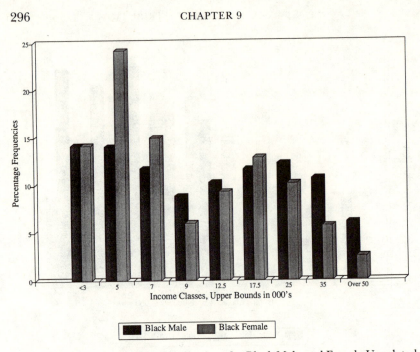

FIGURE 9.47. Money Income Distributions for Black Male and Female Unrelated Individuals, 15 Years or Older, by Income Classes, 1987

The essential outlines of the composition of the three classes in terms of these age cohorts are a repeat of that for all races, with a somewhat smaller concentration of black females over the age of 64 and between the ages of 18 and 24 than was true in the all-race distributions. The pattern of greater relative presence of the youngest category for black males than females and of greater over 65 representation for females is a repetition of the all-race patterns. However, 77 percent of unrelated black males and 53 percent of females between the ages of 15 and 24 are found in these three income groups, and 63 percent of black males and 80 percent of black females over the age of 64 are in these classes. It is the concentration of the female aged in the $3,000 to $5,000 class that accounts for the huge discrepancy in that class for black sexes in figure 9.47.

Only 2.5 percent of black males and 2.7 percent of black females among unrelated individuals have college diplomas or more in the 18-to-24-year cohort, and 4.3 percent of the males versus 6.0 percent of the females over age 64 have this many years of schooling. Also, 44 percent of the males compared with 52 percent of the females have a high school diploma and above in the younger cohort, while 20 percent of the males and 14 percent of the females in the aged cohort have such attainments.

The high school or better educational differentials between the sexes may play a large role in explaining the better showing of young and larger showing of elderly among females in the distributions.

Median income for black unrelated males was $9,555 versus $6,493 for females, increasing to $18,769 and $17,442 respectively for those in full-time employment. Approximately 44 percent of all unrelated black males were in full-time employment in 1987 versus 32 percent of black females. About 59 percent of black unrelated males and 69 percent of females are below the all-race, both sexes median income of $12,559.

5. *Nonfamily Incomes: A Summary.* Among the more important characteristics of income distribution for unrelated individuals, the following have been found to be of interest for the present study:

1. Income inequality, as measured by the Gini coefficient, has been greater in the postwar period for unrelated persons than for family units, whether one considers all races, whites, or blacks. However, this conclusion must be conditioned by the fact that in all three cases the Lorenz curves intersect those for families.

2. The paths of the Gini coefficients in the postwar period were different in the 1960 to 1980 period, when they declined for unrelated individuals and rose for family units. But after 1980 both groups' coefficients rose steeply, registering increasing inequality.

3. Unrelated individuals' Gini coefficients are more volatile in the short run than family units'.

4. In 1987, 85 percent of unrelated persons lived alone and hence had no more than one income earner per household. Moreover, only 42 percent were in full-time employment. Therefore, median income was only 41 percent of that for all-race family income.

5. The role of the very young and the very old in forming the lowest income classes was larger for unrelated individuals than for family units. The dominance of older retired and semiretired persons in these categories and the differences in the median incomes of those working full- and part-time raises the question of the feasibility of supporting large numbers of individuals in retirement at rather early ages.

6. The distributions of white and black unrelated persons' incomes reveal inequalities in the frequencies in the lowest and highest income classes. The differences in median incomes narrow significantly when comparison is made between persons who are employed full-time. Differentials in employment, therefore, are a major factor in these racial inequalities. Contributing to these data are substantial deficiencies in educational attainment by blacks compared with whites. Although these differentials narrow as one moves from older to younger groups, there is a disturbing reversal of the tendency in the 18–24 year age bracket.

7. Persons of Hispanic origin seem to have income distributions intermediate in inequality between whites and blacks. Educational levels are lower than for blacks, but earnings are nonetheless higher for comparable educational attainments. In the poorest and the richest categories Hispanics outperform blacks, in part because of a larger number of earners per household and greater family support systems for the elderly.

8. White and black male unrelated persons show income distributions that are marked by "extremes disparity," or overrepresentation of blacks in the poorest income classes and underrepresentation in the highest, with narrower differentials in the middle-income classes. For both races, the males concentrated in the less than $7,000 annual income classes consisted to a large extent of the very young and very old members of the population, with such persons being relatively more numerous among whites than blacks. Median incomes for blacks was significantly below that for whites.

9. White and black female distributions reveal the same extremes disparities as those for males, but in the lower income classes the disparity is much more marked. The black occupants of these lowest income classes are predominantly aged, while for whites, although those over 64 years are a large segment, the youngest group also plays a large part. The black aged have markedly less educational qualifications than white.

10. All-race male and female distributions once more display extremity inequalities, with narrowing of the differentials in intermediate classes. With males, a smaller proportion of those in the three lowest income classes are aged compared with females, the very young forming a larger segment of these poor. Elderly unrelated females constitute a significant group of the poor.

11. White male–female distribution comparisons parallel closely those for all races, given the predominance of whites in the total category. For black male–female distributions there exists a repetition of the heavy concentration of the female aged in the lowest income classes. The median income levels of females are significantly lower than those of males, even though female educational attainments are higher, in large part because of a smaller full-time employment percentage for females. When median income levels for fully employed black males and females are considered, the differential in median incomes narrows to about $1,300 per year. Both sexes, however, obtain median incomes substantially below those for all races.

LIFE-CYCLE OR DYNAMIC DISTRIBUTIVE ANALYSES

As a final perspective on income distribution in the United States in the postwar period, we must study the patterns of income receipt over age groups for all races, whites and blacks, and by sexes. The age profile of

TABLE 9.19

Median Incomes by Age Groups, Race and Sex, Dollar Amounts and Normalized by
Median Income of All Unrelated Persons, 15 Years and Older, 1987

Group	Age Cohorts						
	15–24	25–34	35–44	45–54	55–64	≥65	≥15
a. Money Incomes							
1. All Races							
a. Both Sexes	9,450	18,226	20,692	17,545	11,527	8,205	12,559
b. Males	10,383	18,646	21,834	19,832	14,390	9,584	15,666
c. Females	8,431	17,735	18,491	15,864	10,563	7,863	10,689
2. Whites							
a. Both Sexes	9,945	19,080	21,603	18,974	12,570	8,706	13,338
b. Males	10,921	19,944	22,873	21,596	16,671	10,548	16,664
c. Females	8,643	18,098	20,010	16,768	11,460	8,296	16,137
3. Blacks							
a. Both Sexes	5,493	13,573	13,239	11,715	8,005	4,990	8,094
b. Males	5,559	12,924	13,504	12,723	10,691	5,899	9,555
c. Females	5,351	14,739	12,884	10,686	6,370	4,783	6,493
b. Normalized Values							
1. All Races							
a. Both Sexes	.75	1.45	1.65	1.40	.92	.65	1.00
b. Males	.66	1.19	1.39	1.27	.92	.61	1.00
c. Females	.79	1.66	1.73	1.48	.99	.74	1.00
2. Whites							
a. Both Sexes	.75	1.43	1.62	1.42	.94	.65	1.00
b. Males	.66	.90	1.37	1.30	1.00	.64	1.00
c. Females	.77	1.63	1.80	1.51	1.03	.74	1.00
3. Blacks							
a. Both Sexes	.68	1.68	1.64	1.45	.99	.62	1.00
b. Males	.58	1.35	1.41	1.33	1.06	.62	1.00
c. Females	.82	2.27	1.98	1.65	.98	.74	1.00

Source: U.S. Bureau of the Census, *Current Population Reports*, Series P-60, no. 162, 73–77.

earnings is best isolated from data on unrelated individuals, since about
85 percent of them are single-earner households. Family data, using the
age of the householder as a criterion, obscures the age pattern because
of variations in numbers of earners per family and number of family
members.

Table 9.19a displays age-cohort median incomes for all households of
unrelated persons—including those employed full-time and those unemployed or with part-time jobs—by sex and race. In table 9.19b these

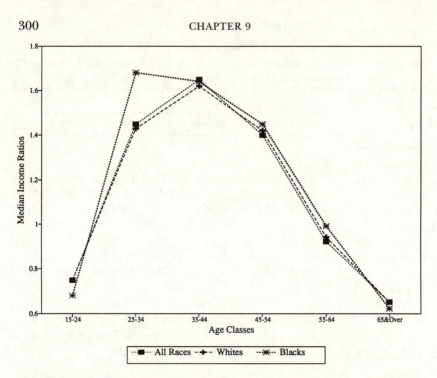

FIGURE 9.48. Median Money Incomes for Unrelated Individuals, 15 Years or Older, for Both Sexes and All-Races, Whites and Blacks, by Age Classes, as Ratios to Own-Group Age-Specific Median Income, 1987

data are normalized by dividing these median incomes in each age class by the median income in the relevant group for all unrelated persons aged 15 years or more.

Figure 9.48 presents a visual display of the life-cycle pattern of income receipt—as reflected in 1987's cross-section data—for all races and both sexes, for whites, and for blacks. Using the all-race data as the baseline for comparison, it is seen that median incomes for unrelated persons jump smartly in the 25- to 34-year-old age group from the 15- to 24-year class, rising from 75 percent of the median for all ages to 145 percent, then rise to a peak of 165 percent in the 35- to 44-year-age group. The decline thereafter is a relatively gentle descent to 140 percent for 45- to 54-year-olds, then sharp descents to 92 percent in the 55- to 64-year cohort and 65 percent after age 65.

Whites, course, follow this profile closely, but blacks depart importantly, when their percentages of median own-group income are compared with the baseline. The youngest age group, at 68 percent, is substantially below the baseline, echoing the concern raised in table 9.16 and accompanying discussion with the increased differential between

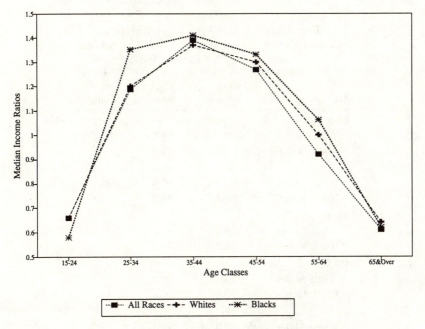

FIGURE 9.49. Median Money Incomes for Unrelated All-Race, White and Black Males, by Age Classes, as Ratios to Own-Group Age-Specific Median Income, 1987

whites and blacks in this class with respect to high school, college, and postgraduate education. More surprisingly, the percentage figure for the 25- to 34-year cohort jumps to 168, or 16 percent above the black baseline figure. As will be seen, most of this is attributable to females in this cohort who, when fully employed, have almost closed the income gap with white, fully employed women (with median incomes of $20,039 versus $20,804). The black percentages then fall to about parity with all-race data for the remainder of the income classes, with some tendency for the ages before retirement to be higher for blacks. Age and experience seem to count for a bit more in their case.

For white and black males the profiles are depicted on figure 9.49. The most striking difference is once more the large differential in blacks' favor between the percentages for the 25 to 34 age cohort. Those percentage differentials remain positive until they turn negative in the post–65 cohort. Blacks have not closed a large gap in median incomes with whites in the 25- to 34-year cohort ($12,924 vs. $19,994 for all persons in the cohort, $17,423 vs. $23,425 for the fully employed), and indeed the median income for both black male employment status subgroups is below that for corresponding female subgroups.

TABLE 9.20
Percentages of Male Age Classes Who Have
Completed at Least Grammar School, High School,
and College Educations, 1987

Age Cohort	Grammar School	High School	College
15–24			
White Males	96.7	54.4	5.3
Black Males	83.8	43.4	2.5
25–34			
White Males	97.2	86.5	26.2
Black Males	98.1	83.2	12.1
35–44			
White Males	96.6	87.2	32.0
Black Males	94.9	75.2	15.4
45–54			
White Males	94.4	78.9	25.5
Black Males	90.3	60.2	11.9
55–64			
White Males	92.0	69.0	20.7
Black Males	67.7	35.8	6.3
65 and Over			
White Males	84.9	53.6	13.5
Black Males	48.1	20.2	4.3

Source: U.S. Bureau of the Census, Education Attainment in the
United States: March 1987 and 1986, Current Population Reports,
Series P-60, no. 428 (Washington, D.C., 1988), table 1, 3–16.

Table 9.20 lists the percentages of each male age class, by race, that
have completed at least the grammar school, high school, and college
thresholds. Figure 9.50 presents the high school and college threshold
levels graphically. For the first of these thresholds, although the steady
and rather dramatic lessening of the gap between whites and blacks as
one moves from the oldest age group to the 25–34-year-old group is encouraging, its marked widening in the youngest age group is discouraging. The curve does peak in the 25–34-year cohort, and no doubt provides some of the explanation for the wide difference in median income
ratios for that category shown in figure 9.49.

Comparisons of the college diploma profiles on figure 9.50 is not so
clear-cut. The disparities in percentages for the 25–34 through 55–64
classes remain rather steady, with a slight widening in the 35–44 age
category. Some narrowing is revealed in the oldest cohort, possibly re-

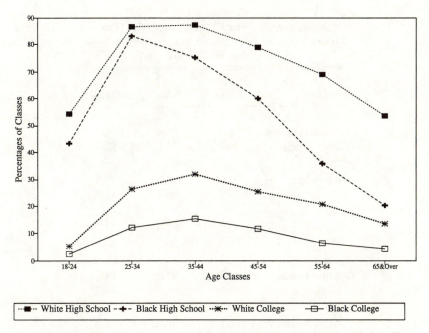

FIGURE 9.50. School Attainment, White and Black Unrelated Males, by Age Class, as Percentages of Total Numbers in Each Own-Group Age Class, 1987

flecting the favorable effect on higher education for blacks of the G.I. bill after World War II. No doubt the slight tendency for reduction of the differential had some contribution to make to the narrowing of the median income ratios in the upper age categories revealed in figure 9.49, but the extent is not determinable.

The median income profiles for white and black females are displayed in figure 9.51, from which the pattern for white and black males is reproduced with even greater concentrations of income in the peak earning cohorts. Young black women in the 25–34 and 35–44 year cohorts earn substantially larger median incomes than younger and older cohorts and more relatively than their counterpart whites. From table 9.19 it can be seen that black women have been more successful in closing the median income gaps with white women, especially in the 25–34-year class, than have black men with white men, in part because of the nature of the service jobs held by women.

Table 9.21 presents the data on percentages of white and black females in terms of schooling completed by age classes. Several important features are worth noticing. First, note how black females in the age range 15 to 44 have essentially closed the gap between whites in terms of

TABLE 9.21
Percentages of Female Age Classes Who Have
Completed at Least Grammar School, High School,
and College Educations, 1987

Age Cohort	Grammar School	High School	College
15–24			
White Females	97.8	59.0	6.1
Black Females	96.7	52.1	2.7
25–34			
White Females	97.6	88.1	24.0
Black Females	98.7	80.4	12.6
35–44			
White Females	96.9	87.0	22.7
Black Females	96.5	76.7	12.5
45–54			
White Females	95.5	80.0	14.7
Black Females	89.5	61.9	10.4
55–64			
White Females	93.1	80.0	11.0
Black Females	80.5	46.9	6.9
65 and Over			
White Females	86.5	53.8	8.1
Black Females	60.5	27.7	6.0

Source: U.S. Bureau of the Census, Education Attainment in the United States: March 1987 and 1986, Current Population Reports, Series P-60, no. 428 (Washington, D.C., 1988), table 1, 3–16.

acquiring a grammar school education or more. Significant differences occur in the age groups in which many blacks grew up in the South. The urbanization of the black during and after the second world war was clearly important in achieving this degree of educational opportunity. Success was not so noticeable in the case of a high school education and even less for college and postgraduate education. The black has not shared equally the white female's increasing opportunity to achieve a college or postgraduate education. Indeed, the gap tends to widen in the younger cohorts. Finally, comparison with table 9.20 reveals the all but universal dominance of white and black females over their male counterparts in the percentages obtaining a grammar school and a high school education or more. This is reversed, however, in the higher educational spheres.

Figures 9.51 and 9.52 permit a comparison of median income ratios and high school and college educational attainments for white and black

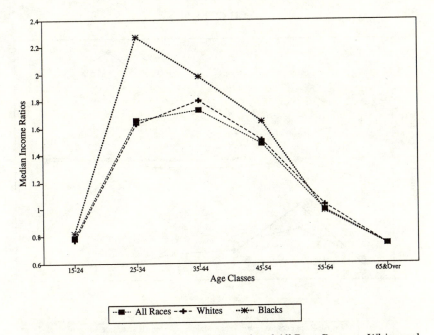

FIGURE 9.51. Median Money Income for Unrelated All-Race Persons, White and Black Females, by Age Classes, as Ratios to Own-Group Age-Specific Median Income, 1987

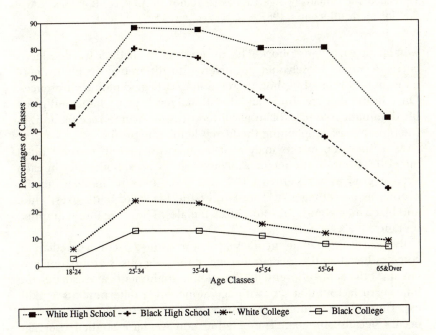

FIGURE 9.52. School Attainment, White and Black Female Unrelated Individuals by Age Class, as Percentages of Total Numbers in Each Own-Group Age Class, 1987

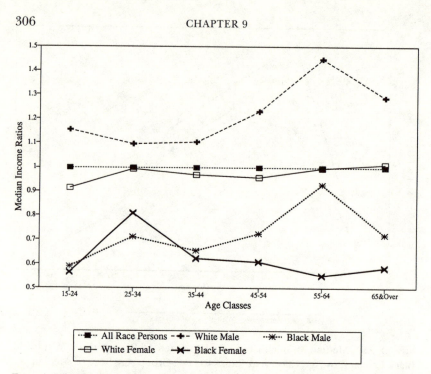

FIGURE 9.53. Median Money Incomes for White and Black Male and Female Unrelated Individuals, by Age Classes, as Ratios to All-Race, Both Sexes Age-Specific Median Incomes, 1987

women in each age cohort. The differences in median income levels correlate rather closely and negatively with differences in high school education or more, but show no relation to college diploma differences. Once more, then, we find that educational levels play a large and possibly dominant role in explaining differences in income receipt, and, in the present case, explaining the life-cycle income profile.

As a final step in the analysis of income distribution in the United States, I have used the median income for all races, both sexes in each age category as a baseline of 100, and computed the median income profiles as percentages of it for whites and blacks of both sexes, white and black males, and white and black females. These are found graphed on figure 9.53.

By measuring median incomes against baseline age-cohort median income rather than the median income of the race or sex group, one lessens the effects of differential educational attainments and isolates the impacts of factors that vary with age alone. Such determinants as skill, experience, and seniority are mirrored in the resulting profiles. This occurs because the patterns of education we have studied over age groups tend to move up and down together for races and sexes. Hence, the baseline median incomes for each age class rise and fall with the race and sex median incomes for those groups, lessening the influence of such correlated factors. On the other hand, measuring age-bracket median incomes against own-group median income averages out age in the base and allows such age-cohort differences as education to gain prominence.

In these profiles, males, both white and black, peak in median income relative to the baseline in the 55- to 64-year class. This does not occur significantly because of a rise in the relative numbers of women in each group as those groups age, with a consequent depressing of the baseline median income. The proportions of males to females in the all-race classes does not change drastically in the 25–34 through 55–64 classes. This pattern, distinctively different from females' profiles, is explained primarily by the acquisition of greater amounts of experience, skill, and seniority by males, by virtue of their longer employment tenure, greater unionization, and greater likelihood of possessing jobs in which skills are required that are honed by learning and experience.

The profiles for males of both races rise rather steadily from the 25–34 year age group to the 55–64 year group, which runs counter to the education profiles, whereas women seem to benefit most in employments where youthfulness is more rewarded. The profile for white women is markedly horizontal remaining just below the baseline over all classes, substantially below white male ratios in every group. Black males and females remain below the baseline for all classes, although black men in the 55–64 year group approach to within 7 percent of baseline median income.

A Summary

The multifaceted presentation of both static and dynamic income distributions necessitated by the complexity of the concepts makes it difficult to grasp their essential outlines through the burden of detail. Let us try to pull together some of the main threads of the fabric as a preliminary to addressing the problems of redistribution implicit in the dualistic individualism theory of economic justice presented in chapter 8.

1. In postwar American society, for both families and unrelated individuals, and within both groups, for races and sexes, the distribution of money incomes is extremely unequal.

    a. For all-race families, the Gini coefficient in 1987 was about .400, but for black families the coefficient was .455, versus .379 for white families. Black family money income is significantly more unequally distributed than white.

b. For unrelated individuals the Gini coefficient in 1987 was about .460, or substantially above that for families. For black unrelated individuals the coefficient was .490, compared with .442 for whites. As in the case of families, the black unrelated individual income distribution was markedly more unequal than the white.

c. For families, the lowest 40 percent received in 1987 a somewhat smaller proportion of total money income than the highest 5 percent.

d. For families, in 1987, the lowest 40 percent received 15.4 percent of money income, the highest 20 percent received 43.7 percent.

e. For unrelated individuals, in 1987, the lowest 40 percent of the persons received 12.4 percent of money income, the highest 20 percent about 48.4 percent.

f. For families in 1987, the lowest 40 percent of blacks received 11.7 percent of money income and the highest quintile 48.3 percent, versus 16.3 percent and 42.9 percent respectively for white families. In general, comparisons between white and black distributions reveal these "extremes disparities."

g. For unrelated persons, the lowest two quintiles for blacks received 10.4 percent of money income and the highest quintile 51.5 percent. Corresponding data for whites are 12.9 percent and 47.8 percent respectively.

h. When family incomes are adjusted for tax burdens, support payments in kind, private benefits, and family size, the inequality is lessened considerably. The Gini falls from .36 in 1984 to .28, and the lowest 40 percent of families receive 20.7 percent of income (versus an unadjusted level of 15.7 percent) and the highest quintile 36.8 percent (compared with 42.9 percent preadjustment).

2. The degree of inequality as measured by the Gini coefficient has been remarkably stable over the postwar period. Although patterns over time differ for the various groups mentioned above, in general the tendency has been for the Gini to fall from 1947 to about 1970, then to rise gently to the early 1980s, at which point the rate of rise accelerated greatly.

a. The Gini tends to be sensitive cyclically, showing a rise in periods of recession and a fall in prosperity. This cyclicity is greater for unrelated individuals than for families, for lower quintiles than for higher, and for blacks than for whites. For black families and unrelated individuals, however, this cyclicity has been reduced substantially since the 1970s.

3. In 1987 the median income per family member was about $9,733 and for unrelated individuals about $12,559.

a. About 21 percent of all-race families received less than 50 percent of median family income, incorporating about 40 million persons. All-race median family income was $30,853.

b. Approximately 44 percent of black families have incomes less than 50 percent of median family income.

    c. For Hispanic families, 39 percent receive less than 50 percent of median family income.

    d. Only about 19 percent of white families receive less than 50 percent of median family income.

4. About 9.3 percent of white families earn less than $10,000 in money income, versus 30 percent of black families.

    a. About 41 percent of unrelated individuals earn less than $10,000 in money income, although for those in full-time employment median incomes are much higher.

    b. However, over 50 percent of persons earning less than $10,000 are 65 years of age or more and 16 percent are under the age of 24. Only 27 percent are in the prime earning ages of 25 to 54.

    c. Blacks are more heavily concentrated in the lowest income classes and less represented in the highest quintile compared with whites—another example of the extremes disparities—but for those fully employed the gap between whites and blacks closes rapidly. For all individuals over the age of 14, the median income is $13,330 for whites and $8,094 for blacks, but for the family with fully employed family head, values are $21,916 and $18,220.

    d. Hispanics have a median income that is 12 percent above that for blacks and the concentration in income classes below $10,000 per year is smaller than that for blacks.

5. Educational achievement and age are highly correlated with income receipt.

    a. Blacks with a high school education or more have a frequency of 82 percent that of whites with the same attainment. For college the percentage is 50 percent and for postgraduate education only 42 percent. The differential for grammar school completion is not large. The impact on employment and income rather clearly begins at the level of secondary school educational achievement.

    b. Educational levels among Hispanics is a less important explanatory factor than for blacks and whites, but the numbers attaining higher education rise more rapidly through the older age groups than for blacks.

    c. Greater equalization of the educational levels offers one of the major potentials for achieving greater income equality in a voluntarist market society.

6. Differences among the sexes constitute one of the most significant factors in differential income receipts in the postwar period.

    a. In 1987, over 16 percent of all U.S. families were headed by a female with no husband present. Although 13 percent of white families fit this description, fully 43 percent of black families were so constituted. This latter group constitutes one of the major problem groups in terms of income support. In 1984, 50 percent of all black families with heads under the age of 35 were headed by women, of whom 75 percent had never married.

1. Median incomes of such families were $14,620 for all races, $17,018 for whites, but only $9,710 for blacks.
2. About 54 percent of black children were being brought up in such female-headed families.

b. The sharp rise in black families headed by females is a prominent factor in the explanation of a first quintile share of income of only 3.2 percent in 1987, versus 5.1 percent for whites.

c. Apart from the important female-headed family issue, in 1987, 31 percent of white unrelated females and 53 percent of black unrelated females earned less than $7,000 annually in money income. These classes for both whites and blacks are dominated by the very young and the very old, and, in the case of blacks, the presence of the elderly is significantly higher than for whites.

1. Median income for all unrelated black females is only 58 percent of that for whites, but for black females in full-time employment that percentage rises to 87 percent, substantially above the 79 percent figure for like comparisons for males.

d. Among blacks, especially women, persons over the age of 65 constitute an important poverty group. Fully 43 percent of black unrelated women over the age of 65 received less than $7,000 in money income in 1987.

7. For life-cycle incomes, earnings peak in the 35- to 44-year-old cohorts for all races, but for blacks, because females have about closed the income gap with whites in the 25- to 34-year-old group, the peak incomes come in this earlier cohort.

a. Earnings decline rather steadily from the peak earning age group until retirement age, when the earnings fall off steeply.

b. Because this profile corresponds closely with educational attainments, job experience, seniority, and, presumably, productivity, much of this inequality must be judged just in a voluntarist society.

But which of these present inequalities are justifiable within the context of the dualistic individualism theory of economic justice and which unjust? In which cases should the compassionate social concern be expressed in the form of social aid? And were these actions to be taken, what implications do they have for redistribution and how feasible must they be judged to be within the ruling ethos? Answers to these questions must be sought in chapters 10 and 11.

THE FEASIBILITY OF REDISTRIBUTIVE PROGRAMS UNDER THE DUALISTIC INDIVIDUALISM THEORY OF ECONOMIC EQUITY

INTRODUCTION

Within the context of the American ethos and the distribution patterns of the market mechanism discussed in chapter 9, are the potential redistributive implications of the dualistic individualism theory of economic justice, as developed in chapters 7 and 8, feasible? If so, what are the limits to such feasibility in the short and long terms? The questions concerning short-run feasibility are addressed in this chapter, and chapter 11 deals with longer-term feasibility.

It is desirable to emphasize once more the limited ends of the analysis. First, only the narrow distributive implications of the theory will be analyzed within the framework of present political and economic institutions. The ambitious framework of reform proposed in chapter 7 with policy implementation can be instituted only in a period of time much longer than that under discussion here and in chapter 11. However, in accordance with the bill of economic rights and obligations proposed in chapter 7, it will be assumed in these chapters that the incremental tax burdens imposed by the redistributive policies discussed will be borne by individual and corporate income taxes, that current in-kind payments will be converted to money income, and that payments to the undereducated for human capital purposes will be restricted to such usage.

Second, the goals of the analyses are those of a feasibility study, bracketing within rather broad limits of tolerance the incremental amounts of taxation on nonbeneficiaries that would be necessary to implement redistribution policies at various thresholds of support. Those aims are sufficiently challenging, but they do not encompass the full range of subtleties that a deeper analysis of the impacts of the programs uncovers. To explore them in depth would require an extensive analysis of the interactions among such factors as federal, state, and local income taxes, earned-income tax credits on federal taxes, and dependent care expense credits for a large variety of families with differing characteristics. These would include the number of adults and children in the family and their ages, places of residence (states, metropolitan or nonmetropolitan areas, and so forth), the number of earners per household, educational attainments, and a host of others.[1]

Three programs are proposed to bracket the domain of the potentially feasible programs. As a lower bound, in the following section, the study addresses the current poverty program in the United States, describing its defining features and gauging the gross cost of bringing all households up to its prescribed income levels. The analysis continues by estimating the gross cost of lifting households below 50 percent of the relevant median income levels (hereafter, "50 percent program") to those thresholds. Then a similar analysis is undertaken of a program designed to attain 60-percent-of-median-income thresholds (hereafter, "60 percent program"). I then go on to refine the estimates of gross costs of the three programs to arrive at the net tax increments implied for nonbeneficiary or "nonthreshold" taxpayers. These estimates are qualified by a number of simplifications and omissions made in their calculation. Finally, in the last section, final estimates of feasible income support programs for the short and medium term are ventured.

ESTIMATING THE GROSS COSTS OF A POVERTY THRESHOLD PROGRAM

A first set of estimates to gauge the gross costs of the three bracketing threshold programs will focus on a well-known measure: that which would raise each household to its relevant official poverty level as a minimum. In a later section, the net incremental tax burdens on nonthreshold income recipients will be computed under assumptions that either the full costs will be levied in the form of increased individual income taxes or that they will be shared with corporate income taxpayers. In both situations, ceteris paribus conditions are assumed; that is, no other changes in tax programs are introduced simultaneously with the incomes programs.

The Official Poverty Program

As introduced in chapter 8 the official definitions of poverty, developed in the Social Security Administration in 1963 and revised by Federal Interagency Committees in 1969 and 1980, are based on a set of multipliers applied to the estimated cost of food for households with a variety of characteristics. The food budget used in the estimates was based on the Department of Agriculture 1961 Economy Food Plan: because families of three or more were found to spend about one-third of their income on food, the poverty level was set at three times the cost of that plan. The

TABLE 10.1
Poverty Thresholds in 1987, by Size of Family, Number of
Related Children under 18, and Age of Householder

Size of Unit (Persons)	Related Children								
	0	1	2	3	4	5	6	7	≥8
1									
Under 65	$5,909	—	—	—	—	—	—	—	—
65 or Older	5,447	—	—	—	—	—	—	—	—
2									
Under 65	7,606	7,829	—	—	—	—	—	—	—
65 or Older	6,865	7,799	—	—	—	—	—	—	—
3	8,884	9,142	9,151	—	—	—	—	—	—
4	11,714	11,906	11,519	11,558	—	—	—	—	—
5	14,127	14,333	13,894	13,554	13,347	—	—	—	—
6	16,249	16,313	15,978	15,655	15,176	14,892	—	—	—
7	18,697	18,813	18,411	18,130	17,608	16,998	16,330	—	—
8	20,911	21,096	20,715	20,383	19,911	19,312	18,688	18,529	—
9	25,155	25,276	24,940	24,658	24,195	23,557	22,980	22,837	21,958

Source: U. S. Bureau of the Census, *Measuring the Effects of Benefits and Taxes on Income and Poverty: 1986, Current Population Reports*, Series P-60, no. 164-RD-1 (Washington, D.C.: U.S. Government Printing Office, 1988), table A-1, 216, with 1986 data adjusted to 1987 levels by Consumer Price Index-U.

multiplier for smaller families was slightly higher to include the higher fixed costs of smaller families.[2]

The poverty thresholds in 1987, as defined by size of family unit, number of related children under the age of 18, and by age of householder, are given in table 10.1. These thresholds are based wholly on money income and neglect all noncash benefits (food stamps, Medicaid, public housing subsidies, school lunch subsidies, and so forth). They include, however, all government cash benefits, notably Social Security payments, government pensions, and Supplemental Security Income (SSI), which encompasses payments by federal, state, and local welfare agencies to low income persons who are aged 65 years or over, blind, or disabled.

The detail of the forty-eight thresholds in current use, as displayed in table 10.1, can be compressed into the weighted average data over the number of related children of table 10.2 for use in estimating the costs of implementing the poverty program for all eligible persons. The data consist of such averages by size of family up to seven persons, the median income for families of relevant size in 1987, and the percent of such median income that the poverty benefit represents.

TABLE 10.2

Weighted Average Poverty Levels of Income in 1987 by Size of
Household, Median Incomes of All Households of Equal Size, and
Poverty Levels as Percentages of Median Income

Size of Family (Persons)	Weighted Average Poverty Level	Median Income	Poverty Level as % of Median Income
1	$ 5,910	$12,743	46.4%
2	7,398	26,522	27.9
3	9,060	32,433	27.9
4	11,612	37,054	31.3
5	13,737	35,731	38.4
6	15,507	33,478	46.3
7	17,523	31,166	56.2

Source: U.S. Bureau of the Census, *Poverty Status in the United States: 1988, Current Population Reports,* Series P-60, no. 166 (Washington, D.C.: U.S. Government Printing Office, 1989), table A-2, 88; 19–22.

Estimating the Gross Costs

A first step in derivation of estimates of the budgetary costs of bringing all persons below such thresholds to their levels is to gather estimates of the numbers of persons affected. These data are listed in table 10.3.

The data are distressing but contain no large surprises in the light of chapter 9's analysis. It is noteworthy nonetheless that one-third of blacks are below poverty thresholds, that an equal percentage of families headed by women are in poverty, and that 34 percent of female-headed white families and 57 percent of such black families are impoverished. Given the extremely minimalist nature of the poverty level definitions, even in light of the need to augment such money income measures by in-kind benefits and to interpret them in life-cyle terms, the data heighten awareness of the magnitude of the problem the nation faces.

A last datum needed in the calculation of the money income necessary to lift all such persons to their poverty thresholds is the average amount of income shortfall from such levels. For the relevant income groups, these calculations are reproduced in table 10.4.

Use of the data of tables 10.3 and 10.4 results in the estimates of compensatory income listed in table 10.5. Two such estimates are made for cross-checking purposes: the first, using averages of shortfalls per person in families and for unrelated individuals, and the second using a finer classification of income groups.

It is estimated therefore that in 1987 it would have imposed a gross budgetary burden of between $50 billion and 53 billion to have lifted all

TABLE 10.3

Persons below Poverty Thresholds, 1987, by Race, Sex, and
Family Status

	Below Poverty Threshold	Poverty Rate
1. Persons		
Total	32,341,000	13.4%
White	21,249,000	10.4
Black	9,577,000	32.6
In Families	24,840,000	12.0
Heads of Households	7,005,000	10.7
Related Children		
under 18 Years	12,391,000	19.9
under 6 Years	4,852,000	22.4
Other members	5,445,000	
In Unrelated Subfamilies	644,000	57.5
Reference Persons	260,000	56.4
Children under 18 Years	374,000	61.0
Unrelated Individuals	6,857,000	20.8
Male	2,683,000	17.5
Female	4,174,000	23.6
2. Families		
Total	7,005,000	10.7
Married Couples	3,011,000	5.8
Male Householder, No wife	340,000	12.0
Female Householder, No Husband	3,654,000	34.2
White	4,567,000	8.1
Married Couples	2,382,000	5.1
Male Householder, No Wife	224,000	9.8
Female Householder, No Husband	1,961,000	26.9
Black	2,117,000	29.4
Married Couples	439,000	11.9
Male Householder, No Wife	101,000	23.4
Female Householder, No Husband	1,577,000	57.1

Source: U.S. Bureau of the Census, *Money Income and Poverty Status in the United States: 1988, Current Population Reports*, Series P-60, no. 166 (Washington, D.C.: U.S. Government Printing Office, 1989), table 17, 57, and table 25, 78.

TABLE 10.4

Average Amount of Money Income Required to Raise Poor
Families and Persons to Respective Poverty
Thresholds, 1987

Income Group	Income Shortfall
1. All Poor Families	$4,635
a. Per Family Member (3.46 persons)	1,340
2. Poor Families with Female Head of Household, No Spouse Present	4,999
a. Per Family Member (3.27 persons)	1,529
3. All Married Couple Families	4,256
a. Per Family Member (3.82 persons)	1,115
4. Unrelated Individuals	2,512
a. Women	2,222
b. Men	2,942

Source: U.S. Bureau of the Census, *Money Income and Poverty Status in the United States: 1988, Current Population Reports*, Series P-60, no. 166 (Washington, D.C.: U.S. Government Printing Office, 1989), 8. The data in 1988 dollars have been adjusted to 1987 dollars by deflation with the CPI-U.

TABLE 10.5

Estimates of Compensatory Poverty Threshold Amounts, 1987

Income Unit	Number of Units	Per Unit Amount	Total (thousands)
A. Aggregate Estimate			
1. Family Persons	24,237,000	$1,340	$32,477,580
2. Unrelated Persons	8,104,000	2,512	20,357,248
Total			$52,834,828
B. Detailed Estimate			
1. Female Households, No Spouse Present	3,654,000	4,999	18,266,346
2. Married Couples	3,011,000	4,256	12,814,816
3. Other Families	340,000	4,635	1,575,900
Total, Families			$32,657,062
4. Unrelated Persons	6,857,000		
a. Male	2,683,000	2,942	7,893,386
b. Female	4,174,000	2,222	9,274,628
Total, Unrelated Persons			$17,168,014
Total, Households			$49,825,076

Source: Tables 10.3 and 10.4.

persons below the poverty thresholds at that time up to those levels. As noted, these transfers are in *cash* benefits alone. In 1986, means-tested government cash transfers, which include aid to families with dependent children, other welfare payments, and SSI, were $23 billion, or, in 1987 dollars, $23.8 billion.[3] These payments are included in money income levels before shortfalls are computed. In that year, government means-tested noncash benefits, including Medicaid, food stamps, free or reduced-price school lunches, and rent subsidies, amounted to an additional $26 billion in 1986 dollars, or about $27 billion in 1987 dollars.[4]

Hence, in 1987, the total of means-tested noncash transfers to the poor equaled about one-half the incremental amount I estimate would have been necessary to meet poverty thresholds. It should be repeated that the money incomes of the poor include such cash benefits as Social Security payments, government retirement pensions at all levels, Aid to Families With Dependent Children (AFDC), SSI, and the like. These must be understood to be existing burdens on the taxpayer that are not included in the incremental estimates above.

GROSS COSTS OF A
50-PERCENT-OF-MEDIAN-INCOME THRESHOLD

To probe more generous implications of the dualistic individualism theory of economic equity, and the upper bound of program feasibility, I have chosen next a threshold of 50 percent of the relevant median income levels computed in chapter 9. For this suggested program, using similar calculations to those of the poverty threshold program used earlier, and employing both an aggregate and detailed analysis, the gross cost estimates detailed in table 10.6 are derived.

My estimate of the gross money income increment necessary to lift persons to 50 percent of the relevant per capita median incomes in 1987 is about $100 billion, or about four times the amount of means-tested noncash transfers in 1986 expressed in 1987 dollars. Adjustments will be necessary to reduce these gross needs to net needs, but the magnitude of the former suggest that implementation of such a program would require a substantial short-term change in the American ethos.

GROSS COSTS OF A
60-PERCENT-OF-MEDIAN-INCOME THRESHOLD

To gauge the rate of rise in gross costs as thresholds mount above 50 percent, I assume that each household is given money income equal to 60 percent of its relevant per capita median income under 1987 condi-

TABLE 10.6
Estimates of Compensatory Threshold Amounts to Bring All
Persons to 50 Percent of Median Incomes, 1987

Income Class	Number of Units	Persons	Shortfall Per Person	Total (thousands)
A. Aggregate Estimate				
1. Families, All Races				
Under $2,500	1,172,394	3,446,838	$4,441	$15,307,408
2,500–4,999	1,706,485	5,170,650	3,628	18,759,118
5,000–7,499	2,351,301	7,194,981	2,824	20,318,626
7,500–9,999	2,435,974	7,234,843	1,920	13,890,899
10,000–12,499	2,963,552	8,712,843	1,039	9,052,644
12,500–14,999	2,898,419	8,318,463	75	623,885
Total, Families, All Races				$77,952,580
2. Unrelated Individuals, All Races				
Under $2,000	1,845,000	1,845,000	4,840	8,929,800
2,000–2,999	679,000	679,000	3,340	2,267,860
3,000–3,999	1,067,000	1,067,000	2,340	2,496,780
4,000–4,999	2,038,000	2,038,000	1,340	2,730,920
5,000–5,999	1,802,000	1,802,000	340	612,680
Total, Unrelated Individuals, All Races				$17,038,040
Aggregate Estimate				$94,990,620
B. Detailed Estimate				
1. Families, White				
Under $2,500	756,594	2,163,859	$4,441	$ 9,609,698
2,500–4,999	1,042,418	3,054,285	3,628	11,080,946
5,000–7,499	1,642,089	4,844,163	2,824	13,679,916
7,500–9,999	1,793,408	4,985,674	1,920	9,573,494
10,000–12,499	2,342,639	6,629,668	1,039	6,888,225
12,500–14,999	2,443,518	6,792,980	75	509,474
Total, White Families				$51,341,753
2. Families, Black				
Under $2,500	356,697	1,084,359	4,441	4,815,638
2,500–4,999	610,763	1,966,657	3,628	7,135,032
5,000–7,499	620,811	2,073,509	2,824	5,855,589
7,500–9,999	558,371	1,937,547	1,920	3,720,090
10,000–12,499	508,132	1,697,161	1,039	1,763,350
12,500–14,999	386,840	1,303,651	75	97,774
Total, Black Families				$23,387,473

TABLE 10.6 (*cont.*)

Income Class	Number of Units	Persons	Shortfall Per Person	Total (thousands)
3. Families, Net Other-Race				
Under $2,500	64,626	202,926	4,441	901,194
2,500–4,999	98,850	343,010	3,628	1,244,440
5,000–7,499	139,958	492,652	2,824	1,391,249
7,500–9,999	134,987	492,703	1,920	945,990
10,000–12,499	147,033	574,899	1,039	597,320
12,500–14,999	133,458	476,445	75	35,733
Total, Net Other-Race Families				$ 5,115,926
Total, All Families				$79,845,152
4. Unrelated Individuals, White Male				
Under $2,000	587,328	587,328	4,840	2,842,668
2,000–2,999	229,824	229,824	3,340	767,612
3,000–3,999	280,896	280,896	2,340	657,297
4,000–4,999	459,648	459,648	1,340	615,928
5,000–5,999	421,344	421,344	340	143,257
Total, Unrelated Individuals, White Male				$ 5,026,761
5. Unrelated Individuals, White Female				
Under $2,000	755,972	755,972	4,840	3,658,904
2,000–2,999	277,704	277,704	3,340	927,532
3,000–3,999	509,124	509,124	2,340	1,191,350
4,000–4,999	1,033,676	1,033,676	1,340	1,385,126
5,000–5,999	1,064,532	1,064,532	340	361,941
Total, Unrelated Individuals, White Female				$ 7,524,853
6. Unrelated Individuals, Black Male				
Under $2,000	234,475	234,475	4,840	1,134,859
2,000–2,999	60,175	60,175	3,340	200,985
3,000–3,999	101,675	101,675	2,340	237,920
4,000–4,999	190,900	190,900	1,340	255,806
5,000–5,999	118,275	118,275	340	40,214
Total, Unrelated Individuals, Black Male				$ 1,869,784
7. Unrelated Individuals, Black Female				
Under $2,000	182,868	182,868	4,840	885,081
2,000–2,999	82,104	82,104	3,340	274,227
3,000–3,999	139,950	139,950	2,340	327,483
4,000–4,999	311,622	311,622	1,340	417,573
5,000–5,999	156,744	156,744	340	53,293
Total, Unrelated Individuals, Black Female				$ 1,957,657

TABLE 10.6 (*cont.*)

Income Class	Number of Units	Persons	Shortfall Per Person	Total (thousands)
Total, Unrelated Individuals				$16,379,055
Detailed Estimate				$96,224,207

Source: Tables 9.7, 9.8, 9.9, 9.10, 9.14, 9.18. Shortfalls were computed from mean incomes in each class less 50 percent of median income for all race families and unrelated individuals. These were $4,866 per member of families and $6,280 for unrelated individuals. Other-race families are estimates of those families not counted in the black and white family categories.

tions. The computations—similar in all respects to those of table 10.6—are reproduced in table 10.7.

The estimate of the gross cost of lifting all households below the 60-percent-of-median-income threshold to its levels is about $150 billion annually, or about six times current means-tested in-kind subsidies.

ESTIMATES OF CETERIS PARIBUS TAX BURDENS

The best available study of the distribution of tax burdens specifies twelve different definitions of income that permit the computation of such burdens and the receipt of means-tested and non-means-tested, cash and noncash government transfer payments by quintiles. Because it is based on calendar year 1986 data,[5] all calculations will be done in terms of that year and then projected into dollars of the study year 1987. Unfortunately, 1986 does not reflect the effects of the Tax Reform Act of 1986 which took effect in 1987, but because that act was designed to be tax neutral overall, and because our concern is simply that of feasibility, it was deemed preferable to employ the extensive results of the study and project one year forward rather than to initiate a much less intensive and detailed analysis.

The Official Poverty Threshold

From the detailed estimate of table 10.5, about $49,825 million in additional cash income would have been necessary in 1987 to bring households up to official poverty thresholds. A closer look must now be given to the net incremental tax burden that such a commitment would inflict on nonbeneficiaries. From the gross amount of supplement must be deducted the cash value of the means-tested noncash benefits received by these households (hereafter, the thresholders), because as indicated

TABLE 10.7
Estimates of Compensatory Threshold Amounts to Bring All
Persons to 60 Percent of Median Incomes, 1987

Income Class	Number of Units	Persons	Shortfall Per Person	Total (thousands)
A. Aggregate Estimate				
1. Families, All Races				
Under $2,500	1,172,394	3,446,838	$5,415	$ 18,664,628
2,500–4,999	1,706,485	5,170,650	4,602	23,795,331
5,000–7,499	2,351,301	7,194,981	3,798	27,326,538
7,500–9,999	2,435,974	7,234,843	2,894	20,937,636
10,000–12,499	2,963,552	8,712,843	2,013	17,538,953
12,500–14,999	2,898,419	8,318,463	1,049	8,726,068
15,000–17,499	3,158,951	9,192,547	256	2,353,292
Total, Families, All Races				$119,342,446
2. Unrelated Individuals, All Races				
Under $2,000	1,845,000	1,845,000	6,535	12,057,075
2,000–2,999	679,000	679,000	5,035	3,418,765
3,000–3,999	1,067,000	1,067,000	4,035	4,305,345
4,000–4,999	2,038,000	2,038,000	3,035	6,185,330
5,000–5,999	1,802,000	1,802,000	2,035	3,667,070
6,000–6,999	1,883,000	1,883,000	1,035	1,948,905
7,000–7,999	815,015	815,015	35	28,526
Total, Unrelated Individuals, All Races				$31,611,016
Aggregate Estimate				$150,953,462
B. Detailed Estimate				
1. Families, White				
Under $2,500	756,594	2,163,859	$5,415	$ 11,717,296
2,500–4,999	1,042,418	3,054,285	4,602	14,055,820
5,000–7,499	1,642,089	4,844,163	3,798	18,398,131
7,500–9,999	1,793,408	4,985,674	2,894	14,428,541
10,000–12,499	2,342,639	6,629,668	2,013	13,345,521
12,500–14,999	2,443,518	6,792,980	1,049	7,125,836
15,000–17,499	2,650,881	7,475,484	256	1,913,724
Total, White Families				$ 80,984,869

TABLE 10.7 (*cont.*)

Income Class	Number of Units	Persons	Shortfall Per Person	Total (thousands)
2. Families, Black				
Under $2,500	356,697	1,084,359	$5,415	$ 5,871,804
2,500–4,999	610,763	1,966,657	4,602	9,050,556
5,000–7,499	620,811	2,073,509	3,798	7,875,187
7,500–9,999	558,371	1,937,547	2,894	5,607,261
10,000–12,499	508,132	1,697,161	2,013	3,416,385
12,500–14,999	386,840	1,303,651	1,049	1,367,530
15,000–17,499	454,304	1,526,461	256	390,774
Total, Black Families				$33,579,497
3. Families, Other-Race				
Under $2,500	64,626	202,926	5,415	1,098,844
2,500–4,999	98,850	343,010	4,602	1,578,532
5,000–7,499	139,958	492,652	3,798	1,871,092
7,500–9,999	134,987	492,703	2,894	1,425,882
10,000–12,499	147,033	574,899	2,013	1,157,272
12,500–14,999	133,458	476,445	1,049	499,791
15,000–17,499	114,529	412,304	256	105,550
Total, Net Other-Race Families				$7,736,963
Total, All Families				$122,301,329
4. Unrelated Individuals, White Male				
Under $2,000	587,328	587,328	6,535	3,838,188
2,000–2,999	229,824	229,824	5,035	1,157,164
3,000–3,999	280,896	280,896	4,035	1,133,415
4,000–4,999	459,648	459,648	3,035	1,395,032
5,000–5,999	421,344	421,344	2,035	857,435
6,000–6,999	510,720	510,720	1,035	528,595
7,000–7,999	239,081	239,081	35	8,368
Total, Unrelated Individuals, White Male				$ 8,918,197
5. Unrelated Individuals, White Female				
Under $2,000	755,972	755,972	6,535	4,940,277
2,000–2,999	277,704	277,704	5,035	1,398,240
3,000–3,999	509,124	509,124	4,035	2,054,315
4,000– 4,999	1,033,676	1,033,676	3,035	3,137,207
5,000–5,999	1,064,532	1,064,532	2,035	2,166,323
6,000–6,999	1,095,388	1,095,388	1,035	1,133,727
7,000–7,999	503,493	503,493	35	17,621
Total, Unrelated Individuals, White Female				$14,847,710

TABLE 10.7 (*cont.*)

Income Class	Number of Units	Persons	Shortfall Per Person	Total (thousands)
6. Unrelated Individuals, Black Male				
Under $2,000	234,475	234,475	6,535	1,532,294
2,000–2,999	60,175	60,175	5,035	302,981
3,000–3,999	101,675	101,675	4,035	410,259
4,000–4,999	190,900	190,900	3,035	579,382
5,000–5,999	118,275	118,275	2,035	240,690
6,000–6,999	126,575	126,575	1,035	131,005
7,000–7,999	51,875	51,875	35	1,816
Total, Unrelated Individuals, Black Male				$ 3,198,427
7. Unrelated Individuals, Black Female				
Under $2,000	182,868	182,868	6,535	1,195,042
2,000–2,999	82,104	82,104	5,035	413,394
3,000–3,999	139,950	139,950	4,035	564,698
4,000–4,999	311,622	311,622	3,035	945,773
5,000–5,999	156,744	156,744	2,035	318,974
6,000–6,999	123,156	123,156	1,035	127,466
7,000–7,999	76,640	76,640	35	2,682
Total, Unrelated Individuals, Black Female				$ 3,568,029
Total, Unrelated Individuals				$ 30,532,363
Detailed Estimate				$152,833,692

Source: Tables 9.7, 9.8, 9.9, 9.10, 9.14, 9.18. Shortfalls were computed from mean incomes in each class less 60 percent of median income for all race families and unrelated individuals. These were $5,840 per member of families and $7,535 for unrelated individuals. Other-race families are estimates of those families not counted in the black and white family categories.

above these benefits will be assumed to be paid in cash under the new policy and will contribute toward the supplement. A second deduction from the amount that must be paid will be the federal income taxes that will be forthcoming on that cash supplement from the thresholders. After these deductions are made, the remaining amount of the supplement is the net incremental tax payment that will be paid by nonthresholders.

Because the Census study for 1986 (hereafter, the Census study) will be drawn on to make these estimates, it will be necessary to convert 1987 dollars to those of 1986 through use of the Consumer Price Index-U series. The gross supplement in such value units is $48,071 million. The first step is to estimate the amount of the means-tested noncash benefits that accrued to thresholders in 1986.

TABLE 10.8

Household Income Brackets, by Quintiles,
with Amounts of Means-Tested Noncash
Benefits Received, 1986

Quintile	Brackets	Means-Tested Noncash Benefits (thousands 1986 dollars)
1Q	$0–10,373	$14,298,904
2Q	10,374–19,717	6,442,560
3Q	19,718–30,601	2,612,816
4Q	30,602–45,995	1,020,072
5Q	45,996–	1,091,656
Total		$25,466,008

Source: U.S. Bureau of the Census, Measuring the Effects of Benefits and Taxes on Income and Poverty: 1986, Current Population Reports, Series P-60, no. 164-RD-1 (Washington, D.C.: U.S. Government Printing Office, 1988). (Hereafter, Benefits and Taxes.)

Table 10.8 lists, by income quintiles, the brackets of cash income within the quintiles and the value of noncash benefits received. Each quintile contains 17,896,000 households. Table 10.5's detailed estimates include 13,862,000 households under official poverty income limits, or about 77 percent of a quintile's households. On the assumption that the thresholders are included in 1Q, and that they receive 77 percent of the quintile's benefits (which is, no doubt, an underestimate), we estimate that the amount of means-tested noncash benefits received was $11,010 million. The pretax net amount of the threshold supplement, therefore, is $37,061 million.

Thresholders will be required to pay federal income taxes on the whole of the incremental $48,071 million, which will reduce the tax burden shifted to nonthresholders. In 1986, households in 1Q had a mean income of $5,904 and paid a mean income tax of $36. Since the mean income of poverty thresholders is estimated to have been $3,541,[6] or about equal to 60 percent of 1Q mean income, I shall use 60 percent of this mean income tax, or $22, as representative of the amount paid by them. With the proposed supplemental income, the average household income for beneficiaries will rise to $6,980, or 47 percent of the 2Q mean income in 1986. The mean income tax paid by 2Q occupants was $633, and we assume that the income tax paid by poverty thresholders would be 47 percent of that, or $297. Subtracting $36 from this to obtain an estimate of the mean incremental tax, a figure of $261 per threshold household is arrived at. Multiplying that by the estimated 13,862,000 households affected yields an estimate of federal income tax reclama-

TABLE 10.9

Distribution of Nonthresholder Personal Income Taxes, 1986,
with Estimated Burdens of Poverty Threshold Policy on nonthresholders
(thousands of dollars)

Unit	Fed. Income Tax	% of Taxes	Incremental Policy Taxes	Total Taxes
1Q Nonthresh.	$ 148,179	.04%	$ 13,182	$ 161,361
2Q	11,328,168	3.14	1,007,787	12,335,955
3Q	36,955,240	10.26	3,287,648	40,242,888
4Q	78,044,456	21.66	6,943,066	84,987,522
5Q	233,864,928	64.90	20,805,317	254,670,245
Totals	360,340,971	100.0	33,443,000	393,783,971

Source: U.S. Bureau of the Census, Benefits and Taxes, 18.

TABLE 10.10

Estimated Tax Burdens of Poverty Threshold Policy
as Percentages of Money Income, 1986

Unit	Total Money Income (thousands 1987 dollars)	Actual Tax as % of Income	After-Policy Tax as % of Income
1Q Nonthresh.	$ 25,188,246	.61%	.66%
2Q	276,196,675	4.25	4.65
3Q	466,696,329	8.21	8.97
4Q	685,965,698	11.79	12.89
5Q	1,314,391,967	18.44	20.15
Total/Aggregate %	2,768,438,915	13.49	14.74

tion of $3,618 million from the threshold supplement. Therefore, I estimate that the posttax net incremental amount of the income tax burden to be borne by nonthresholders is $33,443 million.

Table 10.9 reveals the federal income taxes paid in 1986 by nonthresholders (with the figure for nonthresholders in 1Q estimated as simply proportionate to their household numbers). On the assumption that nonthresholders will share the additional burden in the same proportions as they shared the total 1986 federal tax levies, the incremental taxes they would be forced to pay and the total hypothetical tax burden they would have borne in 1986 are listed in table 10.9.

Table 10.10 presents total money income received in 1986, converted to 1987 dollars with the CPI-U, and burdens computed as percentages of those incomes. The policy implies an overall rise of 9.3 percent in the percentage of income taken in federal individual income taxes, with

TABLE 10.11
Tax Burdens on Nonthresholders of Poverty Threshold Policy
Assuming Corporate Income Taxes Bear 19 Percent
of the Incremental Taxes, in 1987 Dollars

Unit	Total Money Income (thousands 1987 dollars)	Actual Tax as % of Income	After-Policy Tax as % of Income
1Q Nonthresh.	$ 25,188,246	.61%	.65%
2Q	276,196,675	4.25	4.57
3Q	466,696,329	8.21	8.90
4Q	685,965,698	11.79	12.68
5Q	1,314,391,967	18.44	19.83
Total/Aggregate %	2,768,438,915	13.49	14.51

equivalent rises in each of the quintiles, and the same percentage rise in total taxes paid.

The direct impact of the tax increment on individuals could be lessened if the poverty threshold supplement were borne in part by corporation income taxes. In 1987–88, of total federal income tax collections of $495,376 million, corporations paid 19 percent.[7] Were this same percentage of the incremental after-tax burden to be paid by corporations, the personal income tax portion would be reduced to $27,089 million, and were this distributed among nonthresholder units in the same manner as that assumed in table 10.9, the personal tax burdens would be reduced to those shown in table 10.11. Comparison of the data with those of table 10.10 reveal that individual income taxes would rise by 7.6 percent.

The 50-Percent-Median-Income Threshold

In the calculations above, 11,860,337 families with threshold income requirements of $15,426 and 7,958,240 unrelated individuals with threshold levels of $6,280 were identified for the 50 percent threshold. This involves 19,818,577 households, therefore, with a weighted mean threshold of $11,749 in 1987 money. I have again used the CPI-U series to deflate throughout the analysis, and doing so reduces that weighted mean to $11,336 at 1986 prices. All dollar values hereafter will be in 1986 dollars unless stated otherwise. The total money income needed to give each threshold household that floor income was $224,733 million, of which about $128,568 million was obtained by those households through the market mechanism and by means-tested and non-means-tested government cash transfers. This implies a shortfall of $96,165 million in 1986.

TABLE 10.12
Money Income Brackets, Including Cash Transfers,
Incomes Received, and Federal Income Taxes Paid, 1986

Quintile	Brackets	Income Received (thousands)	Fed. Income Taxes (thousands)
1Q	$ 0–10,373	$ 105,657,984	$ 644,256
2Q	10,374–19,717	266,471,440	11,328,168
3Q	19,718–30,601	450,263,360	36,955,240
4Q	30,602–45,995	661,811,976	78,044,456
5Q	45,996–	1,268,110,560	233,864,928
Totals		2,752,315,320	360,837,048

Source: U.S. Bureau of the Census, Benefits and Taxes.

Table 10.12 lists the brackets of money incomes for each quintile, the total income received, and federal income taxes paid by the quintiles. The poverty households will include 1Q recipients plus that portion of 2Q recipients that accounts for $22,910 million, or the shortfall of income received by 1Q occupants below the threshold requirement. Assuming a uniform distribution within 2Q of recipients over the bracket, with each quintile containing 17,896,000 households, I find that we need the lowest 2,097,420 households with incomes ranging from $10,373 to $11,469 to obtain the necessary additional income receipts. These householders account for 11.7 percent of the total in the quintile and have a mean income of $11,469. The total of threshold households in the first two quintiles—19,993,420, or slightly more than was calculated for 1987—will constitute the "thresholders" hereafter.

Suppose again that the program to raise thresholders to the 50 percent level were financed wholly by increases in individual federal income taxes. On the assumption that 50 percent of the 1986 means-tested noncash receipts in 2Q went to thresholders, I estimate that of the $25,466 million in such payments a total of $17,520 million went to thresholders. As in the poverty threshold exercise, these payments must be deducted from the $9,165 million gross incremental threshold requirement, to obtain a pretax amount of $78,645 million necessary for distribution to thresholders.

To estimate the net incremental tax burden on nonthresholders it is necessary once more to deduct the income taxes that would be paid by thresholders on their supplements. In terms of 1986 tax structure an estimate of this amount can be made in the following manner. The mean income of individuals in 2Q was $14,890, and the mean income for

TABLE 10.13

Distribution of Nonthresholder Personal Income Taxes, 1986,
with Estimated Burdens of 50-Percent-of-Median Income Policy on
Nonthresholders (thousands of dollars)

Unit	Fed. Income Tax	% of Taxes	Incremental Taxes	Total Taxes
2Q Nonthresh.	$ 8,780,062	2.42	$ 1,719,821	$ 10,499,883
3Q	36,955,240	10.39	7,383,862	44,339,102
4Q	78,044,456	21.80	15,492,606	93,537,062
5Q	233,864,928	65.39	46,470,711	280,335,639
Totals	357,644,686	100.0	71,067,000	428,711,686

Source: U.S. Bureau of the Census, Benefits and Taxes, 18.

thresholders in that quintile is estimated at $11,469, or 76 percent of the 2Q mean income. The mean federal income tax payment for households in 2Q was $633, or 4.2 percent of mean income. Applying this percentage to thresholders' mean income yields a mean tax payment of $481 per household. Thus, thresholders in 1Q paid $644 million and the thresholders in 2Q are estimated to have paid $1,009 million, so actual mean thresholder income taxes per household are estimated to have been $83. Mean threshold income is estimated to be $11,749, or 78 percent of 2Q income. This percentage of actual 2Q tax paid is $446 per household. Therefore, the incremental tax per household is estimated at $446 less $83, or $363. For all threshold households this amounts to $7,578 million. Hence, the net tax burden to be shouldered by nonthreshold taxpayers is $71,067 million. Table 10.13 lists the absolute and percentage amounts of taxes paid in 1986 by thresholders and nonthresholders, and the incremental tax burdens on the latter implied by the 50 percent program are given on the assumption that they are distributed proportionately to total taxes paid in 1986.

Under this distributive scheme, federal income taxes borne by nonthresholders would rise about 20 percent, with each quintile unit bearing the same proportionate increase. Not surprisingly, this is about double the proportionate increase required for the poverty program. In table 10.14 these 1986 dollars are converted into 1987 dollars, and the total tax burden is calculated as a percent of income received. Taxes would rise from about 13.8 percent of total nonthresholder money income to 16.5 percent, or by about 19.8 percent.

As developed earlier, were corporations to bear 19 percent of the supplemental burden, the personal income tax portion would be reduced to $54,693 million, and were this distributed among nonthresholder

TABLE 10.14

Estimated Total Tax Burdens of 50-Percent-of-Median-Income Threshold
as Percentages of Total Money Income, 1986, in 1987 Dollars

Unit	Total Money Income (thousands 1987 dollars)	Actual Tax as % of Income	After-Policy Tax as % of Income
2Q Nonthresh.	$ 225,478,689	4.04%	4.83%
3Q	466,696,329	8.21	9.85
4Q	685,965,698	11.79	14.13
5Q	1,314,391,967	18.44	21.11
Total/Aggregate %	2,692,532,683	13.77	16.50

TABLE 10.15

Estimated Total Tax Burdens of 50-Percent-of-Median-Income Threshold as
Percentages of Total Money Income, 1986, Assuming Corporate Income Taxes
Bear 19 Percent of the Incremental Taxes, in 1987 Dollars

Unit	Total Money Income (thousands 1987 dollars)	Actual Tax as % of Income	After-Policy Tax as % of Income
2Q Nonthresh.	$ 225,478,689	4.04%	4.84%
3Q	466,696,329	8.21	9.54
4Q	685,965,698	11.79	13.69
5Q	1,314,391,967	18.44	21.41
Total/Aggregate %	2,692,532,683	13.77	15.98

units in the same manner as that assumed in table 10.13, the personal tax
burdens would be reduced to those shown in table 10.15. Comparison of
the data with those of table 10.14 reveals a tempering of the rise in tax
payments as a proportion of income from 19.8 to 16.0 percent on the
average.

The 60-Percent-Median-Income Threshold

Computation of the tax burden for the 60 percent program repeats the
methodology of the 50 percent program. Table 10.7's detailed estimates
identified 17,000,906 families with an average shortfall of $7,194 and
9,925,764 unrelated persons with mean shortfall of $3,076 for this
threshold category. For the total of 26,926,670 households, therefore,
the weighted average shortfall was $5,676 in 1987 dollars. The threshold
income levels (at 60 percent of relevant median incomes) were $12,626

TABLE 10.16

Distribution of Nonthresholder Personal Income Taxes, 1986, with Estimated
Burdens of 60-Percent-of-Median-Income Policy on Nonthresholders
(thousands of dollars)

Unit	Fed. Income Tax	% of Taxes	Incremental Taxes	Total Taxes
2Q Nonthresh.	$ 4,531,267	1.28	$ 1,551,872	$ 6,083,139
3Q	36,955,240	10.46	12,681,704	49,636,944
4Q	78,044,456	22.08	26,769,792	104,814,248
5Q	233,864,928	66.18	80,236,632	314,101,560
Totals	353,395,891	100.0	121,240,000	474,635,891

Source: U.S. Bureau of the Census, Benefits and Taxes, 18.

for the average family and $5,024 for unrelated individuals. The weighted average household threshold income was $9,758. Therefore, the money income needed to reach the 60 percent threshold for all persons was $287,744 million, of which the thresholders earned $134,910 million, leaving a gross shortfall of $152,834 million.

In 1986 dollars these convert to a threshold income of $277,615 million, private income of $130,161 million, and a gross shortfall of $147,454 million. From table 10.12, such households would include those in 1Q and and that portion of the lowest earners in 2Q accounting for $171,957 million under the assumptions made in the section above on the 50 percent program. This includes 12,495,967 households earning between $10,374 and $17,159, with a mean income of $13,767. The thresholders in this category, therefore, include all of the households of 1Q and the households in this portion of the households of 2Q.

A first deduction from the gross shortfall of the thresholders is their receipt of means-tested noncash transfers on their reported 1987 incomes. I will assume that all such transfers would have accrued to thresholders in 1Q. Also, thresholders would have accounted for almost 70 percent of the 2Q households and I will assume that fully 90 percent of noncash transfers would have been received by them. The data of table 10.8 provide an estimate then of $20,097 million in means-tested noncash benefits to be deducted from the gross shortfall of $147,454 million to yield a pretax burden of $127,357 million.

From table 10.12, the thresholders' $277,615 million income would have yielded $7,441 million in federal income taxes if I assume their share of 2Q receipts was only 60 percent rather than the 70 percent of households among thresholders. With earned income of $130,161 million in 1986 dollars, however, about $1,324 million was actually paid, so

TABLE 10.17

Estimated Total Tax Burdens of 60-Percent-of-Median-Income Threshold
as Percentages of Total Money Income, 1986, in 1987 Dollars

Unit	Total Money Income (thousands 1987 dollars)	Actual Tax as % of Income	After-Policy Tax as % of Income
2Q Nonthresh.	$ 110,476,927	4.25%	5.71%
3Q	466,696,329	8.21	10.02
4Q	685,965,698	11.79	15.84 .
5Q	1,314,391,967	18.44	24.77
Total/Aggregate %	2,577,530,891	14.21	19.09

TABLE 10.18

Estimated Total Tax Burdens of 60-Percent-of-Median-Income Threshold as
Percentages of Total Money Income, 1986, Assuming Corporate Income Taxes
Bear 19 Percent of the Incremental Taxes, in 1987 Dollars

Unit	Total Money Income (thousands 1987 dollars)	Actual Tax as % of Income	After-Policy Tax as % of Income
2Q Nonthresh.	$ 110,476,927	4.25%	5.43%
3Q	466,696,329	8.21	10.49
4Q	685,965,698	11.79	15.07
5Q	1,314,391,967	18.44	23.57
Total/Aggregate %	2,577,530,891	14.21	18.16

that the incremental taxes would be $6,117 million. The net incremental
tax burden on nonthresholders, therefore, is the gross threshold income
less money income of beneficiaries, less means-tested noncash benefits,
less income tax paid on the shortfall income. This amounts to an estimated $121,240 million.

Table 10.16 estimates the nonthresholder tax burdens were they to be
borne entirely by individuals and distributed in the same proportions
among the quintiles as ruled in 1986. This is a 34.3 percent overall tax
rise for nonthresholders. Table. 10.17 converts these burdens into 1987
dollars and reports the burdens in terms of incomes received.

Finally, on the assumption that corporate income taxes would bear 19
percent of the net burden, table 10.18 reproduces the reductions in direct individual tax burdens. Such a policy would reduce direct individual
tax impacts on nonthresholders from 34.3 percent to about 27.8 percent
of money income.

Some Caveats

It is worthwhile to stress once again that these estimates of tax burdens should be considered rough estimates only, suitable for gauging feasibility, but necessary of refinement for more accurate estimates of tax burdens for other purposes. Some important reasons for this reservation will be given below.

First, the Census Bureau model that computed the estimates of means-tested noncash benefits included Medicaid benefits at their "fungible" value, not the actual tax value of the services rendered. The computation attempted to value such services at the extent to which they freed up resources that could have been spent on medical services. Therefore, the estimates of such noncash benefits understate the tax burdens they impose on nonthresholders. School lunch subsidies are included at their full tax cost, however.

Second, I have not taken into account changes that would occur in state and local income taxes if the investigated policies were implemented. For example, changing Medicaid noncash benefits to federal cash benefits would lower the state income taxes currently paid to provide a portion of such subsidies. Similarly, converting housing subsidies to cash payments at the federal level would lessen burdens on states and localities. In ignoring these reductions my figures may overestimate the tax burdens suffered by nonthresholders. Alternatively, it is also a fairly safe assumption that uses other than tax remissions will be found to absorb the freed funds.

Third, the estimates given in the section on 50-percent-of-median-income thresholds assume that the cash and noncash benefits now being enjoyed by nonthresholders would continue at their full value were the social policies installed. I have argued in chapter 7 that the dualistic individualism theory of economic equity would recommend that many of these be put on a means-tested basis. Social Security income payments, for example, are a prime example of important entitlements that would be scaled back considerably under such a scheme, providing important tax savings to many nonthresholders. Agricultural subsidies and mortgage interest subsidization also should be included in means-tested programs.

Therefore, were the threshold support policies analyzed to be introduced along with such accompanying reforms, net tax burdens could be substantially lessened. Of course, the political feasibility of instituting such reforms in the short run would have to be considered alongside the economic feasibility of the threshold programs. In the short run the changes are deemed to be infeasible, especially in the light of recent failures to reduce such middle class entitlements to obtain federal budget reductions.

Fourth, the ceteris paribus estimates of tax burdens also neglected the possibility that substantial resources would be freed because of cutbacks in existing programs, notably, at the present time, the defense budget. An analysis of the prospective extent of such reductions and the potential extension of other programs to absorb them would obviously carry us far beyond the confines of this study. I assume implicitly that any such reductions would be absorbed wholly by other social needs.

Fifth, the location of thresholders within the income quintiles should be more closely researched. I have assumed that they lie wholly within the first and second quintiles, that the thresholders who are fractional occupants of a quintile are arrayed in ascending order of income, and that income recipients are uniformly distributed within quintiles. These are only approximations, of course, and could be improved with closer research.

Last, by assuming that incremental burdens will be shared proportionately among quintiles, I have ignored the fact that increased taxes will be levied disproportionately on upper income brackets, so that their marginal tax rates would rise much more than average. This potentiality would greatly increase the real burden through disincentives and would also have unclear implications for the political feasibility of the programs.

A Judgment of Feasibility

There remains the difficult task of judging the feasibility of the proposed social support programs within the context of what has been interpreted as the American ethos. This is inescapably a subjective judgment, although it can be guided by the experience of the 1980s and early 1990s in the reluctance of Congress and the executive branch to raise taxes to reduce what is all but universally recognized to be an unacceptable budget deficit. A fear of tax increases on the part of both branches of government has all but paralyzed governmental action on fiscal policy and promoted scandalous misrepresentations of the ineffective measures that were adopted. Indeed, this inability of democratic government to design rational fiscal policy for fear of public reaction to tax hikes must be labeled one of its historic failures, which raises serious questions concerning its ability to function under modern political and economic conditions.

Minimally, the experience reinforces the sentiment that in the short run the ability of the egoistic strand of the individualist ethos to accom-

TABLE 10.19
A Summary of the Increases in Net Federal Tax Burden on Private
Taxpayers Implied by the Threshold Programs

Threshold Program	Incremental Net Taxes (millions 1986 dollars)	Percent Rise in Taxes	
		Without Business	With Business
Poverty Threshold	$ 33.443	9.3%	7.6%
50% Threshold	71.067	19.8	16.0
60% Threshold	117.833	34.3	27.8

Source: Tables 10.9–10.18.

modate a larger role for the social strand is quite limited. Table 10.19 summarizes estimates of incremental federal income tax burdens for the three alternative programs under policies of corporation sharing and nonsharing.

My belief is that in the short run—say for the next decade—the poverty threshold program which implies an 8 to 9 percent rise in personal income taxes is at the upper limit of political feasibility, and only if the growth of affluence during the period is sufficiently strong to help overcome the egoistic urges of the ethos and if the public is philosophically convinced of the urgency of the need. With respect to the obtaining of that public conviction, it must be accepted that the reluctance to institute a greater role of compassionate justice to be expected from the strong strain of egoistic individualism will be complicated by the fact that a large portion of the recipients will be minority members, immigrants, and/or unmarried mothers. Experience with the policy proposal to institute universal health insurance in the mid-1980s at a cost of about $60 billion suggests that such incremental taxes—even when spent in large part to benefit the taxpayers bearing the burden—are not feasible. The above-mentioned difficulties in the late 1980s and in 1990 in raising $50 billion to help reduce the budget deficit reinforce this judgment.

Note that the percent-of-median-income programs have escalating features that would lead to their retaining a relatively constant share of income. Hence, economic growth would not provide a rapid rise in feasibility as it would were the programs stated in fixed real terms, as is the poverty threshold program. But even in the short run it is doubtful that such an absolute target can be sustained in an increasingly affluent society.

In the short run, therefore, I believe the goal of those who wish to expand the role of the social strand of individualism should be limited to a program of raising all households to poverty thresholds, with perhaps some improvement in presently defined levels. In the long run, with the aging of the population and the rise in associated health care costs, that goal may expand to a percent-of-median-income program threshold for some fractional standard. The study of long-run feasible programs is the substance of chapter 11.

Chapter 11

THE LONGER-TERM IMPLICATIONS
OF DUALISTIC INDIVIDUALISM

INTRODUCTION

Having gauged within broad limits the feasibility of an economic justice system based on dualistic individualism within the present social context, I will end the consequentialist analysis with a look ahead. With present trends and the likelihood of their continuance, what magnitudes of tax-payer burdens are implied for the long run if a 40-percent-of-median-incomes policy is adopted and maintained? Does it offer the prospect of feasibility, given the capacity of the ethos to yield greater scope to the social strand of individualism and the potential lessening of the burden through the growth of the economy?

The first part of this chapter focuses in more detail on the most vulnerable groups in U.S. society than was done in chapters 9 and 10 in order to isolate those groups whose growth patterns over the next thirty years will be strategic in dictating needs. Race, sex, age, family head, and education are the relevant characteristics, as demonstrated in the earlier chapters, and the recent (i.e., 1986) income status of groups so defined will be presented in this section. This will provide a baseline from which to project future income requirements.

The next section, "The Future of the Vulnerable Groups," on the basis of demographic and educational projections, seeks to project future tax burdens brought about by the implementation of dualistic individualism policies based on the analysis of the previous section.

The final section draws conclusions about the prospective long-term feasibility of such tax burdens within the context of the American ethos and economy.

THE VULNERABLE GROUPS

Families

From the Bureau of the Census's extensive study of poverty in 1986, table 11.1 presents a profile of those family groups most vulnerable to poverty. The data list the characteristics of the groups and the percentages of the total number of families with those characteristics (reproduced in column 4) that fell below poverty thresholds under three different definitions of income. Those definitions are private cash income only before government transfers; private cash income plus government *cash* transfers (the standard Bureau of the Census Current Population Survey measure of money income used throughout this book); and private cash income plus government *cash* and *noncash* transfers.

1. *All Races.* Of the roughly 65 million families of all races in the United States in 1986, 18.6 percent failed to achieve relevant poverty thresholds if private cash income only is taken into account. Government cash transfers reduced that substantially to about 11 percent (and this income basis is the one normally used in citing the incidence of family poverty). Finally, if government noncash transfers (the fungible value of Medicare and Medicaid, food stamps, housing and school lunch benefits) are included, the figure falls to 7.9 percent.

The first potentially vulnerable group identified is the aged. Almost 40 percent of persons 65 years of age or older would have fallen below poverty thresholds had private income only been taken into account. The huge role that government cash transfers—overwhelmingly Social Security pensions, of course—play in eliminating poverty among this group is displayed dramatically by the fall in the percentage to 7 percent when included. About one-third of all families headed by a householder in this age category has been lifted above poverty thresholds by such government programs. When noncash benefits are factored in poverty is all but eliminated, falling to less than half its proportion in the general population of families. Poverty among the aged, therefore, is not widespread among family households, but rather among female unrelated individuals over 65 who are primarily widows.

A second candidate group for projection of needs consists of families headed by women with no husband present. Overall, fully 44 percent of such families are below poverty thresholds if private income only is taken into account. These percentages rise to 52 percent for all such families with children under the age of 18 and 65 percent for those with children under six years of age. Government cash transfers reduce these percentages, but in no manner comparable to those received by the elderly: for all such families such payments reduce the impoverished by about 10 percentage points and for families with children by about 5 percentage points. Government noncash transfers are more effective, reducing the percentages to 24 percent overall, about 35 percent for families with children under 18, and about 46 percent for those with children under 6. This group of families is identified as the group most vulnerable to poverty.

A last category of vulnerability is the undereducated. Families whose householder was over the age of 25 and had fewer than 12 years of com-

TABLE 11.1
Percentages of Families in Poverty, by Income Definitions,
Race, and Selected Characteristics, 1986

| Characteristics | Percentages by Income Type | | | Families |
	1 Private Cash Income	2 Plus Govt. Cash Transfers	3 Plus Govt. Noncash Trans.	4 (Base of Percentages)
1. All Race	18.6%	10.9%	7.9%	64,491,000
a. Househ. >65	39.6	7.0	3.3	10,229,000
b. Female HH., No Husband	44.2	34.6	24.0	10,445,000
1. Child. <18	51.9	46.0	34.9	7,094,000
2. Child. <6	65.0	60.6	46.0	2,971,000
c. HH. <12yrs. Schooling	40.4	21.6	15.1	15,857,000
2. White	16.3	8.6	6.7	55,676,000
a. Househ. >65	37.2	5.4	2.9	9,201,000
b. Female HH., No Husband	38.2	28.2	19.6	7,227,000
1. Child. <18	46.0	39.8	28.2	4,552,000
2. Child. <6	59.7	55.0	41.3	1,760,000
c. HH. <12yrs. Schooling	37.1	18.0	12.8	12,939,000
3. Black	37.3	28.0	19.3	7,096,000
a. Househ. >65	64.9	22.1	7.6	886,000
b. Female HH., No Husband	58.8	50.1	34.5	2,967,000
1. Child. <18	63.0	58.0	42.2	2,386,000
2. Child. <6	72.6	68.9	53.3	1,149,000
c. HH. <12yrs. Schooling	56.1	37.9	25.2	2,558,000
4. Hispanic	30.9	24.7	18.7	4,403,000
a. Househ. >65	49.9	17.3	7.2	334,000
b. Female HH., No Husband	58.7	51.2	36.0	1,032,000
1. Child. <18	65.9	59.5	41.9	822,000
2. Child. <6	74.2	69.1	54.1	435,000
c. HH. <12yrs. Schooling	45.2	35.8	27.2	2,232,000

Source: U.S. Bureau of the Census, *Money Income and Poverty Status in the United States:
1988, Current Population Reports,* Series P-60, no. 166 (Washington, D.C.: U.S. Government
Printing Office, 1989), table 5, 158–161.

pleted schooling placed 40 percent of their members below poverty levels considering only cash income. Government cash transfers lowered this substantially to about 22 percent and noncash transfers to about 15 percent. Of course, there is a good deal of overlap between the second and third categories.

2. *Whites.* Table 11.1 reveals what one would suspect concerning white families: their dominance in numbers (86 percent of the total) assures that the percentages for the vulnerable groups track those for all families rather closely with favorable 5 to 6 percentage point differences with the interesting exception of the elderly. Social Security payments have leveled out poverty incidence between the races so that whites have less than a 2 percentage point differential from all-race percentages after government cash transfers and only a .4 percentage point difference when noncash benefits are added in. Among the vulnerable groups, differences between white and nonwhite families are least in evidence among the elderly.

3. *Blacks.* For all black families, considering only private cash income, 37 percent fall below relevant poverty thresholds, or double the percentage for all-race families and about 2.3 times that for white families. Black families as a whole, therefore, constitute a major vulnerable group. Government cash transfers reduce the percentage to 28 percent, and the addition of noncash benefits lowers the figure to 19 percent—a major multiple of both all-race and white levels.

About 65 percent of black families headed by the aged were in poverty in private cash income terms in 1986, but government cash benefits reduced that to 22 percent and noncash benefits to about 8 percent. As in the case of whites, the extent of government payouts to this group marks it as an important element in the projection of future needs.

As noted in chapter 9, the black family headed by a female is among the most desperately impoverished in the nation. In cash income terms 59 percent of such families fall below the poverty floor, and government cash transfers reduce this only to 50 percent. Noncash transfers are somewhat more helpful, but nonetheless about 35 percent of all such families remain below poverty levels after they are included.

For those families with children the situation is bleaker still. In those with children under 18 fully 63 percent are impoverished on a cash income basis, 58 percent after government cash transfers, and 42 percent with the inclusion of all government transfer payments. But worst off are those families with youngsters under 6: 73 percent are in private cash income poverty, 69 percent after cash benefits, and 53 percent remain in poverty after all government transfers are considered. These are substantially above the corresponding white categories, although, as was shown above, even these latter were extremely high. The black unmarried or

abandoned mother is a substantial burden on the society and will become even more so if support levels rise to 40 percent of relevant median
incomes. These families accounted for fully 41.8 percent of black families and 4.6 percent of all-race families in 1986, and are expected to rise
over the period in prospect.

Finally, black families with householders who have completed less
than a high school education fall short of poverty thresholds in about 56
percent of the cases, or about the same as for female-headed families.
However, government cash benefits are somewhat more effective, reducing the poverty level to 38 percent. These government benefits were
about equally split between Social Security payments and Aid to Families
With Dependent Children, indicating the dominance of the elderly and
the single-parent family in this category.

4. *Hispanic Origin.* As a whole, families of Hispanic origin are somewhat better off in receiving private cash income than are blacks, but have
lessened advantages after government cash and noncash entitlements
are included. About 19 percent of such families remain below poverty
levels after all three types of income are included, or about the same
proportion as blacks.

Families headed by women track the black family percentages very
closely. These two groups and their subgroupings could be merged with
little loss of accuracy in computing tax burdens.

As noted in the analysis of chapter 9, lower educational attainment is
not so punishing among Hispanics as it is among blacks, but nonetheless
45 percent of families headed by a householder with less than a high
school education were in poverty in 1986. Government cash payments
reduced that percentage to 36 percent—slightly less than that for black
families in this category—and noncash benefits resulted in a further
decline to 27 percent, or about 2 percentage points more than black
families.

Unrelated Individuals

1. *All Races, Both Sexes.* When one studies unrelated individuals of both
sexes and all races with respect to their relation to poverty thresholds,
one notes that the percentages falling below those levels for all three
measures of income are about double those for families. This must be
discounted, of course, for the large numbers of single young persons
who are climbing the first rungs of their career ladders or are in the
process of obtaining an education. On a life-cycle basis, therefore, the
profile is not so bleak.

However, when one studies in table 11.2 the two problem subgroups
at risk, the disproportion does not disappear. Fully 68 percent of those

TABLE 11.2
Percentages of Unrelated Individuals in Poverty, by Income
Definition, Race, and Selected Characteristics, 1986

	Percentages by Income Type			Persons
	1	2	3	4
Characteristics	Private Cash Income	Plus Govt. Cash Transfers	Plus Govt. Noncash Trans.	(Base of Percentages)
1. All Race—Both Sexes	36.5%	21.6%	18.0%	31,679,000
a. Househ. >65	68.2	25.2	17.0	9,184,000
b. HH. <12yrs. Schooling	71.3	38.9	29.0	7,918,000
2. All Race—Male	26.4	17.5	17.3	14,481,000
a. Househ. >65	63.1	19.6	13.5	2,098,000
b. HH. <12yrs. Schooling	60.0	33.9	28.0	2,947,000
3. All Race—Female	45.1	25.1	20.0	17,198,000
a. Househ. >65	69.7	26.8	17.9	7,086,000
b. HH. <12yrs. Schooling	78.0	41.9	29.6	4,971,000
4. White—Both Sexes	34.8	19.2	16.0	27,143,000
a. Househ. >65	66.2	22.1	14.9	8,259,000
b. HH. <12yrs. Schooling	70.4	34.6	25.4	6,347,000
5. White—Male	23.7	15.1	13.5	12,111,000
a. Househ. >65	59.5	16.7	11.7	1,819,000
b. HH. <12yrs. Schooling	57.2	29.2	23.3	2,217,000
6. White—Female	43.8	22.5	18.0	15,032,000
a. Househ. >65	68.1	23.7	16.0	6,439,000
b. HH. <12yrs. Schooling	77.4	37.5	28.6	4,130,000
7. Black—Both Sexes	49.7	38.5	32.4	3,714,000
a. Househ. >65	87.5	53.9	36.0	833,000
b. HH. <12yrs. Schooling	76.6	58.0	45.2	1,432,000
8. Black—Male	42.0	31.0	28.4	1,917,000
a. Househ. >65	90.0	39.8	26.6	244,000
b. HH. <12yrs. Schooling	71.0	50.1	44.5	663,000

TABLE 11.2 (cont.)

Characteristics	Percentages by Income Type			Persons
	1 *Private* *Cash* *Income*	*2* *Plus Govt.* *Cash Transfers*	*3* *Plus Govt.* *Noncash Trans.*	*4* *(Base of* *Percentages)*
9. Black—Female	58.0	46.6	36.6	1,798,000
a. Househ. >65	86.4	59.7	39.8	589,000
b. HH. <12yrs.				
Schooling	81.5	64.8	45.8	769,000
10. Hispanic—Both Sexes	40.1	32.8	25.6	1,685,000
a. Househ. >65	84.5	50.1	37.6	221,000
b. HH. <12yrs.				
Schooling	64.2	51.3	41.2	633,000
11. Hispanic—Males	32.6	26.8	24.6	1,001,000
a. Househ. >65	n.a.	n.a.	n.a.	n.a.
b. HH. <12yrs.				
Schooling	53.3	42.8	39.0	333,000
12. Hispanic—Females	51.2	41.7	31.7	684,000
a. Househ. >65	86.6	55.3	29.0	158,000
b. HH. <12yrs.				
Schooling	76.5	60.9	43.1	299,000

Source: U.S. Bureau of the Census, *Money Income and Poverty Status in the United States: 1988, Current Population Reports*, Series P-60, no. 166 (Washington, D.C.: U.S. Government Printing Office, 1989), table 7, 170–181.

over the age of 65 fall below poverty thresholds in terms of private cash income. Social Security largely is effective in reducing this to about 25 percent, and noncash transfers suppress this further to 17 percent, or about the average for all unrelated individuals. These figures are substantially higher than the corresponding measures for families headed by aged householders. The single aged constitute a significant problem group, in largest part because of widowed women.

A second vulnerable group of single persons is that containing persons whose completed schooling constitutes less than a high school education. On a private cash income basis 71 percent of unrelated individuals over the age of 25 with fewer than 12 years of schooling fall below poverty thresholds (compared with only 40 percent of families with such a householder). This is reduced to 39 and 29 percent respectively when government cash and noncash transfers respectively are factored in, but these are roughly double the family figures.

2. *All Races, Male versus Female.* For all categories of income the male impoverished are relatively less plentiful than female, but government cash transfers and, to a greater degree, noncash transfers reduce the discrepancy to small numbers. About 26 percent of all male unrelated individuals fall below the poverty standards with respect to private cash income, compared with 45 percent of females. But when government cash benefits are added these percentages fall to 18 percent and 25 percent, and with total government benefits added, to 17 percent and 20 percent respectively.

For householders over 65 about 63 percent of males and 70 percent of females have deficient private cash incomes. Social Security payments (primarily) reduce these figures to about 20 percent and 27 percent respectively, and noncash benefits to about 14 percent and 18 percent. However, an important consideration in identifying female unrelated individuals in this category as especially important in trend estimation for the future is their numerical dominance of men. The total number of women is 3.38 times that of men, so that despite the closeness of the percentages in poverty after all government transfers are included, in absolute terms there are 1,268,000 aged women in poverty and only 283,000 men.

A similar if less disparate situation holds with respect to undereducation. In the marketplace women with less than a high school education are much more likely to experience poverty than are men, with probabilities of about .8 to .6. Government entitlement programs reduce the two sexes to about equal probabilities at .30 for women and .28 for men. But 1,471,000 women remain below poverty thresholds after government entitlements versus 825,000 men.

In summary, women in the disadvantaged groups suffer most in the acquisition of private cash income, but are the beneficiaries of greater government cash and noncash benefits, particularly the latter. Nonetheless, although both sexes must be accounted at risk, the relative differentials remaining after government programs and the larger numbers of women in the relevant subgroups mark them as an extremely important vulnerable group.

3. *Whites.* Instead of projecting growth patterns for all-race males and females, however, one may obtain greater precision by disaggregating the sexes by race or Hispanic origin. The percentages of whites in poverty, sex disregarded, are very close to those for all races, though, of course, a bit lower. A similar statement holds for the two sexes, as does the absolute predominance of females in the two vulnerable subgroups. Hence I will signalize both male and female unrelated individuals over the age of 65 or with less than 12 years of completed schooling as warranting special attention in projecting time patterns.

4. *Blacks, Both Sexes.* On a private cash income basis about 50 percent of black unrelated individuals are in poverty, a fraction about 43 percent higher than for whites. Cash benefits reduce poverty to 39 percent and all government benefits to 32 percent, both of which figures are double the corresponding white percentages. For the aged, 88 percent of single persons would be below poverty thresholds in the absence of government programs, but these reduce the percentages to 54 for cash benefits and 36 for cash and noncash payments. These figures, however, remain about 142 percent of corresponding white levels.

5. *Black Males.* Unrelated black men are, on a total basis, somewhat less impoverished than black women, but about 28 percent remain below thresholds after all income sources are considered. For aged males, 90 percent receive private cash incomes below poverty levels, but government cash benefits reduce that to about 40 percent and supplementary noncash benefits to 27 percent. Uneducated black males over 25 suffer impoverishment on a 71 percent basis in terms of private cash income, reduced to 50 percent by government cash benefits. Noncash benefits are ineffective in reducing the percentage by only an additional 5 points. In all categories, of course, black males are relatively much more subject to poverty than their white counterparts. In the projection of social benefits requirements for the next 30 years, black male unrelated individuals in general and the aged and undereducated among them in particular should be singled out as vulnerable groups.

6. *Black Females.* The plight of black unrelated women is even more bleak than for males: 58 percent with deficient private cash incomes, lowered only to 47 percent by cash payouts and 37 percent by all government benefits. These two percentages for government transfers are about double the respective figures for white females—the same relation borne by these percentages for black males relative to white males. Although a smaller percentage of aged black females receive poverty-level private cash incomes, the great disadvantage they suffer from smaller Social Security payments is revealed in the fact that 60 percent remain impoverished after such payments compared with only 40 percent of their male counterparts. Social security payments to widows of covered husbands typically fall by about one-third at the death of the husband, and, of course, those who are themselves in covered employment typically have earned less over the years of their labor force participation. Even after noncash government transfers, about 40 percent of aged black unrelated women remain in poverty. Finally, undereducated black females are a large segment of the poverty-ridden, and all government programs succeeded in reducing the poverty percentages from 82 percent to 46 percent.

7. *Hispanic Origin.* In all three sex groupings—both sexes, male, and female—and for both the aged and the undereducated, such data as exist indicate that the poverty experience of those of Hispanic origin is quite close to their black counterparts. Moreover, since they are captured in either the white or black racial blocs to an almost complete degree, I shall not make separate projections of the benefit requirements. But because, as noted in chapter 9, they are a rapidly growing segment of the U.S. population they should be signalized as a vulnerable poverty group closely linked in terms of needs to the those of similar black categories.

The Future of the Vulnerable Groups

The Aged

One fact about the income condition of individuals 65 years of age or older in the United States that emerges from the data of chapters 9 and 10 is that on a mean or median basis they are better off—not worse off—than the population in general when government cash benefits are added to private cash incomes. Their relative advantage grows even greater if the imputed equity from home ownership is factored into the income measure or if bequeathable wealth is considered as a source of supplements to income flows.[1] But that relative advantage over younger income recipients, despite disadvantages in income earning, health status, and susceptibility to uncertainty—springs largely from government entitlement programs. And it is these burdens on the taxpayer that our projections must quantify.

Table 11.3 illustrates this forcefully by listing the percentage of elderly households with varying degrees of dependence on specific income sources in 1986. Since these data were collected for individuals over the age of 55 or 60, rather than 65, they understate the dependence on government benefits and also omit such important noncash entitlements as Medicare and Medicaid payments.

Nonetheless, fully 57 percent of such households relied for 50 to 100 percent of their income on Social Security, and 24 percent for 90 to 100 percent. Notably, private pensions (including annuities) are minor sources of support: 74 percent of the aged households received no such income. Exactly 13 percent received government pensions, so that only 39 percent of these individuals had any pension income and for only 7 percent did it provide as much as 50 percent of total income. Only 19 percent had any employment earnings and for only 8 percent did they provide as much as 50 percent of income. Finally, 70 percent received

TABLE 11.3
Percentage Distribution of Elderly Households by
Dependence on Income Sources, 1986

Income Source	Percentage Dependence	Percentage of Households
Earnings	0%	81%
	1–49	11
	50–100	8
	90–100	2
Social Security	0	8
	1–49	35
	50–100	57
	90–100	24
Private Pensions	0	74
	1–19	13
	20–49	11
	50–100	2
Government Pensions	0	87
	1–49	8
	50–100	5
Income from Assets	0	40
	1–19	30
	20–49	18
	50–100	12

Source: Michael D. Hurd, "Research on the Elderly: Economic Status, Retirement, and Consumption and Saving," *Journal of Economic Literature*, 28 (1990/2): 588.

less than 20 percent of their total income from property earnings, and only 12 percent received as much as 50 percent or more from such sources. Even after taking account of estimates that the elderly underreport income by about 37 percent, most of that derived from property whose ownership is highly concentrated, the importance of Social Security payments is clear.[2] This is especially true for those households at the lower end of the elderly income distribution. For example, in 1984, when family income was adjusted for size of family, in the lowest quintile Social Security benefits accounted for 78 percent of family income, property income for 4 percent, earnings for 2 percent, and all other sources for 16 percent.[3]

To estimate the burden implied in the year 2020 by lifting all elderly individuals—in families and in unrelated households—to the 40-percent-of-median-income levels, I will proceed in the following steps:

Step 1. Estimation of the number of elderly household units in 2020 disaggregated by race, sex, and age.

Step 2. Estimation of median cash and noncash income in 1987 dollars for such household units in 2020.

Step 3. Estimation of 40-percent-of-median-income levels in 1987 dollars for such household units.

Step 4. Estimation of implied tax burden in 1987 dollars to meet government program goals and to raise elderly household units to the 40-percent-of-median-income thresholds.

1. *Estimates of Elderly Population.* The middle series projections for the elderly population of the U.S. Census Bureau produce the data listed in table 11.4.[4]

Projections of the population percentages that will fall in the Social Security Area in 2020, classified by age group, sex, and marital status, are reproduced in table 11.5. In the absence of more detailed projections it is assumed that all unmarried persons in the age groups listed in the table live in unrelated person units. That overestimates the size of the latter group by ignoring the number of the aged who live with family members, but this segment of the population has declined dramatically in recent years and will probably continue to do so over the next three decades.[5]

Tables 11.4 and 11.5 permit us to project the total numbers of elderly persons 65 years of age or more living in 2020 and to classify them by age, sex, and marital status. The first step is then completed.

2. *Estimates of Cash and Noncash Income for Elderly Units.* As shown in table 11.3 the most important component of elderly incomes is that derived from Old Age and Survivors' Insurance and Disability Insurance (OASDI). Our first task, therefore, is to project the costs of these entitlements in the target year under the assumptions that they will retain the same real values as they did in 1986, and that in 2020 all individuals 65 years of age or more will receive OASDI benefits.[6] To obtain greater accuracy two estimates of the payments to the elderly from two different bodies of data using two different classifications of recipients are derived.

a. 1986 Income Study. In 1986 the median dollar incomes from Social Security benefits for those 65 years of age or older were the following:[7]

Group	Number of Units	Median Social Security Benefit	Total Social Security Benefit ($ Millions)
Married couples	7,920,000	$9,070	$ 71,834.40
Nonmarried men	2,608,000	5,790	15,100.32
Nonmarried women	8,942,000	5,100	45,604.20
Totals	19,470,000		132,538.92

TABLE 11.4
Projections of the Aged U.S. Population, by Age, Sex, and Race:
1988 and 2020, Middle Series (in thousands)

	1988			2020		
	Both Sexes	Male	Female	Both Sexes	Male	Female
1. All Races						
65–69	9,977	4,531	5,446	17,467	8,316	9,151
70–74	7,896	3,392	4,503	13,506	6,176	7,330
75–79	5,887	2,313	3,574	8,981	3,830	5,151
80–84	3,623	1,268	2,354	5,462	2,116	3,345
85–89	1,934	584	1,349	3,459	1,168	2,291
90–94	799	203	596	2,061	582	1,479
95–99	231	53	178	864	197	667
≥100	54	11	42	266	44	223
All	246,048	120,054	125,995	294,364	144,035	150,329
≥62	36,832	15,337	21,495	63,936	28,206	35,731
≥65	30,399	12,356	18,043	52,067	22,430	29,637
2. White						
65–69	8,880	4,050	4,830	14,517	6,976	7,541
70–74	7,103	3,061	4,042	11,454	5,285	6,168
75–79	5,309	2,084	3,225	7,631	3,284	4,346
80–84	3,318	1,156	2,163	4,696	1,837	2,859
85–89	1,768	528	1,240	2,988	1,012	1,976
90–94	729	182	547	1,808	509	1,299
95–99	206	46	160	762	171	591
≥100	46	9	36	229	35	194
All	207,696	101,689	106,007	234,330	115,227	119,103
≥62	33,070	13,777	19,293	53,972	23,965	30,007
≥65	27,358	11,117	16,242	44,084	19,110	24,974
3. Black						
65–69	896	392	504	2,141	980	1,161
70–74	649	268	381	1,439	634	804
75–79	474	183	291	906	378	529
80–84	250	90	160	501	193	308
85–89	141	46	95	314	108	206
90–94	62	18	44	178	54	124
95–99	22	6	16	77	21	56
≥100	7	2	5	31	7	24
All	30,287	14,414	15,874	42,128	20,188	21,939
≥62	3,082	1,264	1,818	7,025	3,046	3,979
≥65	2,502	1,005	1,497	5,587	2,376	3,212

TABLE 11.4 (*cont.*)

	1988			2020		
	Both Sexes	Male	Female	Both Sexes	Male	Female
4. Other Races						
65–69	201	89	112	809	360	449
70–74	144	63	80	613	256	358
75–79	104	46	58	444	168	276
80–84	55	22	31	265	86	178
85–89	25	10	14	157	48	109
90–94	8	3	5	75	19	56
95–99	3	1	2	25	5	20
≥100	1	0	1	6	2	5
All	8,065	3,951	4,114	17,906	8,620	9,287
≥62	680	296	384	2,939	1,195	1,745
≥65	539	234	304	2,396	944	1,451

Source: U.S. Bureau of the Census, *Projections of the Population of the United States by Age, Sex and Race: 1988 to 2080*, by Gregory Spencer, *Current Population Reports*, Series P-25, no. 1018, 1989, table 4. Other-race data has been obtained as residuals.

Unfortunately the estimates in the last column were based on the median benefits rather than mean amounts, and therefore are probably underestimates. This will be corrected for downward bias in the last stage of the analysis.

In 1986 the estimates of private incomes for those 65 and older, including government and nongovernment pensions, earnings, and property income, are the following:[8]

Group	Non-SS Income
Married couples	$9,997
Non-married persons	3,093

Finally, in 1986, for single-person households with members aged 65 or more, the following amounts of government means-tested or non-means-tested cash or noncash benefits were received:[9]

Benefit	Total Amount ($ thousands)
AFDC or non-SSI cash assistance	$130,480
SSI	1,329,952
Food stamps	223,802
Housing assistance	1,718,757
Medicare	12,108,176
Medicaid	1,336,336
Total	16,623,925

TABLE 11.5

Projected Distribution of the Population in the Social Security
Area, Year 2020, by Age Group, Sex, and Marital Status

| Age Group | Percentages of Total Number | | | |
and Sex	Married	Single	Divorced	Widowed
60–64				
Male	74.6%	12.2%	10.1%	3.1%
Female	64.6	8.4	16.0	11.0
65–69				
Male	76.6	9.1	9.0	5.3
Female	59.5	6.5	16.5	17.6
70–74				
Male	76.5	6.0	8.5	9.0
Female	51.5	5.3	16.1	27.0
75–79				
Male	75.3	3.9	6.9	13.9
Female	41.2	4.6	14.1	40.1
80–84				
Male	71.4	2.9	5.2	20.4
Female	29.5	3.8	11.6	55.1
85–89				
Male	63.1	2.1	4.8	30.1
Female	18.6	3.3	9.5	68.5
90–94				
Male	50.8	1.3	5.1	42.7
Female	10.9	3.0	8.5	77.4
95 and Over				
Male	34.5	1.0	5.1	59.4
Female	5.4	2.3	8.1	84.3
65 and Over				
Male	74.2	6.1	7.8	11.9
Female	43.9	5.0	14.3	36.7

Source: U.S. Department of Health and Human Services, Social Security
Administration, Office of the Actuary, *Social Security Area Population Projections: 1989*, Actuarial Study No. 105, June 1989. Alternative II projections—the intermediate case estimates—were used in the table.

Hence, the average benefit to single households is $1,439. Lacking finer
data I will assume that married couples received 1.5 times the level of
single households, or $2,159, from these supplemental sources.

To summarize, the estimates of incomes received from all sources by
Social Security beneficiaries 65 years of age or older are gathered from
the results above and presented in table 11.6.

TABLE 11.6

Estimates of Money Income Sources for Social Security
Beneficiaries 65 Years of Age or Older, 1986

	1 Total Money Income	2 SS Benefits	3 Other Earnings	4 Other Govt. Transfers	5 Total Income
Units					
1. All Units	$12,051	$6,150	$5,901	$1,732	$13,783
2. Married					
Couples	19,067	9,070	9,997	2,159	21,226
3. Unmarried					
a. Men	9,795	5,790	4,005	1,439	11,234
b. Women	7,927	5,100	2,827	1,439	9,366

Source: U.S Department of Health and Human Services, Social Security Administration, *Income of the Population 55 or Older, 1986*, SSA Publication No. 13-11871, June 1988, tables 14, 17, 18, 19, 22, 24, and 27. Estimates are based on median measures of the income types and are therefore subject to error as estimates of means. Some adjustments have been made when appropriate to maintain data consistency.

TABLE 11.7

Estimates of Money Income Sources for Social Security Beneficiaries 65 Years of
Age or Older, 1986, Corrected for Median Income Downward Bias

	1 Total Money Income	2 SS Benefits	3 Other Earnings	4 Other Govt. Transfers	5 Total Income
Units					
1. All Units	$13,859	$ 7,073	$ 6,786	$1,732	$15,591
2. Married					
Couples	21,927	10,431	11,497	2,159	24,086
3. Unmarried					
a. Men	11,264	6,659	4,606	1,439	12,703
b. Women	9,116	5,865	3,251	1,439	10,555

Source: Table 11.6, with columns 2, 3, and 4 multiplied by 1.15.

Because the data in columns 1, 2, and 3 of table 11.6 are median data and therefore downward biassed, a correction factor should be applied to them. A 15 percent factor has been chosen on the grounds that income data throughout this study have revealed the medians to fall between 15 and 20 percent below means. Table 11.7, therefore, contains the corrected values.

Through use of the projections of population in 2020 by sex in table 11.4 and the married versus unmarried (single-divorced-widowed) projections by sex in the Social Security Area in table 11.5, estimates of the number of married couples and unmarried persons classified by sex are obtained. They are displayed in table 11.9.

TABLE 11.8

Projections of Population of Persons Aged 65 or
Older, by Marital Status and Sex, in Year 2020

Unit	Number of Units
Married Couples	16,643,000
Single Persons	
a. Male	5,786,940
b. Female	16,626,357
Total Households	22,413,297

Sources: Tables 11.4 and 11.5.

Under the assumption that the real values of Social Security and other governmental cash and noncash benefits will remain the same for units in 2020 as in 1986, the projections of table 11.8 were obtained in 1987 dollars. The projection of private income for the aged is a more difficult operation. I shall assume that private retirement and annuity income, earnings from labor, and property income will rise in real terms at the same rates over the period as projected GNP. Over a 33-year period (1987–2020) small changes in assumed growth rates can cumulate to large changes in projected GNP and other income magnitudes. For example, the Social Security Administration (SSA) projected that real GNP would rise from $4,476 billion in 1987 to $9,987 billion in 2020, or at an average annual growth rate of 2.43 percent.[10] I will be more optimistic and assume an average growth rate at the historic 3 percent level, which leads to a year 2020 GNP projection of $12,046 billion in 1987 prices—a value about 21 percent higher than the SSA value. Private income includes nongovernment and government retirement payments, earnings from work, and property income, and I have assumed that they will rise at the per capita rate of growth of GNP, calculated as 3 percent less the SSA projection of population growth at .57 percent per year over the period.

Table 11.9 compares the total incomes (as corrected in table 11.7) received by Social Security beneficiaries 65 years of age or more in 1986, inflated to 1987 prices, to the projections of such incomes in 2020 under the assumptions that (1) government payments retain the same real values as they had in 1986 and (2) private income rises at 2.43 percent per year in real terms. Table 11.9 yields estimates of mean total incomes of $24,965 for married couples, $13,167 for unmarried men, and $12,324 for unmarried women for the year 2020.

Social Security benefits to the aged are projected to be about $321 billion in 1987 dollars in the year 2020, with other benefits bringing the

TABLE 11.9
Total Income Receipts by Household Units 65 Years of Age or Older, 1986,
and Projected Incomes for the Year 2020 (millions of 1987 dollars)

	1 Total Money and In-Kind Income	2 Total Money Income	3 SS Benefits	4 Private Income	5 Other Govt. Trans.	6 Total Govt. Trans.
Units						
a. Estimated 1986 Receipts						
1. Married						
Couples	$197,723	$180,000	$ 85,624	$ 94,376	$17,723	$103,347
2. Nonmarried						
a. Men	34,339	30,449	17,999	12,450	3,890	21,889
b. Women	97,829	84,492	54,359	30,132	13,337	67,696
Totals	329,891	294,941	157,982	136,958	34,950	192,932
b. Estimated 2020 Receipts						
1. Married						
Couples	$415,494	$378,250	$179,930	$198,320	$37,244	$217,174
2. Nonmarried						
a. Men	76,196	67,565	39,938	27,626	8,631	48,569
b. Women	204,897	180,098	101,072	56,026	24,799	125,871
Totals	696,587	625,913	320,940	281,972	70,674	391,614

total of government transfers to about $392 billion. This represents a 103 percent rise in the former and the latter compared with 1986.

b. 1987 Annual Supplement Data. To provide another approach to the 2020 projections, data have been drawn from the Social Security Bulletin's Annual Supplement for 1989, which gives data for the year 1987.[11] These data permit us to break down the data for the elderly by sex alone and to include the burden of the children of the elderly in the Social Security area. Table 11.10 records these data. This method yields an estimate of Social Security retirement, survivor, and disability benefits paid to *aged* beneficiaries in 1987 at about $173 billion, compared with about $158 billion in 1986 from the first estimate.

Projections of Social Security costs are made in table 11.11 straightforwardly by applying the per person benefits of table 11.10 to projections of relevant population sizes in year 2020.

The estimates in table 11.11 do not include projections of the costs of supporting the children of the aged population, and I shall simply add the $1,137.87 million cost in 1987 recorded in table 11.10. Hence, projected Social Security costs for the aged in 2020 using the second method are about $312 billion, before considering administrative costs and reclaimed income taxes from the benefits. This compares with $321 billion from table 11.9's projection, which used the first method.

TABLE 11.10
Social Security Benefits Received by Households with at Least One Member
65 Years of Age or Older, by Sex, 1987

Age	Men	Women	Children
1. Whites			
65–74	$45,142,366,000	$46,804,505,000	
Persons	6,237,895	8,222,450	
Per Person	$7,237	$5,692	
75–84	21,496,667,000	30,062,016,000	
Persons	3,069,157	5,211,533	
Per Person	$7,004	$5,941	
85 and Over	4,344,917,000	9,801,830,000	
Persons	695,026	1,794,794	
Per Person	$6,251	$5,461	
Totals	$70,983,950,000	$87,568,351,000	$ 902,878,000
Persons	10,002,078	15,228,777	330,136
Per Person	$7,097	$5,750	$2,734
2. Blacks			
65–74	$ 3,095,328,000	$ 3,308,108,000	
Persons	524,009	708,166	
Per Person	$5,907	$4,671	
75–84	1,411,103,000	1,930,861,000	
Persons	252,923	386,082	
Per Person	$5,579	$5,001	
85 and Over	275,534,000	520,233,000	
Persons	55,951	125,804	
Per Person	$4,925	$2,418	
Totals	$ 4,781,965,000	$ 5,759,202,000	$ 179,151,000
Persons	832,883	1,220,052	80,155
Per Person	$5,741	$4,720	$2,235
3. Other Races			
65–74	$ 857,414,000	$ 944,848,000	
Persons	139,084	185,164	
Per Person	$6,165	$5,103	
75–84	395,426,000	292,822,000	
Persons	63,546	90,003	
Per Person	$6,223	$3,253	

TABLE 11.10 (*cont.*)

Age	Men	Women	Children
85 and Over	67,434,000	64,980,000	
Persons	12,580	14,091	
Per Person	$5,360	$4,611	
Totals	$ 1,320,274,000	$ 1,302,650,000	$ 55,841,000
Persons	215,210	289,258	28,905
Per Person	$6,135	$4,503	$1,931
Grand Total	$172,854,262,000		
Persons	27,427,454		
Per Person	$6,302		

Source: See endnote 11.

TABLE 11.11
Projections of Social Security Benefits for Households with at Least One Member 65 Years of Age or Older, by Race and Sex, Year 2020, 1987 Dollars

Age Group	Men Number (thousands)	Men Benefits (millions)	Women Number (thousands)	Women Benefits (millions)	Totals Number (thousands)	Totals Benefits (millions)
1. White						
65–74	12,261	$88,732,857	13,709	$78,031,628	25,790	$166,764,485
75–84	5,121	35,867,484	7,205	42,804,905	12,326	78,672,389
85 and Over	1,727	10,795,477	4,050	22,171,660	5,787	32,967,137
Totals	19,109	135,395,818	24,974	143,008,193	44,083	278,404,011
2. Black						
65–74	980	$ 5,788,860	1,161	$ 5,423,031	2,141	$ 11,211,891
75–84	571	3,185,609	837	4,185,837	1,408	7,371,446
85 and Over	191	940,675	409	988,962	600	1,929,637
Totals	1,742	9,915,144	2,407	10,597,830	4,149	20,512,974
3. Other Races						
65–74	617	$ 3,803,805	807	$ 4,118,121	1,424	$ 7,921,926
75–84	254	1,580,642	454	1,476,862	708	3,057,504
85 and Over	73	391,280	191	880,701	264	1,271,981
Totals	944	5,775,727	1,452	6,475,684	2,396	12,251,411
Grand Total	$311,168,396					
Persons	50,628					
Per Person	$6,146					

Source: Table 11.10 and U.S. Bureau of the Census, *Projections of the Population of the United States by Age, Sex and Race: 1988 to 2080, Current Population Reports*, Series P-25, no. 1018 (Washington, D.C.: U.S. Government Printing Office, 1989), table 4, 86–87.

TABLE 11.12

Total Income Receipts by Household Units 65 Years of Age or Older,
Projected for the Year 2020 (millions of 1987 dollars)

Units	Total Money and In-Kind Income	Total Money Income	SS Benefits	Private Income	Other Govt. Trans.	Total Govt. Trans.
Persons	$664,952	$594,278	$312,306	$281,972	$70,674	$382,980

Sources: Tables 11.9 and 11.11.

I will assume that the private income and other government transfer estimates for 1986 and 2020 listed in table 11.9 will apply in the aggregate to the projections in table 11.11. Expanded income estimates projected for 2020 for the second method are given in table 11.12 and are comparable to the projections from method 1 in table 11.9, panel b.

Hereafter, in the calculations to follow, I will adopt the "worse-case scenario" and use the projections of the first method given in table 11.9.

3. *Estimates of the 40-Percent-of-Median-Income Threshold.* If median incomes rise at the projected average annual rate of per capita GNP growth median incomes in 2020 will be $43,400 for married couples and $28,006 for an unrelated individual in 1987 prices. The 40 percent support levels therefore would be $17,360 for a married couple and $11,202 for a single individual. Under our perhaps overly optimistic assumptions concerning the course of nongovernment cash income for the elderly,[12] large additional support payments to reach the thresholds should not be required in the aggregate, given the mean projections of table 11.9. Of course, the distribution of incomes about these medians will leave some recipients below the threshold and require some net outlays, but the overall outlay on the 40-percent-of-median-income program should not be a great burden.

4. *Estimates of the Tax Burden on Nonelderly Taxpayers.* The series of optimistic assumptions made in this analysis of the plight of the elderly, assumed to hold over the next thirty years, include the following:

1. the inclusion of all retirees in the Social Security retirement, survivorship, and disability fold;
2. the average annual real rise in GNP and other total income measures at 3 percent;
3. the average annual real rise in private income receipts by Social Security beneficiaries of 2.43 percent, implying a total population rate of increase of .75 percent per year;
4. the continuance of Social Security benefits on a non-means-tested basis at their real 1987 values;

5. the continuance of means-tested governmental cash and noncash benefits at their real 1987 values;

6. the expansion of the 65-and-over population by about 71 percent, or at an average annual rate of 1.68 percent;

7. the maintenance of age-retirement rates at their 1987 patterns.

Under these assumptions the attainment of a 40-percent-of-median incomes should impose only a small incremental burden. However, as noted in chapter 10, private pensions and property income are highly concentrated in upper income brackets of the aged, so that some support would be likely in lower fractiles as well.

But in the long run it is necessary to expand our definition of incremental burdens to allow for changes in the sizes of beneficiary populations which in terms of judging actual with hypothetical present or near-past periods could be ignored. Moreover, changes in numbers of nonbeneficiary taxpayers and their incomes must also intrude into the analysis. Under the projections of population growth adopted, the aged population will rise by 103 percent by 2020. However, the total U.S. work force is projected to reach its peak by about 2010 and to total 133,426,000 by 2020—an increase of only 17.6 percent over that of 1987.[13] The *aged dependency ratio*—the ratio of the number of persons 65 years of age or more to the number of persons aged 20 to 64—will be .311 in 2020, compared with .203 in 1987. That is, in 1987 about 5 workers in the labor force existed to support each aged person, but in 2020 that will decline to 3.2 workers. The burden of support for each retired person will be magnified by a smaller wage-earner base.

I assume that OASDI benefits will be paid on a current basis from payroll taxes split equally between employer and worker. In 1987 Social Security benefits to aged beneficiaries averaged per worker were $564. That will rise in 2020 to about $993, or by 76 percent. Per capita income per worker should rise by 123 percent over the period, however, lessening the impact of the increased tax burden. In general, the total transfer payments to the aged to be borne by nonbeneficiary taxpayers will rise by 103 percent, while per capita GNP rises by 123 percent. Despite the rise in the aged dependency ratio and the size of the aged population, therefore, were government transfer programs held constant at 1987 levels, the real taxpayer burden relative to income should not make such programs infeasible.

But are the seven assumptions realistic for a 2020 agenda? One potential violation of assumption 5 would be a large growth in Medicare and Medicaid costs. The median age of the relevant population will actually decline between the first and last years of the time period—from 73.1 to 73.0 years—and those in the 75–84 year bracket will actually decline from 31.2 percent of the aged in 1987 to 27.7 percent in 2020.[14] However, the very old—85 years of age and over—will increase from 9.6 percent to 12.8 percent, imposing a prospective large jump in government-financed health care.

In 1986 the mean Medicare outlay per enrollee age 65 or over was $2,313 and the mean Medicaid outlay per beneficiary was $1,324.[15] In 1985, 2,290,000 households with householder 65 years or older, or 10.6 percent, received Medicaid benefits. At a 3 percent per year rate of rise, these benefits would escalate to $6,649 for Medicare and $3,806 for Medicaid in 1987 dollars. Given the rapid rise in real health costs in recent years and the large increase in end-of-life medical costs that can be expected with the growth in the over-80 population these estimates seem conservative. Assuming 100 percent of the aged population in 2020 will be enrolled in Medicare and 10.6 percent—the 1986 datum—will receive Medicaid benefits, other government transfers in table 11.6 will rise to $4,325 for a single household and $6,488 for a married couple. Total government transfer payments rise $59,306 billion, a 15 percent jump over the table 11.9 projection and a 134 percent rise over 1987 levels. This is in excess of per capita personal income growth.

Finally, in estimating tax burdens on nonbeneficiaries I must make two adjustments. The first is for income taxes on benefits paid to the aged which will reduce benefits paid by the nonaged. In 1987 taxation of retirement, survivors, and disability payments totalled $3,221 million, or about 1.9 percent of the benefits computed by method 2 in table 11.10. Application of this percentage to method 1 projections for 2020 in table 11.9 yields a tax recapture estimate of $5,969 million, and a net tax burden of $314,971 million.

But administrative expenses offset these gains. In 1986 administrative costs for the retirement, survivors, and disability programs of OASDI were $2,209 million, or 1.12 percent of benefits paid. For the 2020 projection of Social Security benefits to the aged this forecasts costs of $3,599 million.

In summary, estimates of the cost projections for 2020 to provide (1) government transfers to the aged population equal per household to those granted in 1987, (2) adjustment for income taxes paid on benefits, (3) adjustment for administrative costs, and (4) government transfers that anticipate sizable increases in medical costs are presented in table 11.13.

Female-Headed Families with Minor Children

The second vulnerable group in my analysis consists of families with children under the age of 18 headed by a woman with no husband present. I will proceed in the same stepwise fashion as employed in the analysis of the aged.

TABLE 11.13

Summary of Net Tax Burden to Achieve Programs for the
Aged, in Year 2020 (millions of 1987 dollars)

Program	Total Transfer Payments
1. 1987 Benefits per Household	$391,614
2. Net of Income Tax Paid on Benefits	385,645
3. Plus Inclusive of Administrative Costs	389,244
4. Plus Increased Medical Benefits	444,951

TABLE 11.14

Distribution of Number of Children in Female-Headed Households with
Children under 18 Years of Age, by Race, 1986

	(Thousands of Households)							
Number of Children	*Whites*		*Blacks*		*Other Races*		*Total*	
	No.	%	No.	%	No.	%	No.	%
0	3,071	—	940	—	95	—	4,106	—
1	2,084	51.6	1,719	37.2	54	41.2	2,857	46.8
2	1,362	33.7	654	33.8	45	34.4	2,061	33.8
3	421	10.4	336	17.4	21	16.0	778	12.7
4	119	2.9	152	7.9	8	6.1	279	4.6
5	36	1.0	57	2.9	3	2.3	96	1.6
6 or more	18	.4	15	.8	—	—	33	.5
Totals	7,111	100.0	2,873	100.0	226	100.0	10,210	100.0
Total with Children	4,040		1,933		131		6,104	
Total Children	6,757		3,843		267		10,867	
Average Children per Family with Children	1.67		1.99		2.04		1.78	

Source: U.S. Bureau of the Census, *Household and Family Characteristics, March, 1986, Current Population Reports*, Series P-20, no. 419 (Washington, D.C.: U.S. Government Printing Office, 1987), table 12.

1. *Estimates of Population of Families with Female Householders and Children under 18.* Table 11.14 presents the recent distribution of the subject population by race and number of children.

To aid in the projection of the number of female-headed households in the year 2020, Table 11.15 lists such householders by age and sex, including in the category women who are married with no spouse present, widowed, or divorced. They may or may not have children. The

TABLE 11.15

Female-Headed Households, by Race and Age of Householder,
in Absolute Terms and as Percentages of All Women of That Race in
That Age Group, 1986 (thousands of households)

Age Group	All Races		White		Black		Other	
	No.	%	No.	%	No.	%	No.	%
15–19	78	.87	71	.97	7	.51	—	—
20–24	631	6.40	534	6.54	85	6.02	12	4.23
25–29	1,384	12.65	1,138	12.54	205	14.10	41	9.93
30–34	1,810	17.15	1,383	15.72	366	27.13	61	14.99
35–44	3,584	20.96	2,754	18.90	727	37.24	103	17.76
45–54	2,747	23.15	2,032	20.08	629	46.28	86	22.28
55–64	3,329	28.68	2,671	26.23	572	49.70	86	31.73
65 and Over	9,072	55.32	8,006	54.30	935	66.98	131	50.78

Source: U.S. Bureau of the Census, *Poverty in the United States: 1986, Current Population Reports*, Series P-60, no. 160 (Washington, D.C.: U.S. Government Printing Office, 1988), table 8.

percentages are based on the ratio of such women in a given age group to all women in that age group.

Finally, the projections of the female population in 2020 and of the number who will be heading households, assuming that the proportions by age group and race will be the same as those ruling in 1986 as given in table 11.15, are displayed in panels a and b of table 11.16 respectively. The total number of households headed by women, therefore, is projected to rise from 10.210 million to 34.188 million, or by 225 percent. In table 11.14, 59.8 percent of these households had one or more children under the age of 18 in 1986. Applying that percentage to the 2020 projection of table 11.16 yields the forecast that 20.526 million female-headed households will exist with one or more children under the age of 18. These will consist of 15.003 million white households, 4.414 million black households, and 1.109 other-race households. If the average number of children per such households remains the same as in 1986, there will be 36.101 million children under the age of 18 living in such female-headed households, compared with 10.867 million in 1986. This averages to 1.76 children per family with children.

2. *Estimates of Cash and Noncash Income for Female-Headed Households with Children under 18.* Receipts by such families of government cash transfers (means- and non-means-tested), and of noncash transfers in 1986, inflated to 1987 dollars, are given in table 11.17.

In 1986, the distribution of such households by number of children under the age of 18 is given by race in table 11.14. Estimates of 1986

TABLE 11.16
Projections of Female Population and Households
Headed by Females, by Age and Race, Year 2020
(thousands of persons or households)

Age Group	All Races	White	Black	Other
a. Female Population				
15–19	8,613	6,488	1,520	605
20–24	8,866	6,762	1,486	618
25–29	9,459	7,286	1,520	653
30–34	9,997	7,745	1,566	686
35–44	18,821	14,644	2,839	1,338
45–54	18,480	14,649	2,672	1,159
55–64	20,981	17,163	2,775	1,043
65 and Over	29,637	24,974	3,212	1,451
Totals	124,854	99,711	17,590	7,553
b. Female-Headed Households				
15–19	74.93	62.93	7.75	—
20–24	567.42	442.23	89.46	26.14
25–29	1,196.56	913.66	214.32	64.84
30–34	1,714.49	1,217.51	424.86	102.83
35–44	3,944.88	2,767.72	1,057.24	237.63
45–54	4,278.12	2,941.52	1,236.60	258.23
55–64	6,017.35	4,501.85	1,379.18	330.94
65 and Over	16,395.19	13,560.88	2,151.40	736.82
Totals	34,188.94	26,408.32	6,560.81	1,757.43

Source: U.S. Bureau of the Census, *Projections of the Population of the United States by Age, Sex, and Race: 1988 to 2080, Current Population Reports,* Series P-25, no. 1018 (Washington, D.C.: U.S. Government Printing Office, 1989), table 4, Middle Series, 86–87, and table 11.15.

median incomes received by these households are recorded in table 11.18.

On the assumption employed earlier that per capita incomes throughout the economy will expand at an annual rate of 2.43 percent over the period 1986–2020, median private incomes for these families will rise to levels 2.28 times their 1986 values.

But let us return for a moment to the situation with the subject households in 1986 and their relation to poverty levels. From table 11.14, 46 percent of families headed by females with children under 18 years of age fell below poverty thresholds in 1986, or 3,264,000 families. From table 11.19, therefore, it would have required in 1986, in addition to all government cash and noncash means-tested and non-means-tested pay-

TABLE 11.17

Government Cash and Noncash Transfers to Female-Headed Families
with Children under the Age of 18, 1986, in 1987 Dollars

Benefit	No. of Families	Mean Amount	Total (thousands)
1. Social Security	1,033,000	$5,591	$5,775,360
2. Medicare	992,000	2,442	2,422,450
3. Medicaid	1,423,000	1,786	2,541,312
4. AFDC or Other Non-SSI Cash Assistance	2,400,000	3,785	9,085,683
5. SSI	374,000	3,286	1,228,849
6. Food Stamps	2,708,000	1,577	4,269,192
7. Housing Assist.	1,361,000	2,108	2,869,306
8. School Lunch Subsidies	2,849,000	528	1,503,066
Total			29,694,218
Total Families	7,094,000		
Total Families in Poverty	3,264,000		

Source: U.S. Bureau of the Census, *Measuring the Effect of Benefits and Taxes on Income and Poverty: 1986, Current Population Reports*, Series P-60, no. 164-RD-1 (Washington, D.C.: U.S. Government Printing Office, 1988), table 9, 206–208.

TABLE 11.18

Estimates of 1986 Median Incomes Received by Families
Headed by Females with Children under 18, with Projection for 2020
in Parentheses, in 1987 Dollars

Group	Private Income	Govt. Cash and Noncash Transfers	Total Cash Income	Taxes (Income and Payroll)
All Races	$8,087 ($18,476)	$3,729	$11,816	$1,050
White	9,481 (21,660)	2,870	12,351	1,287
Black	2,099 (4,795)	6,706	8,175	586

Source: U.S. Bureau of the Census, *Measuring the Effect of Benefits and Taxes on Income and Poverty, Current Population Reports*, Series P-60, no. 164-RD-1 (Washington, D. C.: U.S. Government Printing Office, 1988), table D, 8.

ments made in that year, as reproduced in table 11.17, an additional
$11.4 billion in benefits to bring all such families up to poverty thresh-
olds. Total government payouts, therefore, from table 11.19, would have
amounted to $7,729 per poverty family on the average, in 1987 dollars,
for a total of $25,227 million.

TABLE 11.19

Weighted Mean Income Deficits of Families in Poverty Headed
by Females with Children under 18 Years of Age, 1986, in 1987 Dollars

Income Deficit	All Races	White	Black
Mean Deficit in Private Income	$7,729	$7,124	$8,615
Mean Deficit after Government Cash Transfers	5,062	4,542	5,794
Mean Deficit After Government Cash and Noncash Transfers	3,494	3,327	3,700

Source: U.S. Bureau of the Census, *Measuring the Effect of Benefits and Taxes on Income and Poverty, Current Population Reports*, Series P-60, no. 164-RD-1 (Washington, D.C.: U.S. Government Printing Office, 1988), table 6, 162–167. Weights for different numbers of children are taken from table 11.15. Poverty thresholds are listed in table 10.2.

As we saw in chapter 9, median family income in 1987 was $30,853 for a mean family size of 3.17 members. From table 11.15 mean family size for female-headed families with children under 18 was 2.78, including the head of household and mean number of children, or 88 percent of the size of all families. Let us reduce median income proportionately to stand at $27,057 per family, so that the 40-percent-of-median-income threshold would be $10,823. Because the weighted poverty threshold level for this set of families was $9,158, attainment of the goal would entail an average additional benefit of $1,665. Hence, the total transfer cost, before tax recapture, would be $30,662 million. In 1986, households in the $10,823 income range paid about $376 in 1987 dollars, so that gross transfers to subject families in poverty would net to about $29,435 million.

But the 40 percent standard would include some families above the poverty level. It is necessary to make highly speculative estimates of the additional burden imposed by such families. From table 11.18, for all races, the median income specifies that 50 percent of these families received cash incomes below $11,816. The poverty threshold of $9,158 is the upper bound for 46 percent. Hence, I assume that the domain $9,158 to $11,816 includes about 4 percent of the total, or 244,160 families. On the assumption of a uniform distribution of families over this interval, since I wish to include families between $9,158 and $10,823, or 63 percent of the domain, a total of 152,945 families headed by female householders with children under 18 will be added to those below the poverty level when a 40 percent standard is adopted.

Mean income in the income bracket is $9,991. From table 11.18 median income received by all families is $8,087, which I adopt as a rough measure for the 4 percent of families under analysis. Hence, present government transfers (cash and noncash) are estimated to be $1,904 per family. An additional $832 will be necessary to lift such families on the average to the desired 40 percent threshold, so that total government cost before tax recapture is $2,736 per family. Families in the $10,823 income neighborhood paid about $511 in federal income taxes in 1986 (1987 dollars), so I estimate the net tax burden to average to $2,225 per family. The total additional tax burden, therefore, for families above subsistence but below the 40 percent threshold is $340 million, which, when added to the amount necessary to boost impoverished families to that level, yields a total cost of $29,775 million, or, roughly, $30 billion. From table 10.9, line 2, I conclude that about 63 percent of the $48 billion necessary to fully implement a 40-percent-of-median income program under 1986 conditions would be necessary to support female-headed families with minor children.

3. *Estimates of the 40-Percent-of-Median-Income Threshold.* Let us turn now to the estimate of the gross cost of the 40 percent threshold in 2020 in terms of the subject population. With a 2.43 percent annual rate of growth in all forms of income, the median family income should equal $68,795 for a hypothesized family size of 3.17 persons. Since the projected mean family size for the subject population is 1.76, the median income is reduced proportionately to family size to about 56 percent of the stated median income, with $38,195 as projected relevant median income. This sets the mean target at $15,278 in 1987 dollars.

Applying the same rate of growth to private income in table 11.18, I find projected median incomes for all races and for whites to be substantially above the mean median target. The female-headed households with children under 18 that are seriously at risk are blacks, who reveal a median income deficit of $10,483. With a projected number of 4.414 million households, to which will be added other-race families of 1.109 million, a total of 5.523 million families will require total government transfers of $10,483 per family. This yields a payout of $57.898 million before tax recapture. This is undoubtedly an underestimate because I ignore the amounts necessary to bring white families below this median income level up to the standard. In rough, and conservative, estimate, therefore, the gross tax cost in 2020 should be about $58 billion, compared with an estimated cost of $31 billion in 1986.

4. *Estimate of the Tax Burden on Nonbeneficiaries.* Finally, on the basis of 1986 tax payments by families in the $15,278 neighborhood, tax recapture should amount to about $656 per household, for a total of $3.623 billion. Hence, my final estimate of the net tax burden on nonbeneficiaries to bring female-headed households with children under 18 up to a 40-percent-of-median-income threshold is $54.275 billion. This is an underestimate in ignoring the need to support some white families and in failing to take into account administrative costs. The data are summarized in table 11.20.

TABLE 11.20

Summary of Net Tax Burden to Achieve 40-Percent-of-Median-Income
Standard for Female-Headed Households with Children under the Age of 18,
Year 2020 (millions of 1987 dollars)

Program	Total Transfer Payments
40-Percent-of-Median-Income Standard	$54,275

The Undereducated

The last of the large poverty-candidate groups to be considered is that of
the undereducated. Projecting the extent of its existence and its penalization thirty years hence raises some especially troublesome questions.
The first is definitional. While the designation of "aged" has been specified rather clearly in legal conventions, and the notion of female-headed
households with minor children affords no ambiguity, "undereducated"
is a relative expression. It gains definition only with a specification of the
demands of an environment which in the present case can be seen only
dimly a generation away.

A second problem is that within a generation present attitudes of segments within the current population toward education could alter drastically and completely nullify expectations based on current perceptions.
These problems confront us, of course, with respect to age and women
heads of households: attitudes toward retirement age and the factors
leading to formation of single-parent families may well alter. But I expect
them to do so more slowly and with greater continuity than the desire for
education, driven as it is by economic expediency.

Third, it is difficult to disentangle the undereducated from female-
headed households with minor children to prevent double counting of
tax burdens. Many unmarried teenage mothers do not continue their
schooling and join the ranks of the undereducated. It is necessary when
computing the tax charges of the undereducated to eliminate these
women whose burden has been included in that determined in the section "Female-Headed Families with Minor Children."

And last, unlike most members of the other two groups, almost all of
the undereducated will be full-time participants in the labor force and
completely subject to the market's valuation of their deficiencies. Pre-
dicting what those judgments will be thirty years hence requires a gift of
prescience no one possesses.

Nonetheless, in judging the feasibility of a 40 percent standard it is
necessary to gauge the burden that an undereducated underclass might
impose on the American society. I will somewhat arbitrarily identify two
subgroups of the undereducated: those with less than a grammar school
education (less than eight years of schooling) and those with less than a

TABLE 11.21

Percentage Distribution of Years of Schooling Completed by
Persons 20 Years of Age and Older, by Age, Race, and Sex, 1987

Age Group	Both Sexes Less Than		Males Less Than		Females Less Than	
	8 Yrs.	12 Yrs.	8 Yrs.	12 Yrs.	8 Yrs.	12 Yrs.
1. All Races						
20–24	2.2%	15.3%	2.4%	16.6%	1.9%	14.0%
25–34	2.6	13.5	2.8	14.0	2.4	13.0
35–44	3.5	14.1	3.6	13.9	3.3	14.3
45–54	5.6	22.4	6.0	22.7	5.3	22.1
55–64	9.2	32.2	10.4	34.0	8.2	30.7
25 and Over	7.0	24.5	7.2	24.0	6.8	24.8
2. Whites						
20–24	2.1	14.4	2.5	15.8	1.8	13.0
25–34	2.7	12.8	2.9	13.6	2.4	11.9
35–44	3.3	12.9	3.4	12.8	3.2	13.0
45–54	5.0	20.5	5.6	21.1	4.5	20.0
55–64	7.3	29.4	8.0	31.0	6.6	28.0
25 and Over	6.2	23.1	6.3	22.7	6.0	23.3
3. Blacks						
20–24	2.0	21.0	1.6	22.9	2.4	19.6
25–34	1.6	18.4	1.9	16.9	1.4	19.6
35–44	4.1	23.9	4.7	24.4	3.6	23.3
45–54	10.2	38.8	9.9	40.0	10.4	37.9
55–64	25.2	58.0	32.3	64.2	19.6	53.2
25 and Over	13.0	36.5	14.5	36.9	11.8	36.1

Source: U.S. Bureau of the Census, *Educational Attainment in the United States: March, 1987 and 1986, Current Population Reports*, Series P-60, no. 428 (Washington, D.C.: U.S. Government Printing Office, 1988), table 1.

high school education (under twelve years of schooling). To anticipate future trends in attitudes toward the importance of education, the present percentages in the two subgroups are adjusted downward to predict improvements in its attractiveness. And I will assume, more optimistically, that the undereducated will retain relative income position in the economy of 2020, with their median incomes rising at an annual per capita rate of 2.43 percent.

1. *Estimates of the Undereducated Population.* Table 11.21 reproduces the percentage distribution by age group of the educational attainments of persons by race and sex in 1987. As noted in chapter 9 the encouraging

outlook on expansion of the educated as one moves from older to younger age groups is clouded by the fall in high school completion by the 20–29 year age groups, especially among males in general and black males in particular.

Assume that by 2020 all age groups below the age of 34 will have achieved dropout rates half those shown in table 11.21. This group includes those born between 1986 and 2000, and I am somewhat optimistic concerning the prospects for the rather impressive changes in culture and educating proficiency that would have to occur to achieve it.

For those in the 34–44 year bracket educational experience will have been in the 1980s or mid-1990s and should largely reflect the problems the society confronts currently in education and cultural attitudes toward it. These persons in 1987 ranged up to 11 years of age and hence are not represented in the data of table 11.21. I will assume, again optimistically, that dropout rates will fall to 75 percent of their 1987 values.

The age group 45–54 in 1987 ranged between 12 and 21 years of age and hence offers the prospect of little improvement over current experience at the grammar school level but the possibility of a reduction in high school dropout rates in the next few years. I will therefore adopt the 1987 rates for the 20–24 age group for grade school dropouts and 75 percent of the high school dropout rates for that age bracket and apply them to the 45–54 age group.

For the preretirement bracket, ages 55–64, born between 1956 and 1965, with education behind them, I will assume the rates are those for the 25–34 year group in table 11.21. They range in age between 22 and 31 in 1987, and should reflect the attainments of that age bracket.

It will also be assumed that differentials will continue to exist between the races and the sexes, but that they will narrow somewhat. In the case of blacks, development of greater opportunity through a lessening of discrimination and the continuing growth of a middle class should improve cultural attitudes toward schooling and increase incentives to acquire an education. But the stresses on the black family and its tendency to concentrate in the inner cities should prevent the racial gap from being eliminated. I will reduce the rates derived in the previous paragraph by 15 percent for blacks in the 20–24 and 25–34 age brackets and the high school dropout rate for blacks in the 35–44 year group to compensate for these expectations.

The greater attraction and opportunity for education in the lower levels for women are expected to persist, I believe, given the higher pay that will characterize entry-level jobs for males and the greater temptations that will continue to exist to lure them away from school at an early age. But if the nation is successful in enhancing public education, the differential should narrow. I will therefore reduce male dropout rates deter-

TABLE 11.22

Projections of the Percentages of Population 20 Years of Age and Older Lacking Grammar and High School Educations, by Race and Sex, Year 2020

	Males		Females	
Age Group	0–7 Years	8–11 Years	0–7 Years	8–11 Years
1. Whites				
20–24	1.13%	5.98%	.90%	5.60%
25–34	1.31	4.81	1.20	4.75
35–44	2.55	6.09	2.40	7.35
45–54	2.50	9.35	1.80	7.95
55–64	2.90	10.70	2.40	9.50
2. Blacks				
20–24	.61*	8.15	1.02	7.31
25–34	.73*	5.73	.60*	7.73
35–44	3.53	10.47	2.70	12.16
45–54	1.60	15.58	2.40	12.30
55–64	1.90	15.00	1.40	18.20

Source: Table 11.21. The computation of the percentages differs from those in table 11.21 in that the double-counting of persons who lack a grammar school education is eliminated in the table above. That is, those who have 8 to 11 years of schooling are those who, in addition to having a grammar school education have gone beyond.

*These data are biased downward by the failure of the absolute numbers of persons to reach a threshold level. They were recorded as zero.

mined above by a further 10 percent for the 20–24 and 25–34 age brackets and the high school dropout rate by the same percentage for the 35–44 year bracket. The final results of these adjustments in dropout rates are summarized in table 11.22.

Projections of the population in these race, sex, and age categories are given in table 11.23. The projections of the undereducated in 2020, derived by multiplying the forecasts of table 11.23 by the percentages of table 11.22, are also presented in the table.

2. *Estimates of Cash and Noncash Income for the Undereducated.* Table 11.24 details the mean money income and mean money earnings in 1986 (in 1987 dollars) of the age groups with which I have been dealing. The differences between these data yield an estimate of government cash transfers, but omit noncash transfers. These are listed under "cash transfers" in the table.

TABLE 11.23

Projections of Populations and Undereducated by Age, Sex,
and Race, Year 2020 (thousands of persons)

Age Group	Males	0–7 Yrs.	8–11 Yrs.	Females	0–7 Yrs.	8–11 Yrs.
1. All Races						
20–24	9,265	97	587	9,076	84	534
25–34	17,697	216	876	17,479	192	917
35–44	17,543	471	1,173	17,530	492	1,418
45–54	20,469	490	2,068	20,758	391	1,776
55–64	16,475	459	1,842	17,431	397	1,843
Totals	81,449	1,733	6,546	82,274	1,493	6,488
2. Whites						
20–24	7,758	88	464	7,542	68	422
25–34	14,998	196	721	14,587	175	693
35–44	15,158	387	923	14,839	356	1,091
45–54	17,996	450	1,683	17,863	322	1,420
55–64	14,635	424	1,566	15,276	367	1,451
Totals	70,545	1,545	5,357	70,107	1,288	5,077
3. Blacks						
20–24	1,507	9	123	1,534	16	112
25–34	2,699	20	155	2,892	17	224
35–44	2,385	84	250	2,691	73	327
45–54	2,473	40	385	2,895	69	356
55–64	1,840	35	276	2,155	30	392
Totals	10,904	188	1,189	12,167	205	1,411

4. Summary

Male Population 25 and over	81,449
Female Population 25 and over	82,274
Total Population 25 and over	163,723
Total Population Less than 7 Years Schooling	3,226
Total Population with 8 to 11 Years Schooling	13,034
Total Undereducated Population	16,260

Source: U.S. Bureau of the Census, *Projections of the Population of the United States by Age, Sex and Race: 1988 to 2080, Current Population Reports*, Series P-25, no. 1018 (Washington, D.C.: U.S. Government Printing Office, 1989), table 4, 86, Middle Series, and table 11.22.

TABLE 11.24

Mean Money Income and Mean Money Earnings, Persons 18 Years
and Older, by Age and Sex, 1986 (1987 Dollars)

| | Males | | Females | |
Age Group	0–7 Yrs.	8–11 Yrs.	0–7 Yrs.	8–11 Yrs.
18–24				
1. Income	n.a.	n.a.	n.a.	n.a.
2. Earnings	$ 7,672	$ 5,745	$4,245	$ 3,639
25–34				
1. Income	9,717	13,586	4,279	5,772
2. Earnings	8,861	12,774	2,810	4,215
3. Cash Trans.	856	812	1,469	1,557
35–44				
1. Income	11,345	17,274	5,398	6,827
2. Earnings	8,743	16,253	3,780	5,781
3. Cash Trans.	2,602	1,021	1,618	1,046
45–54				
1. Income	13,491	21,260	4,590	7,262
2. Earnings	11,868	19,514	4,206	5,830
3. Cash Trans.	1,623	1,746	384	1,432
55–64				
1. Income	11,640	19,428	8,975	13,085
2. Earnings	8,185	15,436	1,131	2,316
3. Cash Trans.	3,455	3,992	7,844	10,769

Source: U.S. Bureau of the Census, Money Income of Households, Families and
Persons in the United States: 1986, Current Population Reports, Series P-60, no. 159
(Washington, D.C.: U.S. Government Printing Office, 1988), tables 35 and
36, 133–142. Data on income and earnings have been made comparable by
averaging both over *all* persons in the age bracket, whether or not they had
earnings.

Estimates of the total government cash transfers are obtained straightforwardly by multiplying the number of persons in each category in 1986
by the relevant per person transfer. The results are summarized in table
11.25. The total amounts to about $72 billion, perhaps half of it Social
Security retirement and survivors benefits. These latter have not been
captured, however, in estimates of the Social Security payments to those
65 years of age and over determined earlier.

The estimation of noncash transfers by government to these households is somewhat less accurate because of data limitations. Four categories of such benefits must be considered: Medicaid, food stamps, school
lunch subsidies, and rent or housing assistance. Medicare benefits can
be ignored as accruals almost exclusively to the aged.

TABLE 11.25

Estimated Government Cash Transfers to the Undereducated,
1986 (in millions of 1987 dollars)

Age Group	Males		Females	
	0–7 Yrs.	*8–11 Yrs.*	*0–7 Yrs.*	*8–11 Yrs.*
25–34	$ 497	$ 1,825	$ 741	$ 3,439
35–44	1,650	1,890	894	1,979
45–54	1,227	3,232	257	2,967
55–64	3,980	9,828	8,828	29,098
Totals	7,354	16,775	10,720	37,483
Grand Totals:				
Males	24,129			
Females	48,203			
Both Sexes	72,332			

Sources: U.S. Bureau of the Census, *Poverty in the United States: 1986, Current Population Reports*, Series P-60 (Washington, D.C.: U.S. Government Printing Office, 1988), table 1, 10, and table 11.24.

TABLE 11.26

Government Noncash Transfers to Households Whose Head
Completed Less Than 12 Years of Schooling, 1986
(in millions of 1987 dollars)

Benefit Type	Households Receiving	Amount Per Receiving Household	Total Received
Medicaid	4,343,000	$ 885	$ 4,110
Food Stamps	3,586,000	1,196	4,289
School Lunch Subsidies	2,754,000	576	1,587
Rent Subsidies	1,802,000	1,868	3,601
Total			13,587

Source: U.S. Bureau of the Census, *Poverty in the United States: 1986, Current Population Reports*, Series P-60, no. 160 (Washington, D.C.: U.S. Government Printing Office, 1988), table 8.

Table 11.26 lists the benefits received in 1986 by households whose heads had less than 12 years of schooling. From table 11.9.a the total amount of such transfers received by those 65 years of age or older was $34,950 million in 1986. In that year, 6.14 percent of the aged had less than 12 years of education, and so to obtain an estimate of the amount of in-kind benefits that went to them the total was multiplied by that percentage to obtain $2,146 million. Subtracting that from the total of

TABLE 11.27

Estimates of the Number of Female-Headed Families with Children under 18
Years of Age with Household Head among the Undereducated, 1986

Age Group	1 No. of Households[a]	2 No. of Households with Children[b]	3 Percent Undereducated[c]	4 No. of Households Undereducated
25–34	3,194,000	1,910,000	13.0%	248,000
35–44	3,584,000	2,143,000	14.3	306,000
45–54	2,747,000	1,643,000	22.1	363,000
55–64	3,329,000	1,991,000	30.7	611,000
Totals	12,854,000	7,687,000		1,528,000

[a] Table 11.15.

[b] Obtained by multiplying column 1 by .598, the proportion of single female-headed families households having minor children. From table 11.14.

[c] From U.S. Bureau of the Census, *Poverty in the United States: 1986, Current Population Reports*, Series P-60, no. 160 (Washington, D.C.: U.S. Government Printing Office, 1988), table 1, 10.

$13,587 million in table 11.26 yields an estimated $11,441 million of government noncash transfers to households with heads between 25 and 64 who have completed less than 12 years of schooling, or $704 per undereducated person. The estimate of total government cash and noncash payments in 1986 (1987 dollars) to that category is then $83,773 million, or $5,152 per person.

A last step in the computation of nonoverlapping transfer costs with the aged and female-headed households with minor children is to subtract out the costs of those of the latter incorporated with the undereducated. Eliminating the latter under the age of 25 effectively eliminates many teenage mothers with children who are counted in the female-headed families with minor children estimates. Nonetheless, a substantial overlap persists.

Table 11.27 estimates that in 1986 about 1,528,000 of the undereducated persons between 25 and 64 years were female heads of household with children under 18. Multiplication of this number by the mean total transfer payments to the undereducated leads to an estimated overlapping payment of $7,872 million. Subtraction of this from the prior gross estimate of $83,773 million leads to the final total government transfer cost to the undereducated who are neither aged nor female heads of families with minor children of $75,901 million in 1986 (1987 dollars). From tables 11.23 and 11.27 I estimate that 14,688,000 persons between the ages of 25 and 64 fell in this category.

TABLE 11.28

Incremental Government Transfers Necessary to Attain the 40 Percent Standard
for the Undereducated in 1986, 1987 Dollars

Age Group	Median Income	Target Income	Total Income of Female Undereducated[a]		Deficit Females	
			0–7 Yrs.	8–11 Yrs.	0–7 Yrs.	8–11 Yrs.
25–34	$18,266	$7,306	$4,983	$ 6,476	$2,323	$830
35–44	20,692	8,277	6,102	7,531	2,175	746
45–54	17,545	7,018	5,294	7,966	1,724	—
55–64	11,527	4,034	9,679	13,789	—	—

Source: Tables 9.19 and 11.25.
[a] Includes earnings plus government cash and noncash transfers.

Suppose in 1986 a 40-percent-of-median-income standard had been in effect for the undereducated? What additional government transfers would have been required? Table 11.28 details the deficits, and shows that the only needs on an aggregate basis would have been to cover the women in the first three age groups. Earnings plus existing government transfers would bring males of all age groups and both categories of undereducation and females in the other categories up to the 40 percent standard and beyond.

Table 11.29 completes the computation by obtaining the net numbers of women in the three deficit groups and multiplying those numbers by the relevant deficits. The necessary transfer increment is $5,925 million, for a total transfer cost of $81,826 million. The sum of government cash and noncash transfer benefits to the undereducated in 1986 was almost sufficient to lift them as a group above the 40 percent standard.

It is now necessary to project the net cost of the 40 percent standard in year 2020. I start with the projections of table 11.23.1 for the undereducated and the mean money earnings data for 1986 in table 11.24. If I apply our assumption that earnings in 1987 dollars will grow at 2.43 percent per year over the intervening period, those mean earnings per undereducated person in each category should rise to the levels recorded in table 11.30. Shortfalls and required transfer payments are detailed in table 11.31. Under the assumption of earnings growth males in the aggregate in each age-education category should rise above the 40 percent thresholds. But women in all categories will fall below relevant thresholds. Total transfer payments will be $41,092, or a little less than the government cash transfers to such women in 1986 (table 11.25).

These projections are quite sensitive to the projection of earnings growth. If the jobs in which the undereducated concentrate grow in pay

TABLE 11.29

Number of Undereducated Females Corrected for Number of Mothers
with Minor Children, and Total Additional Transfer Cost of
40 Percent Standard, 1986 (1987 Dollars)

Age Group	Income Deficit	No. Females With Indicated Education[a]	Females With Minor Child.[b]	Support Numbers	Cost (Millions)
25–34					
a. 0–7 Yrs.	$2,323	505,000	39,000	466,000	$1,083
b. 8–11 Yrs.	830	1,892,000	147,000	1,745,000	1,448
35–44					
a. 0–7 Yrs.	2,175	553,000	47,000	506,000	1,101
b. 8–11 Yrs.	746	1,892,000	162,000	1,730,000	1,291
45–54					
a. 0–7 Yrs.	1,724	669,000	88,000	581,000	1,002
Total					5,925

[a] U.S. Bureau of the Census, *Poverty in the United States: 1986, Current Population Reports*, Series P-60, no. 160 (Washington, D.C.: U.S. Government Printing Office, 1988), table 1, 10.
[b] See reference b and column 3 in table 11.27.

TABLE 11.30

Projections of Mean Money Earnings, Undereducated Persons 25 Years of Age
and Older, by Age and Sex, 2020, and Projected Median Incomes
(1987 Dollars)

Age Group	Males		Females		Median Income	Target
	0–7 Yrs.	8–11 Yrs.	0–7 Yrs.	8–11 Yrs		
25–34	$20,244	$29,184	$6,420	$ 9,630	$41,731	$16,692
35–44	19,974	37,132	8,636	13,207	47,273	18,909
45–54	27,114	44,582	9,609	13,319	40,084	16,034
55–64	18,699	35,265	2,584	5,291	26,335	10,534

Source: Table 11.24

at substantially less than our assumed 2.43 percent rate, these transfer payments would rise substantially. For example, if the rate of growth was half the assumed rate, or 1.22 percent per year, the total transfer cost would rise to $68,312 million, with the two youngest and least educated male categories receiving aid.

To net out of the projections of table 11.31 the transfers that would accrue to women who head households with minor children, the following approximative procedure was followed, as depicted in table 11.32. Column 1 contains the projected female undereducated, including both

TABLE 11.31

Projected Deficit Incomes for 40 Percent Standard and Total Expenditures
Required, 2020, 1987 Dollars

	Deficits				Total Transfers	
	Males		Females		0–7 Yrs.	8–11 Yrs.
Age Group	0–7 Yrs.	8–11 Yrs.	0–7 Yrs.	8–11 Yrs.	(in millions)	
25–34	—	—	$10,272	$7,062	$ 1,972	$ 6,476
35–44	—	—	10,273	5,702	4,407	8,085
45–54	—	—	6,425	2,715	2,512	4,822
55–64	—	—	7,950	5,243	3,156	9,662
Totals					12,047	29,045
Grand Total					41,092	

Source: Tables 11.23.1, 11.30.

TABLE 11.32

Computation of Government Transfers Necessary for 40 Percent Standard Net
of Female-Headed Families with Minor Children, 2020

	1	2	3	4
Age Group	Projected Female Undereducated (0–11 Yrs.)[a]	Female-Headed Households[b]	Households With Children	Projected Undereducated[c]
25–34	5,109,000	2,911,000		
35–44	1,847,000	3,945,000		
45–54	2,167,000	4,278,000		
55–64	2,240,000	6,017,000		
Totals	11,363,000	17,151,000	6,658,000	1,073,000

[a] Table 11.23.1.
[b] Table 11.16.
[c] 16.1 percentage figure from table 11.27.

those without grammar school and high school diplomas. The projected
female-headed households are taken from table 11.16.b and reproduced
in column 2. To obtain an estimate of the proportion of these households with minor children it was necessary to work with a figure of 59.8
percent of female-headed households derived from table 11.14 for 1986.
This was applied to households whose female heads were within the first
three age groups, omitting those between 55 and 64 years of age. These
operations yielded a projection of 6,658,000 female-headed households
with minor children. From the third column of table 11.27 a weighted
average of the first three age groups' percentages of undereducated

TABLE 11.33

Estimation of Federal Income Tax Reclamation
in Year 2020 from Undereducated Beneficiaries
in the 40 Percent Program, 1987 Dollars

Age Group	1 Target Income	2 Estimated Tax	3 Weights
25–34	$16,692	$ 916	.239
35–44	18,909	1,691	.239
45–54	16,034	881	.284
55–64	10,534	578	.238

Source: Tables 11.30 and 11.23, and U.S. Bureau of the Census, *Measuring the Effects of Benefits and Taxes on Income and Poverty, Current Population Reports*, Series P-60, no. 164-RD-1 (Washington, D.C.: U. S. Government Printing Office, 1988), table 1, 16.

yielded a value of 16.1 percent in the aggregate which, when applied to the total of households with minor children, projects 1,073,000 female-headed households.

Finally, the employment of the projections of table 11.23 to obtain a weighted average of projected deficits for the 40 percent standard in the first three age groups of table 11.31 is $5,537. Applied to the estimate derived in column 4 of table 11.32, I am led to project an overlap of $5,980 million in transfer payments. Subtraction of this from the $41,092 million projection of table 11.31 yields a net transfer cost before tax reclamation of $35,112.

4. *Estimate of the Tax Burden on Nonbeneficiaries.* To estimate the tax reclamation by federal income taxes from beneficiaries of the 40 percent program, an aggregate procedure is necessary because of the inability to break down the number of female-headed households with minor children in table 11.32. In table 11.33, column 1 records the target income under the program for each age group and column 2 the estimated income tax in 1986 (1987 dollars). To obtain a weighted mean income tax, I have used the weights in column 3 which were derived from the projected female undereducated population by age group in table 11.23. This yields a weighted average income tax of $1,011. Multiplying this by the projected undereducated female-headed families with minor children of 1,073,00 yields a reclamation estimate of $1,085 million.

The tax-adjusted, female-household adjusted transfer cost of the 40 percent program for the undereducated in 2020 is projected to be $34,027 million. It is recorded in table 11.34, together with the cost of the same program were the assumed rate of growth in earnings assumed to be half of that employed in the estimation just concluded.

TABLE 11.34
Summary of Net Tax Burden to Achieve 40-Percent-of-Median-Income
Standard for Undereducated Persons, Year 2020
(in billions of 1987 dollars)

Program	Total Transfer Payments
40-Percent-of-Median-Income Standard with 2.43% Annual Growth in Earnings	$34.027
40-Percent-of-Median-Income Standard with 1.22% Annual Growth in Earnings	74.221

SUMMARY AND CONCLUSION

I have attempted to project the program costs in 2020 of supporting the three most vulnerable groups in American society isolated—the aged, single mothers, and the undereducated—at defined levels of support. Those levels are to maintain the aged at 1986 benefits in real terms (which for all practical purposes meet the 40-percent-of-median-income standard) and to raise the remaining two groups to 40-percent-of-median-income thresholds in 2020. The goal is to gauge the feasibility of such programs within broad tolerances. One need not belabor the dangers of projecting data thirty years into the future, but with the limited aims of gauging the ability of the American ethos to tolerate such programs some perspective is accessible.

The projection parameters have been optimistic, most notably in assuming an average annual growth rate of 3 percent for all total income and earnings measures and 2.43 percent for per capita income measures. I have also assumed that it will be possible to limit the benefits to the aged to the 1986 levels thirty years in the future in the face of substantial income growth. In other decisions where data was unavailable or fuzzy, I have attempted to be conservative in the sense of leaning toward the underestimation of costs.

The results of the analyses are summarized in table 11.35. In 1987 dollars, it is projected that the total transfer costs of these three programs alone will lie between $478 billion and $573 billion, compared with costs in 1986 of $305 billion. That is an increase of between 57 percent and 88 percent.

During this period from 1986 to 2020, however, GNP in 1987 dollars under the assumption of a 3 percent growth rate is projected to rise from $4,344 billion to $12,046 billion, or by 177 percent, and per capita GNP from $18,232 to $41,654, or by 128 percent. Population, on the other hand, is projected to rise at a rate of .57 percent per year, to total only a 21 percent rise over the 34-year period.

TABLE 11.35

Summary of Projected Transfer Costs in Year 2020 of Programs to Supplement
Incomes of the Three High Poverty Risk Groups (billions of 1987 dollars)

	Total Transfer Payments	
Group and Program	1986	2020
1. Aged (65 Years or More)		
a. Maintaining 1986 Benefits plus Administrative Costs (which essentially meets or exceeds 40-Percent-of-Median-Income Standard)	$201.499	$389.244
b. Maintaining 1986 Benefits with a 3 Percent Rise per Year in Real Medical Costs		(444.951)
2. Female-Headed Households with Children under 18 Years		
a. 40-Percent-of-Median-Income Standard	29.775	54.275
3. Undereducated		
a. 40-Percent-of-Median-Income Standard with 2.43% Growth Rate in per Capita Earnings	81.826	34.027
b. 40-Percent-of-Median-Income Standard with 1.22% Growth Rate in per Capita Earnings		(74.221)
Totals	304.533	477.546
		(573.477)

As indicated in chapter 10, I do not believe this package would be feasible in the short run, despite the fact that the program for the aged is currently funded. However, the annual $88 billion cost in 2020 of the other two programs is 40 percent above the cost in 1987 of the 40 percent standard, as computed in table 10.7. If earnings growth fell to 1.22 percent annually, that cost could escalate to $128 billion, or 114 percent of 1987 costs.

With a work force projected to be 133,426,000 persons in 2020, the burden on the worker of the $478 billion package would be $3,579, or, were the package cost to rise to $573 billion, fully $4,298. These estimates do not incorporate the redistributive costs of programs other than the three dominant ones I have dealt with in this chapter.

Weighted mean per capita income in 1987 was approximately $13,857. At a 2.43 percent growth rate, that will rise to $30,897 in 2020, or by 123 percent. At 1.43 percent per year growth the figure would be $20,726, a 50 percent rise. The per person cost of the three programs would absorb from 11.6 billion to 17.3 percent of pretax income at the $478 billion cost level, or between 13.9 percent and 20.7 percent at the $573 billion cost level.

In fiscal year 1987–1988 per capita personal federal income taxes were $1,632 and federal payroll taxes added $1,301 for a total federal income burden of $2,933. Additions of state and local personal taxes yielded a total of $1,991 for income taxes and $3,719 for income and payroll taxes.[16] In studying the feasibility of the proposed 2020 programs, therefore, we are facing costs that may well exceed per capita income-plus-payroll tax burdens at all government levels currently by substantial amounts.

The current fiscal crisis in the United States, which has required eight years to impose an initial annual tax rise of $50 billion, or a per capita tax increase of $203, is an index of the strength of the egoistic strand of individualism in the American ethos. The three programs in table 11.35 would impose incremental tax costs of between $588 and $914. Under current economic and attitudinal conditions such increases are completely outside the realm of feasibility, especially because of their direct application to redistributive uses.

The willingness to pay taxes does not rise proportionately with income, for income earners benchmark their living standards continuously with income growth. To argue that rises in per capita income of between 50 percent and 123 percent over the next thirty years would eliminate serious resistance to the adoption of the 40 percent standard is naive. But over the long run affluence does raise the weight a society gives to the social strand of individualism: one need only compare the rise of social welfare programs in the last sixty years to establish that. Nonetheless, it is always a painful social process, and the size of the proposed tax increments seen in the light of potential income growth ensures political and economic struggle even in the long run.

Feasibility hinges largely, I believe, on the growth rate for income over the next thirty years. If it is as high as 3 percent or even 2.5 percent, I believe the 40 percent standard lies on the edge of feasibility in the American society. If growth is less, I would believe that feasibility is moot. However, given the prospects for the American society, and given the rising social demands that will be made by vested interests who will amplify their voting voices in the period, I feel that the 40 percent standard is one that could be achieved in 2020, but that it marks the upper bound of the social strand's potential for support.

PART IV

Reprise and Prospect

Chapter 12

COMPASSIONATE CAPITALISM

THE THREE E'S

Any economic mechanism adopted by a society to allocate its scarce resources among goods productions and to distribute those goods among its citizens must be judged by the three E's: efficiency, ethos, and equity.

Ideal economic efficiency is attained when, with fixed amounts of factor services available to the society, (1) resource allocations are made in such manner as to permit the production of more of any good or group of goods only if one or more other goods are reduced in quantity; (2) goods distributions among recipients are such that it is impossible to benefit one or more persons unless one or more others are negatively impacted; and (3) when conditions 1 and 2 hold it is impossible to move to another resource allocation and goods distribution meeting the same conditions such that a different allocation of goods among consumers and factors to goods production would leave all consumers at least as well off and one or more better off.

These conditions for economic efficiency, the means of implementing them, the degree to which realistically functioning economic systems attain or approach them, the important sets of situations in which such systems fail to perform acceptably in their regard, the supplementary economic systems or corrective measures necessary to attain such performance, and judgments as to the circumstances in which the costs of such supplementation or correction outweigh the inefficiency costs: these are the traditional concerns of the economist whose interests lie in microeconomics. Modern microeconomic theory is almost wholly concerned with such problems of efficiency in its judgments of economic systems, comfortable with the rather weak commitment to values such analysis enjoins. After all, how many would quarrel with the assumption that more satisfaction derived from economic goods is better than less? Some, to be sure, have challenged the proposition, but given the challenges facing societies that can be met successfully only with enhanced goods availability, it is difficult to take such criticism seriously. Concerns about excessively consumerist societies and the frivolity of power toothbrushes ring hollow in face of the enormous demands on resources that confront the world's societies.

But the citizens of a society and their social policymakers do not have the ability to ignore the more controversial dimensions of an economy's performance. That controversy arises because decisions in these domains require value judgments—choices among alternative axioms of what constitutes the "good" and the "right." Does the operation of this economic system lead to economic solutions that conflict with the deep-seated ideals and beliefs that shape the society's vision of communal life and inform and design noneconomic social institutions? Does the command economy constrict unacceptably the highly valued freedom of the individual? Does the market economy require or instill an excessive individualism in the face of the organic nature of other values and beliefs in the society? To what extent can this form of economy be altered to conform to the social *Geist* or to what extent can the latter be changed to accommodate an economy believed to have compensating advantages? More deeply, which of the plurality of values, beliefs, folkways, and mores that are current in a society at any time should be accepted by decision makers as dominant in their appeal or desirable of reinforcement and thereby as incorporated into the "ethos"?

Any economic system, given the social importance of the decisions that it must make and effect, must implicitly instill patterns of consciousness, belief, and outlook that are at once necessary for its functioning and potentially inimical to components of the ethos. I have emphasized three such patterns that the market mechanism seeks to instill or reinforce: individualism, materialism, and rationalism. The Grand Experiment currently under way in Eastern Europe, where abrupt transitions from command to free market economic systems are being attempted, yields daily testimony to the difficulties of introducing such instrumental values in societies whose ethos has been antagonistic to many of such values for forty-five to seventy-five years. It is not at all clear at the present writing that such transformations will be successful by virtue of the inertia of ethos.

A still different though related variety of painful value judgments concerning economic systems attends the decision maker and the society he or she serves. Is it "just" that the economy distributes more goods to Jones than to Smith? If so, how much more is sanctioned? Does the "social value" of Jones or the class of Joneses demand his or its economic support contrary to the economy's dictates? Which Smith or class of Smiths should suffer diversion of goods for this purpose? What body of values should constitute the society's principles of economic justice providing guidelines for such decisions to assure consistency and continuity? What set of principles should distinguish the unfortunate from the unjust, the moral from the just, charity from justice? In short, does this economic mechanism conform to the society's notions of equity in its distributive and allocative decisions, and, if not, what corrective measures can be instituted? To what extent would such measures be conformant to goals of economic efficiency and be consistent with the ethos? At which points would the extents of such measures become infeasible in view of such efficiency and ethos constraints? These are the questions any society must address in its design of an economic system, and it is these concerns I have addressed directly in this book.

Efficiency

The body of evidence is now all but indisputable: as an economic mechanism for the efficient allocation of resources and the distribution of goods for the large bulk of individualistic economic decisions, the free market mechanism as it operates in realistic contexts cannot be surpassed by currently available alternatives. Not only in its short-run slice-of-time operation, but in its dynamic or intertemporal allocations, as they affect the effective economic introduction of scientific and technical discoveries and the consequent growth in output, capitalism has displayed a historical record that puts the efficiency performance of alternative systems to shame.

No worthwhile substitute has been found to coordinate the mind-stupefying complex of interrelated decisions of millions of agents into a self-consistent pattern of allocation and distribution that has important optimality features and that functions so cheaply in terms of administrative resources. The entire mechanism is integrated into a self-subsistent decision maker and effectuator by an inexpensive flow of easily understood, one-dimensional information: prices. For good or for evil, no substitute for egoistic self-interest has been found for energizing a society's economic strivings. Societies which have felt that communal dedication, fraternal empathy, or antimaterialist values were preferable have experienced their economies foundering on the rocks of barely submerged self-interest.

Nor am I speaking of the potentials of an abstract theoretical idealization of the market mechanism. Much nonsense is written by economists concerning the efficiency of unrealistic and infeasible theoretical mock-ups of the market economy in antiseptic surroundings. When one leaves those simplistic environments it is true that what economists can assert objectively about conformity to the efficiency conditions cited earlier is quite limited. Rather, my assertions are in reference to the functioning of real world market economies with warts-and-all: markets in which buyers and/or sellers have pricing power, conditions in which participants have imperfect information possibly asymmetrically distributed among them, and nonexistence of facilities for all agents to undertake and shift risks to the extents they desire. The work-a-day market mechanism, with its continuous pressure to minimize costs, to remain within budget, to satisfy customers' demands, to permit consumers to purchase goods that conform to their individual preferences, and to minimize the production of unwanted goods has demonstrated empirically its functional superiority to nonmarket alternative systems in efficiency.

But this is not to assert that the market can function without supplemental economic mechanisms and efficiency-corrective external regulation. In general, the market mechanism is incapable of producing goods whose consumption cannot be restricted to paying users: national defense or police protection, for example. In other cases while the restriction on use could be enforced the market may not be able to provide goods efficiently. For example, where consumption of goods is nonrivalrous—my benefiting from consumption of the good does not restrict your usage, as, for example, use of a highway in noncongestion periods or enjoyment of a television program—the efficient price of such goods is zero. However, no firm could survive if it produced and distributed the good at such an efficient price, and hence it may be judged preferable that the government provide such goods gratis. Finally, at various stages of its development a market economy may find it infeasible to produce certain products that society may deem vital for noneconomic reasons. The high cost of labor, reflecting the high marginal productivity of labor in the mature American economy, has rather clearly made the production of low-income housing impossible in the absence of external subsidy. For the same reasons the production of merchant ships is not feasible in wholly unprotected, unsubsidized conditions. For motives of social concern for the needy and of national security, government may use nonmarket means to remedy the deficiency.

Where the market can function there are some inherent disabilities that lead to outcomes that are inefficient or judged to be unacceptable on other grounds by a society. The market mechanism cannot capture real costs of production that do not pass through a market, that is, costs that are "external" to the market system. Polluting effluents are the classic case, where the total social costs of producing products are not captured in those products' costs and prices but may be inflicted as costs on other products or on the society at large. Users of these products, therefore, face prices that do not reflect true costs, leading to malallocation of resources. Cigarettes provide another example where the market does not capture the health costs their usage inflicts on society and their price therefore understates social costs. In such instances governments may "internalize" such external costs via taxation or other measures in a corrective role. And, of course, where firms' pricing power is judged to be excessive in the light of resource allocation efficiency or equity, the government may act correctively. Other regulatory functions of government on corrective account also are asserted on the same grounds.

My concern in this work has not been with the efficiency of the market mechanism except insofar as it is relevant to economic justice and the constraints on such principles imposed by the ethos. But my conclusion is that the efficiency of the free market mechanism is so predominant over alternatives that only were it found to be excessively and incorrigibly contradictory to the ethos or inconsistent with a desirable theory of economic equity conforming to that ethos could the prospect be entertained of abandoning it. That said, we turn to the questions of ethos and equity.

Ethos

In a similar vein, my major concern is not in delineating in great detail that core of values that constitutes the American ethos, nor in discussing its evolution over time or its general adaptability. My interest in it springs wholly from its role in constraining the choices among principles of economic justice intended to function as operational precepts shaping distributive policy in American society. While it is true that economic justice concerns the "ought" rather than the "is," and though the "ought" cannot be derived from the "is," to the extent one wishes to have realistic relevance the "is" constrains one's choice of the "ought." Conceptions of economic equity in radical nonconformance to the most fundamental values and beliefs shaping a nation's communal consciousness may have some long-term use in steering that nation's course, but like the stars that often function in that capacity, they are ultimately unattainable. They remain pious affirmations on the lips of visionaries. What alternative principles of economic justice are feasible in the context of that ethos, therefore, is not an incidental question in my search for operational guidelines.

I have stressed three strands of the American ethos of direct relevance to the acceptability of a theory of economic justice. Most fundamental is that of *individualism*, which postulates the separable and unique being of the human person, his or her rational and emotional identity, and the right to be accorded a dignity in keeping with those properties. On the one hand from them arises the acceptability of egoistic striving for goals of his or her choosing, subject to recognition of the rights of others to elect the same conduct. This I have termed the *egoistic* strand of individualism.

On the other hand there derives from the same body of human qualities the obligation of society to protect the individual unable to attain a level of dignity through self-effort. These implications of individualism, which conflict with the egoistic strand, I have termed the *compassionate* strand. At the core of the American ethos, therefore, is the tension that exists in these coexisting but contending implications of individualism, motivating social policy to seek an equilibrium between their claims for recognition. The weights accorded to these strands or asserted by their proponents to be appropriate for such a balance is the single most contentious issue in the debate over American economic justice.

A second component of the ethos I have stressed is that of materialism. The recognition of the material standard of life as one of the major sources of human well-being, and the rightness of individual efforts to achieve it in abundance, are well emplaced in the American ethos. The goal seeking of individuals in American society is in very large part comprised of the search for improved material welfare either directly, in order to enjoy the consumption of goods, or indirectly as a means of improving family position, social status, or security in the face of the risks of an individualistic and voluntarist society.

Money—the fungible material good—becomes both a material token and an abstract symbol of social success, the ability to enjoy goods, the performance of duty to one's dependents and, in general, the dominant measure of social worth. It may be decried as "excessive" by critics of the culture, but it must be reckoned with when one is considering redistributive policies whose feasibility hinges on the ability to induce the original recipients of such material wherewithal to yield it up to other claimants on the bases of economic justice. Further, in defense of these values, critics may fail to understand that for many of the nation's citizens "getting ahead" or earning and saving for the childrens' educations or paying off a home that anchors a family and reinforces the feeling of self-worth may constitute the major source of spiritual fulfillment in their lives.

The last component of the American ethos that I have dealt with is the gestalt of attitudes and outlooks I have termed *rationalism.* The living of the life of "right reason" which seeks to steer the individual along a steady path of clearly foreseen goals unobscured by the passions is the ideal it urges for the individual. The systematization and routinization of action in seeking to obtain these goals; the rather rigorous separation of mystical final-cause explanations of phenomena from a dominant proximate cause-and-effect outlook; the depreciation of tradition as a legitimizer of social institutions or mechanisms and their judgment by standards of usefulness; planning and optimization, benefit-cost and the bottom line, hard science and technology rather than soft intellectualism: all of these are facets of the habits of thought and the vision of reality fostered by this strain of the ethos.

My position has been that any theory of economic justice developed to provide operational guidelines for the designation of individual rights and obligations and the shaping of economic and social policy must conform to these cultural artifacts, where conformance includes the potential for them to be altered in directions necessary for acceptance of the theory's dictates. The adoption of this filter leads me initially to ignore theories of economic justice that are grossly inconsistent with the ethos. For example, theories that ground justice in the perfection of the human race or the development of supermen can be dismissed out of hand. Less summarily, but compellingly, so can theories that rely on mystical religious injunctions involving God's sovereign desires or the obligation to work out His will, somehow divined. Remaining candidate theories have been screened for essential compatibility with these tenets of the ethos.

One recognizes the danger of so doing, of course. The peril exists that only such theories that bolster the legitimacy of the status quo can survive such scrutiny. But the opposite danger is one I believe to be demonstrated by much ethical thought: by ignoring the constraints of the ethos and, indeed, their moral desirability as social guidelines, its precepts become elegant but abstract irrelevance. I have attempted to steer a median course through the perils by assuming that the ethos, at least in the long run, can be changed in the direction of a broadly acceptable theory. The success or failure of that effort must be judged ultimately by the reader's choice of ethical values.

A final consideration is the additional support the ethos gives to the wisdom of retaining the market mechanism as the form of economy appropriate to American society. The implicit value system that inheres in the market's decision criteria and that it seeks to reinforce by its operation are conformable to all but one of these constituents of the ethos. The market economy's organization and its operability are grounded solidly in the rightness of egoistic individualism, and enforce such derivatives as the duty to treat the individual on the basis of relevant merit only. It maximizes the freedom of choice of agents within the constraints of their genetic and acquired abilities. And it reinforces the rightness of property ownership—without which it could not function—as a projection of the individual's moral sovereignty.

Further, it is fully in accordance with and, indeed, necessitous of exploiting, the materialistic and rational characteristics of the culture. Its allocation of resources in the face of voluntarism requires for effective implementation that monetary rewards and sanctions, with accompanying status changes, be valued highly by society. The scope of its effectiveness obviously is dictated by the priorities persons give to possessing its products.

Its dependence on rational principles of systematization, optimization, planning, and technical progress need not be labored. Its innate drives toward efficiency, which I have already asserted to be at least a preliminary recommendation for its retention as an allocative mechanism, can be effective only in a society that has been rationalized and disciplined in manners I have indicated.

However, the important facet of the ethos with which the market economy conflicts is the compassionate strand of individualism. It simply has no means of incorporating in its decision making the compassionate and custodial implications of the notion of the sanctity of the individual that forms the underpinning of all liberal societies. Its individualism is an impersonal egoistic individualism, blind to the human being's existence as an end in him- or herself, and cognizant of his or her meaning only as a means to fulfill its productive ends. Any theory of economic justice that proposes the need to correct the market's distribution of income in order to effect this dual strand of individualism must expect a resistance from the ethos strongly reinforced by the value system of the market. Such equity considerations are externalities to the market economy although they are internal to the ethos.

The question of economic justice, therefore, is highly involved in the liberal society with the extent to which the demands of economic equity are or are not constrained to the point where the market can continue to function effectively. What degree of interference with the market's complexly intertwined allocation and distribution decisions can be tolerated by a market economy in the name of economic justice before it must be replaced by an economic form that can accept a more organic social ethos? What are the limits of feasibility of schemes of economic justice that require alterations of the market economy's distributions within the context of the market-supportive ethos?

Equity

With such questions I have reached the third criterion for the functioning of an economy: within some definition of the principles of the right and the good, how *equitable* is its operation? Does it conform to accepted or acceptable principles of commutative and distributive justice? To what extent would principles of economic justice interfere with economic efficiency, or individuality, or the equality of competition for reward, and what are the relative priorities society should accord to each?

The inability of the market mechanism to incorporate communal considerations without external constraints has made it peculiarly vulnerable to criticism from those concerned with economic justice. Some of those assertions fail to take into account the high dependence on voluntary commitment a market economy has. Glib arguments that in a liberal society political institutions must be based on civil equality and that economic inequality is anomolous do not take into account the intensity of effort required of the individual in both capacities, the necessity to induce persons to devote a major portion of their lives to economic pursuits, as well as to subject themselves to the rigid discipline most economic activity requires. Political involvement of the citizen of a liberal society generally is quite minimal, although even in such occasional tasks as voting the lack of incentives occasions low voter turnout. Where such participation is not minimal but remains nonprofessional it is undertaken wholly voluntarily and is subject to withdrawal at the citizen's discretion; where the participation is professional it assumes the dimensions of an economic commitment and must be incentivized by receipt of income. The involvements in both terrains are of a qualitatively different nature, the incentivization requirements equally disparate, so that equality in one sphere does not argue for equality in the other.

Moreover, inequality of reward plays an important role in the very functioning of the market economy. As noted above, efficient resource allocation is accomplished by differential pricing. The political mechanism of a liberal society does not have like needs: indeed, in realistic governmental matters, unequal or disproportionate power exerted by well-organized lobbies constitutes one of the important causes of dysfunction in democracy.

It is also frequently ignored by critics that most of the problems of poverty in the United States occur among groups that for one reason or another do not participate in the market economy or who are not prepared to offer skills commensurate to the needs of an advanced economy. It exists not because persons are in the market economy but because they are outside it. Poverty is largely external to the market economy, and in that respect is more a social than an economic problem. The infusion of equity into such problem areas becomes in largest part the preparation of such groups for full involvement in the market mechanism where possible through external policies, or, failing that, to employ external subsidies. Those who would blame the market economy for failing to provide jobs for the undereducated and unskilled are deploring the very success of the instrument in conquering poverty: rapid growth through technological innovation that has obsolesced such labor. To decry it is to complain that automobiles have outmoded horse-drawn transportation, that combines have displaced hand harvesting, or that automotive street cleaners have replaced the "white wings" of yesterday.

But after having dealt with these broad-brush indictments, the nation cannot ignore more reasoned questions about equity and justice in a market society. Inequality of wealth and income that is brought about to a high degree as a by-product of the market economy's operation may result in agglomerations of political power that threaten political equality. Individuals who are excluded from participation in a market economy or who have not developed the necessary skills for full participation may have a claim in justice against the society. Economic efficiency is merely one social goal, and some sacrifice in its level of involvement may be judged worthwhile if a closer approach to some ideal standard of economic justice results therefrom. The exclusive expression of egoistic individualism in the market's distributive decisions may well be judged by a society to be needful of countervailing by some intrusion of the compassionate implications of individualism.

These considerations of economic justice in American society have a special urgency in my view for several reasons developed in the foregoing chapters. In the next thirty years there looms the necessity for redistribution of income on a scale that will be a substantial change from what we are now undertaking. The important pockets of economic need have every prospect of increasing in size and substantially increasing their relative burden on the productive. Indeed, I project that the economic concerns of justice will dominate those of efficiency over that time frame, and for the first time in our history will be the continuing and major concern of social policy.

The conceptual preparation necessary for the society to confront these problems with consistent guidelines that protect the productive and permit justice to be received by the unproductive; the role of the ethos and desire for economic efficiency in constraining such principles to assure their relevance; and the practical limits of redistributive programs to implement the principles in the short and long runs have constituted the core concerns of this work. A summary of the major results of my analyses follows in the remainder of this chapter.

The Necessity of a Charter

If the scope of redistributive problems has the dimensions I foresee, it becomes extremely important that a consensus be achieved in American society concerning an acceptable theory of economic equity. Such notions that are now discernible are the cumulative result of thousands of ad hoc political decisions that have been shaped much more by the purposeful exercise of power by vested interests than any set of principles. No formal definition of the economic rights and obligations of individuals, or establishment of economic mechanisms and institutions, exists to constrain executive or legislative branches in their policy formation—a situation in marked contrast to that of the protections afforded political and civil rights by the Constitution. The lack of a well-formulated theory of economic justice—principles that permit a society to distinguish the unfortunate from the unjust—place it at the mercy of every aggrieved interest group that clothes its selfish interests in the vestments of justice.

To seek to initiate a debate on what principles would be accepted by the nation in the light of the ethos that ultimately shapes its policy courses, I have proposed another form of intellectual experiment so frequently used by ethical philosophers to derive principles of justice. Instead of an "initial position" or a social contract assemblage I propose a notional convention of the most able minds to draft a bill of economic rights and obligations that they would recommend be incorporated into the Constitution with the recognition that such a document would require the acceptance by a large majority of the American people. What principles would emerge from such a conclave to serve as a formalized statement of economic justice for the nation?

After an intensive study of important theories of social justice now current, in chapter 7 I have ventured ten articles of amendment to the Constitution that I believe likely to attain consensus, and propose their adoption by policymakers to guide decisions in areas of economic justice. These principles rest heavily on the essential rightness of the individualistic and voluntarist economy, and, therefore, of the basic distribution of income yielded by it. To contravene this dominant theme in the American ethos would not only be futile and render the document impractical but would deny an attractive quality in the American character.

Egoistic individualism—with its affirmation of the individual's right to exploit fully his or her abilities and preferences within the limitations of his or her individuality, with its correlative obligation to support his or her dependents and to honor contracts—is the indispensable foundation of liberal society. While its surface manifestations of a dedication to material goods and the chase after the dollar may appear excessive and unattractive to critics, its deeper implications for the liberty of the individual, the development in him or her of a sense of responsibility and accountability, and the pride of independence from state largesse are of far greater importance.

In these respects the document is heavily indebted to Nozick's entitlements theory of economic justice, with its great stress on voluntarist action, but it departs radically in its recognition of the dual strand of individualism which dictates an active concern for the welfare of those who are incapable of gaining a threshold livelihood in the market. Income support and the opening of doors of opportunity through education, the provision of basic forms of catastrophe insurance, and the assumption of the obligations to provide each citizen the opportunity for a life of dignity are accepted as communal obligatons. I have termed the theory of economic justice contained in the bill of economic rights and obligations a *dualistic individualism* theory to emphasize the two faces of a doctrine that is grounded in the preciousness of human life.

In formally endorsing the market mechanism as the basic tool of individualistic goods production, subject to corrective oversight by government where necessary or advisable and to alteration of its distributive results to achieve the goals of compassionate support, the bill gives social and legal standing to what has been an informally accepted institution whose legitimacy has been subject to the idealogical predilections of jurists. It is much as if the judiciary felt free to question the legitimacy of Congress to fashion legislation for the nation, interpreting it rather as an informal assemblage of interested parties whose enactments are useful guidelines for social policy but with no special claim to primacy over alternative methods of policy formulation. Though decentralized and abstract, the free market economy is as vital to a liberal society in the economic area as representative legislatures are in the political and should be as specifically legitimized as the latter.

THE COMPASSIONATE STRAND OF INDIVIDUALISM

Much has been written about the claims of "economic justice" by interest groups of right or left persuasion without any indication of basis in some integrated and consistent theory of economic justice from which such claims can be deduced. Economists especially are prone to assume that a movement toward greater static or dynamic income equality is prima facie an approach to a more just distribution, without any compunction about the lack of a framing ethical philosophy whose precepts imply this. Such ad hoc assertions provide much heat to social debate but little light, and underline the compelling need for the United States as a nation to adopt a consensual theory of economic justice with which to guide policy.

It is this charter that I have sought to achieve in the dualistic individualism theory of this work. Its acceptability rests ultimately on its conformance to dominant American ethical values, which I have explored in an attempt to define the relevant ethos of the nation. A more tangible if partial method of judging that acceptability is to examine the consequences of policies that implement the theory in the area of income distribution. With that task in mind I have narrowed focus from the broad and overarching theory of dualistic individualism to judgments concerning the feasibility of redistributive policies that are implied by the compassionate strand of individualism. To what extent will the ethos permit the elevation of that strand at the expense of the egoistic in the short run and the long run?

Current Inequalities

As a preliminary to seeking answers to these questions, I have given a detailed description of present income distribution in the United States, driven dominantly by the egoistic individualism of the market but tem-

TABLE 12.1
Family Money Income Percentages, by Quintiles,
with Median Incomes, 1987

Quintile	All-Race	White	Black
First	4.6%	5.1%	3.2%
	(7.2)		
Second	10.8	11.2	8.5
	(12.2)		
Third	16.9	17.0	15.3
	(17.8)		
Fourth	24.1	23.8	24.8
	(24.3)		
Fifth	43.7	42.9	48.3
	(38.7)		
Median Income	$30,853		
Gini	.392	.379	.455

Source: Tables 9.1 and 9.6, 9.7 and U.S. Bureau of the Census, *Current Population Reports*, Series P-60, no. 162, table A, 2–4. Parenthesized figures are 1984 distribution adjusted for federal income and payroll taxes, state income taxes, state and local sales taxes, and state and local property taxes, as well as Medicare, Medicaid, and food stamp receipts. See table 9.4.

pered by governmental intrusion of the compassionate strand. I have emphasized the inadequacies of measures of inequality with few dimensions, but I will repeat some of the outstanding conclusions of chapter 9.

1. *Family Distributions.* Static distributions of family money incomes, which include government means-tested and non-means-tested cash entitlements but exclude all noncash subsidies, are extremely unequal when measured against population quintiles. Table 12.1 summarizes such distributions for all-race, white, and black families, and lists median family incomes for such groups in 1987. It is noteworthy that the concentration of blacks in the lower three quintiles is less and the concentration in the upper two quintiles, especially the highest, is greater for blacks than for whites. The optimistic explanation is that middle class blacks have made great progress in raising themselves over the last two decades but have left a hard core of inner city brethren behind in the ghettos. Median income statistics are nonetheless disheartening: the black figure is only about 56 percent of white.

Poverty figures for families reveal a somewhat less sanguine outlook when the races are compared. Table 12.2 summarizes the percentages of families by race and sex of householder who fell below defined poverty levels in 1987. Among married couples of all ages and for both races the poverty rate is well beneath the average for all households at less than 6

TABLE 12.2

Families below Poverty Thresholds, by Race and Sex of
Householder, as Percentages of Relevant Group Totals, 1987

Description	All-Race	White	Black
Married Couples	5.8%	5.1%	11.9%
Male Householder, No Wife	12.0	9.8	23.4
Female Householder, No Husband	34.2	26.9	57.1

Source: Table 10.3.

percent. But racially the distribution is quite shocking: married couple black families as a group have a poverty rate about 2.33 times that of whites, with about 12 percent impoverished. For families headed by a male the ratio is about 2.4 times the white rate. But the truly telling statistics concern the occurrence of poverty in families headed by women. For all races, fully 34 percent of such families are so situated, with whites at 27 percent but blacks at a level of 57 percent, or about 2.1 times the white rate. More distressing, the median income for black families headed by women was only $9,710, or about 57 percent of the corresponding figure for whites.

Clearly I have located an important locus of need for compassionate support in the female-headed family, most particularly the black family of this type. Before taking account of the money value of noncash benefits, all-race female-headed families would have required an average of $5,000 in 1987 to lift them above the poverty level (table 10.4), or a total gross incremental tax burden of over $18 billion in 1987 dollars before taking into account the money value of in-kind benefits and the recapture of a minor portion of the increment from federal income tax.

Male householders in the aggregate offer challenges in these respects but do not pose a major social problem in two regards: percentage-wise they are less numerous and in absolute terms they have fewer members. But black families of this description are 2.4 times as numerous as whites and number about a quarter of all such families.

When the money income data of table 12.1 are adjusted for taxes and noncash benefits the inequality is somewhat diminished, with quintile percentages in 1984 listed in table 12.1. But when measured against a static equality standard, as the Gini measure does, such data yield a Gini value of .298 compared with a measure of .365 when both are computed on the basis of the five quintile values in table 12.2.

As a final indication of the inequality of family income distributions table 12.3 presents the percentages of families, by race, at three percent-

TABLE 12.3
Families below Selected Income Thresholds, 1987

Threshold	All-Race	White	Black
Below $10,000			
(27.7% of median income)	11.8%	9.3%	29.9%
Below $15,427			
(50% of median income)	20.9	18.7	43.5
Below $18,512			
(60% of median income)	27.5	24.5	50.9

Source: Table 9.12.

TABLE 12.4
Money Income Percentage Distributions, by Race,
Unrelated Persons, with Median Incomes, 1987

Quintile	All Races	White	Black
First	3.6%	3.9%	2.7%
Second	8.8	9.0	7.7
Third	15.0	15.2	13.5
Fourth	24.2	24.1	24.6
Fifth	48.4	47.8	51.5
Median Income	$12,559	$13,338	$8,094
Gini Coefficient	.420	.412	.458

Source: Table 9.13.

age levels of median incomes. About 19 percent of white families earn money incomes below 50 percent of median all-race family income, but black families in relative terms are 2.3 times more likely to be in such straits compared with white families. Even more disturbingly, however, black families are about 3.2 times more likely to be living at incomes below $10,000 than white families.

2. *Unrelated Individual Distributions.* Households with unrelated individuals reveal the same money income inequality patterns as families, but with even higher Gini coefficients. Table 12.4 reveals the quintile distributions in 1987 for all races, whites, and blacks. The Gini coefficients compare with an all-race family value, computed on the same five-observation basis as the unrelated households, of .365. Black unrelated individual households are more dispersed than white, with lower concentrations in the lowest three quintiles and markedly higher concentrations in the highest quintile.

Considering unrelated individuals over the age of 14, one reason for the differential earnings of whites and blacks is the markedly smaller percentages of blacks in each age category who obtain full-time employment, despite the higher concentrations of blacks in the more productive age bracket from 35 to 54 (see table 9.15). This, in part at least, is explained by blacks' lower educational attainments. For all black unrelated persons 15 years of age or older, those who earned a high school diploma or more were only 82 percent of the number of whites who did so, and those whose educational attainments included a college diploma or more were only 50 percent of whites in the same category. Black median income for those over age 15 was only 61 percent of white (see table 9.16). The undereducated form a pocket of concern in the compassionate society: a high school education has become an important preparation for earning a satisfactory legal income.

Another classificatory attribute of importance in defining problem groups is that of sex: although higher proportions of white and black women finish grammar school and high school than their male counterparts, smaller proportions go beyond high school. Women tend to earn about 68 percent of male median incomes, whether black or white, part of which is accounted for by a larger proportion of women who are employed part-time, but a larger part can be explained by less higher education (see table 9.18).

Short-Run Compassionate Program Costs

In order to gain some indications of the cost of potential programs to implement the theory of dualistic individualism, and their feasibility at the present time in terms of their compatibility with the ethos, I have estimated the net incremental tax burdens on nonbeneficiaries of three such policies. These are the lifting of all households up to current poverty thresholds, to a 50-percent-of-median-income threshold, and to a 60-percent-of-median-income threshold. I feel that these programs define a spectrum of relevance in the next decade or so for the implementation of the compassionate strand. My conclusions are summarized in table 12.5 in the form of net tax increments over 1987 personal income tax payments.

Interpreting the resistance to tax increases against the backdrop of attempts during the last decade to lower the budget deficit by $50 billion or so, I have concluded that a 60 percent threshold is far out of the range of feasibility. The upper bound I have located somewhat short of the 50 percent threshold. That level implies a 19 percent rise in tax burden on nonbeneficiaries which, given the strength of the egoistic strand of the ethos and the always-suspect nature of redistributive programs, does not appear to be a feasible goal. I have concluded that the poverty threshold,

TABLE 12.5
Estimated Net Tax Burdens on Nonbeneficiaries to
Implement Three Threshold Programs
(billions of 1987 dollars)

Program	Net Tax Increment	Percentage Tax Rise Over Actual 1987 Taxes
Poverty Threshold	$33.443	9.3%
50-Percent Threshold	71.067	19.8
60-Percent Threshold	121.240	34.3

Source: Tables 10.9, 10.10, 10.13, 10.14, 10.16, 10.17.

with implied rise of about 9 percent in tax burden, is the best that can be sought in the next decade as a rise in the priority afforded the compassionate strand of the ethos.

Long-Run Compassionate Program Costs

In assessing the feasibility of long-run policies—I adopted a thirty-year time horizon ending in 2020—a somewhat different approach was adopted in the face of the extremely difficult task of forecasting the path of all entitlements. Because earlier analysis permitted the isolation of those groups that are likely to make the major claims on social compassion in 2020, assuming the causes shaping those changes continue essentially unchanged, the feasibility study can be limited to these groups. They are the aged—65 years and older—families headed by women, and the undereducated. By projecting the demands of these persons at an assumed threshold level of support it becomes possible to cost such programs and to gauge their feasibility.

Caveats are rife in the presentation of the results. I have assumed historically average rates of growth for total and per capita GNP. Population projections derived from detailed Census forecasts are always subject to challenge. Social attitudes toward the family, early retirement, and educational attainment may not remain constant as I have assumed. Other demands for social expenditure—defense, notably, or repair and extension of infrastructure—may ease or increase the noncompassionate burdens on American society. And increasing affluence among other causes may enhance the priority given the dual strain of individualism in the ethos to an extent not foreseen in my assumptions and render threshold programs feasible that I have labeled infeasible.

One point that somewhat lessens the importance of all but large departures from these assumptions is that my goals are not those of prediction within narrow bounds of precision. I am interested only in gauging feasibility, a qualitative characteristic, and have some hopes that the inertia of the ethos and offsetting errors in projections of the groups' demands will permit that task to be fulfilled successfully.

That said, I proceed once more to estimate the net total tax burden on nonbeneficiaries of threshold programs for the three groups, taking care to eliminate overlapping of individuals in them. For the aged I project the 1987 transfers per aged household for the expected aged population in 2020, adjusting for administrative costs and for increased medical benefits expected to accompany the aging of the population. The projection of 1987 levels of support assumes that the essential non-means-tested character of such entitlements will continue into the long run and benefits will not be adjusted upward as median incomes of the population rise. Both assumptions may be incorrect, but on net I suspect that the assumptions give a conservative bias to the projections, in that there is a greater likelihood that a relative standard will be adopted than that such benefits will become significantly means-tested.

For families headed by females and for the undereducated I have estimated the net tax burden on nonthresholders if a 40-percent-of-median-income threshold were instituted. This permits a generous rise in the priority currently given the compassionate strand over the thirty-year period, so that some adaptability in the ethos is assumed.

The results of the analyses—repeated from table 11.35—are contained in table 12.6 measured in 1987 dollars. Expenditures on these groups in 1986 (in 1987 dollars) are listed to permit comparisons with current conditions.

I project that the total net tax burden imposed by these high-risk poverty groups could fall between $478 billion and $573 billion, under highly optimistic assumptions. This compares with costs of about $305 billion in 1986. If per capita income expands over the time period at an optimistic 2.43 percent annual rate, these three programs alone could absorb between 11.6 percent and 13.9 percent of per capita income. If that income expands at only half that annual rate, the three programs would require between 17.3 percent and 20.7 percent of per capita income. Federal, state, and local income and payroll taxes per capita amounted in fiscal year 1987–1988 to $3,719. With the projected work force in 2020, the programs analyzed would place a burden on members of the labor force of between $3,579 and $4,298. Per capita these

TABLE 12.6

Summary of Projected Transfer Costs in Year 2020 of Programs to Supplement
Incomes of the Three High Poverty Risk Groups (billions of 1987 dollars)

Group and Program	Total Transfer Payments	
	1986	*2020*
1. Aged (65 Years or More)		
a. Maintaining 1986 Benefits plus Administrative Costs (which essentially meets or exceeds 40-Percent-of-Median-Income Standard)	$201.499	$389.244
b. Maintaining 1986 Benefits With a 3 Percent Rise Per Year in Real Medical Costs		(444.951)
2. Female-Headed Households with Children under 18 Years		
a. 40-Percent-of-Median-Income Standard	29.775	54.275
3. Undereducated		
a. 40-Percent-of-Median-Income Standard with 2.43% Growth Rate in per Capita Earnings	81.826	34.027
b. 40-Percent-of-Median-Income Standard with 1.22% Growth Rate in per Capita Earnings		(74.221)
Totals	304.533	477.546
		(573.477)

Source: Table 11.35.

burdens are $1,622 or $1,948, or a rise above 1986 levels of 44 to 52 percent.

The strains potential in such relatively modest programs can be gauged by comparing the *incremental* per capita tax costs of $588 to $914 with the $203 increment implied by the $50 billion tax rise imposed by Congress for fiscal 1990 to reduce the budget deficit. The latter was passed after eight years of travail and trepidation. While per capita incomes under my assumptions will rise between 50 percent and 123 percent over the thirty-year period, and the growth in affluence tends to make the public more sensitive to poverty conditions, willingness to pay taxes in an individualistic society grows much more slowly than income. Moreover, the claims of other impoverished groups and other social needs will increase over the period, and I have not taken account of them.

I conclude that if a high growth rate in GNP is sustained on average over the thirty-year period, the 40 percent threshold is a potentially achievable upper bound on programs in compliance with the compassionate strand of individualism. If that growth rate is low, it would not be. If at an intermediate level of about 1.5 percent per year per capita its feasibility is questionable.

THE FUTURE MARKET SOCIETY

The major economic debates in affluent capitalism will increasingly concern distributive justice. Those debates have already begun under the guise of the "necessity" to increase tax burdens to meet social ends, and, increasingly, the needs to provide a minimum standard of life to the under- or nonproductive. Those social debates must increasingly move the focus of economic concern away from questions of efficiency into the more contentious domain of equity. Resolution of such conflicts, if it is to occur in accordance with a consistent and well-considered structure over time, must depend on a consensual social decision concerning the concept of economic justice that should guide American economic policy. The alternative is a succession of ad hoc, unintegrated legislative and executive decisions and judicial interpretations reflecting nothing more satisfying than the relative power of contending and egoistically-motivated interest groups. The implicit notions of economic justice that arise from such egoistic process is simply not an acceptable basis on which a democratic nation builds its ethical structure.

These considerations recommend an attempt to formalize principles of economic justice in a constitutional form to furnish guidelines for executive, legislative, and judicial participants in policy formation and interpretation. The almost complete lack of economic content in the definition of rights and obligations in the American Constitution, and its success in providing such guidelines in political and civil areas, leads us to advocate the devising of such an amendatory document. Although the hope of enacting it in the form of amendments might be fanciful, its formulation and public debate might well provide informal guidance to the solution of the future's dominant economic problems. In its formulation, the body of existing social ethics and the scholarship that exists defining the American ethos should be probed in the search for design consensus and operationalism.

But this much is clear. The press of demographic changes and the political awakening of the impoverished must increase the priority given the dual strand of individualism currently in American economic policy.

The distributive mechanism of the market society will be markedly different fifty years hence from its egoistically driven configuration today, although the economy will be identifiably capitalistic. That movement toward a more compassionate capitalism will be less or more painful as a consensus does or does not emerge concerning American principles of economic justice.

NOTES

PREFACE

1. John Stuart Mill, *Utilitarianism, Liberty, and Representative Government* (London: J. M. Dent & Sons, 1910), 38.

CHAPTER 1
THE IMPLICIT ECONOMIC ETHIC IN
THE MARKET ECONOMY

1. This point has been well made by John Rawls, *A Theory of Justice* (Cambridge, Mass.: Harvard University Press, 1971), 230, 361.

2. See, for example, Max Weber, *The Protestant Ethic and the Spirit of Capitalism* (New York: Scribner's, 1958), 75–78.

3. Thorstein Veblen, *The Theory of Business Enterprise* (New York: New American Library, 1958), 13.

4. Ibid., chap. 10.

5. Joseph A. Schumpeter, *Capitalism, Socialism and Democracy*, 3d ed. (New York: Harper, 1950), 152–155.

6. See Henry Nash Smith, "The Search for a Capitalist Hero," in Earl F. Cheit, ed., *The Business Establishment* (New York: Wiley, 1960), 77–112.

7. See, for example, Herbert Marcuse, *One-Dimensional Man* (Boston: Beacon, 1964). For a good presentation of the Institute's approach, see H. Stuart Hughes, *The Sea Change* (New York: Harper & Row, 1975).

8. John Stuart Mill, *Principles of Political Economy*, 5th ed. (New York: Appleton, 1901), 1:257–258.

9. Arthur Okun, *Equality and Efficiency* (Washington, D.C.: Brookings, 1975), 47–48.

10. John Rawls has termed this equality when compensated "fair equality of opportunity." He argues that because differential natural talents are distributed randomly as gifts of nature, individuals should not fairly be asked to suffer from less advantageous endowments nor be permitted to benefit from those prized more highly by the market. The latter, therefore, should devote their gifts to society via subsidies to those who suffer from lesser native talents. See John Rawls, *A Theory of Justice*, 103–104.

11. Milton Friedman, *Capitalism and Freedom* (Chicago: University of Chicago Press, 1962), 21.

12. Ironically, in the realistic economy in which factor service markets are not perfectly competitive, the strong nondiscriminatory motivation of business firms is lending support to what is perceived by many to be socially desirable *corrective* discrimination in the United States. This concerns so-called *affirmative action* or *reverse discrimination* measures instituted by legislation or activist court rulings.

The programs form one of the socially condoned goals referred to in the discussion that provide exceptions to the strong adherence to horizontal equity.

Recently, in several 1989 Supreme Court rulings—*Richmond vs. Croson, Wards Cove vs. Antonio, Martin vs. Wilks,* and *Patterson vs. McLean Credit Union*—some loosening of prior interpretations has moved the Court away from strong judicial support for these exceptions to horizontal equity. However, many large businesses have announced intentions to continue their affirmative action programs on the basis that it would be disturbing to disestablish the programs but also because 80 percent of the increase in the labor force between the present and the year 2000 will consist of women, minorities, and immigrants. Curtailing of discriminatory outreach programs, therefore, might place firms at a disadvantage in competing for labor in the near future. The profit motive in this instance is supportive of continued discrimination. See *Business Week,* July 3, 1989, 61–62.

13. The conflict has interested social philosophers for centuries. For example, in the eighteenth century, English moral philosophers sought to explain the fact that although man had an undeniably strong egoistic drive (as Thomas Hobbes had indicated so starkly in *Leviathan*) he was capable of living peacefully in a society infused with Lockian harmony. Moreover, the Age of Enlightenment philosophers were convinced that it was possible to discover or create the institutional bases for the perfectly harmonistic society. How could this potential coexist with the instincts that led men, in the absence of the sanctions of an absolute rule, to the Hobbesian "war of all against all"?

The sentimental school of philosophers, which included its founder Lord Shaftesbury as well as Adam Smith and his mentor, Francis Hutcheson, found countervailing emotions ("sentiments") that balanced the egoistic motivation of man with a social motivation. In the case of Shaftesbury that was a "moral sense" that monitored man's actions to exclude the antisocial acts springing from excessively egoistic motivations. For Hutcheson it was an inborn sense of virtue that performed the same function. And Adam Smith, in his *Theory of Moral Sentiments*—his first book, rarely read today—located the corrective factor in man's ability to empathize with his fellows.

In his later work, *The Wealth of Nations,* Smith wrote that in the economic sector the harmonistic society is created by the "invisible hand" of the free market, and did not call on the empathetic sense to bring about the social balance. In the competitive market, each person acting egoistically helped to create an aggregate pattern of allocation which harmonized the interests of all by maximizing social output. The analysis of social welfare, based as it was almost wholly on total output and ignoring its distribution, was a primitive one.

The concern about creating the institutions that would blend and modify or suppress the self-interested motivations of persons in the interests of maximizing social welfare was the core concern of Jeremy Bentham's utilitarian theory of social ethics and of the utilitarian school to which it gave rise. Finally, in the review of important theories of social equity that will be conducted in Part 2, it will be shown that modern social philosophers are wrestling with the same problems.

CHAPTER 2
THEORIES OF SOCIAL EQUITY:
EGOISTICALLY ORIENTED THEORIES

1. For an interesting probing into those characteristics upon which the moral constraints that protect the individual are based see Robert Nozick, *Anarchy, State and Utopia* (New York: Basic Books, 1974), 48–51.

2. Hence, I will ignore such "perfectionist" theories as those of Aristotle or Nietzsche and any number of organic state theories of the fascist type.

3. John Bates Clark, *The Distribution of Wealth* (New York: Macmillan, 1938), v, vii.

4. See, for example, Paul T. Bauer, *Equality, The Third World and Economic Delusion* (Cambridge, Mass.: Harvard University Press, 1981), and *Reality and Rhetoric: Studies in the Economics of Development* (London: Weidenfeld, 1984), for arguments supporting this proposition.

5. As will be indicated, Marx's analysis of capitalistic distribution led him to assert that although living labor created the total net value of the social product, property institutions of capitalism that permitted private ownership of the means of production permitted capitalists to confiscate a portion of the product—so-called "surplus value"—for their private use. The dispute revolves about the question of whether Marx's broader theory of social evolution permitted him to criticize capitalism as an *unjust* system on the basis that the worker's contribution was not received in full in the form of wages. This exploitation of the worker is the result of capitalism's core institutions and will exist as long as the capitalist mode of production exists. But does Marx view the exploitation as "unjust"?

Marx wrote, for example:

The justice of transactions which go on between agents of production rests on this fact that the transactions arise as natural consequences from the relations of production. The juristic forms in which these economic transactions appear as voluntary actions of the participants, as expressions of their common will and as contracts that may be enforced by the state as a single party, cannot, being merely forms, determine this content. They merely express it. The content is just whenever it corresponds to the mode of production, is adequate to it. It is unjust whenever it contradicts that mode. Slavery, on the basis of the capitalist mode of production is unjust; so is fraud in the quality of commodities. (Karl Marx, *Capital* [New York: International Publishers, 1967], 3:339ff.)

Notions of justice, like all other value and belief systems and their supporting institutional apparatus in the Marxist system, are products of the mode of production that is relevant to the technological achievement of the time. In an important sense, therefore, Marx is a captive of his own intellectual framework in foreclosing the possibility of condemning capitalism in moral terms. Justice is a juridical concept appropriate to the capitalist mode of production whose institutions, like those of every other mode of production, are designed to protect the class that possesses the means of production appropriate to that mode. This view is also stated explicitly in the marginal notes to the program of the German Workers' Party in *The Critique of the Gotha Program*.

In this interpretation then, supported by the quotation above, exploitation of the laborer is neither right nor wrong, just nor unjust in any absolute or criticizable sense: lying at the core of capitalist production it is appropriate to that mode of production and hence is just within the juridical framework necessary for that productive process. Thus, redistributing the surplus value from capitalist to labor would be unjust. Marx the revolutionary, therefore, in this interpretation, cannot logically call for abolition of capitalism on the basis of its injustice: that is the path of the despised Utopian socialists who did not possess the deeper understanding of social process that Marxism gave its adherents. For supporters of this interpretation of Marx's concept of equity see Robert C. Tucker, *The Marxian Revolutionary Idea* (New York: W. W. Norton, 1969), and *Philosophy and Myth in Karl Marx* (Cambridge: Cambridge University Press, 1961), as well as Allen C. Wood, "The Marxian Concept of Justice," and "Marx on Right and Justice: A Reply to Husami," in Marshall Cohen, Thomas Nagel, and Thomas Scanlon, eds., *Marx, Justice, and History* (Princeton, N.J.: Princeton University Press, 1980), 3–41, 106–34. This thesis has come to be labeled the Tucker-Wood thesis, and will be referred to as such in the discussion to follow.

This view of Marx's concept of justice has been challenged on two grounds. The first is that Tucker and Wood view Marx's sociology of morals only at the level of its social origins and fail to consider it in the context of the class conflict implicit in those origins. In terms of class conflict Marx can adopt a concept of the just that transcends modes of production and, in this interpretation, did so in *The Gotha Program*, the major source of his views on distribution. This argument has been put forward by Ziyad I. Husami, "Marx on Distributive Justice," in Cohen, Nagel, and Scanlon, eds., *Marx, Justice, and History*, 42–79. The argument is unconvincing because classes also are determined by modes of production and are appropriate to them. Class conflict also assumes the character of an institution that cannot be challenged in terms of morality.

A second challenge is more sustainable. Marx does make a distinction between two types of goods—the *moral* (e.g., justice) and the *nonmoral* (freedom of the individual to develop a multifaceted personality or self-realization). The first type of good is mode-of-production conditioned, but the second reflects deep human needs and interests. To the extent that any mode of production alienates the individual in the sense of interfering with the development of the personality, it can be criticized on grounds that transcend modes of production. That criticism assumes the character of inequity in the terms of this book. See George C. Brenkert, "Freedom and Private Property in Marx," and Allen W. Wood, "Marx on Right and Justice: A Reply to Husami," in Cohen, Nagel, and Scanlon, eds., *Marx, Justice, and History*, 80–105, 106–34.

This interpretation, however, is based on the more humanistic work of the young Marx in the *Economic and Philosophical Manuscripts* and *The German Ideology*. In these works he put forward his theory of alienation in capitalism, interpreting this concept as the crushing of certain "species powers" within human nature whose presence and need for expression distinguished men from animals. The problem arising from this basis for the argument is that it is unclear to what extent the mature Marx of *Capital* regarded the alienation argument as relevant in the face of the exploitation theory present in the later book, especially because alienation depended on the existence of a "human nature" unaffected by modes of production—a concept Marx explicitly rejected in later work.

Despite these academic disputes, several points are quite clear with respect to its relevance to the task ahead. First, Marx himself quite frequently referred to exploitation in words that were heavily weighted with moral connotations: "usurpation," "embezzling," "plunder," "theft," "swindling," and the like. See, for example, R. G. Peffer, *Marxism, Morality and Social Justice* (Princeton, N.J.: Princeton University Press, 1990), 145, 176, for explicit references to such characterizations of exploitation by Marx. Second, Marx's followers, less interested in the consistency of a holistic theory of social evolution, and concerned with promulgating a program for the rising labor and socialist movements, used his exploitation theory as a "scientific proof" of the insufferable inequities of capitalism.

6. This narrowly economic interpretation is actively challenged by Marxist and Marxist-sympathetic moral philosophers, as is the Tucker-Wood thesis. The most recent and extensive treatment of Marxist moral philosophy is that of Peffer, *Marxism.* Peffer asserts (1) that Marx was not a moral philosopher and made no attempt to construct a systematic moral theory, but (2) that such a theory can be constructed from his moral pronouncements. That theory was "mixed deontological," asserting that the autonomy of the individual within a caring community permitting achievement of the fully dimensioned person was the good that was important, but that duties springing from a Kantian notion of men as ends in themselves and the attainment of human dignity resulting from these duties were overriding.

The Tucker-Wood thesis is not incorrect, Peffer believes, but the reason Marx failed to criticize capitalist institutions on moral grounds was because he viewed such institutions as inevitable given the mode of production (Peffer, *Marxism,* chap. 5) However, Marx should be seen as rejecting the possibility of justice in a nonjuridical sense incorrectly on the basis of his own principles (chap. 5, 137, 334, 336–338). Marx himself provided the transhistorical moral grounds for condemning capitalism as unjust. Moreover, in Peffer's view the implicit moral judgments in Marx's early writings persisted into his mature works, so that alienation theory was not abandoned for exploitation theory. He cites the *Grundrisse* as evidence of this continuity, although he believes that the continuity is clear without this writing (63, 75). He writes: "The prescription that all members of society ought to act on the basis of the common good and, in general, would act on this basis in a rationally constructed society, occurs in one form or another in all the rest of Marx's works [i.e., from 1843 on]" (43).

7. Peffer, *Marxism,* 137. See 137–165 for an extended discussion of modern Marxist views of exploitation.

8. Ibid., 164.

9. Allen E. Buchanan, *Marx and Justice: The Radical Critique of Liberalism* (Totowa, N.J.: Rowman and Littlefield, 1982), 46.

10. Interestingly, Lenin believed that "scientific socialism" was not vitally concerned about distribution of income, but rather concentrated on production. He wrote:

Marx contrasts vulgar socialism to scientific socialism, which does not attach great importance to distribution, and which explains the social system by the organization of relations of *production* and which considers that the given system of organization of relations of production already includes a definite system of distribution. The idea . . . runs like a thread through the whole of Marx's teachings. (*Selected Works* [London: Martin Lawrence, 1936], 1:460)

11. Compare Alasdair MacIntyre, *A Short History of Ethics* (New York: Macmillan, 1966), 155–156.

12. Hobbes's references to the drive for power in human nature are frequent and unambiguous (Thomas Hobbes, *Leviathan* [London: J. M. Dent & Sons, 1914]). For example:

Honourable is whatsoever possession, action, or quality is an argument and signe of Power. (46)

Nor does it alter the case of Honour, whether an action (so it be great and difficult, and consequently a signe of much power,) be just or unjust: for Honour consisteth onely in the opinion of Power. (47)

I put for a generall inclination of all mankind, a perpetuall and restlesse desire of Power after power, that ceaseth only in Death. (49)

13. Compare Hobbes, *Leviathan*, 63.

This vision of "natural man" is closely congruent to the view of the human psyche in Sigmund Freud's analysis of the relation of individuals to society in *Civilization and Its Discontents* (London: Hogarth Press, 1951), 85–86. Men are led by their inner drives of sex and aggression to rape, plunder, and murder. They can be restrained only by the force and wiles of the state, which punishes their transgressions and subverts the energy of the ego by in-building the super-ego to serve as a guilt-inflicting preempter of antisocial actions. Justice and morality, therefore, can only be established by an effective state whose foundations, however, because of the strength of the libido and the instinct of aggression, are always in danger of collapsing. The state is at once the problem and the answer, the repressor of the individual and the guarantor of civilization. The unrelieved pessimism with respect to the instinctual drives that shape the human spirit is strikingly similar in both works.

14. Hobbes, *Leviathan*, 144.

15. Ibid., 74.

16. Hence, the absolute sovereign serves the role of the philosopher in Plato's *Republic*. In that work the common man is viewed as egoistic and incapable of just actions because of his inability to understand the abstract Idea. Only the philosopher has the intelligence to abstract from objects to comprehend through the use of the dialectic process the notion of the eternal essence immanent in the ephemeral objects. Hence, justice is imposed by the philosopher-king on the populace, which is incapable of realizing its rationale. The common man is to be educated in the "objects" of just actions but cannot be expected to understand the underlying principles of justice. Religion is to be used to aid the state in instilling a respect for the decrees concerning justice of its ruling philosophers.

17. Compare Henry Sidgwick, *Outlines of the History of Ethics*, 6th ed. (Boston: Beacon Press, 1960 [1931]), 163–170.

18. Hobbes, *Leviathan*, 132–133.

19. Ibid., 80.

20. Sidgwick, *History of Ethics*, 170–174.

21. John Locke, *An Essay Concerning Human Understanding* (London: J. M. Dent & Sons, 1947), 4: chaps. 10 and 17, 297–298, 325–329.

22. John Locke, *Of Civil Government* (London: J. M. Dent & Sons, 1924), 2 (Second Treatise): chap. 4, section 21, 127.

23. "For a man, not having the power of his own life, cannot by compact or his own consent enslave himself to any one, nor put himself under the absolute, arbitrary power of another to take away his own life when he pleases" (ibid., 128). From this Locke reasons that absolute monarchy is inconsistent with natural law, and hence that Hobbes's arguments for the nature of civil society are incorrect. Compare 2: section 137, 186–187.

24. Care must be taken in interpreting the use of the term "property" in the treatises. Locke explicitly defines the term to include the life, liberties, and possessions of individuals, not simply ownership of assets. See Locke, *Of Civil Government*, 2:179–180, 206.

25. Ibid., 2: section 26, 130. Italics furnished.

26. Compare: "As much as any one can make use of to any advantage of life before it spoils, so much he may by his labour fix a property in. Whatever is beyond this is more than his share, and belongs to others." (ibid., 2: 131).

27. Ibid., 140.

28. Ibid., 214.

29. Locke, *Of Civil Government*, 1 (First Treatise): section 42, 30.

30. Robert Nozick, *Anarchy, State, and Utopia* (New York: Basic Books, 1974).

31. It must be noted that Nozick is not asserting that the Lockian state of nature actually existed at any point in history and that social institutions evolved from it. It is, rather, like Rawls's initial position, an intellectual construct from which the analyst, using procedures that are conformant to some set of ethical precepts, can simulate the emergence of institutions and principles for the operation of those institutions in order to study their structure and functioning. Criticisms of such constructs for being "unrealistic" and therefore irrelevant to real problems misunderstand their nature and purpose.

32. Nozick, *Anarchy, State, and Utopia*, 32–33.

33. Ibid., 178.

34. Ibid., 182.

35. Ibid., 160.

36. Ibid., 114.

37. Compare: "As liberals we take freedom of the individual, or perhaps the family, as our ultimate goal in judging social arrangements" (Milton Friedman, *Capitalism and Freedom* [Chicago: University of Chicago Press, 1962], 12). This book should be read in conjunction with Milton and Rose Friedman, *Free to Choose* (New York: Avon, 1979). The later book is an update of the reasoning of the earlier work, with some changes of emphasis, but also employs more extensive discussions of examples to illustrate the points made in the earlier volume.

38. Rather surprisingly, the only other school of ethical philosophy to place such emphasis on the individual's freedom of choice is *existentialism*, especially the secular variety espoused by Jean-Paul Sartre. He sought to detach the importance and inescapability of individual choice from religion, as Kierkegaard had defined it, and defined man's essence as inhering in this complete freedom to choose his moral beliefs, his definition of truth, and thereby his complete life experience. Man, the *être-pour-soi*, as distinguished from the object, *être-en-soi*, is free and is conscious of that freedom. Only in accepting this complete freedom of choice could man find meaning in a life without meaning, that is, incapable of being given direction or understanding by any formal framework. Acceptance of any body of existing beliefs in the name of religion or science undermined the individual's duty to choose the nature of his being. "Liberty is the stuff of his being," Sartre wrote. It is not simply a desirable characteristic of life to be given as a gift or to be striven for. One's duty to oneself is to choose that which we define as the good, and by the very act of choice it becomes the good.

Sartre attempted to show that when the individual chooses actions in his own selfish interest he also chooses for others, and thus that individual actions were conformant to the social good. But choosing for others violates their own absolute freedom of choice and would seem to be an act of bad faith. In short, Sartre's attempt to demonstrate that egoistic choice invariably involves a consideration of the good of others is unconvincing, and his existentialism remains very much an egoistically oriented theory of social ethics. Sartre's best presentation of his philosophy is found in *Existentialism and Humanism* (London: Eyre Methuen, 1973).

39. "But as I have studied economic activities in the United States, I have become increasingly impressed with how wide is the range of problems and industries for which it is appropriate to treat the economy as if it were competitive." Friedman, *Capitalism and Freedom*, 120. And: "Important as private distortions of the price system are, these days the government is the major source of interference with a free market system." Milton and Rose Friedman, *Free to Choose*, 9. The second quotation seems to sound a bit of retreat from the earlier assertion, in that it implies that monopolistic price departures from marginal cost are somewhat more frequent than the earlier book indicated. But the existence of a strict monopoly—in the sense of one supplier—generally hinges on overt or covert government collusion (ibid., 45).

40. Compare: "Yet the conclusions I shall reach are that liberal principles do not justify licensure even in medicine and that in practice the results of state licensure in medicine have been undesirable" (Friedman, *Capitalism and Freedom*, 138). This statement is qualified by a recognized need to restrain physicians whose activities have externalities that extend beyond the individual contractual relation of patient and doctor (e.g., if a physician's activities start an epidemic).

In chapter 8 of the later book, the discussion of physician licensure seems somewhat less firm about the nonnecessity of such state supervision, but in the last chapter, among suggested amendments to the U.S. Constitution is the following: "No State shall make or impose any law which shall abridge the right of any citizen of the United States to follow any occupation or profession of his choice" (Milton and Rose Friedman, *Free to Choose*, 293).

Is licensing a contravention of such rights? The answer is not clear.

41. More exactly, Friedman opposes government legislation or rules against discrimination, believes affirmative action or right-to-work laws are interferences with the freedom of contract, but would reluctantly accept forced school integration to correct segregation in the absence of his school voucher plan which he believes avoids both. See Friedman, *Capitalism and Freedom,* 110–118.

42. Thus, Friedman endorses the elimination of what Locke termed "prerogative," or the privilege granted to the executive authority to exercise, when necessary, "the power of doing public good without a rule" (John Locke, *Of Civil Government* [London: J. M. Dent & Sons, 1924], 2: chap. 14, 202).

43. See Friedman, *Capitalism and Freedom,* 85.

44. See Milton and Rose Friedman, *Free to Choose,* 110–114.

45. Ibid., 123.

46. Friedman, *Capitalism and Freedom,* 161–162.

47. Ibid., 164–165.

48. Ibid., 167.

49. Friederich von Hayek, *The Constitution of Liberty* (Chicago: University of Chicago Press, 1960), 87–88.

50. John F. Nash, "Two-Person Cooperative Games," *Econometrica* 21 (1953): 128–140.

51. See David P. Gauthier's contribution in E. F. Paul, J. Paul, and F. D. Miller, Jr., eds., *Ethics and Economics* (Oxford: Blackwell, 1985). I have drawn substantially from this paper in the discussion of bargaining theories. See also David P. Gauthier, *Morals by Agreement* (Oxford: Clarendon, 1986), chap. 5, 113–156.

52. Ibid.

CHAPTER 3
THEORIES OF SOCIAL EQUITY:
SOCIALLY ORIENTED THEORIES

1. Immanuel Kant, *Fundamental Principles of the Metaphysics of Morals* (New York: Liberal Arts Press, 1949).

2. Henry Sidgwick, *Outlines of the History of Ethics,* 6th ed. [Boston: Beacon Press, 1960 (1931)], 115–116.

3. Francis Hutcheson, *An Inquiry Concerning Beauty, Order, Harmony, Design,* Peter Kiug, ed. (The Hague: Martinus Nijhoff, 1973 [1725]), section 3, paragraph 8.

4. John Locke, *An Essay Concerning Human Understanding* (London: J. M. Dent & Sons, 1947), 107. See also 125, 133.

5. Ibid., 176.

6. David Hume, *Treatise of Human Nature,* L. A. Selby-Bigger, ed. (Oxford: Clarendon, 1958 [1739–40]), 2:3, 3.

7. Ibid., 3:1, 2.

8. Ibid., 3:2, 1.

9. David Hume, *An Inquiry Concerning the Principles of Morals* (New York: Liberal Arts Press, 1957 [1751]), 5:2.

10. Sidgwick, *History of Ethics,* 237–239.

11. Jeremy Bentham, *The Principles of Morals and Legislation* (New York: Hafner, 1948 [1789]), 1.

12. A *teleological* theory is one which asserts that an action is morally right if it brings into being as much or more good—defined in the theory—as any other alternative action available to the agent. By contrast, a *deontological* theory holds that an action may be known to be right without consideration of the good of anything, that is, its consequences. See W. K. Frankena, *Dictionary of Philosophy*, D. D. Runes, ed. (New York: Littlefield, Adams & Co., 1958), 76.

13. Bentham, *Morals and Legislation*, 19. Italics supplied.

14. John Stuart Mill, *Utilitarianism* (London: J. M. Dent & Sons, 1947), 4.

15. Ibid., chap. 4.

16. Ibid., 29.

17. Ibid., 58–59.

18. Ibid., 8.

19. Ibid., 55.

20. Ibid., 50.

21. Ibid.

22. See, for example, his famous essay, *On Liberty*, written in 1859, for his classic statement of individualism. In it, for example, he asserts that the *only* just basis for state restrictions on the individual is to prevent harm to others. This would seem to stop short of substantial redistributive exactions.

23. See Anthony Quinton, "Utilitarian Ethics," in W. D. Hudson, ed., *New Studies in Ethics* (London: Macmillan, 1973), 2:113–115. For another indication that Mill was aware of the distinction between rule- and act-utilitarianism, see John Harsanyi, "Rule Utilitarianism, Equality, and Justice," in E. F. Paul, J. Paul, and F. D. Miller, Jr., *Ethics and Economics* (Oxford: Blackwell, 1985), 115–127. Harsanyi's definition of rule-utilitarianism, however, is closer to the notion of generalized utilitarianism given above, although the distinction is not important in the present context.

24. John Rawls, *A Theory of Justice* (Cambridge, Mass.: Harvard University Press, 1971). This major work should be read in conjunction with two subsequent articles which contain substantial revisions in large part as responses to his critics. See "Kantian Constructivism in Moral Theory," *Journal of Philosophy* 77 (1980): 515–572, and "Justice as Fairness: Political not Metaphysical," *Philosophy and Public Affairs* 14 (1985): 223–251.

25. This evolution is well treated in Robert P. Wolff, *Understanding Rawls* (Princeton, N.J.: Princeton University Press, 1977).

26. See Rawls, "Kantian Constructivism in Moral Theory," 518–522, and idem, "Justice as Fairness: Political not Metaphysical," 224–225. In the latter Rawls indicates that in the *Theory of Justice* he did not stress sufficiently that justice as fairness is intended as a political conception of justice for a modern constitutional democracy.

27. See Thomas Nagel, "Rawls on Justice," in Norman Daniels, ed., *Reading Rawls* (Stanford, Calif.: Stanford University Press, 1989), 1–16. Peffer points out that Rawls's notion of achieving this consensus in reflective equilibrium is consistent with the views of such Marxist and Marxist-sympathetic philosophers as Habermas.

28. Rawls has written that his earlier work did not stress these views sufficiently. See "Justice as Fairness: Political not Metaphysical," 224.

29. Immanuel Kant, *Metaphysics of Morals*, 37. See also Jeffrie G. Murphy, "Marxism and Retribution," in Marshall Cohen, Thomas Nagel, and Thomas Scanlon, eds., *Marx, Justice, and History* (Princeton, N.J.: Princeton University Press, 1980), 166.

30. See Rawls, "Kantian Constructivism in Moral Theory," 526.

31. "The essential thing is not to allow the principles chosen to depend on special attitudes toward risk. For this reason the veil of ignorance also rules out the knowledge of these inclinations: the parties do not know whether or not they have a characteristic aversion to taking chances" (Rawls, *A Theory of Justice*, 172). The prohibition is repeated on 530.

32. Rawls's original formulation of the theory was in terms of bargaining theory. See John Rawls, "Justice as Fairness," *The Philosophical Review* 57 (1958). Wolff, *Understanding Rawls*, believes that Rawls's desire to derive principles from bargaining theory among individuals in full knowledge of their position in society was abandoned in successive retreats only reluctantly as he recognized defects in his derivations of the principles. Nonetheless, Rawls seems to continue to view the original position as one of bargaining. For example, he defines a "thin" veil of ignorance as one which rules out only that knowledge that would give a participant a "threat advantage" ("Kantian Constructivism in Moral Theory," 549).

33. Rawls concedes that this is an unsatisfactory solution, his preference being for a proof that the principles adopted would be uniquely determined from all possible alternatives. But he felt this was not possible at the present time.

34. Rawls, *A Theory of Justice*, 118–119.

35. See "Kantian Constructivism in Moral Theory," 531.

36. A lexicographic ordering is one that follows that used in a dictionary. All words beginning with "a" are selected. Then all those starting with "aa," and within that group those beginning with "aab" and so forth. In terms of a preference ordering, all those alternatives containing the most favored choice are ranked ahead of all others. In that grouping, those alternatives that contain both the first and second choices are ranked ahead of those that contain both the first and third choices, and so forth. The alcoholic's preferences are an example of a lexicographic ordering. All consumption baskets containing whiskey are preferred to all baskets containing no whiskey. In the former category, all those containing food as well may be preferred to all those containing other goods, and so forth.

37. Rawls, *A Theory of Justice*, 82.

38. Ibid., 78.

39. Ibid., 104.

40. Ibid., 319.

41. Ibid., 73.

42. Ibid.

43. Ibid., 84.

44. Nagel believes that Rawls's reflective process transcends an intuitionist constraining of the principles derived from the original position. See Nagle, "Rawls on Justice," as well as R. Dworkin, "The Original Position," in Norman

Daniels, ed., *Reading Rawls* (Stanford, Calif.: Stanford University Press, 1989), 1–16 and 16–53.

45. See Dworkin, 34–35.

46. I am indebted to Professor Elizabeth Kiss of Princeton University for pointing out the bearing of reflective equilibrium on my own efforts.

47. Rawls, *A Theory of Justice*, 258.

48. Ibid., 285.

49. See Rawls, "Kantian Constructivism in Moral Theory," 552–553.

Chapter 4
A Framework for Judgment

1. John Stuart Mill, *Utilitarianism* (London: J. M. Dent & Sons, 1910, [1863]), 46–47.

2. Compare Henry Sidgwick, *The Methods of Ethics*, 7th ed. (Chicago: University of Chicago Press, 1962 [1907]), 2–4.

3. Compare Alexis de Tocqueville, *Democracy in America* (New York: Appleton, 1899), 2:615: "In America the passion for physical well-being is not always exclusive, but it is general; and if all do not feel it in the same manner, yet it is felt by all."

4. A notable critic of the market society in these respects was the sociologist Georg Simmel. See his *The Philosophy of Money* (London: Routledge and Regan Paul, 1978 [1900]), especially 365–366, 380, 390–392, 407.

5. Fred Hirsch, *Social Limits to Growth* (Cambridge, Mass.: Harvard University Press, 1978), 101, 143.

6. Michael Walzer, *Spheres of Justice* (New York: Basic Books, 1983), 97, 119.

7. This work has been innovated by Gary Becker in a number of articles.

8. For works that are associated with this "new economic sociology" which stresses the sociological matrix within which the market economy is embedded and the interpenetration of the market's norms and values with it, see Viviana A. Zelizer, "Beyond the Polemics on the Market: Establishing a Theoretical and Empirical Agenda," *Sociological Forum* 3 (1988): 613–634; Mark Granovetter, "Economic Action and Social Structure: The Problem of Embeddedness," *American Journal of Sociology* 91 (1985): 481–510; and "Toward a Sociological Theory of Income Differences," in Ivar Berg, ed., *Sociological Perspectives on Labor Markets* (New York: Academic Press, 1981), 11–47; Bernard Barber, "The Absolutization of the Market: How We Got From There to Here," in G. Dworkin, G. Bermant, and P. Brown, eds., *Markets and Morals* (Washington, D.C.: Hemisphere, 1977), 15–31; and Richard Swedberg, "Economic Sociology: Past and Present," *Current Sociology* 35 (1987): 1–221.

Chapter 5
A Critique of the Egoistically Oriented Theories

1. See R. G. Peffer, *Marxism, Morality and Social Justice* (Princeton, N.J.: Princeton University Press, 1990), for the discernment of an implicit moral theory in Marx's writings that defines the concept of the good and the right.

2. As indicated in note 5 of chapter 2, I am ignoring the debate about the issue of "justice" in Marx's theory of history, and concentrating on the usage that has been made by Marxists of his theory of exploitation.

3. Marx attributes capital's physical productivity to a rather mystical property of direct labor services:

It is the natural property of living labor to transmit old value, whilst it creates new. Hence, with the increase in efficacy, extent and value of its means of production, consequently with the accumulation that accompanies the development of its productive power, labor keeps up and eternises an always increasing capital-value in a form ever new. (Karl Marx, *Capital* [New York: International Publishers, 1967], 1:606)

Paul Sweezy, the leading American Marxist economist, is more direct in describing the role of capital in the productivity scheme:

It is, of course, true that materials and machinery can be said to be *physically* productive in the sense that labor working with them can turn out a larger product than labor working without them, but physical productivity in this sense must under no circumstances be confused with value productivity. From the standpoint of value there is no reason to assure that either materials or machinery can ultimately transfer to the product more than they themselves contain. This leaves only one possibility, namely that labor power must be the source of surplus value. (Paul Sweezy, *The Theory of Capitalist Development* [London: Dennis Dobson, 1946], 61)

The modern economist, drawing on neoclassical marginalist theory, would be able to interpret Sweezy's argument only if the marginal value product of capital equaled its depreciation; that is, if the last dollar of capital returned no *net* return in the form of interest. In this case the society would be satiated in capital goods and they would be free goods, in the nature of air. Air in the blast furnace is productive in the sense that in its absence no pig iron would be forthcoming, yet it does not create value *in the sense of possessing a positive marginal net revenue* because it is a free good in excess supply. But no society has ever existed—certainly not in the capitalist era—in which capital was a free good, and it must be treated symmetrically with all other factors that enter into the production complex. That is, it is productive in the sense of possessing a positive marginal net value product.

4. That is, it will be impossible to produce more of any one good without reducing the output of one or more others. Also, given the perfectly competitive market structure, production will be efficient in the sense that for any particular menu of goods produced in the efficient manner defined above it will be impossible to benefit one or more consumers by shifting resources among goods productions without hurting one or more others.

5. When the production function that specifies the maximum product that can be obtained from any feasible basket of inputs is *linear and homogeneous*, the exhaustion-of-product phenomenon does hold, but only under these conditions. Euler's theorem asserts that if the marginal products of each factor service (the partial derivatives of the function) are multiplied by the respective number of

units of factors employed and the products are summed, the result is the function itself: this is proof of the exhaustion-of-product proposition. Linear homogeneous production functions yield constant costs at constant factor prices. Such functions yield zero output when all input quantities are zero, and reveal *proportionality* and *additivity*. That is, multiplying all inputs by a positive factor α increases output by that same factor, and the combined output from two different baskets of inputs is simply the sum of the baskets' outputs taken singly. Although such functions are approximated in reality for certain domains of input, they cannot be assumed to be the universal or even general case. Hence, the exhaustion-of-product theorem is not general.

6. Two important studies of such efficiency effects are the pioneering analysis by Arnold Harberger and, in response to that effort, the work of Keith Cowling and Dennis C. Mueller, "The Social Costs of Monopoly Power," *Economic Journal* 88 (1978): 727–748.

7. Of course, these notions of voluntarism may rest on some notion of natural rights on which the sanctity of the individual is based, from which in turn derives the rightness of voluntarism. Certainly Nozick begins his construction in the context of the social contract which is a rights-based concept. My point, however, is that the immediate validation of concepts of distributive fairness, among other aspects of social justice, rests directly on the degree of voluntary motivation of actions. Coercion of the individual violates his moral sanctity, which may rest on a variety of moral bases besides natural rights, as, for example, Kantian rational autonomy.

8. See Erich Fromm, *Escape from Freedom* (New York: Rinehart, 1941).

CHAPTER 6
A CRITIQUE OF THE SOCIALLY ORIENTED THEORIES

1. "It is every man's duty to be beneficent, that is to promote, according to his means, the happiness of others who are in need, and this without hope of gaining anything by it.

"For every man who finds himself in need wishes to be helped by other men. But if he lets the maxim of not being willing to help others in turn when they are in need become public, i.e., makes this a universal permissive law, then everyone would likewise deny him assistance when he needs it, or at least would be entitled to. Hence the maxim of self-interest contradicts itself when it is made a universal law—that is, it is contrary to duty. Consequently, the maxim of common interest—of beneficence towards the needy—is a universal duty of men, and indeed for this reason: that men are to be considered fellow-men—that is rational beings with needs, united by nature in one dwelling place for the purpose of helping one another" (Robert Paul Wolff, ed., *Metaphysics of Morals* [Indianapolis: Bobbs-Merrill, 1969], 33). This is admittedly an ambiguous passage. It begins by asserting the duty of one to give material benefits to those in need without the prudent consideration of reciprocity, yet goes on to justify the actions on the grounds of potential self-benefit. Yet, the gist of the passage is to establish such charity as a categorical imperative—that is, one whose nonuniversalization would result in a contradiction.

2. John Stuart Mill, *Utilitarianism* (London: J. M. Dent & Sons, 1910 [1863]), 3–4.

3. R. E. Peffer seems to share this opinion of Kantian moral theory in asserting that Kant is a deontological theorist despite his bringing into his detailed arguments for practical moral maxims certain consequentialist features. See *Marxism, Morality and Social Justice* (Princeton, N.J.: Princeton University Press, 1990), 83.

4. Hegel raises a similar objection to Kant's argument that if men refused to pay back deposits left with them for which no receipts had been issued there could be no deposits. But in such an assertion Kant assumes the existence of private property and yet says nothing about why private property should exist. See H. B. Acton, "Kant's Moral Philosophy," in W. D. Hudson, ed., *New Studies in Ethics* (London: Macmillan, 1974), 1:330–331.

5. This is the translation given by H. B. Acton, ibid., 341. Other translations differ somewhat, especially with respect to the degree to which others can be treated as means.

6. But see Charles Fried, *Contract as Promise: A Theory of Contractual Obligation* (Cambridge, Mass.: Harvard University Press, 1981). Fried opposes the arguments of the "Death of Contract" legal school which views the obligation imposed by contract as community-imposed rather than moral. Damages should be assessed for breach of contract, therefore, on the basis of actual loss or restitution.

Fried argues that the basis of contract lies deep within the moral soil of liberalism:

> It is a first principle of liberal political morality that we be secure in whatever is ours—so that our persons and property not be open to exploitation by others, and that from such a foundation we may express our will and expend our powers in the world. (7)

The moral autonomy of the individual is basic. The trust implicit in contracts is a manner of conforming to Kant's Second Formulation, permitting us to benefit from the use of others as means at the same time that we honor and benefit them as autonomous ends in themselves. Not to honor a contract is to use another as a means exclusively. Hence, a contract is a promise with legal as well as moral force, that is, a concern of justice, and hence the penalty for failure to conform to it should be the *expectation* of gain from it by the injured party, not merely damages. Hence, in the formulation by Fried, Kantian theory is used as the basis for enforcement of a fundamental capitalist institution.

7. Henry Sidgwick, *The Methods of Ethics*, 7th ed. (Chicago: University of Chicago Press, 1962 [1907]), 121.

8. Rawls makes this point but asserts more narrowly that Mill's statement in the quotation is actually an assertion of the Rawlsian principles of justice as fairness. See John Rawls, *A Theory of Justice* (Cambridge, Mass.: Harvard University Press), 302.

9. Mill, *Utilitarianism*, 58–59.

10. Ibid., 57–58.

11. Abba P. Lerner, *The Economics of Control* (New York: Macmillan, 1944), 25–40.

12. Rawls makes this criticism of utilitarianism quite explicit:

It is customary to think of utilitarianism as individualistic, and certainly there are good reasons for this. The utilitarians were strong defenders of liberty and freedom of thought, and they held that the good of society is constituted by the advantages enjoyed by individuals. Yet utilitarianism is not individualistic, at least when arrived at by the more natural course of reflection, in that, by conflating all systems of desires, it applies to society the principle of choice for one man. (*A Theory of Justice*, 29)

13. See, for example, John C. Harsanyi, "Rule Utilitarianism, Equality, and Justice," in E. F. Paul, J. Paul, and F. D. Miller, Jr., eds., *Ethics and Economics* (Oxford: Blackwell, 1985), 115–127. Harsanyi's rule-utilitarianism gives great weight to the need to preserve incentives and economic efficiency, and seems to be willing to accept a large departure from the goal of maximizing straightforwardly calculated social utility of the utilitarian type in order to achieve it. He argues that social and economic equality are not intrinsic moral values in utilitarianism, and advocates the introduction of such other social goals as protection of the family, the rights of property, and, one senses, a rather large set of additional constraints. Harsanyi recognizes the substantial deviation that rule-utilitarianism makes from the classic form by asserting that it places itself between that classic form and certain forms of intuitionism.

14. I borrow the term from Christopher Morley. It is defined as a love of the underdog. See his preface, "In Memoriam: Sherlock Holmes," in A. Conan Doyle, *The Complete Sherlock Holmes* (Garden City, N.Y.), xi.

15. Rawls, *A Theory of Justice*, 280.

16. Peffer, *Marxism, Morality and Social Justice*, 371–372.

17. Ibid., 384.

18. See John Rawls, "A Kantian Conception of Equality," *Cambridge Review* 96 (1975): 94–99.

Chapter 7
The Bases for Economic Justice in America

1. Arthur Okun, *Equality and Efficiency* (Washington, D.C.: Brookings, 1975), 117.

Chapter 8
Measuring Inequality

1. Morton Paglin, "The Measurement and Trend of Inequality: A Basic Revision," *American Economic Review* 65 (1975/4): 603.

2. Frank Levy, *Dollars and Dreams* (New York: W. W. Norton, 1987), 158–159.

3. Amartya Sen, *On Economic Inequality* (Oxford: Clarendon), 2–3.

4. That is, $y_i = x_i / \Sigma_i \, x_i$. I shall use these symbols to denote income shares (y) and dollar incomes (x) throughout the discussion.

5. Graham Pyatt, "On the Interpretation and Disaggregation of Gini Coefficients," *Economic Journal* 65 (1976): 243–255.

6. Insights into such decompositions have been given by N. Bhattacharya

and B. Mahalanobis, "Regional Disparities in Household Consumption in India," *Journal of the American Statistical Association* 62 (1967/317): 143–161; M. Mangahas, "Income Inequality in the Philippines: A Decomposition Analysis," *World Employment Programme Research Working Papers No. 12* (Geneva: International Labor Office, 1975); V. M. Rao, "Two Decompositions of Concentration Ratios," *Journal of the Royal Statistical Association, Series A,* 132 (1969); Paglin, "Measurement and Trend of Inequality"; and Pyatt, "Gini Coefficients."

7. Sheldon Danziger, Robert Haveman, and Eugene Smolensky, "The Measurement and Trend of Inequality: Comment," *American Economic Review* 67 (1977): 508, n. 5.

8. Joseph J. Minarik, "The Measurement and Trend of Inequality: Comment," *American Economic Review* 67 (1977): 513–516.

9. C. John Kurien, "The Measurement and Trend of Inequality: Comment," *American Economic Review* 67 (1977): 517–519.

10. See Bhattacharya and Mahalanobis, "Regional Disparities in Household Consumption"; Pyatt, "Gini Coefficients"; and Henri Theil, *Economics and Information Theory* (Amsterdam: North-Holland, 1967), 94–96.

11. See Kurien, "Measure and Trend of Inequality," 517.

12. Ibid.

13. Theil, *Economics and Information Theory,* 91–134.

14. See U.S. Bureau of the Census, *Current Population Reports,* P-60–119, 206 and P-60–134, 31.

15. See Department of Health, Education and Welfare, *Characteristics of Low Income Population* (Washington, D.C.: U.S. Government Printing Office, 1976).

Chapter 9
The Distribution of Income
in the United States in the Postwar Period

1. Regression equations for trend lines with t-distribution values in parentheses below regression coefficients and with relevant parameters are the following:

For the white Gini:

$$WGINI = .36483 - .00156 \; TIME^2 + .000003 \; TIME^3 + .000001 \; TIME^4$$
$$(120.55) \quad (-2.35) \qquad\qquad (.08) \qquad\qquad (1.85)$$

$R^2 = .797$ Standard Error of Estimates = .005

$\bar{R}^2 = .780$ Durbin-Watson = 1.28

Mean of WGINI = .355

Standard Deviation of WGINI = .011

For the black Gini:

$$BGINI = .40202 + .00082 \; TIME - .00014 \; TIME^2 + .000004 \; TIME^3$$
$$(68.24) \quad (.64) \qquad\quad (-1.81) \qquad\qquad (3/02)$$

$R^2 = .708$ Standard Error of Estimate = .010

$\bar{R}^2 = .684$ Durbin-Watson = 1.15

Mean of BGINI = .406

Standard Deviation of BGINI = .018

2. U.S. Bureau of the Census, *Current Population Reports*, Series P-60, no. 162 (Washington, D.C.: U.S. Government Printing Office), table A, 2.

3. After interpolation into the sixth income class population ratio (column 1) on the assumption of a uniform distribution of incomes within that class.

4. U.S. Bureau of the Census, *Current Population Reports*, Series P-60, no. 162, table B, 4.

5. Frank Levy, *Dollars and Dreams* (New York: W. W. Norton, 1987), 158.

6. The regression equation for the trend line for unrelated individual household Gini coefficients is the following:

$$\text{UNGINI} = .51050 - .00529\ \text{TIME} + .00078\ \text{TIME}^2 = .00004\ \text{TIME}^3 + .0000006\ \text{TIME}^4$$
$$(58.37)\quad (-1.70)\qquad (2.43)\qquad\qquad (-3.27)\qquad\qquad (3.78)$$

$R_2 = .829$ Standard Error of Estimate = .01288

$\bar{R}^2 = .810$ Durbin-Watson statistic = 1.38

Mean of UNGINI = .478

Standard Deviation of UNGINI = .030

7. U. S. Bureau of the Census, *Current Population Reports*, Series P-60, no. 166 (Washington, D.C.: U.S. Government Printing Office), 19–22.

8. U.S. Bureau of the Census, *Current Population Reports*, Series P-60, no. 162, table 18, 73–77.

9. Regression equations are the following, with *t*-values and parameters:

Whites:

$$\text{WUNGIN} = .47532 + .00441\ \text{TIME} - .00006\ \text{TIME}^2 - .00001\ \text{TIME}^3 + .0000003\ \text{TIME}^3$$
$$(54.24)\quad (1.53)\qquad\qquad (-.22)\qquad\qquad (-1.14)\qquad\qquad (2.04)$$

The observation for 1947 was omitted from the regression as an extreme item.

$R^2 = .902$ Standard Error of Estimate = .009

$\bar{R}^2 = .891$ Durbin-Watston = 2.01

Mean of WUNGIN = .472

Standard Deviation of WUNGIN = .029

Blacks:

$$\text{BUNGIN} = .45496 + .00332\ \text{TIME} - .000009\ \text{TIME}^3 + .0000002\ \text{TIME}^4$$
$$(55.60)\quad (3.10)\qquad\qquad (-3.38)\qquad\qquad (3.35)$$

$R^2 = .236$ Standard Error of Estimate = .017

$\bar{R}^2 = .174$ Durbin-Watson = 2.13

Mean of BUNGIN = .473

Standard Deviation of BUNGIN = .018

10. U.S. Bureau of the Census, *The Hispanic Population in the United States: March 1988, Current Population Reports*, Series P-20, no. 438 (Washington, D.C.: U.S. Government Printing Office, 1989), table A, 2.

CHAPTER 10
THE FEASIBILITY OF REDISTRIBUTIVE PROGRAMS
UNDER THE DUALISTIC INDIVIDUALISM
THEORY OF ECONOMIC EQUITY

1. For an excellent discussion of the problems involved in such work, and for a presentation of a model to determine the interactions among such factors, see Gordon H. Lewis and Richard J. Morrison, *Income Transfer Analysis* (New York: Immergut and Siolek, 1987).

2. The cost of the Thrifty Food Plan for 1986, adjusted for 1987 prices through use of the CPI-U index, is given below:

Sex and Age of Person	Annual Amount
Child	
1 and 2 years	$536
3 to 5 years	580
6 to 8 years	712
9 to 11 years	846
Male	
12 to 14 years	884
15 to 19 years	917
20 to 50 years	980
51 years and over	889
Female	
12 to 19 years	877
20 to 50 years	880
51 years and over	870
Family Size Adjustment Factors	
1 person	+20%
2 persons	+10%
3 persons	+ 5%
4 persons	± 0%
5 or 6 persons	− 5%
7 or more persons	−10%

Source: U.S. Department of Agriculture, as quoted in U.S. Bureau of the Census, *Measuring the Effects of Benefits and Taxes on Income and Poverty: 1986, Current Population Reports*, no. 164-RD-1 (Washington, D.C.: U.S. Government Printing Office, 1988), 224.

3. U.S. Bureau of the Census, *Measuring the Effects of Benefits and Taxes on Income and Poverty: 1986, Current Population Reports*, Series P-60, no. 164-RD-1 (Washington, D.C.: U.S. Government Printing Office, 1988), 6.

4. Ibid.

5. Ibid.

6. Calculated from weighted average thresholds and shortfalls in 1986.

7. U.S. Bureau of the Census, *Government Finances in 1987–1988*, Series GF-88-5 (Washington, D.C.: U.S. Government Printing Office, 1990), table 4, 4.

CHAPTER 11
THE LONGER-TERM IMPLICATIONS OF
· DUALISTIC INDIVIDUALISM

1. See Michael D. Hurd, "Research on the Elderly: Economic Status, Retirement, and Consumption and Saving," *Journal of Economic Literature* 28 (1990): 588, for a further development of this theme.

2. Daniel Lerner, "Adjusted Estimates of the Size Distribution of Family Money Income," *Journal of Business and Economic Statistics* 1 (1983): 135–146.

3. Daniel Lerner, "Money Incomes of Aged and Nonaged Family Units, 1967–84," *Social Security Bulletin* 50 (1987): table 14.

4. U.S. Bureau of the Census, *Projections of the Population of the United States by Age, Sex and Race: 1988 to 2080*, by Gregory Spencer, *Current Population Reports*, Series P-25, no. 1018 (Washington, D.C.: U.S. Government Printing Office, 1989). The middle series projections assume lifetime births per 1,000 women at 1,800, life expectancy at birth of 81.2 years, and annual immigration of 500,000 persons.

5. For example, in 1960, 14 percent of men over the age of 65 lived with relatives, but by 1988 this had declined to 7 percent. For those over 75, the percentages are 22 and 9 respectively. For elderly women, the decline is even more striking. Those over the age of 65 living with relatives declined from 34 percent in 1960 to 17 percent in 1988, and for those over 75 the figures are 46 and 22 percent respectively. See Hurd, "Research on the Elderly," table 3, 569.

6. The normal retirement age becomes 67 in year 2026. This is the minimum age at which unreduced benefits are payable.

7. U.S. Department of Health and Human Services, Social Security Administration, *Income of the Population 55 or Older, 1986*, SSA Publication No. 13-11871 (Washington, D.C.: U.S. Government Printing Office, June 1988), table 24, 62.

8. Ibid., table 18, 47–48.

9. U.S. Bureau of the Census, *Measuring the Effects of Benefits and Taxes on Income and Poverty, Current Population Reports*, Series P-60, no. 164-RD-1 (Washington, D.C.: U.S. Government Printing Office, 1988), table 9, 206.

10. U.S. Department of Health and Human Services, Social Security Administration, Office of the Actuary, *Projections for OASDI Cost and Income Estimates: 1987*, Actuarial Study No. 101 (Washington, D.C.: U.S. Government Printing Office, May 1988). The projections quoted are its Alternative II-A estimates, which constitute the case intermediate between pessimistic and optimistic parameters.

11. U.S. Department of Health and Human Services, Social Security Administration, *Annual Statistical Supplement, Social Security Bulletin, 1989*, SSA Publication No. 13–11700 (Washington, D.C.: U.S. Government Printing Office, December 1989).

12. Perhaps the most questionable factor is the assumed rise of private pensions and annuities. With the relative decline of manufacturing and the

unions based in that sector and the rise of service industries with smaller size as well as the surge of women in the labor force, pension plans may well continue their relative decline over the next thirty years.

13. U.S. Department of Health and Human Services, Social Security Administration, Office of the Actuary, *Economic Projections for OASDHI Cost and Income Estimates: 1987*, Actuarial Study No. 101 (Washington, D.C.: U.S. Government Printing Office, May 1988).

14. U.S. Bureau of the Census, *Projections of the Population of the United States by Age, Sex and Race: 1988 to 2080, Current Population Reports*, Series P-25, no. 1018 (Washington, D.C.: U.S. Government Printing Office, 1989).

15. U.S. Bureau of the Census, *Measuring the Effects of Benefits and Taxes on Income and Poverty, Current Population Reports*, Series P-60, no. 164-RD-1 (Washington, D.C.: U.S. Government Printing Office, 1988), tables B-3 and B-4, 225–226.

16. U.S. Bureau of the Census, *Government Finances in 1987–1988*, Series GF-88-5 (Washington, D.C.: U.S. Government Printing Office, 1990), table 2.

INDEX

Adorno, Theodore, 12, 115
aged dependency ratio: defined, 357; in 1987, 357; projection for 2020, 357
alienation thesis, 115
analytical framework for theories of justice, 102, 113
Aristotle: and perfection theory, 407n.2
Arnold, Matthew, 11
associationist psychology, 68
Augustine, Saint, 35
Austrian school, 47. *See also* justice-as-freedom theories

bargaining theory: absence of social dimension in, 141; compatibility of, with ethos, 141; concept of good in, 140; critique of, 140–41; and economic justice, 52–55; egoistic motives in, 52, 140–41; Gauthier's model, 54–55, 413n.51; Nash's model, 53–54; principles of right in, 140–41; uncertain relation of, to equity, 52, 58. *See also* Gauthier, David P.; justice-as-fairness theory of equity; Nash, John
Bauer, Paul T., 407n.4
Bentham, Jeremy: act-utilitarianism of, 60, 67–71, 72, 151, 406n.13; penology, 69. *See also* utilitarian theory of equity
bill of economic rights and obligations: as charter of dualistic individualism theory of equity, 393, 402; constituent assembly and, 100–102; content of, 189–97, 392–94; contractarian nature of derivation, 99–102, 113; and economic content of Constitution, 97–99, 402; and entitlement theories of equity, 132, 393; lessening of vested interest power with, 122–23; and marginal productivity theory, 120, 123–24; necessity of, 392–94; policy implications of, 197–204. *See also* dualistic individualism theory of equity Brenkert, George C., 407n.5
Butler, Joseph, 38, 66

Cambridge Platonists, 37, 40. *See also* Cudworth, Ralph; More, Henry

Chicago school, 47. *See also* Friedman, Milton; justice-as-freedom theories of equity; Knight, Frank H.; Simon, Henry C.; Stigler, George
Cicero, 35
Clark, John B., 31–32
coefficient of variation. *See* income distribution, inequality measures
compassion. *See* dualistic individualism theory of equity
competition: imperfect, 122; perfect, 121–22, 412n.39
consequentialism: importance of, for feasible theory of equity, 209–10; and operationalism, 22. *See also* teleological theories of equity
Constitution, U.S.: and economic rights, 3. *See also* bill of economic rights and obligations; dualistic individualism theory of equity
contributory theories of economic equity: axiomatic bases of, 57; compatibility of, with ethos, 123–25, 126, 140–43; concepts of good in, 114–16, 120; concepts of right in, 116–20; deontological nature of, 115; as egoistic theory, 30; and imputations of factor contributions, 117–20, 125–26, 142; marginal productivity theory as, 30–32, 50, 51, 57, 114, 116, 123, 124, 132, 179, 417n.5; Marxist variant of, 32–34, 57, 114, 115, 116, 120–21, 123, 124–25, 173, 417n.3; pricing power and, 120–22; relation of, to entitlement theory of equity, 58; vague formulation of, in American ethos, 15. *See also* market economy; Marx, Karl
Cove vs. Antonio, 405n.12
Cowling, Keith: on pricing power and social welfare, 418n.6
cross-subsidization: in bill of economic rights and obligations, 193; equity aspects of, 185–86
Cudworth, Ralph. *See* Cambridge Platonists
Cumberland, Richard, 64
Cyrenaics, 64